T0359291

K FIND
IDE

For more detail see Contents on page 3

How to use this Directory page 4

Suburbs & Localities Index page 6

Facilities Index page 7

Street Index page 16

Wollongong City Centre Maps 1-2 Scale 1:9 500

Wollongong & Environs Maps 11-96 Scale 1:19 000

University of Wollongong page 98

NSW State Atlas Index page 100 & Maps 53-64

Town Maps page 116

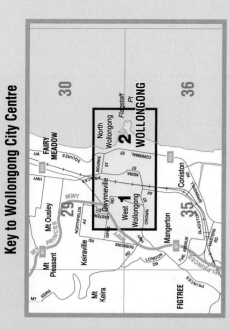

Key to Wollongong City Centre

Published in 2022 by Hardie Grant Explore,
an imprint of Hardie Grant Publishing

Hardie Grant Explore (Sydney)
Gadigal Country
Level 7, 45 Jones Street
Ultimo, NSW 2007

Hardie Grant Explore (Melbourne)
Wurundjeri Country
Building 1, 658 Church Street
Richmond, Victoria 3121

www.hardiegrant.com/au/explore

UBD Gregory's is an imprint of Hardie Grant Explore

Hardie Grant acknowledges the Traditional Owners of the Country on which we work, the
Wurundjeri people of the Kulin Nation and the Gadigal people of the Eora Nation, and recognises
their continuing connection to the land, waters and culture. We pay our respects to their Elders
past, present and emerging.

Publishers note
UBD Gregory's welcomes contributions and feedback on the contents of this directory. Please
e-mail us at upsales@hardiegrant.com.au. Hardie Grant Explore is Australia's largest publisher
and distributor of Street Directories, Maps, Travel and Guide Books.

Wollongong South Coast & Southern Highlands 25th edition
ISBN 9780 7319 3285 6

Cover: Design pfisterer + freeman
          Photo Wollongong Harbour NSW,
          Photograph by Brayden Stanford

Printed in China by Leo Paper Products Ltd

The paper this book is printed on is certified against the Forest Stewardship
Council® Standards and other sources. FSC® promotes environmentally
responsible, socially beneficial and economically viable management of the
world's forests.

Custom Mapping services
For any custom mapping requirements please contact cms@hardiegrant.com.au

Acknowledgments
The revision of the information contained in this street directory could not be carried out without the
assistance given by the following organisations and their representatives Nearmap; Australia Post,
local government authorities, land developers, Federal and State government authorities, tourist
information offices and the general public

CONTENTS

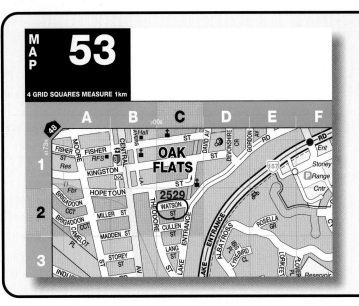

HOW TO FIND A STREET

1. Look up the street name and suburb in the Street Index (e.g. Watson St, Oak Flats).

2. Note its map number and reference (53, C2).

3. Turn to the appropriate map (53) and locate the street by following the grid lines down from the reference letter (c) and across from the number (2) to where they meet, as shown on the diagram above.

WATKINS
cl. Gerringong 70   G2
WATSON
st.   Oak Flats 53   C2
WATTAMOLLA
rd.   Helensburgh 11   P16

CAN'T FIND A STREET?

If the Street Index does not list the street you are seeking under a particular suburb, check to see if the street is actually in an adjoining suburb. To do this, refer to the Suburbs and Localities Index and find on which map the suburb appears. Turn to that map and note the names of surrounding suburbs. Now return to the Street Index and look for the street in one of these suburbs.

MAP FEATURES

Direction

For all practical purposes Grid North and True North are always to the top of the maps. Each map features a directional arrow pointing to the city.

Grid Lines

The blue grid lines serve two purposes:

■ they form the reference squares for locating streets and facilities etc.

■ they allow easy calculation of distances (see Map Scales).

Map Symbols

Most of the map symbols are self-explanatory. However, to ensure that you gain maximum information from the street maps, we recommend that you familiarise yourself with all the map symbols used (see opposite page).

Overlap Areas & Map Borders

The street maps have an overlap area on each edge to assist in maintaining position when moving to an adjoining map. Adjoining map numbers are shown in the borders and corners.

Future Maps

Maps covering areas that may be included in future editions are indicated with white numbers on the Key Map at the beginning of this directory. They allow for future expansion of the directory without renumbering existing maps & still allow sequential map numbering.

Continuing Maps

When map numbers are not in sequential order, then a note will appear under the map number indicating the previous or following map number.

MAP SCALES

The maps are drawn to various scales, allowing more detail to be shown in very congested areas.

▶ Red Borders

Scale 1:9 500 - Grid squares measure 125m
Maps 1 - 2 Wollongong City Centre

▶ Blue Borders

Scale 1:19 000 - Grid squares measure 250m
Maps 11 - 96 Wollongong, Kiama, Nowra, Shoalhaven Heads & Berry

▶ Regional Towns

Scale 1:20 000
Pages 116 – 187

AUSTRALIAN MAP GRID

The small numbers in the map borders refer to the co-ordinates of the Australian Map Grid (AMG) which are spaced at 1000 metre (1km) intervals. The co-ordinates for Wollongong are derived from Zone 56 of the International Universal Transverse Mercator System and is based on the Australian Geodetic Datum of 1966 (AGD66). All of the street maps are aligned with the AMG.

✳	Ambulance Station
⚒	Barbecue
⛽	Boat Fuelling Point
⛵	Boat Ramp
🎳	Bowling Club
▲	Camping Area
🚐	Caravan Park
Ⓟ	Car Park
⅏	Cliffs
■ Cncl Off	Council Office
☎ 861	Emergency Phone & Location Number
✉	Express Post Box
F	Fire Station
♣	Girl Guides
⛳	Golf Course
✚	Hospital
Ⓗ	Hotel
ⓘ	Information Centre
𝑖	Information Centre (accredited)
📖	Library
ⓣ	Lighthouse
☀	Lookout – 360° view
☀	– 180° view
⚔	Masonic Centre
▲	Memorial / Monument
⌂	Motel
⊓	Picnic Area
■ Museum	Place of Interest
⊥	Place of Worship
⋔	Playground
■ PCYC	Pol & Cmnty Youth Club
★	Police Station
✉	Post Office
⬳	Quarry
■ RFS	Rural Fire Service
Ⓢ	School – Private
Ⓢ	– Public
⚜	Scouts
🛢	Service Station
🛒	Shopping Centre
📷	Speed Camera (Fixed)
■ SES	State Emerg. Service
🏊	Swimming Pool
☎	Telephone
Ⓒ	Tertiary Institution – Private
Ⓖ	– Public
🚻	Toilets
Ⓦ	Weighbridge
⚘	Winery

Freeway or Motorway	M1 PRINCES MWY
Highway or Main Traffic Route	PRINCES HWY
Alternate Traffic Route	ALAN ST
Trafficable Road	ALLA RD
Un-Trafficable/Proposed Road	MATTHEW RD
Traffic Light & Red Light Camera	● ✪
Roundabout and Level Crossing	○ ✕
Road, Railway Bridges & Bridge Clearance Heights	
One-Way Traffic Route	→ →
National, State & Tourist Route Numbers	A1 B88 8
House or Building Number	20
Railway Line with Station	*Woonona*
Proposed Freeway	*Proposed* *Freeway*
Proposed Freeway due for completion	*Under Construction*
Direction of Wollongong City Centre	◤CITY◆
Distance by road from GPO	⑧
Suburb Name	**GWYNNEVILLE**
Postcode Number	**2500**
Suburb Boundary	
Locality Name	**Port Kembla North**
Local Government – Name	
– Boundary	
Walking Tracks and Cycleways	🚶 🚴
Park, Reserve, Golf Course, etc	
School or Hospital	
Caravan Park, Cemetery, Shopping Centre, etc	
Mall, Plaza	
Swamp	

Listed below are the suburbs and localities within the area covered by the Street Maps, together with their postcodes and map references. Many localities do not have official boundaries.

With the help of the appropriate authorities we have differentiated between suburbs and localities as follows –

ALBION PARK ..... Suburb   **Bass Point** .... Locality or unofficial suburb   *Primrose Hill* .... Local name or railway station

	Map	Ref

A

ALBION PARK	2527	51	P11
ALBION PARK RAIL	2527	48	C15
AUSTINMER	2515	18	B11
AVON	2574	37	H6
AVONDALE	2530	43	C13

B

Balarang	2529	49	F13
BALGOWNIE	2519	29	B1
BAMARANG	2540	90	C9
BANGALEE	2541	82	L14
BARRACK HEIGHTS	2528	49	N15
BARRACK POINT	2528	50	H16
BARRINGELLA	2540	89	E10
Bass Point	2529	54	L16
BELLAMBI	2518	26	J11
BERKELEY	2506	40	M6
BERRY	2535	96	G11
BLACKBUTT	2529	53	L3
Blue Gum Forest	2508	11	E12
BOLONG	2540	84	M12
BOMADERRY	2541	88	D2
BOMBO	2533	61	N9
BROUGHTON VALE	2535	96	N2
BROWNSVILLE	2530	39	N13
BULLI	2516	22	A8
Bulli Pass	2516	21	N3
Bulli Tops	2516	17	M11
BUNDEWALLAH	2535	96	B1

C

CALDERWOOD	2527	47	K16
CAMBEWARRA	2540	83	B8
CAMBEWARRA VILLAGE	2540	82	M3
CATARACT	2560	17	H9
CLEVELAND	2530	43	P4
CLIFTON	2515	16	L8
COALCLIFF	2508	16	K4
COLEDALE	2515	18	N6
COMERONG ISLAND	2540	95	D16
CONISTON	2500	35	J8
COOLANGATTA	2535	95	B4
CORDEAUX	2526	27	N5
CORDEAUX HEIGHTS	2526	34	B11
CORRIMAL	2518	25	K8
CRINGILA	2502	41	C7
CROOM	2527	52	L10
CURRAMORE	2527	59	M1

D

DAPTO	2530	44	H9
DARKES FOREST	2508	13	C6
DOMBARTON	2526	38	K2
DUNMORE	2529	57	D10

E

EAST CORRIMAL	2518	26	D12

F

FAIRY MEADOW	2519	30	C5
FARMBOROUGH HEIGHTS	2526	33	N16
FERNHILL	2519	25	L16
FIGTREE	2525	34	H7
FLINDERS	2529	53	P9

G

GERRINGONG	2534	70	B5
GERROA	2534	70	D12
GWYNNEVILLE	2500	29	K15

H

HAYWARDS BAY	2530	48	K8
HELENSBURGH	2508	11	K9
HORSLEY	2530	38	N13
HUNTLEY	2530	43	C6

I

ILLAROO	2540	89	J3

J

JAMBEROO	2533	60	B9
JASPERS BRUSH	2535	96	A14
JERRARA	2533	61	C13

K

KANAHOOKA	2530	44	M2
KEIRAVILLE	2500	29	D9
KEMBLA GRANGE	2530	39	D7
KEMBLA HEIGHTS	2526	33	J6
Kemblawarra	2505	41	P16
KIAMA	2533	65	L4
Kiama Blowhole		62	E16
KIAMA DOWNS	2533	61	L2
KIAMA HEIGHTS	2533	65	N13
KOONAWARRA	2530	44	P8

L

LAKE HEIGHTS	2502	41	D12
LAKE ILLAWARRA	2528	50	B6
LILYVALE	2508	12	M2
LONGREACH	2540	90	F1

M

MADDENS PLAINS	2508	16	D7
MANGERTON	2500	35	E8
MARSHALL MOUNT	2530	47	H9
MEROO MEADOW	2540	84	D4
MINNAMURRA	2533	58	C14
Mt Brown		44	F13
MOUNT KEIRA	2500	28	N10
MOUNT KEMBLA	2526	34	A2
MOUNT OUSLEY	2519	29	H8
MOUNT PLEASANT	2519	29	C6
MOUNT ST THOMAS	2500	35	D9
MOUNT WARRIGAL	2528	49	H6
MUNDAMIA	2540	91	B4

N

NORTH NOWRA	2541	87	H1
NORTH WOLLONGONG	2500	30	B9
NOWRA	2541	88	D15
NOWRA HILL	2540	91	E15

O

OAK FLATS	2529	49	C13
O'Briens Gap	2526	27	N12
Omega Flat		69	F7
OTFORD	2508	14	D1

P

PENROSE	2530	43	P12
PORT KEMBLA	2505	41	K4
Port Kembla North	2505	41	Q8
PRIMBEE	2502	46	L8
Primrose Hill		61	K10

R

ROSE VALLEY	2534	69	C4
RUSSELL VALE	2517	25	L3

S

SADDLEBACK MOUNTAIN	2533	65	D13
SCARBOROUGH	2515	16	E12
SHELL COVE	2529	54	J10
SHELLHARBOUR	2529	54	G5
SHELLHARBOUR CITY CENTRE	2529	53	F1
SHOALHAVEN HEADS	2535	95	L8
SOUTH NOWRA	2541	91	N12
SPRING HILL	2500	35	B15
STANWELL PARK	2508	13	M11
STANWELL TOPS	2508	13	N5

T

TAPITALLEE	2540	82	C10
TARRAWANNA	2518	25	E12
TERARA	2540	88	N9
Terragong Swamp		61	C4
THIRROUL	2515	22	A2
Tootawallin Gully		65	B10
TOWRADGI	2518	30	B1
TULLIMBAR	2527	51	B9

U

UNANDERRA	2526	34	M15

W

WARILLA	2528	49	P10
WARRAWONG	2502	41	H14
WERRI BEACH	2534	69	K13
WEST NOWRA	2541	91	G2
WEST WOLLONGONG	2500	35	E1
WINDANG	2528	50	H3
WOLLONGONG	2500	30	B15
WOMBARRA	2515	16	F15
WONGAWILLI	2530	38	G9
WOONONA	2517	26	H2
Woonona Heights	2517	21	M11
WORONORA DAM	2508	11	C6
WORRIGEE	2540	92	N6

Y

YALLAH	2530	48	J5
YELLOW ROCK	2527	51	G14

FACILITIES INDEX

Map Ref

Aged Care, Nursing Homes & Retirement Communities

Anglicare Chesalon, South Nowra
189 Old Southern Rd 92 E9
Woonona
20 Alice St 26 C2
ARV, St Lukes
4 Lindsay Evans Pl, Dapto 44 C11
Berry Masonic Village
41 Albany St 96 G10
Bishop McCabe Village
23 Ziems Av, Towradgi 25 P15
Blue Haven Care, Aged Care Facility
Bonaira St, Kiama 65 Q5
Nursing Home & Retirement Village
55 Thompson St, Kiama 61 P14
Clelland Lodge
201 Illaroo Rd, North Nowra 87 H4
Dumaresq Retirement Village
124 Wallace St, Nowra 92 C3
Farmborough Aged Care Centre
91 Waples Rd, Farmborough Heights 40 E1
Garrawarra Centre
Old Princes Hwy 11 H1
Hammond Care, Horsley
116 Shone Av 38 L16
Hillcrest Village Self Care, UPA
1a Railway Cr, Stanwell Park 13 P9
Hillside at Figtree Aged Care
190 Princes Hwy 34 N10
Illawarra Diggers Aged & Community Care Residence
8 Blundell Pde, Corrimal 25 M8
IRT Birch Villa
47 Underwood St, Corrimal 25 N12
IRT Braeside
155 Gipps Rd, Keiraville 1 C4
IRT Diment Towers
39 Staff St, Wollongong 1 E15
IRT Edwina
4 Underwood St, Corrimal 25 N9
IRT Five Islands
25 Quarry St, Port Kembla 42 E13
IRT Greenwell Gardens
4 Brereton St, Nowra 88 C10
IRT Harbourside
4 Terralong St, Kiama 62 B16
IRT Howard Court
27a Stewart St, Wollongong 2 C15
IRT Keiraview
60 Grey St, Keiraville 29 E14
IRT Links Seaside
1 Ross St, Wollongong 35 Q6
IRT Seaview
49 Park Rd, Woonona 26 D1
IRT Sid Wearne Court
109 Farrell Rd, Bulli 22 C12
IRT Tarrawanna Gardens
2 Foothills Rd, Tarrawanna 25 J15
IRT Towradgi Park
17a Murranar Rd, Towradgi 30 C1
IRT Towradgi Park Lodge
43 Towradgi Rd, Towradgi 30 C1
IRT William Beach Gardens
286 Kanahooka Rd, Kanahooka 39 P15
IRT Woonona
4 Popes Rd 22 A14
Jettys by the Lake
210 Windang Rd, Windang 46 D16
John & Helen Robinson Nursing Home
Mayflower Retirement Village, Belinda St, Gerringong 70 E2
Kennett Home Aged Care
103 The Drive, Stanwell Park 14 C11
Lakeline Estate
Lakeline Dr, Kanahooka 45 C3
Lakeview Village
7 Wallaroo Dr, Shellharbour City Centre 53 J2
McCauley Lodge
10 Tasman Pde, Thirroul 22 H4
Marco Polo Unanderra Care Services
70 Waples Rd 40 E1
Mayflower Retirement Village
Belinda St, Gerringong 70 E2
Multicultural Aged Care Illawarra
1 Eyre Pl, Warrawong 41 H12
Nareena Homes
84 Jacaranda Av, Figtree 34 K3
Opal Shoalhaven
43 Brinawarr St, Bomaderry 88 A2
Osborne House Hostel, UnitingCare
54 Osborne St, Nowra 87 P12
Pioneer Lodge & Boronia Dementia Hostel
Mayflower Retirement Village, Belinda St, Gerringong 70 E2
Rest Point Village
9 Browns Rd, South Nowra 92 A9
Ridgeview Aged Care Facility
95 Daintree Dr, Albion Park 52 B14
Rose Mumbler Village
Judith Dr, North Nowra 87 F5
St Marys Retirement Village
211 Northcliffe Dr, Berkeley 40 K12
The Arbour
10 Victoria St, Berry 96 E8
The Grange at Berry
22 Victoria St 96 F8
Uniting Berry
10 Victoria St 96 D9
UnitingCare Elanora
23 Wallaroo Dr, Shellharbour City Centre 53 K2
Villa Maria Centre
cnr Tannery St & Blackman Pde, Unanderra 34 J16
Warrigal Care Albion Park Rail
2 Pine St 52 K5
Warrigal Care Coniston
91 Bridge St 35 G8
Warrigal Care Mt Warrigal
5 Rowland Av 49 K9
Warrigal Care Warilla
1 Arcadia St 50 C12
Wollongong Nursing Home
12 Suttor Pl, Figtree 34 M9

Airport

Illawarra Regional Airport 48 E14

Ambulance Stations

Barrack Heights
10 Captain Cook Dr 49 M14
Berry
North St 96 E6
Bulli
Hospital Rd 22 C11
Dapto
cnr Emerson Rd & Beltana Av 44 F7
Helensburgh
2 Lilyvale St 11 N11
Kiama
Terralong St 62 A15
Nowra
Bunberra St, Bomaderry 87 N1
Warrawong
First Av S 41 K14
Wollongong
455 Crown St 1 C14

Bays, Beaches, etc

Abernethys Creek 83 M7
Albion Creek 48 G13
Allans Creek 41 B1
Allen Creek 17 C9
American Creek 33 J7
Ash Pond 48 K1
Austinmer Beach 18 G14
Bamarang Dam 89 P11
Barrack Point 50 H15
Barrack Swamp 54 C3
Barringella Reach 89 A2
Beaky Cove 54 Q13
Bellambi Beach 26 G5
Bellambi Creek
Bellambi 26 A7
Cataract 21 B12
Bellambi Harbour 26 K8
Bellambi Lagoon 26 G11
Bellambi Point 26 L9
Bellambi Reef 26 M9
Bells Point 18 H13
Belmore Basin 2 J9
Bensons Creek 50 A11
Berrwarra Point 50 G6
Bevan Island 95 A14
Bevans Island 49 Q3
Big Island 42 L15
Black Beach 62 B16
Black Head 70 F16
Blowhole Point 62 E16
Bomaderry Creek 87 M4
Bombo Beach 62 A12
Bombo Headland 62 D8
Boomberry Point 45 A10
Boonerah Point 49 H7
Boston Point 54 P1
Boyds Beach 62 A3
Branch Creek 34 M3
Brandy & Water Creek 34 D2
Brickyard Point 18 K11
Brooks Creek 44 J5
Broughton Creek 96 H16
Broughton Mill Creek 96 M9
Browns Creek
Cambewarra 82 K1
South Nowra 92 C8
Budjong Creek 40 M7
Bulli Beach 22 H15
Bulli Harbour 22 K7
Bulli Point 22 K9
Bundewallah Creek 96 E3
Burroo Bay 48 P13
Burroo Point 49 G12
Bushrangers Bay 54 P3
Cabbage Tree Creek
Balgownie 29 C1
Mundamia 90 M7
Camp Gully 11 M12
Cape Horn 16 J11
Carricks Creek 18 G4
Cataract Creek 25 D1
Cedar Gully 12 F12
Charcoal Creek 34 E16
Church Point 66 C2
Coalcliff Beach 16 M2
Coalcliff Dam 13 F12
Coalcliff Harbour 16 M4
Coledale Beach 18 M5
Collins Creek 21 N13
Colyers Creek 60 C14
Colymea Creek 89 H9
Colymea Reach 89 E2
Comerong Island 95 E15
Coniston Beach 36 A10
Connar Creek 52 M8
Connollys Creek 96 J1
Cooback Creek 51 L10
Coomaditchy Lagoon 41 Q15
Cordeaux River 27 A11
Corrimal Beach 26 F15
Creole Point 48 N11
Crookhaven Creek 88 L15
Cudgeree Bay 46 D15
Cudgeree Island 50 B1
Dalys Creek 18 H3
Dapto Creek 33 E12
Duck Creek 48 F1
Eastern Basin 35 P15
Easts Beach 66 A9
Elizabeth Point 45 B12
Fairy Creek 1 N3
Fairy Meadow Beach 30 A10
Fishermans Beach 42 G14
Flagstaff Point 2 N9
Flanagans Creek 18 A15
Flat Rock 22 J16
Flatrock Creek 91 D11
Flat Rock Dam 91 F3
Fountaindale Creek 60 H12
Frazers Creek 52 E4
Friars Cave 66 C6
Frys Creek 59 H4
Gardiners Creek 12 B12
Geering Bay 69 L12
Gerongar Point 48 L9
Gerringong Boat Harbour 70 J4
Gibsons Creek 39 Q9
Gills Creek 13 H1
Good Dog Creek 83 B10
Goondarrin creek 27 F2
Greys Beach 87 N8
Griffins Bay 46 J2
Gurungaty Waterway 35 N14
Hacking River 14 A6
Hamiltons Gully 12 G13
Hargrave Creek 13 L8
Haywards Bay 48 K10
Hennegar Bay 49 B12
Herbert Creek 13 P1
Hewitts Creek 22 G5
Hicks Creek 18 D13
Hooka Creek 40 G12
Hooka Island 40 H16
Hooka Point 40 H15
Horsley Creek 52 L1
Horsley Inlet 48 M15
Hyams Creek 59 P12
Inner Harbour 41 N1
Jacky Jones Creek 18 H8
Jenkins Creek 40 D2
Jerrara Creek 60 P13
Jerrara Dam 60 Q16
Joes Bay 46 K3
Judbowley Point 50 C3
Kaleula Point 66 C5
Kanahooka Point 45 E6
Karoo Bay 49 D14
Karoo Point 49 E13
Kellys Creek 13 D5
Kembla Creek 27 E9
Kendalls Beach 66 A4
Kendalls Point 66 B3
Kiama Harbour 62 B15
Killalea Beach 58 D2
Killalea Lagoon 54 E16
Koona Bay 48 L14
Koonawarra Bay 45 A8
Koong-burry Bay 40 F16
Korrongulla Swamp 46 K6
Kully Bay 41 K16
Kurrakwah Bay 50 J6
Kurrura Point 48 M14
Lake Avon 37 H1
Lake Cataract 17 B4
Lake Cordeaux 27 A3
Lake Illawarra 40 L15
Langs Point 40 F15
Little Lake 50 C14
Loddon River 17 F5
Loves Bay 66 A12
McCauley's Beach 22 H7
McKinnons Creek 12 D6
Macquarie Rivulet 51 J2
Maddens Creek 15 H1
Maloneys Bay 54 N16
Marsden Head 66 D8
Marshall Mount Creek 47 D12
Martins Islet 42 Q16
Meemi Gully 33 G2
Minnamurra Beach 58 A8
Minnamurra Point 58 C13
Minnamurra River
Jamberoo 59 E1
Kiama Downs 57 K15
Minnamurra 57 Q10

FACILITIES INDEX 7

Boat Ramps

Bowling Clubs

Caravan, Tourist & Mobile Home Parks

Cemeteries & Crematoria

Churches & Other Places of Worship

Other Congregations

Anglican

Churches & Other Places of Worship

	Map Ref
Albion Park Rail	
cnr Princes Hwy &	
Creamery Rd	48 H15
Austinmer	
49 Moore St	18 E14
Balgownie	
Church St	29 F2
Bellambi	
Gladstone St	26 D9
Berry	
Albert St	96 K7
Bomaderry	
Bunberra St	88 B2
Bulli	
cnr Point St &	
Princes Hwy	22 E8
Corrimal	
cnr Russell &	
Underwood Sts	25 N10
Dapto	
122 Princes Hwy	44 G2
Fairy Meadow	
Daisy St	29 N4
Figtree	
cnr Bellevue Rd &	
Uralba St	34 P4
Gerringong	
Fern St	69 G15
Helensburgh	
Bushland Chapel,	
Parkes St	11 P9
Jamberoo	
Wyalla Rd	60 A7
Kiama	
Manning St	66 A1
Nowra	
cnr Berry & Junction Sts	87 Q12
Oak Flats	
Parkes St	49 A16
Port Kembla	
Fitzwilliam St	42 B12
Shellharbour	
Mary St	54 D7
Thirroul	
cnr Lachlan St &	
Lawrence Hargrave Dr	22 E3
West Wollongong	
Fisher St	35 E2
Windang	
Waratah St	50 E2
Wollongong	
Crown St	2 B12
Woonona	
Princes Hwy	22 A14

Clubs

	Map Ref
Albion Park RSL Memorial	
cnr Tongarra &	
Hamilton Rds	51 P4
Austinmer Surf Life Saving Club	
Lawrence Hargrave Dr	18 G14
Bellambi Surf Life Saving Club	
Morgan Pl	26 G7
Berkeley Sports	
5 Wilkinson St	40 M12
Bomaderry RSL	
5 Bunberra St	88 B2
Bulli Surf Life Saving Club	
Bulli Beach	22 H13
Bulli Workers	
313 Princes Hwy	22 C12
City Diggers Wollongong	
82 Church St	2 A13
Coalcliff Surf Life Saving Club	
Beach Reserve	16 M2
Coledale RSL	
749 Lawrence	
Hargrave Dr	18 L7
Coledale Surf Life Saving Club	
Lawrence Hargrave Dr	18 M6

	Map Ref
Collegians	
Rugby League Football,	
Collegians Balgownie	
Balgownie Rd	29 G2
Collegians City	
3a Charlotte St,	
Wollongong	1 P8
Red Dog on the Green	
147 The Avenue,	
Figtree	35 B9
Corrimal Leagues	
54 Railway St	26 A11
Corrimal RSL Memorial	
168 Princes Hwy	25 P10
Corrimal Surf Life Saving Club	
1 Lake Pde,	
East Corrimal	26 F15
Dapto Leagues	
Bong Bong Rd	44 F2
Fairy Meadow	
Surf Life Saving Club	
Elliotts Rd	30 B6
Fraternity	
11 Bourke St,	
Fairy Meadow	29 N6
German	
636a Northcliffe Dr,	
Kembla Grange	40 E8
Gerringong	
Surf Life Saving Club	
Pacific Av	69 H16
Gerroa Boat Fishermans	
68 Crooked River Rd	70 C11
Helensburgh-Stanwell Park	
Surf Life Saving Club	
Beach Rd,	
Stanwell Park	14 A12
Illawarra Leagues	
97 Church St,	
Wollongong	2 A14
Illawarra Master Builders	
61 Church St,	
Wollongong	2 C8
Kemblawarra Portuguese	
Sports & Social Club	
156 Shellharbour Rd,	
Port Kembla	46 N1
Kiama Downs	
Surf Life Saving Club	
North Kiama Dr	62 A1
Kiama Leagues	
139 Terralong St	61 Q15
Kiama Surf Life Saving Club	
Manning St	66 A2
Koonawarra Bay Sailing	
Kanahooka Rd,	
Kanahooka	45 E6
North Wollongong	
Surf Life Saving Club	
Cliff Rd	2 F2
Port Kembla Leagues	
3 Wentworth St	42 A10
Port Kembla Returned Soliders	
Military Rd	42 B11
Port Kembla Sailing	
6 Northcliffe Dr,	
Berkeley	40 Q13
Port Kembla	
Surf Life Saving Club	
Cowper St	42 D16
Sandon Point	
Surf Life Saving Club	
Point St,	
Bulli	22 J9
Scarborough Wombarra	
Surf Life Saving Club	
Monash St,	
Wombarra	16 E15
Shellharbour Surf Life	
Saving Club	
cnr Beach Rd &	
Wollongong St	54 E4
Shoalhaven Ex-Servicemens	
157 Junction St,	
Nowra	88 A12

	Map Ref
Shoalhaven ExServicemens	
Sports Club	
Greenwell Point Rd,	
Worrigee	92 J3
Shoalhaven Heads	
Surf Life Saving Club	
McIntosh St	95 J9
Steelers	
1 Burelli St,	
Wollongong	2 F14
The Illawarra Yacht	
1 Northcliffe Dr,	
Warrawong	41 F16
The Shellharbour	
cnr Shellharbour &	
Wattle Rds	54 A8
The Sporties,	
Warilla Sports Club	
54 McGregor Av,	
Barrack Heights	50 C14
Thirroul	
Surf Life Saving Club	
Thirroul Beach	22 K2
Towradgi	
Surf Life Saving Club	
Murranar Rd	30 D1
Warilla-Barrack Point	
Surf Life Saving Club	
7 Osborne Pde	50 E10
Warilla RSL	
Shellharbour Rd	50 B11
Wests Illawarra	
Hargreaves St,	
Unanderra	34 J15
Windang Surf Life Saving Club	
Fern St	50 F5
Wollongong AFL	
Pioneer Rd,	
Fairy Meadow	30 B3
Wollongong City	
Surf Life Saving Club	
Marine Dr	2 J10
Wollongong Hellenic	
57 Princes Hwy,	
West Wollongong	35 B6
Wollongong Tennis	
37 Foley St,	
Gwynneville	1 J7
Woonona Bulli RSL Memorial	
455 Princes Hwy	22 B14
Woonona	
Surf Life Saving Club	
Woonona Beach	26 G1

Fire Stations

	Map Ref
Albion Park	
1 Russell St	51 Q5
Albion Park Rail	
180 Princes Hwy	48 H16
Balgownie	
117 Balgownie Rd	29 G3
Berry	
26 Prince Alfred St	96 K8
Bulli	
325 Princes Hwy	22 C12
Coledale	
759 Lawrence	
Hargrave Dr	18 K7
Corrimal	
124 Princes Hwy	25 P9
Dapto	
88 Byamee St	44 H2
Helensburgh	
91 Walker St	11 N13
Kiama	
210 Terralong St	61 N14
Nowra	
69 Bridge Rd	87 Q11
Scarborough	
Wilson St	16 F14
Shellharbour	
Wattle Rd	54 B8

	Map Ref
Shoalhaven	
34 Norfolk Av,	
South Nowra	91 H14
Thirroul	
240 Lawrence	
Hargrave Dr	22 J1
Unanderra	
80 Central Rd	34 K14
Warrawong	
48 King St	41 L13
Wollongong	
32 Denison St	1 L12

Rural Fire Service

	Map Ref
Albion Park	
Tongarra Rd	52 B4
Austinmer	
Buttenshaw Dr	18 E11
Broughton Vale/Berry	
Albert St	96 K7
Bulli	
Dumbrell Rd	22 B12
Calderwood	
Calderwood Rd	47 B14
Cambewarra	
Illaroo Rd,	
Tapitallee	82 A12
Dapto	
Wongawilli Rd,	
Wongawilli	38 H10
Darkes Forest	
Darkes Forest Rd	15 J1
Dunmore	
Shellharbour Rd	57 K3
Farmborough Heights	
Bardess Cr	39 Q4
Gerringong	
Blackwood St	70 E1
Helensburgh	
cnr Collins & Parkes Sts	11 L12
Illaroo Road	
181 Illaroo Rd,	
North Nowra	87 H5
Jamberoo	
Young St	60 B7
Kiama-shellharbour SES	
127 Tongarra Rd,	
Albion Park	52 A4
Mt Keira	
Mt Keira Rd	28 N12
Mt Kembla	
Cordeaux Rd	34 A6
Oak Flats	
Fisher St	53 A1
Otford	
cnr Otford &	
Domville Rds	14 E4
Shoalhaven	
Fire Control Centre	
92 Albatross Rd,	
South Nowra	91 M6
Shoalhaven Heads	
Shoalhaven Heads Rd	95 F7
Stanwell Park	
Lawrence Hargrave Dr	13 P12
Wollongong	
Fire Control Centre	
Dumbrell Rd,	
Bulli	22 B12

Girl Guides

	Map Ref
Albion Park	51 K4
Dapto	44 G7
Fernhill	25 N16
Gwynneville	1 H8
Helensburgh	11 L12
Kiama	62 A15
Lake Illawarra	49 Q9
Nowra	88 A15
Thirroul	22 G4
Unanderra	40 J1
Woonona	22 B13

Golf Courses, Clubs & Driving Ranges

	Map Ref
Boomerang Golf Course	15 Q4
Calderwood Valley	
Golf Course	47 A12
Galloping Golf	40 A9
Gerringong Golf Club	70 E8
Helensburgh	
Golf Driving Range	11 J16
Illawarra Golf Club	15 Q5
Illawarra Golf Complex	46 F12
Jamberoo Golf Club	60 C6
Kiama Golf Club	57 Q15
Nowra Golf Range	92 G3
Nowra Golf &	
Recreation Club	87 M9
Port Kembla Golf Club	46 J7
Russell Vale Golf Course	25 N4
Shoalhaven Heads	
Golf Club	95 J7
The Grange Golf Club	39 N11
The Links Shell Cove	53 N15
Vineyards Golf Links	92 P16
Wollongong Golf Club	35 Q5
Worrigee Links	
Golf Course	92 J1

Hospitals

	Map Ref
Bulli	
Hospital Rd	22 B11
Coledale	
Lawrence Hargrave Dr,	
Wombarra	18 N3
David Berry	
85 Tannery Rd,	
Berry	96 P7
Figtree Rehabilitation	
1 Suttor Pl	34 M9
Lawrence Hargrave Private	
72 Phillip St,	
Thirroul	18 A15
Nowra Private	
Weeroona Pl	92 B5
Port Kembla	
Cowper St,	
Warrawong	41 J13
Shellharbour	
15 Madigan Bvd,	
Mount Warrigal	49 K14
Shellharbour Private	
27 Captain Cook Dr,	
Barrack Heights	49 M14
Shoalhaven District Memorial	
Scenic Dr,	
Nowra	87 N10
Wollongong	
Loftus St	1 H12
Wollongong Private	
Crown St	1 F13

Hotels & Motels

	Map Ref
Adina Apartment Hotel	
Wollongong	2 E12
Archer Resort	
Nowra	92 B2
Avaleen Lodge Motor Inn	
Bomaderry	83 M14
Bangalee Motel	
Berry	96 M7
Beach Park Motel	
North Wollongong	2 D2
Berkeley Hotel	40 L12
Berry Hotel	96 K8
Berry Village	
Boutique Motel	96 H8

Parks, Reserves & Sporting Venues

Parks, Reserves & Sporting Venues

Street Listings

All the streets in this index are listed alphabetically and then by suburb. It is most important to have the correct name when looking for a particular street. If any difficulty is experienced with the suburb name, refer to the Suburbs and Localities Index.

Mc and **Mac:** Names beginning with 'Mc' are treated as though they are spelt 'Mac' and indexed accordingly.

Mt: Names beginning with 'Mt' are treated as though they are spelt 'Mount' and indexed accordingly.

St: Names beginning with 'St' are treated as though they are spelt 'Saint' and indexed accordingly.

The: Names beginning with 'The' are treated with 'The' first and are indexed accordingly.

Streets not Named on Maps

For reasons of clarity it is not always possible to show and name every street on the map itself. Any street or lane that is not shown on the map face is listed in italic (sloping) type and referenced to its approximate position.

Alphabet Indicators

These are the street names in capitals located on the top left and right hand corners of each page of the street index. The indicator on the left page represents the first named street in the first column on this page, while the indicator on the right page represents the last named street in the last column on this page.

ABBREVIATIONS FOR DESIGNATIONS

Alley .... al	Close cl	End ....end	Junction .... jnc	Pocket .... pkt	Street .... st
Approach ...... app	Common ...... cmn	Entrance .... ent	Key ....key	Port/Point .... pt	Tarn .... tn
Arcade .... arc	Concourse ..... cnc	Esplanade ..... esp	Lane .... la	Promenade .. prm	Terrace .... tce
Avenue .... av	Copse .... cps	Expressway ... exp	Link .... lk	Quadrant .... qd	Tollway .... twy
Bend .... bnd	Corner .... cnr	Fairway ....fy	Lookout............ lkt	Quay/s .... qy	Top ....top
Boardwalk...... bwk	Corso .... cso	Freeway .... fwy	Loop .... lp	Ramble .... ra	Tor .... tor
Boulevard ...... bvd	Court .... ct	Frontage .... fr	Mall .... ml	Reach .... rch	Track .... tr
Bowl .... bl	Courtyard ...... cyd	Garden/s .... gdn	Mead .... md	Reserve .... res	Trail .... trl
Brace .... br	Cove .... cov	Gate/s .... gte	Meander .... mdr	Rest .... rst	Turn .... trn
Brae .... br	Crescent .... cr	Gateway ... gwy	Mews .... mw	Retreat .... rt	Underpass ..... ups
Break .... brk	Crest .... cst	Glade .... gld	Motorway .... mwy	Return .... rtn	Vale................ va
Brook .... brk	Cross .... cs	Glen .... gln	Nook .... nk	Ridge .... rdg	Valley.............. vy
Broadway ..... bwy	Crossing .... csg	Grange .... gra	North .... n	Rise .... ri	View .... vw
Brow .... brw	Curve .... cve	Green .... grn	Outlook .... out	Road .... rd	Vista .... vst
Bypass .... bps	Dale .... dle	Grove .... gr	Parade .... pde	Roadway .... rdy	Walk .... wk
Central.............. c	Down/s .... dn	Grovet .... gr	Park .... pk	Route .... rte	Walkway .... wky
Centre .... ctr	Drive .... dr	Haven ....hvn	Parkway .... pky	Row ....row	Way .... wy
Chase .... ch	Driveway........ dwy	Heights .... hts	Pass .... ps	Serviceway ... swy	West .... w
Circle .... cir	East .... e	Highway .... hwy	Pathway .... pwy	South .... s	Wynd .... wyn
Circuit .... cct	Edge .... edg	Hike .... hk	Place .... pl	Square .... sq	
Circus .... crc	Elbow .... elb	Hill ....hill	Plaza .... plz	Strand .... sd	

ABBREVIATIONS FOR SUBURB NAMES

Airport .... Aprt	Crossing .... Csg	Head/s .... Hd	Lower .... Lr	Pocket .... Pkt	South .... S
Basin .... Bsn	Down/s .... Dn	Headland .... Hd	Meadow/s ..... Mdw	Point/Port........... Pt	Terminal ...... Term
Bay .... B	East .... E	Heights .... Ht	Mount .... Mt	Range .... Rge	University .... Uni
Beach .... Bch	Field/s .... Fd	Hill/s .... Hl	Mountain/s .... Mtn	Reach .... Rch	Upper .... Up
Bridge .... Br	Flat .... Fl	Island I	North .... N	Reserve .... Res	Valley .... Vy
Central............Ctrl	Forest .... Frst	Junction .... Jctn	Paradise .... Pdse	Ridge .... Rdg	Vale .... Va
Chase .... Ch	Garden/s .... Gdn	Lagoon .... Lgn	Park .... Pk	River .... R	Village Vill
Corner .... Cnr	Grove .... Gr	Lakes L	Peninsula.....Pen	Rocks .... Rks	Waters .... Wtr
Court .... Ct	Gully .... Gly	Lodge .... Ldg	Plain/s .... Pl	Saint .... St	West .... W
Creek .... Ck	Harbor/our ..... Hbr	Lookout .... Lkt	Plateau .... Plat		

		Map Ref

A

ABBEY
st. Kembla Grange..39 C11
ABELIA
pl. Worrigee...........92 H7
st. Barrack Heights..54 A1
tce. Woonona...........22 A9
ABERCROMBIE
cr. Albion Park....51 M7
st. W Wollongong....35 C4
ABERDARE
pl. Farmborough Ht..39 Q1
ABERGELDIE
st. Nowra.............92 E4
ABERNETHYS
la. Cambewarra....83 J7
la. Meroo Meadow..83 M8
ABERTILLERY
rd. Figtree..........34 L8
ABLETT
ct. Shoalhaven Hd..95 D6
ACACIA
av. Albion Park Rail..52 H4
av. Gwynneville........1 C7
av. Gwynneville.....29 F16
st. Windang...........50 E2
ACER
pl. Worrigee.........92 J4
ACHILLES
av. N Wollongong....1 Q1
av. N Wollongong.....29 N13
ACLAND
dr. Horsley..........38 M12
ACMENA
cl. Shellharbour....54 A5
ACREAGE
st. Kembla Grange..39 E10
ADAM MURRAY
wy. Flinders.........53 N9
ADAMS
av. Unanderra.........34 G15
pde.Woonona...........22 D15
ADDISON
av. Lake Illawarra..49 Q7
la. Lake Illawarra..49 Q6
st. Shellharbour....54 C8
ADELAIDE
pl. Shellharbour....54 E8
pl. Tarrawanna.....25 J12
ADELE
cl. Nowra............92 D5
ADINA
av. Kiama............61 P16
av. W Wollongong...34 Q1
ADMINISTRATION
rd. Port Kembla....41 J9
AGAPANTHA
tce. Woonona.........22 A9
AGARS
la. Berry............96 P9
la. Coolangatta....95 B1
AGNEW
cl. Balgownie.......25 G16
AIR
av. Bulli...........22 F5
AIRPORT
rd. Albion Park Rail..48 F14
AITKEN
cl. Albion Park....52 B7
pl. Lake Heights....41 C12
AJAX
av. N Wollongong..29 N12
AKUNA
st. Keiraville.......1 A6
st. Keiraville......29 E15
st. Kiama...........61 Q16
ALANDALE
av. Figtree.........34 P11
ALANSON
av. Bulli...........21 P10
ALATA
cr. South Nowra....92 G11

ALBAN
st. Corrimal........25 P10
ALBANY
la. Berry...........96 G9
st. Berry...........96 H9
ALBATROSS
dr. Blackbutt.......53 D3
rd. Nowra...........91 J9
rd. Nowra Hill......90 E16
rd. Nowra Hill......90 Q16
rd. Nowra Hill......91 B16
rd. South Nowra....91 G11
ALBERMARLE
st. Farmborough Ht..40 D2
ALBERT
ct. Berry...........96 K7
la. Balgownie.......29 F2
st. Bellambi........26 B7
st. Berry...........96 G7
st. Corrimal........25 Q7
st. Lake Illawarra..50 A8
st. Nowra...........91 Q3
st. Unanderra.......34 K15
st. Woonona.........22 A16
ALCOOMIE
cr. Koonawarra......44 K5
ALCORN
st. Flinders........53 P11
ALDINGA
av. Gerringong......70 F4
av. Koonawarra......44 K5
ALDOUS
pl. Worrigee........92 Q14
ALDRIDGE
av. East Corrimal...26 E12
ALEXANDER
av. Kiama Downs.....61 N4
st. Fairy Meadow....29 L2
ALEXANDER BERRY
dr. Coolangatta.....95 A12
ALEXANDRA
st. Berry...........96 J8
ALFRED
cr. Lake Illawarra..49 Q8
st. Bomaderry.......84 D13
st. Woonona.........22 A16
ALICE
st. Woonona.........26 C2
ALISON
st. Kiama...........61 L14
ALKERA
cr. W Wollongong...35 C3
ALKIRA
cct. Horsley........38 L15
ALLAMBIE
av. Koonawarra......44 L5
av. Kiama...........65 Q5
ALLAN
st. Port Kembla....41 Q12
st. Wollongong......1 F15
st. Woonona.........35 H4
ALLANS CREEK
rd. Port Kembla....41 H2
ALLAWA
pl. Koonawarra......44 L5
ALLAWAH
pl. Dunmore........57 H13
ALLEN
st. Austinmer.......18 G13
st. Mt Keira........28 Q14
ALLENBY
pde.Bulli...........22 E7
ALLENS
la. Shellharbour....54 D7
ALLINGA
dr. Oak Flats.......49 G14
ALLISON
av. Nowra...........92 E1
ALLMAN
la. Mt St Thomas....35 D10
ALLOWRIE
cr. Nowra...........92 E4
st. Jamberoo.......60 B6

ALLUMBA
gr. Cordeaux Ht.....34 G13
ALMA
rd. Helensburgh.....11 J11
ALMOND
gr. Worrigee........92 L4
ALMOND BARK
rd. Worrigee........92 H6
ALNE BANK
la. Gerringong......69 C14
la. Rose Valley.....69 A10
ALPINA
pl. South Nowra....92 F10
ALROY
st. Bulli...........22 H11
ALUKEA
rd. Cordeaux Ht.....34 J11
ALVAN
pde.Mt Pleasant....29 D6
ALVERSTOKE
cl. Bomaderry.......84 B13
ALVIS
av. Dapto...........44 H8
AMALFI
cr. Nowra...........88 D16
AMANDA
pl. Horsley.........39 C15
AMARA
pl. Oak Flats.......49 H15
AMARAL
av. Albion Park....51 N5
av. Dapto...........44 D8
AMAROO
av. Figtree.........34 L11
wy. Shellharbour C C..53 G1
AMBASSADOR
av. North Nowra....87 G6
AMBER
pl. Bomaderry......83 Q13
AMBLESIDE
av. Mt Keira........29 B14
AMINYA
pl. Farmborough Ht..40 B2
AMR
rd. Spring Hill.....35 C14
AMUNDSEN
av. Shoalhaven Hd..95 E6
ANAMA
st. Fairy Meadow....29 M5
ANCHORAGE
pde.Shell Cove......54 D12
ANDERSON
av. Nowra...........87 P12
pl. Kiama Downs.....61 L5
rd. Woonona.........25 P2
ANDERSONS
la. Jaspers Brush...96 A13
ANDREW
av. Keiraville......29 C12
cr. Mt Warrigal.....49 N12
cr. Worrigee........92 H7
ANDROMEDA
rd. Dunmore........53 M13
ANEMBO
cr. Kiama Heights...65 N11
ANGEL
st. Corrimal........25 M12
ANGELO
st. South Nowra....92 E16
ANGOPHORA
cr. Kanahooka......45 F5
ANGUS
av. South Nowra....91 M12
st. Fernhill........25 K16
ANN
st. Thirroul........22 H3
ANNA
av. Warrawong......41 F12
ANNE
st. Gwynneville......1 B3
st. Gwynneville.....29 F14
st. Warilla.........50 C10

ANNEALING
rd. Port Kembla....35 H16
ANNESLEY
av. Stanwell Tops...13 L7
ANNIE
st. Corrimal........25 M8
ANTARES
cl. Nowra...........92 F5
pl. Nowra...........92 F5
ANTHEA
pl. Penrose........44 A9
ANTHONY
av. Farmborough Ht..39 Q1
st. Lake Illawarra..50 B8
ANTRIM
av. Warilla.........50 A13
st. Kiama...........61 Q13
ANZAC
st. Nowra...........92 D5
wy. Port Kembla....42 E13
APOLLO
cr. Worrigee........92 H8
dr. Shell Cove......54 B11
APPERLEYS
la. Worrigee........92 Q3
APPIN
rd. Cataract........17 G1
rd. Cataract........17 L12
APPLEBERRY
cl. Bomaderry......84 C10
APPLEBY
cl. Horsley.........43 N1
AQUATIC
dr. Shell Cove......54 D10
ARAGAN
cct. Bulli..........22 H7
ARALUEN
av. Mt Kembla.......33 N7
tce. Tullimbar......51 H8
ARBOREAL
pl. Horsley.........43 Q2
ARCADIA
st. Warilla.........50 C12
ARCHER
pl. Bangalee........83 A16
ARCHIBALD
rd. Gerringong......70 E3
ARGYLE
pl. Unanderra.......34 E13
ARILLA
st. Nowra...........92 F6
ARINYA
cl. Nowra...........92 E6
ARISTO
cr. Mt Ousley.......29 K9
ARKELL
dr. Figtree.........34 P11
ARMAGH
pde.Thirroul........22 B1
ARMITAGE
av. Horsley.........43 Q2
ARMOUR
st. Bellambi........26 J9
ARMSTRONG
av. Gerringong......70 G1
av. Mt Warrigal.....49 M10
st. Dapto...........39 J15
st. W Wollongong...29 C16
ARNHEIM
cl. North Nowra....87 F7
ARNOLD
cr. Kiama...........65 J3
cr. Lake Heights....41 B13
ARRABI
st. Flinders........53 J8
ARROW
av. Figtree.........35 A7
ARTER
av. Figtree.........34 J4

ARTHUR
st. Corrimal........26 A8
st. Thirroul........22 H1
st. Worrigee........92 H8
ARTIS
st. Bulli...........22 F12
ARUDA
pl. Oak Flats.......49 H13
ARUNTA
cl. Nowra...........92 D2
dr. Thirroul........22 D1
ARVENIS
cr. Balgownie.......29 D4
ARWON
cr. Bangalee........82 N14
ASCALON
cl. Nowra...........92 G3
ASCOT
av. Kembla Grange..40 E7
ASH
av. Albion Park Rail..52 K3
ASHBURTON
dr. Albion Park....52 A14
dr. Albion Park....52 E12
dr. Croom..........52 E12
ASHBURY
av. Horsley.........43 N2
ASHCROFT
pl. Keiraville......29 F9
ASHLEY
av. Farmborough Ht..40 C1
ASHMORE
cr. Kanahooka......45 A1
ASHTON
cl. Albion Park....52 F14
ASHTON VALE
gr. Horsley.........43 N1
ASHWOOD
pl. Horsley.........38 N15
ASMS
rd. Spring Hill.....41 C1
ASPECT
st. Kembla Grange..39 E11
ASPINALL
st. Shoalhaven Hd..95 G8
ASPROMONTE
dr. South Nowra....92 D16
ASQUITH
cl. North Nowra....87 D6
st. Austinmer.......18 D13
ASTERIA
st. Worrigee........92 G7
ASTOR
pl. Shell Cove......53 Q11
ATCHISON
st. Flinders........53 J7
st. Wollongong......1 N16
st. Wollongong......35 L5
ATHANLIN
dr. Haywards Bay...48 F7
ATHENA
cr. Worrigee........92 H8
ATHOL
st. Woonona.........22 A12
ATKINSON
av. Dapto...........44 H7
ATTUNGA
st. Kiama Heights...65 N11
st. Keiraville......29 D15
AUBURN
pde.Cringila.......41 E9
st. Coniston.......35 K8
st. Wollongong......1 M16
st. Wollongong......35 K8
AUGUSTA
pky. Shell Cove.....57 P2
st. East Corrimal...26 B14
AURORA
av. Dunmore........53 M14

AUSTEN
rd. Lake Heights....41 C11
AUSTIN
av. Minnamurra.....58 A13
st. Woonona.........22 C16
AUSTINMER
st. Austinmer.......18 F13
st. Tullimbar......51 J5
AVALON
tce. Figtree........35 A9
AVERY
av. Mt Warrigal.....49 J10
AVIEMORE
pl. Figtree.........28 L15
AVOCA
pl. Albion Park....51 Q12
AVON
cl. Albion Park....52 F12
pde.Mt Kembla......34 A5
AVONDALE
rd. Avondale........43 B12
rd. Dapto...........43 P10
rd. Penrose........43 P10
AVONLEA
st. Dapto...........44 F5
AYERS
la. Oak Flats.......49 B16
AYRSHIRE
la. Calderwood.....51 D5
AYSHIRE
st. Horsley.........38 M12

B

BAAN BAAN
st. Dapto...........44 H1
BACK FOREST
rd. Bolong.........84 Q15
BACKHOUSE
rd. Lake Heights....41 D11
BADGERY
st. Albion Park....52 B7
BAFFLER
pl. Bangalee........82 N15
BAGOT
pl. Port Kembla....41 K11
BAILEYS
rd. Gerringong......70 A2
BAINBRIGGE
cr. Nowra...........87 M15
BAINES
pl. Helensburgh....13 H4
BAKER
cr. Figtree.........34 K6
pl. Mt Warrigal.....49 M9
BAKERS
la. Primbee........46 F11
la. Windang........46 F11
BALARANG
pl. Koonawarra......44 M9
BALFOUR
rd. Austinmer.......18 E13
st. Fairy Meadow....29 K1
BALGOWNIE
la. Tullimbar......51 D7
rd. Balgownie.......29 E2
rd. Fairy Meadow....29 K2
BALIRA
pl. Worrigee........92 K7
BALL
st. Albion Park Rail..48 H14
st. Woonona.........22 A13
BALLANTINE
pl. Horsley.........39 B13
BALLINA
st. South Nowra....92 B16
BALMARINGA
av. North Nowra....87 F6
cl. Cordeaux Ht.....34 J12
BALMER
cr. Woonona.........21 Q12

	Map	Ref

CANTERBURY
rd. Kembla Grange .. 40 D7

CAPRICORN
wy. Shell Cove 53 Q15

CAPTAIN
st. Kembla Grange .. 39 D11

CAPTAIN COOK
dr. Barrack Heights .. 49 M14

CARABEEN
st. Barrack Heights .. 49 P16

CARAVEL
cr. Shell Cove 54 B10

CARBEEN
cr. Cordeaux Ht 34 G12

CARBERRY
av. Kiama Downs 57 Q16

CARCOOLA
st. Mt Keira 28 P15

CARDIFF
st. Berkeley 40 K11

CARDWELL
dr. Nowra Hill 90 P16

CARINMONEY
av. Warilla 49 Q13

CARINYA
wy. Gerringong 69 E14

CARISBROOKE
cl. Bomaderry 84 A14

CARLIE
pl. Woonona 26 A3

CARLON
cr. Farmborough Ht .. 39 P1

CARLOTTA
cr. Warrawong 41 M15

CARLYLE
cl. Dapto 44 F13

CARNARVON
st. Berkeley 40 K10

CAROLE
av. Woonona 21 N14

CAROLINE
st. Corrimal 25 N13

CAROOLA
pde. North Nowra 87 G6

CAROONA
st. Berkeley 40 Q12

CARR
pde. Unanderra 34 J13
st. Towradgi 25 Q16

CARRINGLE
st. Berkeley 40 Q12

CARRINGTON
rd. Cambewarra 83 D1
st. Barrack Heights .. 49 L16
st. Bulli 22 F15
st. Woonona 22 F15

CARRINGTON PARK
dr. Nowra 92 G6
dr. Nowra 92 G6

CARROLL
rd. East Corrimal 26 D14

CARSON
pl. Minnamurra 58 A14

CARTERS
la. Fairy Meadow 29 Q5
la. Towradgi 29 Q5

CARVIE
cl. Shellharbour 54 B5

CASA
cct. South Nowra 92 D15

CASCADE
ct. Albion Park 52 C14

CASCARILLA
st. Figtree 34 H9

CASSANDRA
pl. Stanwell Park 14 A9

CASSEL
av. Towradgi 26 C16

CASSIA
st. Barrack Heights .. 53 P1

CASSIAN
st. Keiraville 29 C13

CASTER
rd. Port Kembla 41 J4

CASTER PARK
rd. Port Kembla 41 K3

CASTLE
ct. Berkeley 40 Q10
gln. North Nowra 87 K5

CASUARINA
cr. Kanahooka 45 F5
pl. Figtree 28 P16
st. Oak Flats 52 M1

CATAMARAN
av. Shell Cove 54 F9

CATER
st. Coledale 18 J6

CATHEDRAL ROCKS
av. Kiama Downs 62 A6

CATHERINE
st. Gwynneville 1 G4
st. Gwynneville 29 J14

CATHIE
cl. Flinders 54 A9

CATO
pl. Mt Keira 29 A13

CATTLE
rd. Calderwood 47 H15

CAVALIER
pde. Bomaderry 83 Q12

CAVANAGH
la. West Nowra 91 J3

CAWDELL
dr. Albion Park 52 B6

CAWLEY
st. Bellambi 26 E11
st. East Corrimal 26 E14

CAY
la. Shell Cove 54 J11

CEDAR
av. Avondale 43 F15
av. Windang 50 D2
gr. Keiraville 29 C12
st. Albion Park Rail .. 52 H5
tce. Woonona 21 P15

CEDAR RIDGE
rd. Kiama 65 L1

CELESTIAL
av. Dunmore 53 M12

CELIA
pde. Shoalhaven Hd .. 95 D11

CEMETERY
rd. Helensburgh 11 L13
rd. Wollongong 35 L8

CENTENARY
rd. Albion Park 51 Q7

CENTENNIAL
ct. Bomaderry 84 B14

CENTRAL
av. Kembla Heights .. 33 M5
av. Oak Flats 49 A14
av. South Nowra 91 N13
rd. Cordeaux Ht 34 J12
rd. Shellharbour C C .. 49 J16
rd. Unanderra 34 J12
rd. Unanderra 34 J13

CENTRAL LAB
rd. Port Kembla 41 H5

CENTRE
av. Nowra 87 P16
rd. Mundamia 91 H5
rd. West Nowra 91 H5

CHADWICK
gr. Helensburgh 11 L12

CHAFFEY
wy. Albion Park 52 D15

CHALMERS
rd. Tapitallee 82 A11
st. Balgownie 29 E2

CHANNON
st. Russell Vale 26 A6

CHAPEL
la. Jamberoo 59 Q5

CHAPLIN
pl. Albion Park 52 C15

CHAPMAN
av. Mt Warrigal 49 L14
st. Fairy Meadow 29 N2
st. Kiama 65 Q4
st. Unanderra 34 M13

CHARCOAL
cl. Unanderra 40 N2

CHARDONNAY
dr. Dapto 44 D13

CHARLES
av. Minnamurra 58 A14
rd. Fernhill 25 M16
rd. Tarrawanna 25 M16
st. Berry 96 F10
st. Port Kembla 42 A13

CHARLOTTE
cr. Albion Park 51 N6
st. Wollongong 1 N8
st. Wollongong 29 M16

CHARLOTTE HARRISON
dr. Woonona 26 D5

CHARLTON
st. Mt Warrigal 49 L7

CHARMIAN CLIFT
pl. Kiama 66 A7

CHATSWORTH
rd. North Nowra 87 H3

CHEBEC
cl. Bomaderry 87 N1

CHEFFINS
pl. Albion Park 52 B5

CHELLOW DENE
av. Stanwell Park 14 A9

CHELTENHAM
dr. Shoalhaven Hd .. 95 F9

CHENHALLS
st. Woonona 26 B1

CHERRY
st. Woonona 21 Q16

CHERRY BRUSH
ct. Berkeley 40 N8

CHERRY PLUM
wy. Worrigee 92 H4

CHERYL
pl. Corrimal 25 K11

CHESHIRE
st. Berkeley 40 H9

CHESTER
st. Bellambi 26 C7

CHESTNUT
av. Bomaderry 83 Q12
st. Barrack Heights .. 53 Q2

CHIFLEY
la. Oak Flats 48 N16

CHILLAWONG
cct. Blackbutt 53 G2

CHINCHILLA
wy. Albion Park 52 E14

CHIPPENDALE
pl. Helensburgh 11 L12

CHIPPEWA
rd. Gerringong 70 E4

CHISHOLM
rd. Gerringong 70 E1
rd. Warrawong 41 F13
st. Shellharbour 54 C8

CHISLEHURST
av. Figtree 34 Q5

CHITTICK
av. North Nowra 87 E1
pl. Gerringong 70 F2

CHOUNDING
cr. Bellambi 26 G9

CHRIS
vw. North Nowra 87 L5

CHRISTIANSEN
pl. Bellambi 26 F8

CHRISTINE
la. Nowra 87 N16

CHRISTLANA
cl. West Nowra 91 J2

CHRISTY
dr. Port Kembla 41 Q4

CHURCH
la. Kembla Heights .. 33 L5
st. Albion Park 51 K5
st. Balgownie 29 G2
st. Port Kembla 42 B13
st. Thirroul 22 G2
st. Wollongong 2 A12
st. Wollongong 2 A16
st. Wollongong 2 B11
st. Wollongong 29 P16
st. Wollongong 35 N7
st. Wollongong 35 P2

CHURCHILL
av. Warrawong 41 L12
cct. Barrack Heights .. 49 Q14
st. Jamberoo 60 A5

CHURINGA
cir. Koonawarra 44 K7

CHURNWOOD
pl. Albion Park Rail .. 52 N7
pl. Cordeaux Ht 34 B14

CIRRUS
st. Dapto 44 J4

CIVIC
av. Shell Cove 54 D11

CLAREMONT
av. Lake Heights 41 C13
pl. Kiama 61 M16

CLARENCE
ct. Berkeley 40 Q10
st. Berry 96 G10

CLARKE
av. North Nowra 87 H7
st. Dapto 39 F16
st. Kiama Downs 57 P16

CLAYTON
st. Kembla Grange .. 39 E10

CLEARY
av. Kanahooka 44 N2
st. Barrack Heights .. 49 P15

CLEMATIS
cr. Barrack Heights .. 53 M1

CLERMONT
cr. Albion Park 52 G13

CLEVELAND
pl. Tullimbar 51 H7
rd. Avondale 43 C11
rd. Cleveland 43 D9
rd. Dapto 43 N6
rd. Huntley 43 D9

CLEVERDON
cr. Figtree 35 A8

CLIFF
av. Barrack Point 50 F15
dr. Kiama Downs 61 Q4
pde. Thirroul 22 J3
rd. N Wollongong 2 E3
rd. Scarborough 16 F14
rd. Wollongong 2 F4
rd. Wollongong 30 A15
st. Coledale 18 K7

CLIFFORD
st. Fairy Meadow 29 N5

CLIFTON SCHOOL
pde. Clifton 16 J8

CLIPPER
av. Shell Cove 54 C11
rd. Nowra 92 F3

CLIVE
av. Warrawong 41 H13

CLIVE BISSELL
dr. Cataract 28 K5
dr. Mt Keira 28 K5

CLOUDY
la. Calderwood 51 D4

CLOVER
ct. Cambewarra Vill .. 82 M6

CLOVERFIELD
pl. Horsley 38 L16

CLOVER HILL
rd. Jamberoo 60 E16

CLUB
la. Helensburgh 11 N11

CLUTHA
pl. Wombarra 16 B15

CLYDE
cl. Thirroul 22 F4
wy. Flinders, off
    Wandella Cr .. 53 M10

COACHWOOD
av. Worrigee 92 J4
dr. Albion Park Rail .. 52 N4
dr. Cordeaux Ht 34 D15
dr. Unanderra 34 D15
st. Kiama 61 L13

COAL
st. Gerringong 70 G3

COAL PREP
rd. Port Kembla 41 K7

COAL STOCK
rd. Port Kembla 41 K4

COAST
st. Thirroul 18 A16
tr. Lilyvale 12 N14

COASTAL WALKING
tr. Werri Beach 69 M8

COBARGO
st. Tullimbar 51 K8

COBBLERS
av. Figtree 34 P12

COCHRANE
rd. Thirroul 18 D16
st. W Wollongong 35 C1

COCKATIEL
ct. Blackbutt 53 E3

COCKATOO
cr. Calderwood 51 C4

COCONUT
dr. North Nowra 87 D2

COCOS PALM
dr. Bomaderry 83 P13

COG
rd. Port Kembla 41 L3

COILA
cl. Flinders 53 N6

COIL DESPATCH
rd. Port Kembla 35 J14

COKE OVENS
rd. Port Kembla 41 J6

COKEWORKS
rd. Coledale 18 J5

COLDEN
dr. Albion Park Rail .. 52 Q4

COLE
st. Balgownie 25 F15
st. Kiama 65 L3

COLEDALE
av. Coledale 18 L7

COLEMANS
la. Bulli 22 E10

COLGONG
cr. Towradgi 26 A15

COLLAERY
av. Fairy Meadow 29 M7
rd. Russell Vale 25 Q4

COLLEEN
gr. Wollongong 35 G5

COLLEGE
av. Blackbutt 53 G6
av. Flinders 53 G6
av. Oak Flats 49 H16
av. Shellharbour C C .. 53 H2
pl. Gwynneville 1 G1
pl. Gwynneville 29 J13

COLLEY
dr. Kiama 61 P13
st. Kiama 61 P14

COLLIE
wy. Albion Park 52 F12

COLLIERY
rd. Helensburgh 12 A9

COLLINS
av. Woonona 22 E15
la. Kiama 62 A15
st. Corrimal 25 M10
st. Corrimal 26 A10
st. Helensburgh 11 L12
st. Kiama 61 Q16
wy. Flinders 53 P11
wy. Nowra 87 Q12

COLO
pl. Albion Park 51 Q9

COLONY
gdn. Horsley 39 B14

COLVILLE
st. Flinders 53 L7

COLVIN
pl. Dapto 44 F12

COLYER
av. Nowra 87 P11

COMERONG ISLAND
rd. Comerong Island .. 95 B16

COMMEMORATION
pl. Shellharbour C C, off
    Memorial Dr 49 G16

COMMERCE
dr. Lake Illawarra 50 D9

COMMERCIAL
rd. Port Kembla 41 H8
rd. South Nowra 92 B16

COMMISSIONERS
st. Bombo 62 A7
la. Kiama Downs 62 A7

COMPTON
st. Dapto 44 F10

CONCORDE
wy. Bomaderry 84 D14

CONDIE
cr. North Nowra 87 J6
cr. North Nowra 87 J6

CONDON
pl. Yallah 48 B7
st. Albion Park 52 D11
wy. Nowra 87 P12

CONDOR
cr. Shell Cove 54 A10

CONIFER
st. Albion Park Rail .. 52 J5

CONISTON
cl. North Nowra 87 E6
gdn. Stanwell Tops .. 13 L8

CONJOLA
cl. Flinders 53 M6

CONNAGHAN
av. East Corrimal 26 F11

CONNECTION
rd. Calderwood 51 D4

CONNORS
vw. Berry 96 A6

CONTRACTOR
rd. Spring Hill 35 D14

CONWAY
cr. Blackbutt 53 D4
cst. Berry 96 A6

COOBA
pl. Wombarra 16 C14

COOBACK
rd. Albion Park 51 K5

COOBY
rd. Tullimbar 51 G9
rd. Yellow Rock 51 G9

COOINDA
pl. Kiama 65 N3

COOK
cl. Albion Park 52 D12
st. Unanderra 34 K14

COOKE
pl. Gerringong 70 H3

COOLABAH
rd. Dapto 39 J16

	Map	Ref

COOLANGATTA
av. Gerringong 69 F13
rd. Berry 96 K14
rd. Coolangatta 95 B1
COOLAWIN
cr. Shellharbour 53 Q6
COOLGARDIE
st. East Corrimal 26 B11
COOLIBAH
av. Albion Park Rail .. 52 H4
COOLUM
pky. Shell Cove 53 Q16
COOMBAH
cl. Tapitallee 82 G13
COOMBE
st. Wollongong 2 C12
st. Wollongong 35 P2
COOMEA
st. Bomaderry 88 B4
COOPER
av. Woonona 22 D15
pl. Albion Park 52 D9
pl. Kiama Downs 61 N5
COORONG
rd. North Nowra 87 A7
COORUNG
cl. Cordeaux Ht 34 C8
COPE
pl. Bulli 21 Q9
pl. Gerringong 69 E15
COPPER LEAF
pl. Worrigee 92 K3
CORAL
cr. Unanderra 34 E13
CORAL GUM
ct. Worrigee 92 L7
CORALIE
cl. North Nowra 87 J4
CORAL SEA
dr. West Nowra 91 L6
CORAL TREE
cr. Calderwood 47 D16
dr. Gerringong 70 E2
CORAL VALE
dr. Wongawilli 38 H9
CORBETT
av. Thirroul 22 H5
CORDEAUX
pde. Tullimbar 51 K9
rd. Cordeaux 33 A3
rd. Cordeaux Ht 34 B6
rd. Dombarton 33 B6
rd. Figtree 34 J10
rd. Kembla Heights .. 33 F9
rd. Mt Kembla 33 M7
rd. Unanderra 34 J10
COREEN
av. W Wollongong 35 A1
cl. North Nowra 87 J7
CORELLA
av. Horsley 43 H3
cl. Shellharbour 53 Q5
CORINDA
rd. Woonona 26 F2
CORKWOOD
cct. Woonona 25 Q1
st. Albion Park Rail .. 52 N4
CORMACK
av. Dapto 44 E15
CORMORANT
pl. Berkeley 41 B10
wy. Shell Cove 54 D10
CORNELIUS
la. Bulli 22 G7
pl. Nowra 92 C5
CORNELIUS O'BRIEN
wy. Woonona 26 D5
CORNFIELD
rd. Calderwood 51 E2
CORNOCK
av. Thirroul 22 C1

CORNWALL
cl. South Nowra 92 D10
rd. Dapto 44 H6
CORNWELL
pl. Berkeley 40 K12
CORONA
av. Lake Illawarra 50 A6
CORONATA
dr. Figtree 34 P1
CORONET
pl. Dapto 44 G11
CORREA
ct. Worrigee 92 L6
CORRIE
rd. Woonona 21 Q11
CORRIMAL
st. Tarrawanna 25 K14
st. Wollongong 2 D15
st. Wollongong 29 Q15
st. Wollongong 35 P8
CORUNNA
cr. Flinders 53 Q8
CORYULE
pl. Kiama 65 M3
COSGROVE
av. Flinders 53 N11
av. Keiraville 29 D11
COSTA
st. Worrigee 92 H8
COTTAGE
gr. Corrimal 25 L10
grn. Mt Ousley 29 G6
COTTERILL
av. Woonona 26 D2
COTTON PALM
dr. North Nowra 87 E2
COTTONWOOD
cr. Figtree 34 N3
COUNSELL
rd. Bangalee 82 M15
COURT
la. Wollongong 2 B12
la. Wollongong 35 P2
COVE
bvd. Shell Cove 53 Q11
COVENTRY
st. Berkeley 40 L9
COVER
dr. Worrigee 92 J3
COVINGTON
grn. Dapto 39 H16
COWAL
ct. Flinders 53 Q10
COWELL
la. Coledale 18 K6
pl. Kiama Downs 61 M6
COWPER
la. Helensburgh 11 N9
st. Fairy Meadow 29 P6
st. Helensburgh 11 P9
st. Port Kembla 41 M13
st. Warrawong 41 H11
COWRIES
av. Shell Cove 54 D12
COX
av. Nowra 88 A16
pde. Mt Warrigal 49 J12
pl. Penrose 44 A11
COXS
av. Corrimal 25 L9
la. Corrimal 25 N9
CRADLE
dr. Bulli 22 C9
CRAIG
cr. Dapto 44 J4
pl. Gerringong 69 F14
st. Thirroul 22 H4
CRAIG-MOR
wy. Keiraville 29 D13
CRAMS
rd. North Nowra 87 A4

CRANA
pl. Wollongong 1 D15
pl. Wollongong 35 G4
CRANESBILL
wy. Figtree 34 K9
CRANFORD
la. Figtree 34 P4
CRAVEN
st. Bulli 22 F6
CRAWFORD
av. Gwynneville 1 L4
av. Gwynneville 29 L14
dr. North Nowra 87 G6
CRAY
st. Horsley 43 K3
CREAMERY
rd. Albion Park Rail .. 48 H15
CREEK
rd. Huntley 38 J14
CREEKRUN
Cordeaux Ht 34 B9
CREOLE
pl. Haywards Bay 48 D8
pl. Albion Park Rail .. 48 G13
CREST
av. North Nowra 87 K6
rd. Albion Park 51 K6
rd. Albion Park 51 N9
st. Farmborough Ht .. 40 C3
CRESTING
av. Corrimal 25 K10
CRESTON
gr. Bomaderry 83 N12
CRIBB
st. Berkeley 40 N9
CRIGHTON
pl. Dapto 44 F11
CRINGILA
st. Cringila 41 E7
CRINGILA CAR PARK
rd. Spring Hill 41 F4
CROFT
pl. Gerringong 70 E2
CROOKED RIVER
rd. Gerroa 70 A12
CROOME
la. Albion Park Rail .. 48 C12
rd. Albion Park Rail .. 52 G4
rd. Croom 52 G4
rd. Croom 52 H11
CROSBY
pl. Bomaderry 83 Q12
CROSS
st. Corrimal 25 Q12
st. Corrimal 25 Q9
CROTON
pl. Albion Park Rail .. 48 F13
CROWN
la. Wollongong 1 P12
la. Wollongong 35 M2
st. W Wollongong 1 A13
st. W Wollongong 35 F3
st. Wollongong 1 A13
st. Wollongong 2 D13
st. Wollongong 35 F3
st. Wollongong 35 Q3
CROWN STREET
ml. Wollongong 2 A12
CROWTHER
pl. Tarrawanna 25 J12
CROZIERS
dr. Jaspers Brush 96 A15
CRUSADE
pl. Shell Cove 54 A10
CRYSTAL
av. Horsley 43 F3
CUBITT
pl. Flinders 53 K6
CUDGEE
cr. Mt Kembla 33 P7
CULBURRA
st. Lake Heights 41 D13

CULGOA
cr. Koonawarra 44 L4
CULLEN
dr. Kiama Downs 61 M5
st. Oak Flats 53 C2
st. Unanderra 40 F1
CUMBERLAND
av. South Nowra 91 K15
st. Berkeley 40 G9
CUMMINS
st. Unanderra 34 F14
CUNNINGHAM
pl. Keiraville 29 B13
st. Kiama Downs 61 M5
CURALO
pl. Flinders 53 M7
CURLEW
av. Shell Cove 54 D9
st. Wongawilli 38 L10
CURRACURRONG
rd. Helensburgh 11 P11
CURRAJONG
pl. Albion Park Rail .. 52 J6
CURRAMBENE
pky. Flinders 53 L8
CURRAMORE
rd. Curramore 59 M1
tce. Tullimbar 51 H6
CURRAWONG
ct. Blackbutt 53 G4
CURTA
pl. South Nowra 92 F10
CUSCUS
cl. Blackbutt 53 J3
CUTHBERT
dr. Mt Warrigal 49 K10
CUTTER
pde. Shell Cove 54 B10
CYGNET
av. Blackbutt 53 F2
av. Shellharbour C C .. 53 F2
CYPRESS
av. Figtree 34 N3

D

DABPETO
rd. Horsley 39 C14
DAINTREE
dr. Albion Park 52 A11
DAIRY FARM
wy. Wongawilli 38 J8
DAIRYMAN
pl. Calderwood 47 D16
DAISY
ct. Calderwood 47 E16
pl. Worrigee 92 L15
st. Fairy Meadow 29 N4
DALBY
st. East Corrimal 26 B11
DALE
st. Penrose 44 A9
DALEY
cr. North Nowra 87 L7
DALLAS
st. Keiraville 29 D9
DALMENY
av. Figtree 28 L15
DALRYMPLE
st. Albion Park 52 D14
DALTON
st. Towradgi 25 Q16
DALTONS
rd. Jamberoo 59 A9
DALWAH
st. Bomaderry 88 B3
DALYS
st. Coledale 18 L4
DAM
rd. Wombarra 16 B15
DAMPIER
cr. Shell Cove 53 Q13

DANANTONIO
cl. South Nowra 92 D16
DANIEL
st. Corrimal 25 L8
DANJERA
dr. Albion Park 52 E15
DANUBE
st. Kiama 65 K2
DAPHNE
st. Barrack Heights .. 53 Q1
st. Corrimal 26 B8
DAPTO
sq. Dapto 44 G2
DAPTO SQUARE
la. Dapto 44 G2
DARCY
rd. Port Kembla 41 Q11
rd. Port Kembla 42 B10
DARIEN
av. Bombo 62 A7
DARKES
rd. Dapto 39 E10
rd. Kembla Grange .. 39 E10
DARKES FOREST
rd. Darkes Forest 13 A14
rd. Darkes Forest 15 K1
DARLEY
st. Shellharbour 54 D8
DARLING
dr. Albion Park 52 E15
pl. Barrack Heights .. 49 M16
st. Wollongong 1 J13
st. Wollongong 35 K2
DARLING MILLS
rd. Albion Park 52 E13
DARLY
av. Kanahooka 39 M16
DARRAGH
dr. Figtree 34 K7
DARREN
av. Kanahooka 44 M1
DAVENPORT
rd. Shoalhaven Hd .. 95 D9
DAVEY
cl. Shellharbour C C .. 53 K1
la. Mt Warrigal 49 H10
DAVID
av. Oak Flats 49 D16
cr. Fairy Meadow 29 L8
pl. Bomaderry 84 A14
st. W Wollongong 1 B10
st. W Wollongong 35 F1
DAVID BERRY
st. Shoalhaven Hd .. 95 G9
DAVID SMITH
pl. Kiama Heights 65 M9
DAVIDSON
av. Woonona 26 D2
dr. Shoalhaven Hd .. 95 E6
st. Warilla 49 P10
DAVIES
cr. Mt Warrigal 49 L12
DAVIS
cr. Kiama Downs 61 M5
DAWES
ct. Horsley 43 Q1
DAWSON
pl. Albion Park 51 Q12
st. Balgownie 29 H5
st. Fairy Meadow 29 H5
DAY
av. Figtree 34 L6
st. Lake Illawarra 49 Q7
DEAKIN
st. Oak Flats 48 P15
DEAN
st. Warrawong 41 H15
st. Wollongong 1 M15
st. Wollongong 35 L4
DEBORAH
av. Thirroul 22 D1

DECORA
pl. Albion Park Rail .. 52 N7
DEENYI
cl. Cordeaux Ht 34 F10
DEESON
pl. Dapto 44 F11
DELEGATE
la. Tullimbar 51 H3
DELMONT
pl. Kanahooka 40 A16
DELTA
pl. Albion Park Rail .. 48 F11
DELTAVIEW
av. Haywards Bay 48 H7
DE MESTRE
pl. Nowra 88 C16
DEMPSTER
st. W Wollongong 1 B10
st. W Wollongong 35 F2
DENBIGH
pl. South Nowra 92 D11
DENHAM
dr. Horsley 43 Q1
DENISE
st. Lake Heights 41 E14
DENISON
av. Barrack Heights .. 49 M15
st. Gwynneville 1 L12
st. Wollongong 1 L12
st. Wollongong 35 L2
DENMARK
st. Wombarra 18 M2
DENNIS
av. Mt Warrigal 49 L11
DENNISS
st. Berkeley 40 M10
DEPOT
rd. West Nowra 91 K4
DERBY
st. Berkeley 40 K10
DEROWIE
cr. Lake Heights 41 E13
DERRIBONG
dr. Cordeaux Ht 34 D9
DERWENT
av. Penrose 44 B9
pl. Albion Park 52 B11
DEVENISH
st. Fernhill 25 J16
DEVITT
av. Mt Warrigal 49 L7
DEVITTS
la. Meroo Meadow .. 84 B1
DEVLIN
av. North Nowra 87 C7
DEVON
av. Dapto 44 H7
st. Berkeley 40 L12
DEVONSHIRE
cr. Oak Flats 49 D16
st. Kiama 62 A14
DIAMANTINA
ct. Albion Park 52 B12
DIANELLA
la. Berry 96 E10
DICK
st. Corrimal 26 A10
DICKSON
av. Mt Warrigal 49 J10
DIDO
st. Kiama 61 L12
DIGBY
cl. Albion Park 51 L8
DILLON
rd. Flinders 53 M10
DIMOND
av. Kanahooka 44 M2
DINAH
pl. Balgownie 25 F15
DISCOVERY
pl. Shoalhaven Hd .. 95 E5

	Map Ref
MALACOOTA	
wy. Flinders	53 Q9
MALBON	
st. Kembla Grange	39 E11
MALCOLM	
av. Cringila	41 F10
MALEEN	
st. Bomaderry	87 Q3
MALIN	
rd. Oak Flats	49 D15
MALL	
la. Dapto	44 H2
MALLEE	
st. Albion Park Rail	48 F13
MALLON	
av. Horsley	43 K2
MALONGA	
pl. Koonawarra	44 L10
MALUA	
st. Tullimbar	51 K10
MANDALAY	
av. Nowra	87 P9
MANEY	
av. Horsley	44 A1
MANGERTON	
rd. Mangerton	35 G5
rd. Wollongong	1 C16
rd. Wollongong	35 G5
MANIKATO	
pl. Kembla Grange	40 C8
MANNA	
av. Figtree	34 K2
MANNING	
pl. Albion Park	52 A12
st. Kiama	65 P5
MANNINGVALE	
pl. Worrigee	92 N13
MANOORA	
wy. Nowra	92 D5
MANSONS BRIDGE	
Albion Park	51 L3
MANUKA	
av. Penrose	44 B10
MANYANA	
la. Tullimbar	51 K8
MAPLE	
st. Albion Park Rail	52 H4
MARANA	
cl. Nowra	92 G4
MARCEAU	
st. Mt St Thomas	35 C10
MARCELLE	
st. Figtree	34 P12
MARCHANT	
cr. Mt Warrigal	49 M11
MARENGO	
av. Figtree	34 N1
MARGARET	
pl. Albion Park	52 D13
st. Balgownie	25 F16
st. Gerringong	70 D1
st. Warrawong	41 K15
MARIA	
pl. Flinders	53 H6
MARIE	
pl. Horsley	39 C14
MARIGOLD	
cl. Bomaderry	83 P10
MARINA	
dr. Shell Cove	54 D11
MARINE	
dr. Wollongong	2 H13
dr. Wollongong	36 B3
pde. Towradgi	30 E1
MARION	
st. Thirroul	22 A4
MARITIME	
dr. Shell Cove	54 G12
MARK	
st. Figtree	28 N16
MARKET	
pl. Wollongong	2 F11
pl. Wollongong	36 A2
st. Wollongong	1 N11
st. Wollongong	2 B11
st. Wollongong	35 M2
st. Wollongong	35 P2
MARKHAM	
dr. Calderwood	51 G3
MARKS	
st. Kiama	65 P7
MARLEN	
pl. Woonona	25 P1
MARLEY	
pl. Unanderra	34 P14
MARLO	
rd. Towradgi	30 A1
MARNE	
st. Port Kembla	42 D13
MAROOTA	
av. Balgownie	29 F1
MARR	
st. Wollongong	2 E8
st. Wollongong	29 Q16
MARRIL	
cct. Cordeaux Ht	34 H11
MARSDEN	
cl. Worrigee	92 J7
st. Kiama	65 P7
MARSH	
pl. Albion Park	52 B7
rd. Nowra	92 H2
MARSHALL	
st. Dapto	44 D6
MARSHALL MOUNT	
rd. Calderwood	47 A12
rd. Marshall Mount	47 A12
rd. Penrose	44 A16
MARTENS	
av. Horsley	43 H4
MARTIN	
st. Dapto	44 E11
st. Warilla	49 N10
MARY	
av. Figtree	34 P6
st. Shellharbour	54 D6
st. Thirroul	22 J1
MARY ANN	
st. Towradgi	25 P15
MARY CALLAGHAN	
cr. Woonona	26 D6
MARY DAVIS	
av. Koonawarra	44 K9
MASON	
st. Thirroul	22 E2
MASSEY	
st. Berkeley	40 M10
MASSINGHAM	
av. Nowra	92 B2
MAST	
wy. Shell Cove	54 F12
MASTERS	
rd. Spring Hill	35 D11
MASTHEAD	
pl. Berkeley	40 L9
MATHEWS	
st. Shoalhaven Hd	95 F10
MATILDA	
wy. Berkeley	40 L12
MATTES	
wy. Bomaderry	87 P5
MATTHEW	
st. Fairy Meadow	29 K7
MATTHEWS	
cr. Port Kembla	42 C14
dr. Mt Warrigal	49 L10
st. Wollongong	1 E12
st. Wollongong	35 H2
MAUREEN	
st. Thirroul	22 C1
MAVIS	
gr. W Wollongong	35 C5
MAWARRA	
av. Dapto	44 F9
MAWSON	
rd. Shoalhaven Hd	95 E6
MAXWELL	
cr. Stanwell Park	14 B10
rd. Austinmer	18 H11
st. Fairy Meadow	29 K3
MAYBERN	
cl. North Nowra	87 G4
MAY BUSH	
wy. West Nowra	91 K3
MAYFAIR	
ct. Bomaderry	83 P11
MAYFIELD	
cct. Albion Park	52 B9
MAYNES	
pde. Unanderra	34 H14
MAYO	
cl. Albion Park	52 A7
MEADOW	
rd. Bomaderry	84 E16
st. Corrimal	25 L12
st. Fairy Meadow	29 J2
st. Fernhill	25 K16
st. Tarrawanna	25 K16
MEADOW BANK	
pl. Barrack Heights	53 Q2
MEADS	
av. Tarrawanna	25 N15
MEALING	
av. Mt Warrigal	49 L11
MEANDER	
dr. Calderwood	51 F3
MEARES	
av. Mangerton	35 G6
pl. Kiama	61 P14
st. Fernhill	25 J16
MEDLOW	
wy. Albion Park	52 E12
MEDWAY	
dr. Mt Keira	29 A14
MEEHAN	
av. Shoalhaven Hd	95 E6
cl. Horsley	39 C14
dr. Kiama Downs	61 L5
MEHAFFEY	
st. Woonona	22 E14
MELALEUCA	
av. Penrose	44 B11
cr. Kanahooka	45 F6
pl. Bomaderry	83 N14
rd. Albion Park Rail	52 M4
MELIA	
pl. Penrose	44 B11
st. Kiama	61 L13
st. Shellharbour	54 A6
MELINDA	
gr. Lake Heights	41 E11
MELROSE	
wy. Horsley	39 A14
MELVILLE	
cr. Shell Cove	54 B13
MEMORIAL	
dr. Bellambi	26 A9
dr. Corrimal	25 Q15
dr. Fairy Meadow	29 M10
dr. Gwynneville	1 H2
dr. Gwynneville	29 J13
dr. N Wollongong	1 H2
dr. N Wollongong	29 J13
dr. Russell Vale	26 A9
dr. Shellharbour C C	53 H1
dr. Towradgi	25 Q15
dr. Woonona	22 D16
MENINDEE	
cl. Flinders	53 L7
MERCURY	
st. Wollongong	1 G10
st. Wollongong	35 J1
MERIMBULA	
cl. Flinders	53 M8
MERINDA	
wy. Tapitallee	82 H12
MERINDAH	
av. Kiama Downs	61 Q1
MERMAID	
pl. Gerringong	70 F5
MEROO	
rd. Bomaderry	88 C1
rd. Meroo Meadow	84 A6
st. Bomaderry	88 C4
MERRETT	
av. Cringila	41 E5
MERRICK	
cct. Kiama	61 K14
MERRIGONG	
pl. Helensburgh	11 N14
MERROO	
cl. Flinders	53 M6
MERYLA	
wy. Flinders	53 L9
MESSENGER	
rd. Barrack Heights	49 P15
st. Barrack Heights	49 N16
METCALF	
pl. Mt Warrigal	49 L8
METROPOLITAN	
rd. Helensburgh	11 Q10
METSERV	
rd. Port Kembla	35 J15
MEYER	
pl. Bomaderry	84 D12
MIALL	
wy. Albion Park Rail	48 E10
MIANGA	
cr. Unanderra	40 E2
MICHAEL	
cr. Kiama Downs	61 K6
st. Albion Park	51 Q8
st. Gwynneville	1 B2
st. Gwynneville	29 F13
MIDDLE HEIGHTS	
rd. Coledale	18 H7
MIDDLESEX	
rd. Berkeley	40 J13
MIDGLEY	
st. Corrimal	25 N9
MILDURA	
st. Nowra	92 G5
MILITARY	
la. Port Kembla	42 B11
rd. Port Kembla	42 B11
MILLAR	
pl. Kiama Downs	58 A16
MILLBANK	
rd. Terara	88 K12
rd. Worrigee	92 N2
MILLBROOK	
rd. Figtree	35 A6
MILLER	
av. Nowra	92 B1
st. Coniston	35 K8
st. Oak Flats	53 A2
st. Werri Beach	69 J11
MILLEWA	
av. Gerringong	70 E5
MILNE	
st. Coniston	35 G9
MILTON	
st. Tullimbar	51 H6
MIMOSA	
wy. Barrack Heights	53 M2
MINDA	
cr. Oak Flats	49 G15
MINERAL	
rd. Oak Flats	52 N2
MINGA	
av. Shellharbour C C	49 G16
MINNAMURRA	
la. Jamberoo	60 C5
la. Jamberoo	60 C7
st. Kiama	61 P13
MINNAMURRA FALLS	
rd. Jamberoo	59 C1
MINNEGANG	
st. Warrawong	41 G15
MINTBUSH	
cr. Worrigee	92 L6
MIRIAM	
pl. Flinders	53 H6
MIRRABOOKA	
rd. Lake Heights	41 E13
MISTY	
la. Jamberoo	59 A13
MITCHELL	
pl. Kiama Downs	61 P4
pl. Woonona	26 C2
MITTAGONG	
st. Tullimbar	51 G6
MOAB	
pl. Figtree	34 L1
MOEYAN	
rd. Berry	96 M16
MOGO	
wy. Flinders	53 K7
MOLES	
st. Albion Park	51 L4
MOLINEAUX	
st. Shell Cove	53 N14
MOLLOY	
st. Bulli	22 D11
MOLLYMOOK	
st. Tullimbar	51 H6
MOLONGO	
st. Albion Park	52 E14
MONAGHAN	
av. Nowra	87 N12
MONARCH	
st. Thirroul	22 B2
st. Wongawilli	38 K10
MONASH	
st. Scarborough	16 E15
st. Wombarra	16 E15
MONCKTON	
av. Mt Warrigal	49 M9
MONIE	
st. Woonona	26 B1
MONK	
cr. Bomaderry	84 B13
MONKHOUSE	
pde. Shell Cove	53 P14
MONTAGUE	
cr. Shell Cove	54 B14
st. Fairy Meadow	29 N9
st. N Wollongong	29 N12
MONTEITH	
st. Cringila	41 F8
MONTEREY	
dr. Nowra Hill	90 K12
MONTGOMERY	
av. Warrawong	41 M13
MOOD	
ct. Albion Park	52 C12
MOOLAWANG	
pl. Shellharbour C C	53 H1
MOOMBARA	
st. Dapto	44 G3
MOONA	
av. Kiama Downs	61 Q2
MOONAH	
wy. Shell Cove	53 P16
MOONDARA	
dr. Bangalee	83 B16
MOORE	
la. Austinmer	18 E14
la. Wollongong	2 D13
la. Wollongong	35 Q2
pl. Warrawong	41 J15
st. Austinmer	18 E14
st. Gwynneville	1 C3
st. Gwynneville	29 G14
st. Oak Flats	48 Q15
st. Werri Beach	69 J12
MOORHEN	
st. Wongawilli	38 L10
MOORINGS	
av. Shell Cove	54 J11
MORAN	
av. Dapto	44 F5
pde. Mt St Thomas	35 C10
MORANDOO	
av. Mt Keira	28 N14
MORANS	
rd. Cordeaux	27 L13
rd. Kembla Heights	27 L13
MORAS	
pl. Lake Illawarra	49 P7
MORAY	
rd. Towradgi	26 C16
MORESBY	
st. Nowra	92 C6
MORETON	
pl. Flinders	53 N11
st. Russell Vale	25 N5
MORETON BAY	
pl. Kiama Downs	61 N4
MORGAN	
av. Mt Warrigal	49 K11
pl. Bellambi	26 G7
MORINDA	
cl. Figtree	34 J9
MORNA	
cl. Shell Cove	54 B10
MORNINGTON	
ct. Shell Cove	53 N14
MORONGA	
ct. Horsley	38 M16
MORRIS	
pl. Warilla	49 Q10
MORRISON	
av. Coledale	18 J5
av. Wombarra	16 C16
MORROW	
st. Gerringong	70 G3
MORSCHEL	
av. North Nowra	87 L7
MORSCHELS	
la. Meroo Meadow	84 C1
la. Meroo Meadow	84 H2
MORSE	
av. Kanahooka	44 Q3
MORSON	
av. Horsley	43 J3
MORTLOCK	
av. Port Kembla	41 K9
dr. Albion Park	52 F13
MORTON	
pde. Nowra	88 B14
st. Kiama	62 A16
wy. Port Kembla	35 N14
MORUYA	
lk. Albion Park	52 C12
MOSS	
st. Nowra	88 A1
MOSS VALE	
rd. Bomaderry	83 D7
rd. Cambewarra	83 D7
MOUNT	
st. Kembla Heights	33 M5
st. Mt St Thomas	35 E10
MOUNTAIN	
av. Woonona	21 Q13
rd. Austinmer	18 D15
rd. Thirroul	18 D15
MOUNTAIN ASH	
pl. Worrigee	92 J4
st. Calderwood	51 G2
MOUNTAIN RANGE	
rd. Woonona	21 L16
MOUNTAIN VIEW	
cr. Figtree	34 N6
pl. Shoalhaven Hd	95 D8
tce. Avondale	43 D16
tce. Avondale	47 E1

ORTON

Map Ref

MOUNTAINVIEW
mw. Albion Park 51 P3
MOUNTBATTEN
st. Corrimal 26 B9
MT BRANDON
rd. Jerrara 60 N16
MT BROWN
rd. Dapto 44 D11
MT GILEAD
rd. Thirroul 17 Q16
MOUNT HAY
rd. Broughton Vale 96 G1
MT KEIRA
rd. Cataract 28 G1
rd. Cordeaux 28 G1
rd. Mt Keira 28 M12
rd. W Wollongong 35 B1
MT OUSLEY
rd. Fairy Meadow 29 H8
rd. Mt Ousley 29 H8
MOUNT VIEW
dr. Gerringong 70 E2
MOUNTVIEW
av. Gwynneville 1 K2
av. Gwynneville 29 K13
MT VISTA
cl. Berry 96 B3
MOWBRAY
la. Warrawong, off Cowper St 41 L13
MUIR
st. Woonona 22 E14
MUIRFIELD
av. Shell Cove 57 Q2
MULBERRY
ct. Calderwood 51 H1
MULDA
st. Dapto 44 J3
MULGARA
pl. Blackbutt 53 J4
MULGEN
cr. Bomaderry 84 C16
cr. Bomaderry 88 C1
MULLERS
la. Berry 96 B16
la. Jaspers Brush 96 B13
MUMBULLA
st. South Nowra 92 B9
MUMMUGA
cl. Flinders 53 N8
MUNDABAN
ct. Bulli 22 G7
MUNDOONEN
cr. Horsley 43 L1
MUNDURAN
cl. Albion Park 52 D14
MUNGO
pl. Flinders 53 Q9
MUNGURRA HILL
rd. Cordeaux Ht 34 D10
MUNMORAH
cct. Flinders 53 N10
MURCHISON
st. Albion Park 52 B11
MURPHYS
av. Gwynneville 1 A1
av. Keiraville 1 A1
av. Keiraville 29 C12
MURRAH
cl. Flinders 53 L4
st. Tullimbar 51 J7
MURRA MURRA
rd. Kanahooka 45 D4
MURRANAR
rd. Towradgi 30 A1
MURRAWAL
rd. Stanwell Park 13 P12
MURRAY
cl. Albion Park 51 Q10
rd. East Corrimal 26 B12
MURRAY PARK
rd. Figtree 34 N7

Map Ref

MURRELL
pl. North Nowra 87 C9
MURRIE
st. Windang 46 F15
MURROGUN
cr. Cordeaux Ht 34 C15
st. Albion Park Rail 52 N4
MUSGRAVE
pl. Figtree 34 N13
MYALL
ct. Nowra 92 G6
MYAMBA
st. Gerringong 70 G1
MYE
pl. Albion Park Rail 48 E10
MYEE
st. Kanahooka 44 M1
MYORLA
la. Tullimbar 51 J7
MYRTLE
st. Coniston 35 J7
wy. Barrack Heights 49 L15
MYSTICS
dr. Shell Cove 54 C13
MYUNA
pl. Kiama 65 M1
wy. Mangerton 1 B14
wy. Mangerton 35 F3

N

NAKINA
pl. Oak Flats 49 H14
NALONG
pl. Oak Flats 49 G14
NAMOI
lk. Albion Park 52 A15
NANNAWILLI
st. Berkeley 40 M10
NAPIER
pl. Albion Park 52 D14
st. Balgownie 29 G2
NARANG
rd. Bomaderry 83 M15
rd. North Nowra 83 M15
NARDOO
cr. Thirroul 17 P16
NAREENA
av. Figtree 34 M5
NARELLE
cr. Woonona 26 B3
NARGAL
st. Flinders 53 P8
NAROOMA
la. Tullimbar 51 F7
st. Tullimbar 51 K8
NARRAN
wy. Flinders 53 L6
NARRAWAN
st. Berkeley 40 N12
NARRIAH
pl. Berkeley 40 L9
NARRIEN
pl. North Nowra 87 H3
NARTON
mw. Bellambi 26 F7
NARVO
st. Barrack Heights 49 Q15
NARWEE
lk. Nowra 92 G6
NATAN
pl. Cordeaux Ht 34 F9
NATIONAL
av. Bulli 22 A6
av. Shell Cove 53 P16
NATTAI
cr. Albion Park 52 A15
NAUTICA
cr. Shell Cove 54 E9
NAVAL
la. Shell Cove 54 E10
NEALE
pl. Bomaderry 84 D13

Map Ref

NEAVE
av. Figtree 34 M10
NEBO
dr. Figtree 34 L2
NEBULA
wy. Dunmore 53 M13
NEESON
rd. Kembla Grange 38 N7
rd. Kembla Grange 39 A7
NEHME
av. Albion Park Rail 52 M2
NELLIGEN
st. Tullimbar 51 K8
NELLORE
pl. North Nowra 87 E4
NELSON
st. Gerringong 69 D16
NEPEAN
pl. Albion Park 51 Q10
NEPTUNE
pl. Worrigee 92 J9
st. Gerringong 70 F4
NEVILLE
av. Russell Vale 26 A4
NEWBOLD
cl. Thirroul 22 G4
NEWCASTLE
st. Cringila 41 F6
NEWCOMBE
st. Berkeley 40 K6
NEW DAPTO
rd. Wollongong 1 G13
rd. Wollongong 35 J3
NEWING
cct. Kiama Downs 61 J4
NEW LAKE ENTRANCE
rd. Albion Park Rail 53 C4
rd. Blackbutt 53 C4
rd. Oak Flats 53 C4
rd. Shellharbour C C 53 C4
NEW MT PLEASANT
rd. Balgownie 29 C5
rd. Mt Pleasant 29 A6
NEWTON
cr. Oak Flats 48 Q14
NICHOLSON
rd. Woonona 22 B15
NICKEL
la. Kanahooka 45 B2
NICOL
pl. Bellambi 26 G9
NICOLLE
rd. Primbee 46 G6
NIELSON
st. Farmborough Ht 40 B1
NIGHTINGALE
cl. Blackbutt 53 E3
NILBAR
cl. Bomaderry 87 Q2
NILE
cl. Gerringong 70 E6
NIMBIN
st. Russell Vale 25 Q5
NIMMITABEL
st. Tullimbar 51 K5
NIMROD
st. Shoalhaven Hd 95 F5
NINEVEH
cl. Nowra 92 E3
NIOKA
av. Keiraville 29 C15
NITA
pl. Bomaderry 87 Q3
NIXON
pl. Helensburgh 12 D4
NOAKES
st. Shoalhaven Hd 95 E5
NOBBLERS
la. Terara 88 K8
NOB HILL
dr. Oak Flats 48 N15

Map Ref

NOBLE
pde. Lake Heights 41 B12
rd. Albion Park 51 K6
st. Gerringong 70 G1
NOEL
st. N Wollongong 2 A2
st. N Wollongong 29 N13
NOLAN
st. Berkeley 40 J9
st. Unanderra 40 H3
NOONGA
pl. Cordeaux Ht 34 H11
NOORAMUNGA
av. Cambewarra Vill. 82 M4
NOORINAN
st. Kiama 61 P16
NOOSA
av. Russell Vale 26 B4
av. Woonona 26 B4
NORFOLK
av. South Nowra 91 G14
cr. Shell Cove 54 A14
st. Berkeley 40 K8
NORMAN
av. Mangerton 35 F5
st. Fairy Meadow 29 N3
NORMANBY
pl. Albion Park 52 C10
NORMAN CLARK
cr. Horsley 38 L16
NORMANDIE
pl. Unanderra 40 H1
NORTH
st. Berry 96 E6
st. Berry 96 H6
st. Minnamurra 57 Q12
st. Nowra 87 M11
st. Nowra 88 A11
tce. Dapto 39 G16
NORTHCLIFFE
dr. Berkeley 40 D7
dr. Kembla Grange 40 D7
dr. Lake Heights 41 F16
dr. Port Kembla 41 M14
dr. Warrawong 41 F16
NORTHCOTE
st. Coledale 18 K7
st. Wollongong 1 F10
st. Wollongong 35 H1
NORTH CURRAMORE
rd. Curramore 59 P1
NORTHERN
av. Shellharbour 54 D5
NORTHFIELDS
av. Gwynneville 29 E11
av. Keiraville 29 E11
av. N Wollongong 29 K11
NORTH KIAMA
dr. Kiama Downs 61 Q4
dr. Kiama Downs 61 Q4
NORTH MACQUARIE
rd. Calderwood 51 A5
NORTH MARSHALL MOUNT
rd. Marshall Mount 47 A6
NORTHMEADOWS
Cordeaux Ht 34 B8
NORTH NOWRA LINK
North Nowra 87 G1
NORTHPOINT
pl. Bombo 62 A8
NORTHSPUR
Cordeaux Ht 34 A9
NORTH TARAWAL
st. Bomaderry 83 Q16
NORTHUMBERLAND
st. Berkeley 40 G9
NORTHVIEW
cl. Coolangatta 95 A5
tce. Figtree 34 Q11
NORTHWOOD
rd. Mt Ousley 29 E8

Map Ref

NOTTINGHAM
st. Berkeley 40 G8
NOWRA
la. Nowra 88 A13
NOWRA HILL
rd. South Nowra 92 A15
NUDJIA
rd. Unanderra 34 K15
NUMBAA
wy. Nowra 92 A2
NUMROCK
st. Bomaderry 87 Q2
NUNDAH
cl. Bomaderry 87 P3
NUNKERI
pl. North Nowra 87 K9
NUTANS
cst. South Nowra 92 G10
NYAN
st. Warrawong 41 G16
NYRANG
st. Keiraville 1 A6
st. Keiraville 29 F15

O

OAK
st. Albion Park Rail 52 J6
OAKBANKS
pl. Worrigee 92 P14
OAK FARM
rd. Calderwood 51 E1
OAKHURST
cl. Penrose 44 B9
OAKLAND
av. Windang 50 D2
OAKS
av. Kanahooka 44 P5
OAKWOOD
pl. Horsley 38 N14
O'BRIEN
st. Bulli 22 F8
O'BRIENS
la. Figtree 34 K7
rd. Figtree 34 J2
OCEAN
av. Woonona 26 F1
st. Bulli 22 G14
st. Kiama 65 P8
st. Lake Illawarra 50 D7
st. Mt St Thomas 35 E10
st. Thirroul 22 H2
st. Towradgi 25 Q16
st. Windang 50 F3
st. Wollongong 2 D4
st. Wollongong 29 Q14
OCEANA
pde. Austinmer 18 E14
OCEAN BEACH
dr. Shellharbour 53 Q6
OCEAN FRONT
dr. Shell Cove 54 G12
dr. Shell Cove 54 M2
OCEANVIEW
pde. Fairy Meadow 29 G6
pde. Mt Ousley 29 G6
O'CONNELL
la. Nowra 88 A13
pl. Gerringong 69 F15
st. Barrack Heights 49 M15
ODENPA
rd. Cordeaux Ht 34 F11
O'DONNELL
dr. Figtree 34 N13
st. Port Kembla 42 A12
O'GORMAN
st. Albion Park 52 A4
O'KEEFE
av. Nowra 88 A12
cr. Albion Park 51 L4
OKEEFE
pl. Kiama 65 Q5

Map Ref

O'KEEFES
la. Jaspers Brush 96 A15
OLD BAMARANG
rd. Bamarang 90 F4
rd. Longreach 90 F4
rd. Mundamia 90 F4
OLD BASS POINT
rd. Shellharbour 54 C8
OLD COAST
rd. Stanwell Park 13 P9
OLD COURTHOUSE
la. Wollongong 2 H10
OLD CREAMERY
la. Berry 96 J10
OLD FARM
rd. Helensburgh 12 C6
OLDFIELD
st. Warilla 49 P8
OLD FIVE ISLANDS
rd. Unanderra 34 M13
OLD ILLAWARRA
rd. Helensburgh 11 H11
rd. Helensburgh 11 H6
OLD PORT
rd. Port Kembla 41 Q6
OLD QUARRY
cct. Helensburgh 11 M13
OLD SADDLEBACK
rd. Jerrara 65 G7
rd. Kiama 65 G7
OLD SOUTHERN
rd. Nowra 92 F7
rd. South Nowra 92 D16
OLD SPRINGHILL
rd. Coniston 35 K9
OLD STATION
rd. Helensburgh 12 B5
OLEANDER
av. Figtree 34 M2
OLGA
st. Helensburgh 11 L11
OLIVER
pde. Nowra 87 N14
pl. Berkeley 40 N9
OLIVIA
pl. Kanahooka 45 B1
OLYMPIC
bvd. Port Kembla 42 E16
dr. West Nowra 91 K2
O'MARA
pl. Jamberoo 59 Q5
OMAROO
pl. Horsley 38 M14
OMEGA
la. Rose Valley 69 G3
st. Tullimbar 51 F7
ONDINE
av. Shell Cove 54 A11
O'NEIL
st. Unanderra 34 N14
O'NEILL
st. Warilla 49 Q11
ORANA
av. Kiama 65 Q4
pde. Unanderra 40 F4
rd. Dapto 44 J6
wy. South Nowra 92 D10
ORANGEGROVE
av. Unanderra 40 F6
ORCHID
av. Albion Park Rail 52 J4
cl. Horsley 43 Q2
ORD
pl. Albion Park 52 B11
O'REILLY
st. Warilla 49 Q10
ORGANS
rd. Bulli 22 B10
ORPHEUS
cl. Kanahooka 45 D5
ORTON
st. Balgownie 25 D16

SAILS

THORNBILL

Map Ref

STANDEN
la. Gerringong 70 F1
STANE DYKE
rd. Kembla Grange 38 Q7
STANFORD
dr. Oak Flats 53 C4
STANHOPE
st. Woonona 26 A1
STANLEIGH
cr. W Wollongong 35 B4
STANLEY
av. Farmborough Ht 40 A1
st. Lake Illawarra 49 Q6
STANTHORPE
dr. Kanahooka 45 A1
STANWELL
av. Stanwell Park 13 P11
STAPLES
st. Shoalhaven Hd 95 H8
STAPLETON
av. Albion Park 52 B4
st. Unanderra 34 G14
STARBOARD
la. Shell Cove 54 J12
STARLING
dr. Calderwood 47 E15
st. Wongawilli 38 M11
STATE
pl. Albion Park 51 Q8
STATION
rd. Albion Park Rail 52 H3
rd. Berry 96 H10
rd. Otford 14 F3
rd. Otford 14 G3
st. Bulli 22 D10
st. Dapto 44 F1
st. East Corrimal 26 B13
st. N Wollongong 1 P1
st. N Wollongong 29 M13
st. Nowra 92 B1
st. Stanwell Park 13 Q10
st. Thirroul 22 G3
st. Wollongong 1 M14
st. Wollongong 35 L3
STEEL
st. Cringila 41 F7
st. Towradgi 29 P1
STEPHANIE
av. Warilla 50 D11
STEPHEN
cr. Barrack Heights 49 N16
dr. Woonona 21 P11
STEPHENS
st. Albion Park 52 C11
STERN
wy. Shell Cove 54 J12
STEWARDS
dr. Kembla Grange 38 Q8
STEWART
pl. Barrack Heights 49 L15
pl. Kiama 65 N7
pl. Nowra 87 Q13
st. Wollongong 2 B15
st. Wollongong 35 P4
st. Woonona 22 B15
STILLNESS
rd. Figtree 34 P5
STIRLING
pl. Albion Park 52 D13
st. Stanwell Tops 13 L7
STOCKLEY
cl. West Nowra 91 H3
STOCKMAN
rd. Calderwood 51 E5
STOCKPILE
rd. Port Kembla 41 P6
STOCKWELL
pl. Figtree 34 L11
STOCKYARD
cr. Horsley 43 J4
STOCKYARD MOUNTAIN
rd. Tullimbar 51 A16

STOKES
la. Bulli 22 D10
STONEGARTH
rd. Mundamia 87 A14
STONEHAVEN
rd. Stanwell Tops 13 M8
STONES
rd. Mt Kembla 34 B5
STOREY
st. Fairy Meadow 29 Q5
st. Oak Flats 53 B3
st. Port Kembla 41 M12
STORK
pl. Helensburgh 11 M13
STRADBROKE
av. Shell Cove 53 Q15
STRATA
av. Barrack Heights 53 P2
STRATFORD
rd. Unanderra 40 F4
STRATHALLEN
st. Fairy Meadow 29 K2
STRATHEARN
av. Wollongong 35 K6
STREETON
pl. Kanahooka 40 A16
STRICKLAND
av. Mt Warrigal 49 J8
STRIKE
la. Bulli 22 B10
STRINGY BARK
pl. Albion Park Rail 52 N8
STRINGYBARK
rd. Nowra Hill 90 J13
STRONE
av. Mt Ousley 29 L8
STUART
rd. Warrawong 41 H16
st. Helensburgh 11 N11
st. Nowra 92 C3
STUBBS
rd. Albion Park 52 E11
STUD
cl. Calderwood 51 F1
STURDEE
av. Bulli 22 E6
st. Towradgi 26 A16
STURT
pl. Bulli 21 P9
STYLES
la. Wongawilli 38 L9
SUBLIME
cr. Mt Pleasant 29 D7
SUFFOLK
st. Berkeley 40 K9
SUGAR GLIDER
dr. Bangalee 82 F13
dr. Tapitallee 82 F13
SUGARGUM
st. Albion Park Rail 52 M4
SUGARWOOD
cl. Farmborough Ht 34 A15
rd. Worrigee 92 H5
SULLIVAN
st. Worrigee 92 J6
SUMMERCLOUD
la. Shell Cove 54 C12
SUMMERFIELD
pl. Barrack Heights 53 Q2
SUMMERSET
la. South Nowra 92 F10
SUMMIT
st. Kembla Grange 39 E11
SUNFLOWER
bvd. Calderwood 51 D4
SUNLEA
st. Dapto 44 E6
SUNNINGHILL
cct. Mt Ousley 29 F7
SUNNY BANK
cr. Horsley 39 D14

SUNRAY
cr. Horsley 44 B1
SUNSET
av. Barrack Heights 50 A15
SUPPLY
ct. Albion Park 51 P6
st. Nowra 92 E5
SURF
rd. Shellharbour 54 E5
SURFERS
pde. Thirroul 22 H4
SURFLEET
pl. Kiama 65 N8
SURFSIDE
dr. Port Kembla 42 B15
SURREY
pl. Dapto 39 H15
SUSAN
av. Warilla 50 B11
pl. Farmborough Ht 34 C16
SUSSEX
la. Tullimbar 51 H4
st. Berkeley 40 J13
st. Woonona 22 C16
SUTHERLAND
dr. North Nowra 87 K3
st. Helensburgh 11 P8
SUTTON
pde. Tullimbar 51 G8
SUTTOR
pl. Figtree 34 M9
SUVLA
st. Port Kembla 42 E14
SWAIN
cr. Dapto 44 G8
SWAMP
rd. Berry 96 K16
rd. Dunmore 57 E13
rd. Jamberoo 60 Q7
SWAN
la. Wollongong 35 K7
pl. Albion Park 52 B10
pl. Kiama 61 P14
st. Wollongong 35 L7
SWEENEY
pl. Wombarra 16 C15
SYLVAN
wy. Thirroul 17 P15
SYLVESTER
av. Unanderra 40 F6
SYLVIA
dr. Calderwood 47 F16

T

TABBITTA
rd. Dunmore 57 G5
TABOURIE
cl. Flinders 53 P7
TABRATONG
rd. Helensburgh 11 N14
TAIT
av. Kanahooka 44 N1
TALINGA
av. Kiama Downs 61 Q2
TALLAWARRA
cr. Haywards Bay 48 E6
cr. Yallah 48 E6
TALLAWONG
cr. Dapto 44 E11
TALLAYANG
st. Bomaderry 88 A3
TALLEGALLA
st. Unanderra 40 J1
TALLIA
st. Shoalhaven Hd 95 G7
TALLIAS
cl. Worrigee 92 L16
TALLIMBA
rd. Tapitallee 82 G12
TALLIMBA
rd. Bangalee 82 G12

TALLON
st. Warilla 49 P11
wy. Worrigee 92 J3
TALLOWA
st. Tullimbar 51 J5
TALLOWOOD
st. Albion Park 51 Q9
TALLOWOODS
cr. Russell Vale 25 Q6
TALLWOOD
pl. Horsley 38 N14
TAMARIND
dr. Cordeaux Ht 34 B14
la. Worrigee 92 J5
pl. Barrack Heights 49 L16
TAMBLIN
st. Fairy Meadow 29 J3
TAMINGA
cst. Cordeaux Ht 34 C10
TAMMAR
pl. Blackbutt 53 H3
TANANG
st. Bomaderry 88 B1
TANNER
pl. Kiama 65 M4
TANNERY
rd. Berry 96 M7
rd. Cambewarra 82 N5
rd. Cambewarra Vill. 82 N5
st. Unanderra 34 J16
TAPITALLEE
rd. Cambewarra 82 F8
rd. Tapitallee 82 F8
TARANA
av. Kanahooka 39 M16
TARANNA
cr. Nowra 92 A4
TARAWA
rd. Helensburgh 11 N15
TARAWAL
st. Bomaderry 87 Q2
TARAWARA
st. Bomaderry 87 P2
st. Bomaderry 88 A3
TARONGA
av. Mangerton 35 D10
av. Mt St Thomas 35 D10
TARRA
cr. Oak Flats 49 H13
pl. Berkeley 40 N9
TARRABA
cr. Nowra 92 F2
TARRANT
av. Kiama Downs 61 M4
TARRAWANNA
rd. Corrimal 25 L12
TARTARIAN
cr. Bomaderry 83 K11
TASMAN
dr. Gerringong 70 J2
dr. Shell Cove 53 Q12
pde. Thirroul 22 H4
TATE
pl. Jamberoo 60 A4
st. Coniston 35 L9
st. Wollongong 35 L9
TAURUS
av. Warrawong 41 M13
TAY
gr. West Nowra 91 H5
TAYLOR
pl. Corrimal 25 L7
rd. Albion Park 51 M4
st. Kiama 65 P4
TAYLORS
la. Cambewarra 83 D10
TEAL
pl. Berkeley 41 A11
pl. Shellharbour 53 Q5
TELEVISION
av. Coniston 35 G9

TELOPEA
pl. Cordeaux Ht 34 D15
TEMPLE
rd. Helensburgh 13 L2
TERANIA
st. Russell Vale 25 Q5
TERARA
rd. Nowra 88 E9
rd. Terara 88 E9
TERESA
pl. Dapto 44 J5
TERILBAH
ct. Flinders 53 Q9
TERMEIL
pl. Flinders 53 N6
TERN
pl. Berkeley 41 A11
pl. Blackbutt 53 G2
TERRA
pl. Figtree 34 P13
TERRAGONG
st. Tullimbar 51 K6
TERRAGONG SWAMP BRIDGE
Dunmore 61 G3
TERRALLA
gr. South Nowra 92 D10
TERRALONG
st. Kiama 61 N14
TERRELL
pl. Balgownie 25 C15
TERRIE
av. Figtree 28 N16
TERRY
av. Warilla 50 B12
st. Albion Park 52 A5
THALASSA
av. East Corrimal 26 E12
THAMES
st. W Wollongong 35 A4
THARKINNA
av. Kiama 65 Q7
THE ARCHES
Kanahooka 45 B2
THEATRE
tce. Kanahooka 45 C5
THE AVENUE
Bellambi 26 C9
Coniston 35 D9
Corrimal 25 L11
Figtree 35 A8
Mt St Thomas 35 D9
THE BILLABONG
Albion Park 52 B12
THE BOULEVARDE
Oak Flats 49 A13
Oak Flats 49 A14
THE BREAKERS
rd. Thirroul 22 H3
THE BURGH
tr. Helensburgh 12 F3
tr. Lilyvale 12 F3
THE CIRCLE
Woonona 26 E1
THE CIRCUIT
Kiama Downs 61 Q4
Shellharbour 53 P5
THE CLIFF
tr. Lilyvale 12 N12
THE CONCOURSE
Cambewarra Vill. 82 M7
THE CRESCENT
Helensburgh 12 A5
Helensburgh 12 A6
THE DRIVE
Stanwell Park 13 Q10
THE ESPLANADE
Mt Warrigal 49 E14
Oak Flats 49 E14
Thirroul 22 J2
THE EXPRESSWAY
Albion Park 51 L4

THE FARM
wy. Shell Cove 54 E13
THE GABLES
Berry 96 D6
THE GARDEN
wk. Worrigee 92 L5
THE GLADE
Balgownie 29 B4
THE GLEN
Mt Pleasant 29 B5
THE GRANGE
Horsley 38 Q15
THE GROVE
Austinmer 18 E13
Shellharbour 53 P6
THEILE
pl. Mt Warrigal 49 K7
THE ISLAND
ct. Shell Cove 54 C12
THE KINGSWAY
Barrack Heights 49 N13
Warilla 49 N13
THE LINKS
Shell Cove 53 P16
rd. South Nowra 91 H15
THE LOOKOUT
Thirroul 22 F1
THE MALL
W Wollongong 35 B5
THEODORE
pl. Bomaderry 83 J11
st. Oak Flats 53 B2
THE PARKWAY
Balgownie 29 E3
Mt Pleasant 29 D4
THE PROMONTORY
dr. Shell Cove 54 E12
dr. Shell Cove 54 F12
THE RIDGE
Helensburgh 11 Q6
Shellharbour 53 N5
THERRY
st. W Wollongong 35 A4
THE SADDLE
Cordeaux Ht 34 B9
THE TERRACE
Cambewarra Vill. 82 M8
THE VALE
Cambewarra Vill. 82 M7
THE VILLAGE
Minnamurra 57 N10
THE WAVES
Thirroul 18 A16
THIRD
av. Port Kembla 42 C14
av. Unanderra 34 M14
av.n, Warrawong 41 J13
THIRROUL
rd. Kanahooka 44 L2
THISTLE
wy. Calderwood 51 F2
THOMAS
cl. Berry 96 C5
st. Corrimal 25 N10
st. Lake Illawarra 49 Q8
st. Wollongong 2 A10
st. Wollongong 35 N1
THOMAS COLLAERY
pl. Woonona 26 F6
THOMAS HALE
av. Woonona 26 E4
THOMPSON
st. Woonona 22 D14
st. Woonona 22 D16
THOMSON
st. Kiama 61 P15
THORN
pde. Bulli 22 B9
THORNBILL
cl. Blackbutt 53 F4
st. Wongawilli 38 K10
st. Wongawilli 38 K11

STREET INDEX 33

		Map	Ref

THORNBURY
av. Unanderra 40 F4
THORNETT
st. Barrack Heights .. 49 Q14
wy. Kiama Downs 61 L4
THROSBY
av. Horsley 43 Q1
dr. Gwynneville 1 J8
dr. Gwynneville 29 K16
dr. Wollongong 1 J8
dr. Wollongong 29 K16
st. Shoalhaven Hd .. 95 H7
THROWER
av. Mt Warrigal 49 J12
THURSDAY
dr. Shell Cove 54 B13
THURSTON
cr. Corrimal 25 P14
TIGWAY
av. Figtree 34 P1
TILBA
cl. Flinders 53 L5
TILGMAN
st. Berry 96 B7
TIMBERI
av. Dapto 44 C9
TIMBER RIDGE
dr. Nowra Hill 91 A13
TIMBS
rd. Oak Flats 49 E14
TIMMS
pl. Horsley 44 A1
TINDALL
pl. North Nowra 87 K6
TINDALLS
la. Berry 96 Q4
TINGIRA
cr. Kiama 66 B8
TIN MILL PARK
rd. Port Kembla 35 K12
TINTO
pl. West Nowra 91 K4
TI-TREE
av. Albion Park Rail .. 52 H3
TOBIN
cl. North Nowra 87 D7
TOBRUK
av. Port Kembla 42 D14
st. Fairy Meadow 29 K2
TODD
st. Warrawong 41 K12
TODD
lk. Albion Park 52 A14
TOLSON
pl. Balgownie 25 G16
TOMBONDA
dr. Kiama 66 A7
TOMERONG
st. Tullimbar 51 K7
TOMLIN
st. Albion Park 52 C12
TOM THUMB
av. South Nowra 91 H14
rd. Port Kembla 35 K10
TONGARRA
rd. Albion Park 51 G5
rd. Albion Park Rail .. 52 B4
rd. Calderwood 51 G5
rd. Croom 52 B4
rd. Tullimbar 51 G5
TOOLANGI
cl. Cordeaux Ht 34 F11
TOOLIJOOA
st. Tullimbar 51 J5
TOOMA
pl. Flinders 53 Q10
TOORAK
av. Mangerton 35 E9
pl. Gerringong 69 E14
TORONTO
av. Dapto 44 K4

TORRENS
pl. Albion Park 52 A11
TORRES
cct. Shell Cove 53 Q12
cct. Shell Cove 54 A13
TORRIDON
st. Nowra 92 E3
TOSHACK
st. Warilla 49 N10
TOWERS
rd. Shoalhaven Hd .. 95 F4
TOWN HALL
pl. Wollongong 2 D14
pl. Wollongong 35 Q3
TOWNS
st. Shellharbour 54 C7
TOWNSEND
av. Fairy Meadow 29 M7
TOWRADGI
rd. Towradgi 25 P16
TOXTETH
av. Austinmer 18 G12
TRACKSIDE
dr. Kanahooka 40 B14
TRAINING SHOPS
rd. Port Kembla 41 L9
TRAMWAY
ct. Bulli 22 F7
TRAMWAY BRIDGE
Gwynneville 1 M7
TREETOP
gln. Thirroul 17 Q15
TRENTHAM
rd. Shoalhaven Hd .. 95 E8
TRESNAN
st. Unanderra 34 J16
TRESSIDER
cl. Berry 96 A7
pl. Bellambi 26 G10
TREVISO
pl. North Nowra 83 D16
TREVOR
av. Lake Heights 41 E15
TRIFECTA
pl. Kembla Grange .. 40 E8
TRIM
av. South Nowra 91 J14
TRINITY
row. Bulli 22 H11
TRIPOLI
wy. Albion Park 51 M3
TRISTAN
av. Woonona 26 A3
TROMAN
pl. Bellambi 26 G9
TROON
av. Shell Cove 57 Q2
TRUMAN
av. Dapto 44 E9
TRUMPER
st. Lake Illawarra ... 49 M7
st. Mt Warrigal 49 M7
st. Warilla 49 M7
TUAN
st. Blackbutt 53 K5
TUCKER
av. Balgownie 25 E15
TUCKERMAN
la. Coledale 18 L6
TUGALONG
la. Tullimbar 51 F8
TUGGERAH
cct. Flinders 53 Q8
pl. Berkeley 40 M9
TULIMBAR
la. Tullimbar 51 C8
TULIP
wy. Woonona 22 A10
TULLA
pl. West Nowra 91 H6
TULLY
cr. Albion Park 52 A12

TUMMELL
cl. West Nowra 91 H5
TUNNEL
rd. Helensburgh 12 B5
TURLEY
av. Bomaderry 87 N4
TURNBERRY
cl. Shell Cove 58 A1
TURNBULL
cr. Penrose 44 A10
la. Bulli 22 F10
TURNER
esp. East Corrimal 26 F11
TURNERS
la. Bolong 84 L2
TURNSTONE
la. Shell Cove 54 C10
vst. South Nowra .. 92 E13
TUROSS
st. Albion Park 51 M7
TURPENTINE
st. Kiama 61 L13
TURPIN
av. Warrawong 41 L12
TURRAMA
st. Mt Keira 28 N15
TUSCAN
pl. North Nowra 83 E16
TWEED
lk. Albion Park 52 A13
TWENTY ONE ENTRY
rd. Spring Hill 35 C16
TYALLA
pl. Cordeaux Ht 34 E11
TYNDALL
pl. Horsley 43 M1
TYRREL
la. Flinders 53 L7
st. Flinders 53 L6
TYRWHITT
av. Bulli 22 D6

U

ULAN
pl. Albion Park 52 G13
ULRICK
pl. Nowra 91 P4
ULSTER
av. Warilla 49 P14
UNARA
rd. Dapto 39 G16
UNDERPASS
rd. Port Kembla 41 K8
UNDERWOOD
st. Corrimal 25 N12
UNDOLA
rd. Helensburgh 11 P13
UNICENTRE
rd. Keiraville 29 H11
UNION
st. Coniston 35 J7
st. Towradgi 25 P16
st. Wollongong 35 J7
wy. Gerringong 70 E4
UNIVERSITY
av. Gwynneville 29 J12
av. N Wollongong 1 K1
av. N Wollongong 29 J12
UNYAH
pl. Kanahooka 45 E6
UPHILL
rd. Albion Park 51 P9
UPLAND
ch. Albion Park 51 M10
UPPER CABBAGE TREE
la. Mt Pleasant 29 D5
URALBA
st. Figtree 34 P3
st. W Wollongong 35 A4
URANA
wy. Flinders 53 L5

URANNA
av. North Nowra 87 H4
URSULA
rd. Bulli 22 E11
URUNGA
pde. Wollongong 1 C13
pde. Wollongong 35 G3

V

VALE
st. Mt St Thomas .. 35 F10
VALETTA
st. W Wollongong ... 35 B4
VALLEY
dr. Figtree 28 L14
wy. Kanahooka 39 Q16
VALLEY VIEW
cr. Albion Park 52 F15
VANCE
st. North Nowra 87 J6
VARDY
ct. Helensburgh 11 M12
VEIGALS
la. Bulli 22 E9
VENDETTA
st. Nowra 92 E5
VENN
st. Berkeley 40 N12
VENOSA
wy. South Nowra .. 92 F11
VENUS
rd. Dunmore 53 M14
VERA
st. Helensburgh 12 B6
VERBENA
wy. Barrack Heights .. 49 L15
VERDELHO
av. Dapto 44 D13
VEREKER
st. Fairy Meadow 29 K7
st. Mt Ousley 29 K7
VERMONT
rd. Warrawong 41 H13
VERONICA
st. Warilla 50 C9
VICKERY
st. Gwynneville 1 F7
st. Gwynneville 29 H16
VICTA
wy. Bomaderry 84 D15
VICTORIA
la. Woonona 22 C16
st. Berry 96 E8
st. Gerringong 70 D1
st. Unanderra 34 K16
st. Wollongong 1 M10
st. Wollongong 35 L1
VICTORIOUS
vw. Cambewarra Vill. 82 M7
VIEW
st. Kembla Heights .. 33 L6
st. Lake Illawarra ... 50 C7
st. Nowra 88 A16
st. Nowra 92 A1
st. Port Kembla 41 P6
st. Wollongong 2 B6
st. Wollongong 29 P15
VINES
av. Shell Cove 54 A16
VIOLA
wy. Barrack Heights .. 49 L16
VIOLET
bvd. Calderwood 51 G2
VIRGINIA
st. N Wollongong 2 B2
st. N Wollongong 29 P13
tce. Thirroul 22 D1
VISITOR
rd. Port Kembla 35 H11
VISTA
av. Farmborough Ht .. 40 A1
pl. Thirroul 18 C15

VIVIAN
st. Kembla Grange .. 39 B12

W

WABBA
pl. Koonawarra 44 K7
WADE
st. Figtree 34 M12
WAGIN
st. Shoalhaven Hd .. 95 G8
WAGONGA
rd. Helensburgh 11 N16
WAGTAIL
pl. Farmborough Ht .. 33 P16
wy. Blackbutt 53 D3
WAITANGI
st. Gwynneville 1 E3
st. Gwynneville 29 H14
WAKEFIELD
st. Bulli 22 F6
WALANG
av. Figtree 34 M1
WALBON
cr. Koonawarra 44 L9
WALDRON
st. Mt St Thomas .. 35 D9
WALEY
av. Bellambi 26 H10
WALKER
la. Helensburgh 11 N11
st. Helensburgh 13 M3
st. Warrawong 41 J15
WALL
la. Kanahooka 45 B2
st. Warilla 49 N8
WALLABAH
wy. Koonawarra 44 M5
WALLABY
st. Blackbutt 53 H5
WALLABY HILL
rd. Jamberoo 59 Q16
WALLACE
rd. Fernhill 25 K16
st. Nowra 92 B4
st. Nowra 92 C3
WALLAGOOT
la. Tullimbar 51 F8
WALLAROO
dr. Blackbutt 53 J2
dr. Shellharbour C C . 53 J2
WALLAWA
st. Figtree 35 A6
WALLBANK
wy. Bulli 22 C9
WALLIS
cl. Flinders 53 Q9
WALSH
cr. North Nowra 87 M5
pl. Albion Park 52 E11
WALTER
st. Mangerton 35 D6
WALTERS
st. Warilla 49 P12
WAMBIRI
av. Koonawarra 44 K8
WANDANDIAN
st. Tullimbar 51 H9
WANDELLA
cr. Flinders 53 M9
WANDOO
pl. Shellharbour 53 Q6
WAPLES
rd. Cordeaux Ht 33 Q16
rd. Farmborough Ht .. 33 Q16
rd. Unanderra 40 F2
WARATAH
av. Albion Park Rail .. 52 J4
st. Helensburgh 11 N10
st. Windang 50 E3
WARATI
pl. Oak Flats 49 F16

WARBY
st. Bomaderry 84 B16
WARD
pl. Balgownie 25 F16
WARDELL
st. Bellambi 26 E9
WAREHOUSE
rd. Berkeley 40 P5
rd. Port Kembla 41 H6
WAROO
pl. Bomaderry 84 B11
WARRAH
rd. Unanderra 40 F3
rd. Bangalee 83 A16
WARRAMUNGA
st. Nowra 92 D2
WARRA WARRA
rd. South Nowra 92 B16
WARREGO
st. Albion Park 52 B13
WARREN
av. North Nowra 87 J3
WARRI
pl. Oak Flats 49 H15
WARRIGAL
st. Nowra 92 G6
WARWICK
st. Berkeley 40 J6
WASDALE
pl. Bomaderry 84 A12
WASHERY
rd. Port Kembla 41 K7
WATERFORD
tce. Albion Park 52 F16
WATERFRONT
prm. Shell Cove 54 D11
WATERGUM
gr. Stanwell Park 13 Q10
rd. Worrigee 92 J6
wy. Woonona 21 P16
WATERLOO
st. Bulli 22 F13
WATERS
pl. Wollongong 1 M12
pl. Wollongong, off
Rawson St 35 L2
WATERVIEW
av. Haywards Bay 48 F7
WATKINS
cl. Gerringong 70 H2
WATSON
st. Oak Flats 53 C2
WATTAMOLLA
rd. Helensburgh 11 P16
WATTLE
rd. Barrack Heights .. 49 L15
rd. Blackbutt 53 K3
rd. Flinders 53 N6
rd. Shellharbour 53 N6
rd. Shellharbour C C . 49 L15
rd. Woonona 21 Q16
st. Helensburgh 11 L10
st. Port Kembla 41 K10
st. Windang 46 K16
WATTLEBIRD
rd. South Nowra 92 D14
WATTS
la. Russell Vale 26 C6
WAUGH
av. Towradgi 25 Q15
WAVERLEY
dr. Unanderra 40 J3
WAYARI
wy. Woonona, off
Corkwood Cct ... 25 Q1
WAYNOTE
pl. Unanderra 41 B2
WEAVER
tce. Bulli 22 H7
WEBB
la. Albion Park 52 A4

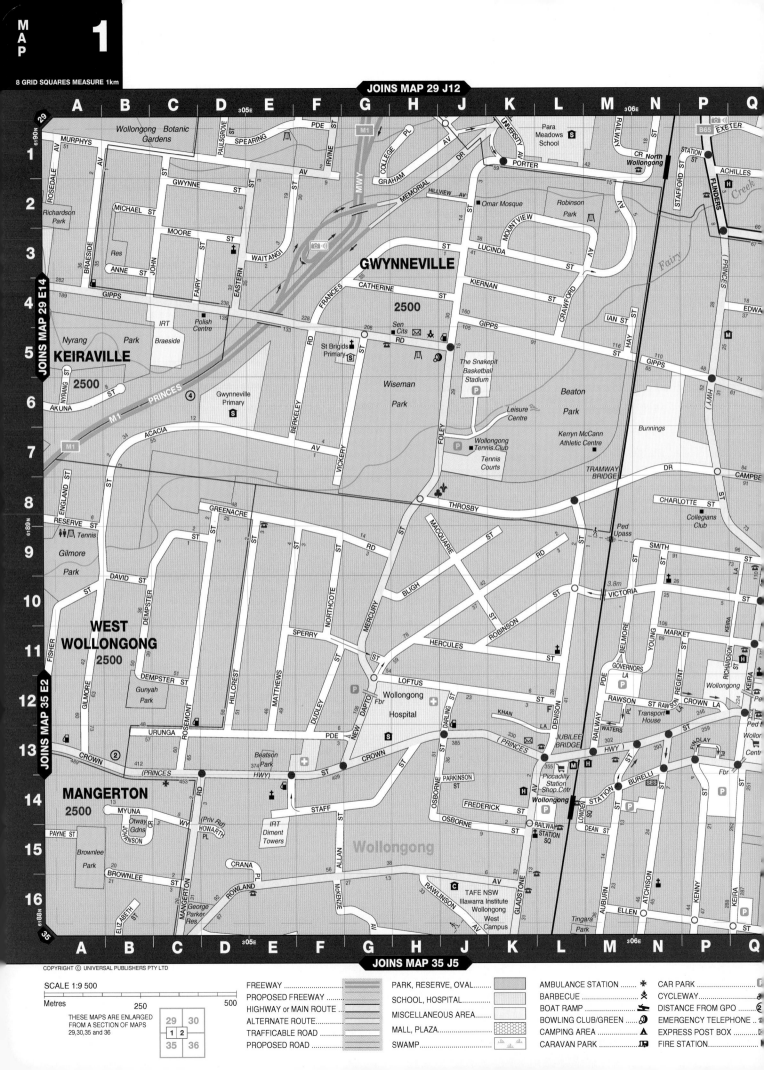

MAP 2

MAP 11 FOLLOWS

8 GRID SQUARES MEASURE 1km

JOINS MAP 30 B12

A B C D E F G H J K L M N P Q

1 2 3 4 5 6 7 8 9 10 11 12 13 14 15 16

30

6190N

308E

307E

JOINS MAP 36 F1

6189N

6188N

NORTH WOLLONGONG
2500

WOLLONGONG
2500

Stuart Park

J P Galvin Park

George Hanley

PLEASANT ST

BODE AV

VIRGINIA ST

BESSELL AV

BLACKET AV

KEMBLA ST

BOURKE ST

BURKE ST

OCEAN ST

PARK ST

CORRIMAL ST

CLIFF RD

North Beach

North Wollongong Beach

Novotel Northbeach Ent

SLSC

Battery Park

George Dodd Res

GEORGES PL

Catholic Convent

MARR ST

DR

WILSON ST

Osborne Park

Brighton Lawn

Rock Pool

TASMAN

SEA

Wollongong Harbour

Belmore

Basin

Fish Co-op

Breakwater Lighthouse

Flagstaff Hill Park

Flagstaff Point

Amphitheatre

Historic Court House

MARINE DR

OLD COURTHOUSE

MAGISTRATES

ROBERTSON ST

HINTON ST

HECTOR ST

ENDEAVOUR DR

Wollongong Foreshore Park

Wollongøng City SLSC

WIN Entertainment Centre

Five Islands Brewery

WIN Sports & Entertainment Centres

WIN Stadium

Salvation Army Centre

Andrew Lysaght Park

Bus Terminal

Market Square

Museum

St Mary Star of the Sea College

Lang Park

PARKSIDE

QUILKEY

MARINE ST

PACIFIC

GRAND

QUEENS

MARKET ST

SMITH ST

CROWN ST

BURELLI ST

STEWART ST

GEORGE ST

BANK ST

EVANS ST

BEATSON ST

HARBOUR ST

CORRIMAL ST

KEMBLA ST

THOMAS ST

FIRST ST

CHURCH ST

MARKET ST

Court House

Mall

NRMA

Simpson

David Jones

Greater Union Cinemas

Leagues Club

Woolworths

Civic Plaza

Arts Centre

Town Hall

Council Office

Steelers Club

IRT Howard Court

ALDI Supermarket

Pioneer Park

Showground

Smiths Hill High

YWCA

Wollongong Primary

Illawarra Master Builders Club

Service NSW

R.O.W.

Market Square

City Beach

Wollongong City Beach

Coombe ST

Moore ST

B65

B65

JOINS MAP 36 B5

COPYRIGHT © UNIVERSAL PUBLISHERS PTY LTD

FIXED SPEED CAMERA
GOLF COURSE
GUIDES / SCOUTS
HOSPITAL
HOTEL / MOTEL
INFORMATION CENTRE
LIBRARY
LOOKOUT 180 , 360
MASONIC CENTRE
MEMORIAL / MONUMENT
ONE-WAY TRAFFIC ROUTE
PICNIC AREA
PLACE OF WORSHIP
PLAYGROUND
POLICE STATION
POST OFFICE
RED LIGHT CAMERA
ROUNDABOUT
SCHOOL - PRIVATE
SCHOOL - PUBLIC
SERVICE STATION
SHOPPING CENTRE
SWIMMING POOL
TELEPHONE
TERTIARY - PRIVATE
TERTIARY - PUBLIC
TOILETS
TRAFFIC LIGHT
WEIGHBRIDGE
WINERIES

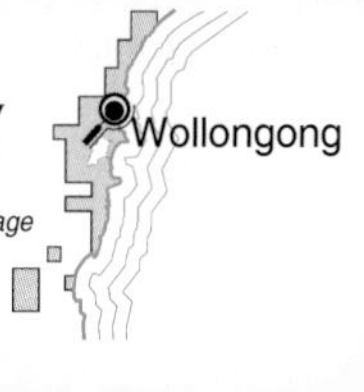

LOCALITY DIAGRAM
Key Map Coverage

Wollongong

MAP 11
PREVIOUS MAP 2
4 GRID SQUARES MEASURE 1km

LIMIT OF MAPS

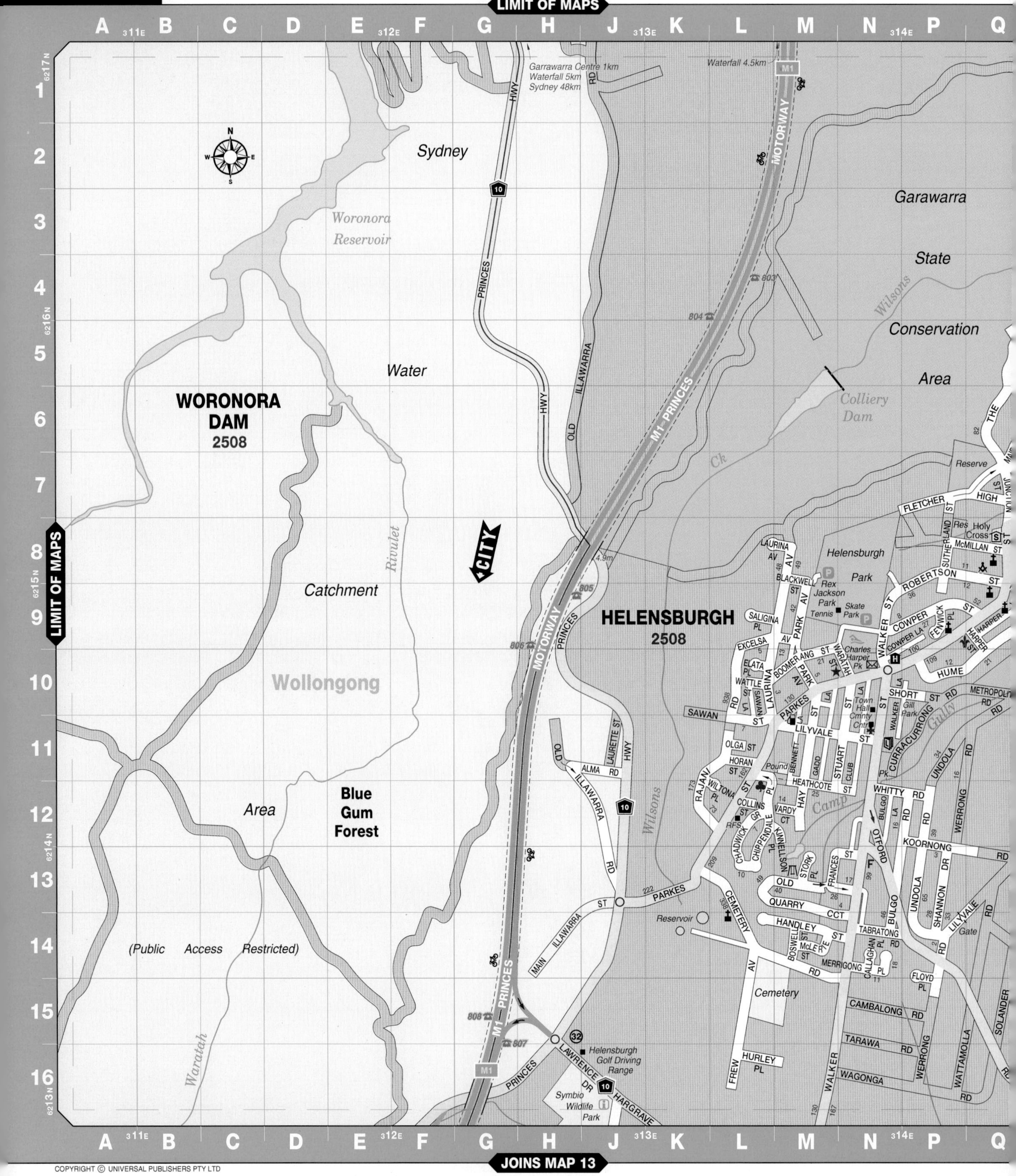

A 311E B C D 312E E F G H J 313E K L M N 314E P Q

LIMIT OF MAPS

Garawarra Centre 1km
Waterfall 5km
Sydney 48km

Waterfall 4.5km

Sydney

Woronora Reservoir

Garawarra

State

Conservation

Area

Water

WORONORA DAM 2508

Colliery Dam

Catchment

CITY

Reserve

HELENSBURGH 2508

Helensburgh Park

Wollongong

Area

Blue Gum Forest

(Public Access Restricted)

Waratah

Reservoir

Cemetery

Helensburgh Golf Driving Range

Symbio Wildlife Park

JOINS MAP 13

COPYRIGHT © UNIVERSAL PUBLISHERS PTY LTD

FREEWAY
PROPOSED FREEWAY
HIGHWAY or MAIN ROUTE
ALTERNATE ROUTE
TRAFFICABLE ROAD
PROPOSED ROAD

PARK, RESERVE, OVAL
SCHOOL, HOSPITAL
MISCELLANEOUS AREA
MALL, PLAZA
SWAMP

AMBULANCE STATION
BARBECUE
BOAT RAMP
BOWLING CLUB/GREEN
CAMPING AREA
CARAVAN PARK

CAR PARK
CYCLEWAY
DISTANCE FROM GPO
EMERGENCY TELEPHONE
EXPRESS POST BOX
FIRE STATION

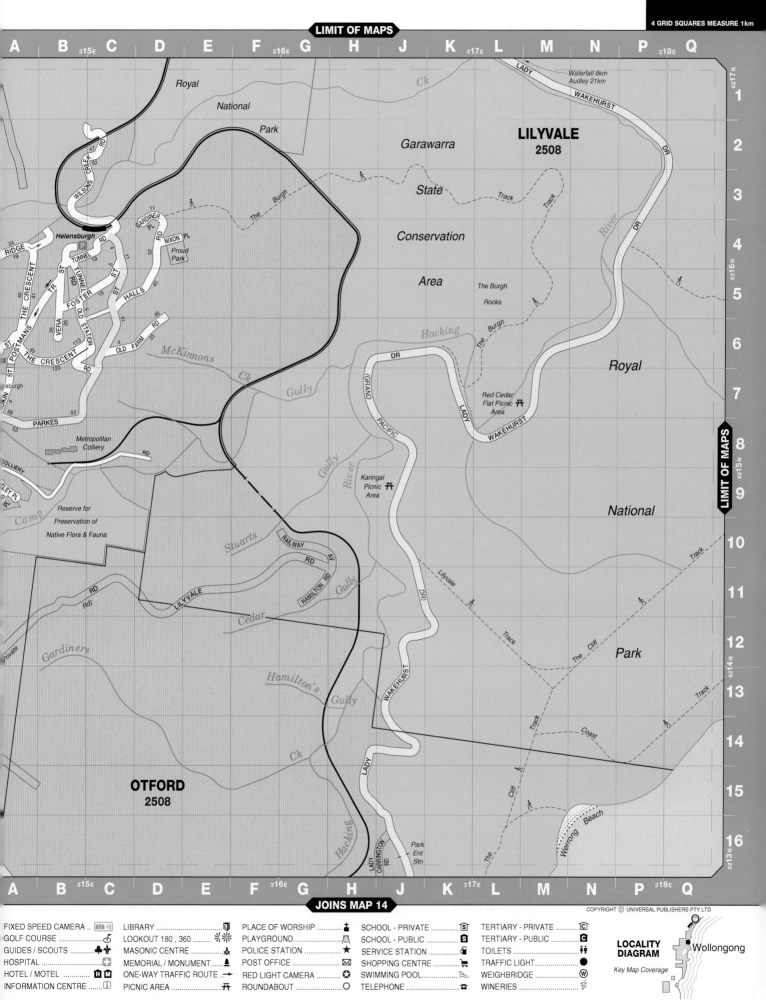

LILYVALE
2508

Garawarra

State

Conservation

Area

Royal

National

Park

Royal
National
Park

Helensburgh

Metropolitan Colliery

Reserve for
Preservation of
Native Flora & Fauna

OTFORD
2508

FIXED SPEED CAMERA .. 📷))) 　LIBRARY .... 🏛　PLACE OF WORSHIP ..... ⛪　SCHOOL - PRIVATE .... Ⓢ　TERTIARY - PRIVATE .... Ⓒ
GOLF COURSE .... ⛳　LOOKOUT 180 , 360 ... 🌸🌼　PLAYGROUND........... 🛝　SCHOOL - PUBLIC .... Ⓢ　TERTIARY - PUBLIC .... Ⓖ
GUIDES / SCOUTS .... ♣♣　MASONIC CENTRE ...... ⚒　POLICE STATION .... ★　SERVICE STATION .... ⛽　TOILETS .... 🚻
HOSPITAL .... ➕　MEMORIAL / MONUMENT..... 🔺　POST OFFICE .... ✉　SHOPPING CENTRE .... 🛒　TRAFFIC LIGHT .... ●
HOTEL / MOTEL .... 🏨🏩　ONE-WAY TRAFFIC ROUTE . →　RED LIGHT CAMERA ..... ✪　SWIMMING POOL .... 🏊　WEIGHBRIDGE .... Ⓦ
INFORMATION CENTRE ...... ⓘ　PICNIC AREA .... 🎋　ROUNDABOUT .... ○　TELEPHONE .... ☎　WINERIES ....

LOCALITY
DIAGRAM
Key Map Coverage

Wollongong

MAP 13

4 GRID SQUARES MEASURE 1km

JOINS MAP 11

A 311E B C D E 312E F G H J 313E K L M N 314E P Q

1
2
3
4
5
6
7
8
9
10
11
12
13
14
15
16

6213N
6212N
6211N
6210N
6209N

LIMIT OF MAPS

Waratah Rivulet

Sydney

Water

Catchment

Area

(Public   Access

Restricted)

WORONORA DAM
2508

DARKES FOREST
2508

Kellys

M1

810 809

M1 PRINCES

PRINCES

812

811

DARKES FOREST RD

M1

Gills

HELENSBURGH
2508

MOTORWAY

HWY

CITY

Symbio i
Wildlife
Park

BARNES

PL
Ford

LAWRENCE

HARGRAVE

TEMPLE RD

WALKER

173

158

ST

Ck

Hindu
Temple

Kellys
Falls

Kellys Falls

Herbert

Ck

STANWELL TOPS
2508

10

69 DRIVE

30

RD

Stanwell Tops

Christian

Conference

Centre

Wollongong

Stanwell Dam

Stanwell

ANNESLEY AV

BENDENA GDN

STIRLING ST

23

34

2

9

PLATEAU

CONISTON GDN

Hargrave

RD

26

26

LONGVIEW CR

STONEHAVEN

Henry
Halloran
Park

The
Garden of
Peace

Stanwell
Tops

LAWRENCE

HARGRAVE

SOUTHVIEW
AV

26

LONGVIEW

Stanwell
Park

RAILWAY

Ck

LAWRENCE

OLD COAST RD

Hillcrest
Village
Self Care
UPA

THE DRIVE

STATION

Stanwell Pa
Pmy

STANWELL
77

Art
Gallery

Res

Ba

Causeway 46

RFS

GRAND

26

10

PACIFIC

MURRAWAL RD

LOWER CO BEACH

DRIVE

Fbr

13

100

11

STANWELL PARK
2508

MADDENS PLAINS
2508

Coalcliff
Dam

COALCLIF
2508

Wodi Wodi Track

Track

Escarpment

Illawarra

LAWRENCE HARGRAVE

75

15

JOINS MAP 16

A 311E B C D E 312E F G H J 313E K L M N 314E P Q

COPYRIGHT © UNIVERSAL PUBLISHERS PTY LTD

SCALE 1:19 000

Metres   500   1000   1km

FREEWAY	PARK, RESERVE, OVAL	AMBULANCE STATION ✳	CAR PARK P
PROPOSED FREEWAY	SCHOOL, HOSPITAL	BARBECUE 🍖	CYCLEWAY
HIGHWAY or MAIN ROUTE	MISCELLANEOUS AREA	BOAT RAMP	DISTANCE FROM GPO 28
ALTERNATE ROUTE	MALL, PLAZA	BOWLING CLUB/GREEN	EMERGENCY TELEPHONE
TRAFFICABLE ROAD	SWAMP	CAMPING AREA ▲	EXPRESS POST BOX ✉
PROPOSED ROAD		CARAVAN PARK	FIRE STATION F

JOINS MAP 12

OTFORD
2508

Govinda
Valley
Retreat
Centre

Otford   Park

Causeway

LLOYD   PL

Ck

104   RD

G.FORGES   RD

LADY
(One lane
bridge)

Otford
Pmy

RFS

DOMVILLE   STATION

STATION   RD

CARRINGTON

LADY   RD

Fbr

FANSHAWE   RD

Otford

BEAUMONT   RD

RD   (GRAND

CARRINGTON   RD

BERESFORD   RD

PACIFIC   DR

DRIVE

Park
Ent
Station

The   Cliff   Track

Otford
Lookout

Royal

National

Park

L   RAWSON   RD

Tall Gums
Environmental
Farm

OTFORD   (Priv   Rd)   RD

Aussie Paintball
Stanwell Tops

DRIVE

10A

28

HARGRAVE

Reserve

DENE

YELLOW   DRIVE

HILLSIDE   CRT

SEAVIEW   CR

MAXWELL   CR

THE   DRIVE

HE   DRIVE

PDE

AV

LADY   WAKEHURST   OTFORD   RD

Bald
Hill

Bald Hill
Lookout

Lawrence
Hargrave
Memorial
Bald Hill
Headland
Reserve
(Hang Gliding
Take off-
Site)

Kennett
Home

Aged
Care

Beach

Undola

Kennett   Home

Stanwell Park
Beach
Reserve

Stanwell
Av Res

Helensburgh-
Stanwell Park SLSC

Stanwell   Park   Beach

TASMAN

SEA

FIXED SPEED CAMERA ..	LIBRARY	PLACE OF WORSHIP	SCHOOL - PRIVATE	TERTIARY - PRIVATE	
GOLF COURSE	LOOKOUT 180 , 360	PLAYGROUND	SCHOOL - PUBLIC	TERTIARY - PUBLIC	
GUIDES / SCOUTS	MASONIC CENTRE	POLICE STATION	SERVICE STATION	TOILETS	
HOSPITAL	MEMORIAL / MONUMENT	POST OFFICE	SHOPPING CENTRE	TRAFFIC LIGHT	
HOTEL / MOTEL	ONE-WAY TRAFFIC ROUTE	RED LIGHT CAMERA	SWIMMING POOL	WEIGHBRIDGE	
INFORMATION CENTRE	PICNIC AREA	ROUNDABOUT	TELEPHONE	WINERIES	

LOCALITY
DIAGRAM
Key Map Coverage

Wollongong

4 GRID SQUARES MEASURE 1km

LIMIT OF MAPS

307E A B C D 308E E F G H 309E J K L M 310E N P Q

1 609N

RFS 2km

DARKES FOREST

DARKES FOREST 2508

814

MOTORWAY

2 M.E.T School Illawarra Campus

813

PRINCES

26

Flat Rock Junctic

Dharawal

3

M1

Nature Reserve 608N

Illawarra

4

Golf Club

Clubhouse

5

816 24

(No Vehicular Access)

Dharawal

6

815

Nature

LIMIT OF MAPS

7 607N

CATARACT 2560

Reserve

Ck

8

Wollongong

CITY

9 607N

10

Sydney Water

11

12 606N

Catchment Area

M1

818 22

13

817

14

(Public Access Restricted)

M1-PRINCES

15

16 605N

22

PRINCES

Illawarra

17

307E A B C D 308E E F G H 309E J K L M 310E N P Q

COPYRIGHT © UNIVERSAL PUBLISHERS PTY LTD

SCALE 1:19 000   1km

Metres   500   1000

FREEWAY	PARK, RESERVE, OVAL
PROPOSED FREEWAY	SCHOOL, HOSPITAL
HIGHWAY or MAIN ROUTE	MISCELLANEOUS AREA
ALTERNATE ROUTE	MALL, PLAZA
TRAFFICABLE ROAD	SWAMP
PROPOSED ROAD	

AMBULANCE STATION	✳	CAR PARK	P
BARBECUE	⚎	CYCLEWAY	
BOAT RAMP		DISTANCE FROM GPO	28
BOWLING CLUB/GREEN		EMERGENCY TELEPHONE	
CAMPING AREA	▲	EXPRESS POST BOX	✉
CARAVAN PARK		FIRE STATION	F

O'Hares Ck

Maddens

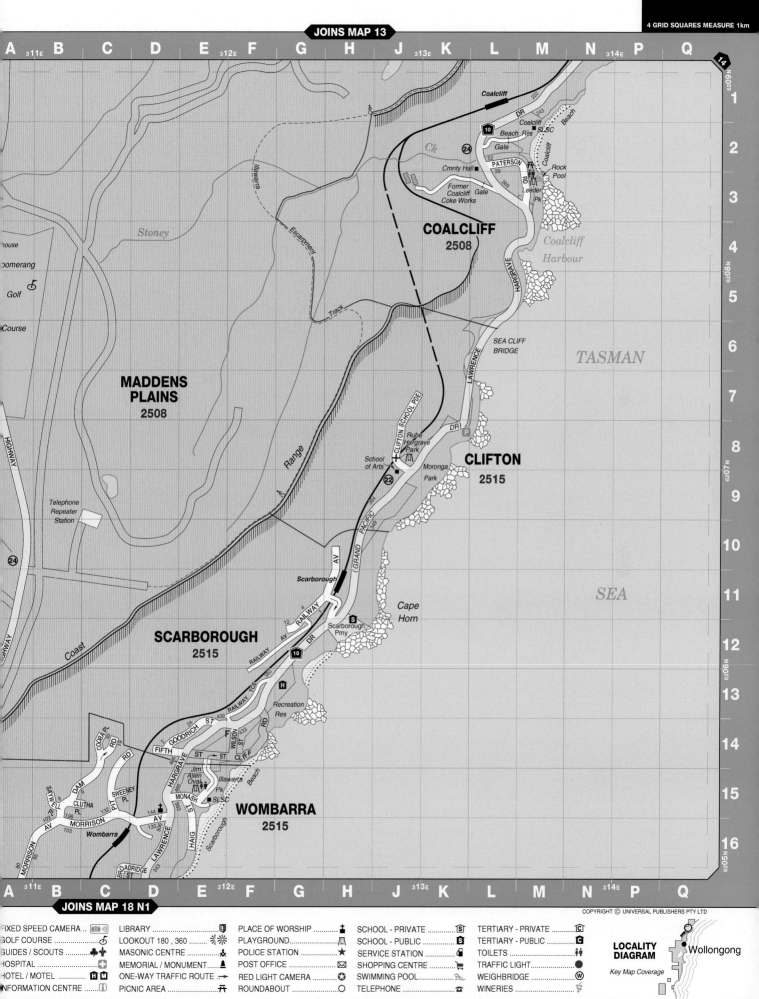

MAP **16**

4 GRID SQUARES MEASURE 1km

JOINS MAP 13

A ₃₁₁ₑ B C D E ₃₁₂ₑ F G H J ₃₁₃ₑ K L M N ₃₁₄ₑ P Q

Coalcliff

COALCLIFF
2508

Ck

Coalcliff
Beach Res
Beach
Gate
Cmnty Hall
Former
Coalcliff
Coke Works
Gate
SLSC
Coalcliff
Rock
Pool
Leeder
Pk
PATERSON

Coalcliff
Harbour

Stoney

Illawarra

Escarpment

HARGRAVE

TASMAN

MADDENS
PLAINS
2508

Track

SEA CLIFF
BRIDGE

LAWRENCE

Telephone
Repeater
Station

Range

Rube
Hargrave
Park
School
of Arts
Moronga
Park

CLIFTON
2515

CLIFTON SCHOOL PDE

GRAND PACIFIC DR

Scarborough

Cape
Horn

Scarborough
Pmy

SEA

SCARBOROUGH
2515

RAILWAY TCE

RAILWAY AV

Recreation
Res

GOODRICH ST
FIFTH ST
WILSON ST
CLIFF RD
ST

COBRA PL
RD
SWEENEY
PIT
DAM
CLUTHA
PL
SAYWELL
AV
MORRISON
AV
MORRISON

Wombarra

HARGRAVE ST
MONASH AV
HAIG ST
LAWRENCE
BROADRIDGE ST

Jim
Allen
Oval
Illawarra
Pk
SLSC

Illawarra Beach

WOMBARRA
2515

Scarborough Beach

FIXED SPEED CAMERA .... 📷
GOLF COURSE .... ⛳
GUIDES / SCOUTS .... ♣♣
HOSPITAL .... ✚
HOTEL / MOTEL .... Ⓗ Ⓜ
INFORMATION CENTRE ..... ℹ

LIBRARY .... 📖
LOOKOUT 180 , 360 ...... ☀❋
MASONIC CENTRE .... ⚒
MEMORIAL / MONUMENT ... ▲
ONE-WAY TRAFFIC ROUTE ... →
PICNIC AREA .... ⅂⌐

PLACE OF WORSHIP .... ✝
PLAYGROUND .... ⛩
POLICE STATION .... ★
POST OFFICE .... ✉
RED LIGHT CAMERA ...... ✪
ROUNDABOUT .... ○

SCHOOL - PRIVATE .... Ⓢ
SCHOOL - PUBLIC .... Ⓢ
SERVICE STATION .... Ⓖ
SHOPPING CENTRE ...... 🛒
SWIMMING POOL .... 🏊
TELEPHONE .... ☎

TERTIARY - PRIVATE ..... Ⓒ
TERTIARY - PUBLIC ...... Ⓒ
TOILETS .... 🚻
TRAFFIC LIGHT .... ●
WEIGHBRIDGE .... Ⓦ
WINERIES .... 🍇

LOCALITY
DIAGRAM
Key Map Coverage

● Wollongong

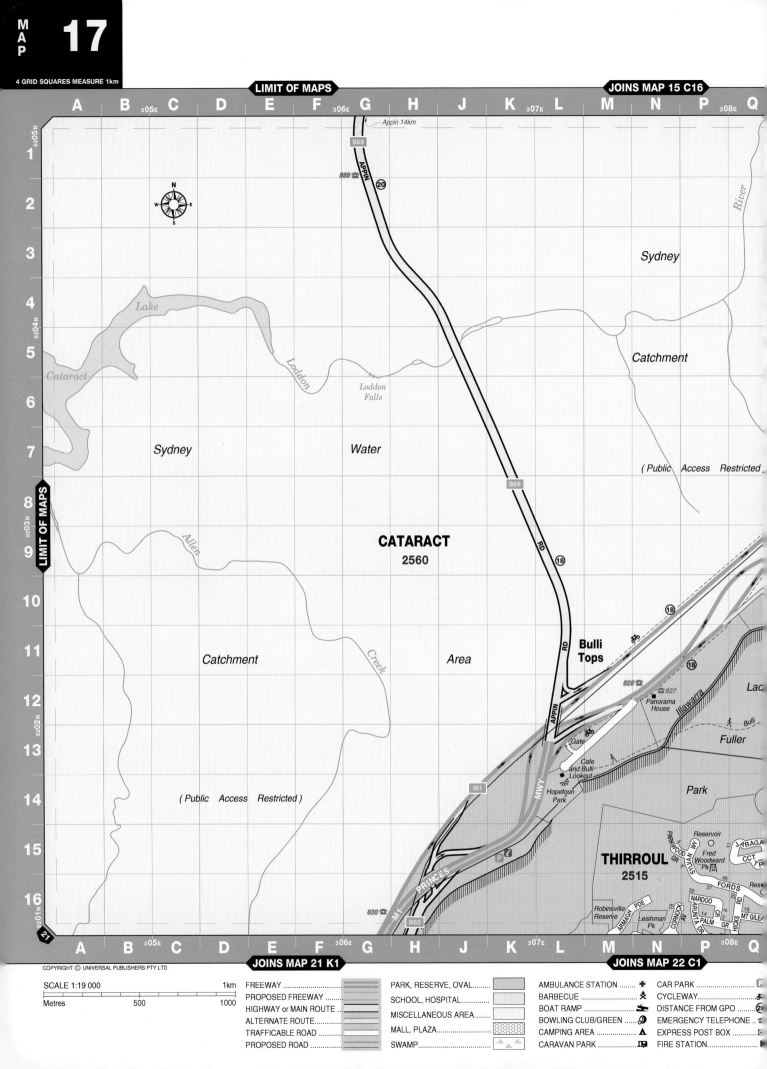

LIMIT OF MAPS

JOINS MAP 15 C16

Sydney

Catchment

(*Public Access Restricted*)

Lake

Cataract

Sydney

Water

Loddon

Loddon Falls

Allen

CATARACT
2560

Catchment

Area

Creek

(*Public Access Restricted*)

Bulli Tops

Panorama House

Illawarra

Lac

Fuller

Gate

Cafe and Bulli Lookout

Hopetoun Park

Park

Reservoir

THIRROUL
2515

Fred Woodward Pk

Robinsville Reserve

Leishman Pk

Appin 14km

LIMIT OF MAPS

JOINS MAP 21 K1

JOINS MAP 22 C1

SCALE 1:19 000

Metres   500   1000   1km

FREEWAY	PARK, RESERVE, OVAL	AMBULANCE STATION	CAR PARK
PROPOSED FREEWAY	SCHOOL, HOSPITAL	BARBECUE	CYCLEWAY
HIGHWAY or MAIN ROUTE	MISCELLANEOUS AREA	BOAT RAMP	DISTANCE FROM GPO
ALTERNATE ROUTE	MALL, PLAZA	BOWLING CLUB/GREEN	EMERGENCY TELEPHONE
TRAFFICABLE ROAD	SWAMP	CAMPING AREA	EXPRESS POST BOX
PROPOSED ROAD		CARAVAN PARK	FIRE STATION

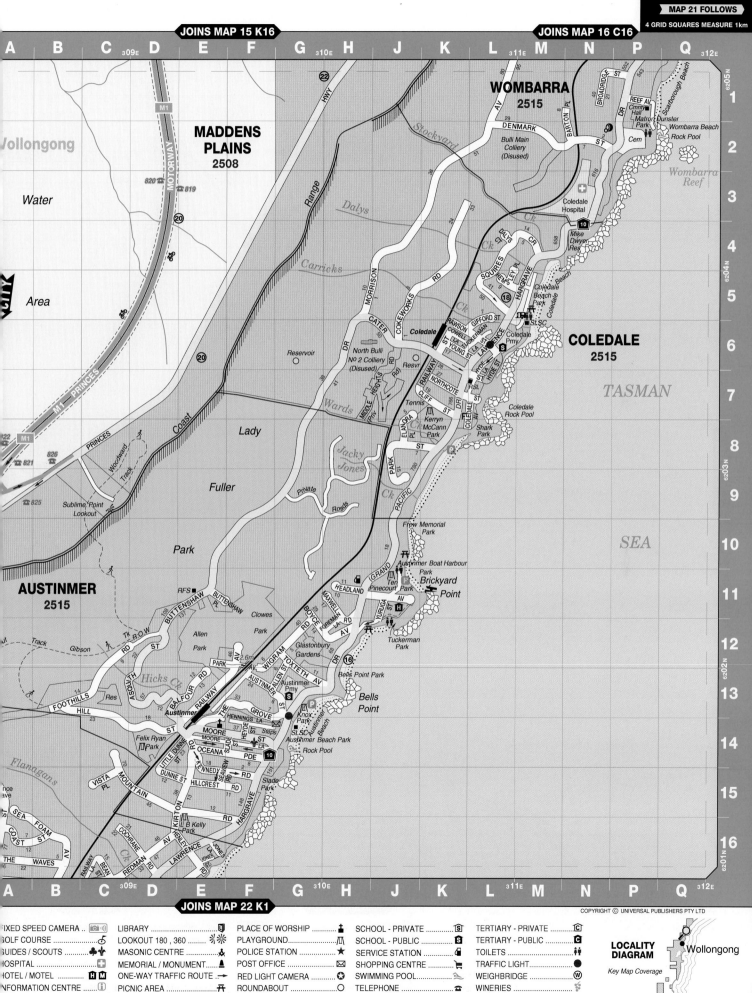

JOINS MAP 15 K16

JOINS MAP 16 C16

A B C 309E D E F G 310E H J K L 311E M N P Q 312E

WOMBARRA
2515

MADDENS
PLAINS
2508

Wollongong

Water

Area

Range

Dalys

Carricks

Coast

Lady

Fuller

Park

Jacky
Jones
Ck

Private
Roads

AUSTINMER
2515

North Bulli
No 2 Colliery
(Disused)

Reservoir

Wards

Tennis

Kerryn
McCann Park

Shark
Park

TASMAN

Coledale
Rock Pool

COLEDALE
2515

Coledale
Hospital

Mike
Dwyer
Res

Coledale
Beach
Park

Bulli Main
Colliery
(Disused)

Stockyard

Wombarra
Reef

Wombarra Beach
Rock Pool

SEA

Frew Memorial
Park

Austinmer Boat Harbour
Park

Brickyard
Point

Tuckerman
Park

Bells Point Park

Bells
Point

Glastonbury
Gardens

Austinmer Pmy

Austinmer Beach

Knox
Park

SLSC

Austinmer Beach Park

Rock Pool

Clowes
Park

Allen
Park

Hicks Ck

Foothills

Felix Ryan
Park

Flanagans

Sublime Point
Lookout

Woodward
Track

PRINCES

Gibson

Track

1
2
3
4
5
6
7
8
9
10
11
12
13
14
15
16

605N
604N
603N
602N
601N

COPYRIGHT © UNIVERSAL PUBLISHERS PTY LTD

FIXED SPEED CAMERA ..
GOLF COURSE ....
GUIDES / SCOUTS ....
HOSPITAL ....
HOTEL / MOTEL ....
INFORMATION CENTRE ....

LIBRARY ....
LOOKOUT 180 , 360 ....
MASONIC CENTRE ....
MEMORIAL / MONUMENT....
ONE-WAY TRAFFIC ROUTE ..
PICNIC AREA ....

PLACE OF WORSHIP ......
PLAYGROUND.............
POLICE STATION ....
POST OFFICE ....
RED LIGHT CAMERA ......
ROUNDABOUT ....

SCHOOL - PRIVATE ....
SCHOOL - PUBLIC ....
SERVICE STATION ....
SHOPPING CENTRE ....
SWIMMING POOL ....
TELEPHONE ....

TERTIARY - PRIVATE ....
TERTIARY - PUBLIC ....
TOILETS ....
TRAFFIC LIGHT...........
WEIGHBRIDGE ....
WINERIES ....

LOCALITY
DIAGRAM
Key Map Coverage

Wollongong

MAP
21
PREVIOUS MAP 18

4 GRID SQUARES MEASURE 1km

LIMIT OF MAPS

JOINS MAP 17 E16

A B C 304E D E F G 305E H J K L 306E M N P Q

1

6201N

Sydney

N
W · E
S

2

830 ☎
B65

Lady

Fuller

829 ☎

Park

RD HIGHWAY

**Bulli
Pass**

14

Bulli

3

Pass

PRINCES

PASS (BULLI)

Scenic

4

834 ☎

833 ☎

Reserve

The Elbow

PRINCES

6200N

5

Water

PRINCES

Illawarra

6

M1

MWY

Wollongong

7

Escarpment

8

LIMIT OF MAPS

6199N

Bellambi

State

Reservoir

Reserve

COPE

9

Catchment

M1

Coast

Conservation   *Area*

STURT PL

HIGHLANDS
KNIGHT PL
62
57
38

Reserve   *Reserve*

CITY

10

ALANSON
20
15

*Woonona
Heights
Park*

11

**CATARACT
2560**

STEPHEN
33
COR

12

6198N

Area

838 ☎

837 ☎

**Woonona
Heights**

JOANNE ST
JUNE
JOSEPH ST
14
PDE
BALMER
CR
DR
16
AV
53
47
88
69

13

Bellambi

Ck

Ck

Collins

POPES LA
MOUNTAIN
POPES
55
50

14

(*Public   Access   Restricted*)

Illawarra

*Carole Avenue
Reserve*

GAHANS
CAROLE
FRETIUS
AV
77
54
AV

PRINCE
AV
GAHANS LA
HIGH
RD

15

M1

PRINCES

BLACKWOOD
24
12
PL
BLUE BERRY CT
WOO

CCT
PERM
INT
PL

CEDAR TCE
26

HOLLYMOUNT
27

16

6197N

M1

MOUNTAIN RANGE
(Private Rd)
RD

FORESTVIEW VW
MAHOGANY WY
WATERGUM
SILKWOOD PL
LAUREL PL
RED ASH
HICKORY
RED WATT
WY

A B C 304E D E F G 305E H J K L 306E M N P Q

JOINS MAP 25

SCALE 1:19 000   1km

Metres   500   1000

FREEWAY	
PROPOSED FREEWAY	
HIGHWAY or MAIN ROUTE	
ALTERNATE ROUTE	
TRAFFICABLE ROAD	
PROPOSED ROAD	

PARK, RESERVE, OVAL
SCHOOL, HOSPITAL
MISCELLANEOUS AREA
MALL, PLAZA
SWAMP

AMBULANCE STATION .... ✳
BARBECUE .... ☈
BOAT RAMP .... ⛴
BOWLING CLUB/GREEN ...... ⊘
CAMPING AREA .... ▲
CARAVAN PARK ....

CAR PARK ....
CYCLEWAY ....
DISTANCE FROM GPO ....
EMERGENCY TELEPHONE ..
EXPRESS POST BOX ....
FIRE STATION...................

MAP 22
MAP 25 FOLLOWS
4 GRID SQUARES MEASURE 1km

A B C D 308E E F G H 309E J K L M 310E N P Q

HIRROUL 2515

BULLI 2516

ABELIA TCE	7
AGAPANTHA TCE	2
CAMELIA TCE	3
GARDENIA TCE	6
GRANDIFLORA TCE	5
MAGNOLIA WY	4
TULIP WY	1

TASMAN

Bulli Harbour

Bulli Point

Sandon Point Res

Waniora Point

SEA

WOONONA 2517

Flat Rock

LEGEND

FIXED SPEED CAMERA	LIBRARY	PLACE OF WORSHIP	SCHOOL - PRIVATE	TERTIARY - PRIVATE		
GOLF COURSE	LOOKOUT 180 , 360	PLAYGROUND	SCHOOL - PUBLIC	TERTIARY - PUBLIC		
GUIDES / SCOUTS	MASONIC CENTRE	POLICE STATION	SERVICE STATION	TOILETS		
HOSPITAL	MEMORIAL / MONUMENT	POST OFFICE	SHOPPING CENTRE	TRAFFIC LIGHT		
HOTEL / MOTEL	ONE-WAY TRAFFIC ROUTE	RED LIGHT CAMERA	SWIMMING POOL	WEIGHBRIDGE		
INFORMATION CENTRE	PICNIC AREA	ROUNDABOUT	TELEPHONE	WINERIES		

COPYRIGHT © UNIVERSAL PUBLISHERS PTY LTD

LOCALITY DIAGRAM
Key Map Coverage

Wollongong

MAP
25
PREVIOUS MAP 22
4 GRID SQUARES MEASURE 1km
JOINS MAP 21

A B C 304E D E F G 305E H J K L 306E M N P Q

Sydney Water Catchment Area
(Public Access Restricted)

M1
MWY
Cataract
Range
Cataract Ck
RIXONS PASS
RD
RIXONS PASS
PRINCES
M1

Rixon Pass

Southern Mines Rescue Stn

RUSSELL VALE 2517

Russell Vale Golf Course

Clubhouse

HICKS ST
Ent

92 DUKE Pk 66
ANDERSON RD

N
W E
S

Wollongong

Coast

Bellambi Colliery
Private
Gate

YARRAN AV
JJ Sweeney Park
Harry Henson Park

MORETON ST
WEST ST
EAST ST
BROKER ST
PRINCES

NRE No1 Colliery

CITY

Reservoirs

KEERONG
Gate
BELLAMBI
Tenpin Bowl

Aspect South Coast School

ALBERT ST

LYNDON ST

CATARACT 2560

CORRIMAL 2518

TAYLOR AV
ROBSON
ANNIE ST
DONCASTER ST
HIGHWAY
JOYCE LA

PARMENTER AV
POWELL AV
BLOOMFIELD RD
WILFORD ST
BLUNDELL PDE
ROTHERY ST
290
313
Corrimal Diggers
301
RONALD

Brokers Nose

DANIEL ST
COXS ST
GLENLEA ST
CRESTING GR
COTTAGE
COXS AV
THOMAS ST
COLLINS
WILLO
IRT
WYNDHAM ST
ALBAN ST
Cem
ROBERT ST

Illawarra Escarpment

JUSTINE AV
FOOTHILLS ST
CHERYL PL
GIRVAN CR
JAMES
Theatre Hall
Centrelink
RSL
Service NSW
Corrimal Memorial Park

State Conservation Area

Illawarra

MEADOW ST
BELLAMBI ST
THE AVENUE
UNDERWOOD
PRINCES
RAILWAY
Gall
PALFREY
GILBERT
HALL

PENDLETON CL
BRADFORD CL
ADELAIDE CL
CROWTHER
HARRIGAN
KAREN PL
ANGEL
TARRAWANNA RD
SHORT ST

TARRAWANNA 2518

Corrimal Colliery

Tarrawanna Soccer Oval

BRISSENDON
Footbridge
WILLIAMSON ST
ST ANDREWS PL
CAROLINE ST
HIGHWAY

Robert Zeims Park

B65

BOND CL
HAWTHORN PL
BERTRAM
BURRA
PROSSER
CORRIMAL
BLAKER PK
Harrigan
HENRY ST
MEADS AV
Baden Powell Pk
Ck

BALGOWNIE 2519

Towradgi

STAINSBY
HOWSON
JORDAN PL
TUCKER ST
DINAH
Doonan Place Park
DOONAN
BRENNAN
BYRNES DR
RD
IRT Tarrawanna Gardens
Tarrawanna Pmy
KEIRA ST
KENDALL ST
LUCCARDA PL

Cabbage Tree Ck

TERRELL PL
FROST ST
COLE ST
WARD PDE
AGNEW
TOLSON
EWING
CHINSON PL
LAHIFF
FOOTHILLS
CALDWELL
MADDEN
DEVENISH
MEARES ST
WALLACE ST
MARY ANN
JULIUS ST
HENRIETTA ST
DALTON ST
MEMORIAL

BOOTIE ST
GORE ST
DUNCAN ST
CHALMERS HILL GR
MARGARET ST
HOCKING
BUCKLAND
WRIGHT ST
BRIAN
ANGUS
MEADOW
FERNHILL 2519
DOUGLAS ST
Dave Masters
Farrell Pk
PRINGLE RD
CHARLES ST
HOPE ST
JOHN
GEORGE
ELIZABETH
UNION
WILLIAM
TOWRADGI
Ziems Pk
OCEAN

28

SCALE 1:19 000
Metres   500   1000   1km

FREEWAY	
PROPOSED FREEWAY	
HIGHWAY or MAIN ROUTE	
ALTERNATE ROUTE	
TRAFFICABLE ROAD	
PROPOSED ROAD	
PARK, RESERVE, OVAL	
SCHOOL, HOSPITAL	
MISCELLANEOUS AREA	
MALL, PLAZA	
SWAMP	
AMBULANCE STATION	✳
BARBECUE	
BOAT RAMP	
BOWLING CLUB/GREEN	
CAMPING AREA	▲
CARAVAN PARK	
CAR PARK	P
CYCLEWAY	
DISTANCE FROM GPO	
EMERGENCY TELEPHONE	
EXPRESS POST BOX	
FIRE STATION	

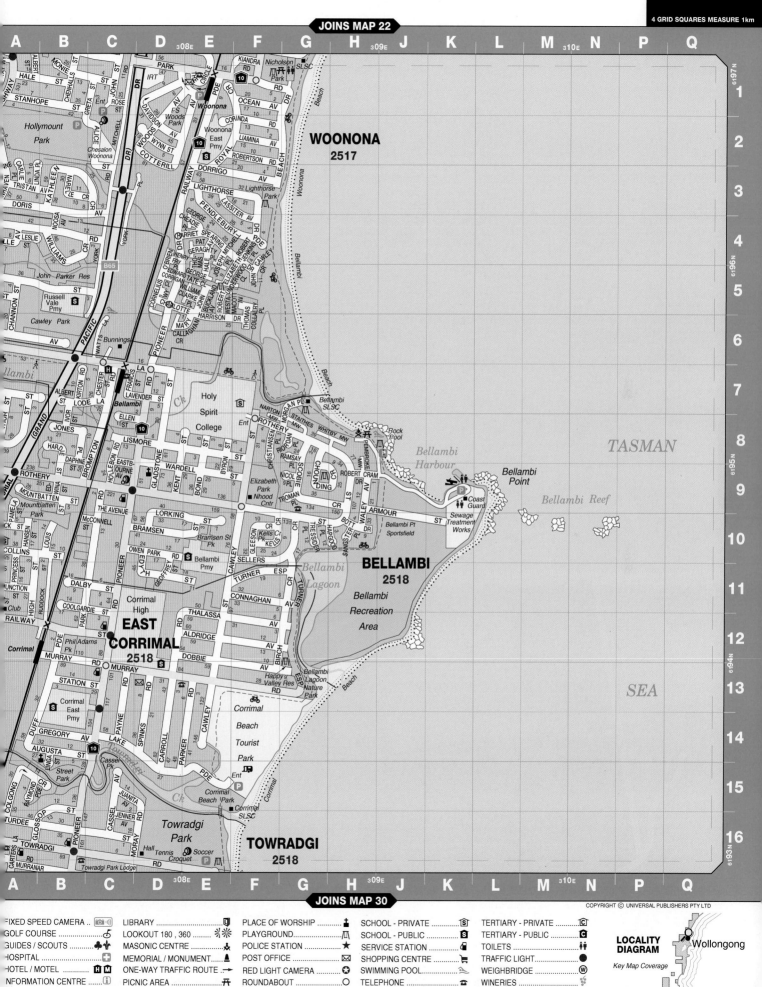

WOONONA
2517

BELLAMBI
2518

Bellambi
Recreation
Area

EAST
CORRIMAL
2518

TASMAN

Bellambi Harbour

Bellambi Point

Bellambi Reef

SEA

TOWRADGI
2518

Corrimal
Beach
Tourist
Park

FIXED SPEED CAMERA .. 📷))
GOLF COURSE ....
GUIDES / SCOUTS ....♣♣
HOSPITAL ....➕
HOTEL / MOTEL ....🄷 🄼
INFORMATION CENTRE ....🛈

LIBRARY ....
LOOKOUT 180 , 360 ....✳✳
MASONIC CENTRE ....
MEMORIAL / MONUMENT....▲
ONE-WAY TRAFFIC ROUTE ...➡
PICNIC AREA ....🛆

PLACE OF WORSHIP ....⛪
PLAYGROUND..................
POLICE STATION ....★
POST OFFICE ....✉
RED LIGHT CAMERA ....✪
ROUNDABOUT ....○

SCHOOL - PRIVATE ....🅂
SCHOOL - PUBLIC ....🅂
SERVICE STATION ....
SHOPPING CENTRE ....🛒
SWIMMING POOL ....
TELEPHONE ....☎

TERTIARY - PRIVATE ....🄲
TERTIARY - PUBLIC ....🄲
TOILETS ....🚻
TRAFFIC LIGHT................●
WEIGHBRIDGE ....Ⓦ
WINERIES ....

LOCALITY
DIAGRAM
Key Map Coverage

Wollongong

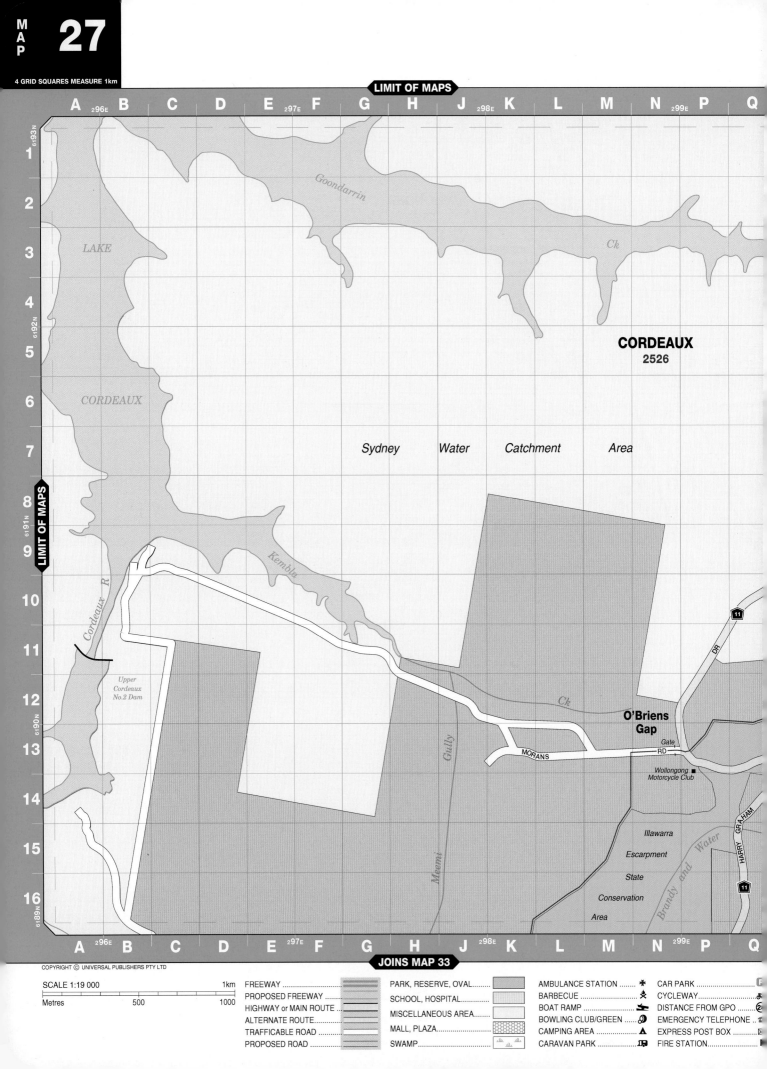

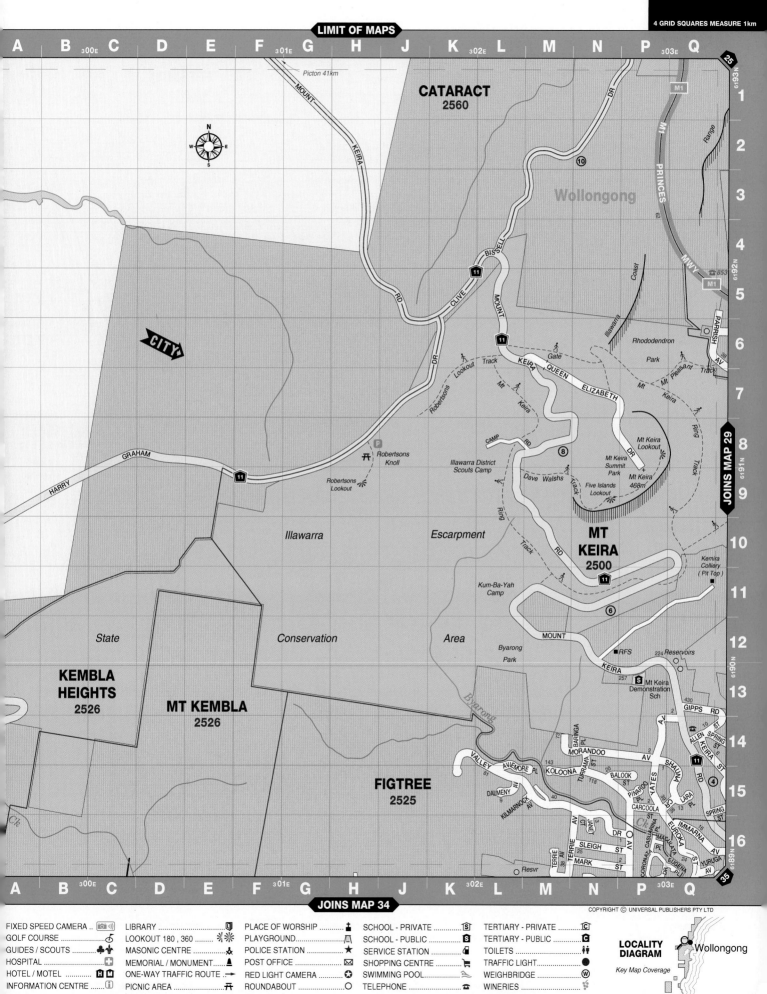

MAP
28
4 GRID SQUARES MEASURE 1km

LIMIT OF MAPS

CATARACT
2560

Wollongong

Picton 41km

CITY

Robertsons Knoll

Robertsons Lookout

Robertsons Lookout Track

Illawarra District Scouts Camp

Mt Keira Lookout

Mt Keira Summit Park

Mt Keira 468m

Five Islands Lookout

Dave Walshs

Kum-Ba-Yah Camp

MT KEIRA
2500

Illawarra   Escarpment

State   Conservation   Area

Byarong Park

KEMBLA HEIGHTS
2526

MT KEMBLA
2526

FIGTREE
2525

Kemira Colliery (Pit Top)

RFS

Reservoirs

Mt Keira Demonstration Sch

GIPPS RD

Resvr

JOINS MAP 29

JOINS MAP 34

FIXED SPEED CAMERA	
GOLF COURSE	
GUIDES / SCOUTS	
HOSPITAL	
HOTEL / MOTEL	
INFORMATION CENTRE	
LIBRARY	
LOOKOUT 180 , 360	
MASONIC CENTRE	
MEMORIAL / MONUMENT	
ONE-WAY TRAFFIC ROUTE	
PICNIC AREA	
PLACE OF WORSHIP	
PLAYGROUND	
POLICE STATION	
POST OFFICE	
RED LIGHT CAMERA	
ROUNDABOUT	
SCHOOL - PRIVATE	
SCHOOL - PUBLIC	
SERVICE STATION	
SHOPPING CENTRE	
SWIMMING POOL	
TELEPHONE	
TERTIARY - PRIVATE	
TERTIARY - PUBLIC	
TOILETS	
TRAFFIC LIGHT	
WEIGHBRIDGE	
WINERIES	

LOCALITY DIAGRAM
Key Map Coverage

Wollongong

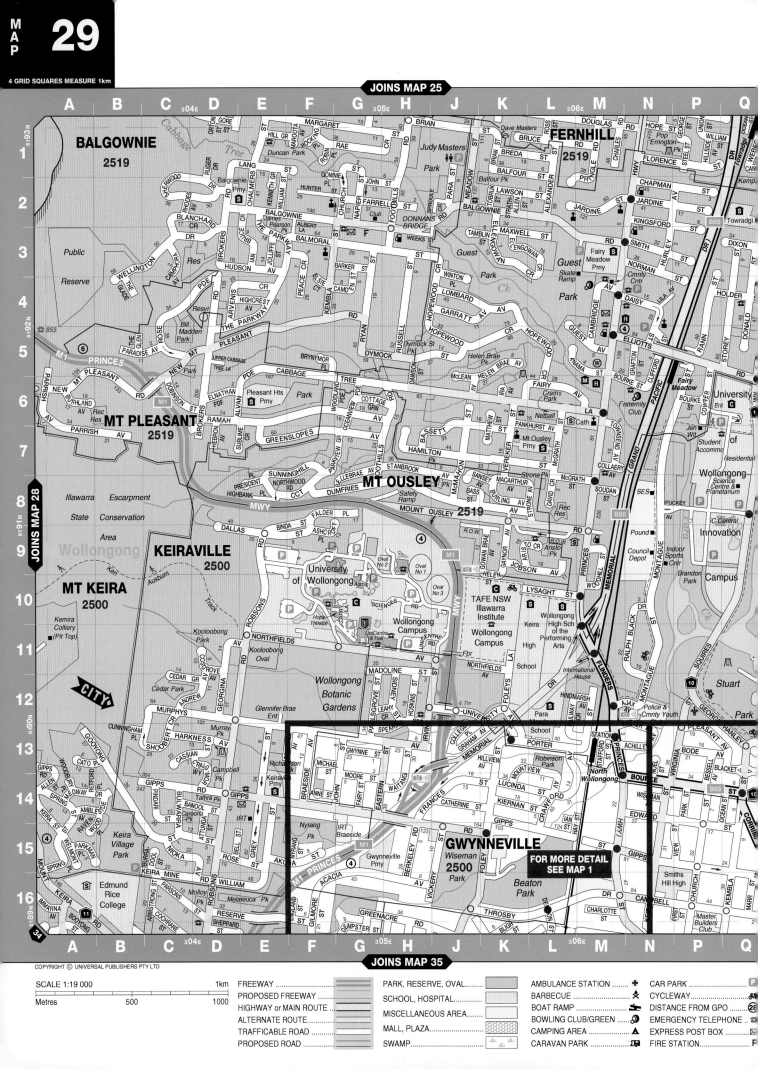

MAP 30
MAP 33 FOLLOWS
4 GRID SQUARES MEASURE 1km

A B C D 308E E F G H 309E J K L M 310E N P Q

6193N — 1
6192N — 2
3
4
5

TASMAN — 6

7
6191N — 8
9
10
11
6190N — 12
13
14
15
6189N — 16

SEA

MURRANAR 92
89
54
TOWRADGI
IRT Towradgi 31
MARLO 56
Park Lodge
RD
EDGAR 52
31 Illawarra
ST 8
Retirement
TOWRADGI
2518
North Dalton Park
Reserve
Wollongong
10
Surf
Ent
Leisure
Wollongong
AFL Club
Resort
Oval
Thomas
Dalton
Park
Fbr
Fairy
Meadow
SLSC
OTTS-RD
FAIRY
MEADOW
2519
Beach
Meadow
uckeys
NORTH
WOLLONGONG
2500
Fairy
ate

Hall Tennis
Soccer
RD
Rock
Pool
Towradgi Point
Illawarra
Towradgi
Towradgi Beach
Beach
Park
Towradgi
SLSC
PDE
MARINE

FOR MORE DETAIL
SEE MAP 2

WOLLONGONG
2500
Rock
Pool
Wollongong
Harbour
Flagstaff Point
10
RGES
WILSON
ST
RD

A B C D 308E E F G H 309E J K L M 310E N P Q

FIXED SPEED CAMERA ..
GOLF COURSE ....
GUIDES / SCOUTS ....
HOSPITAL ....
HOTEL / MOTEL ....
INFORMATION CENTRE ......

LIBRARY ....
LOOKOUT 180 , 360 ....
MASONIC CENTRE ....
MEMORIAL / MONUMENT..
ONE-WAY TRAFFIC ROUTE
PICNIC AREA ....

PLACE OF WORSHIP ....
PLAYGROUND.......................
POLICE STATION ....
POST OFFICE ....
RED LIGHT CAMERA ....
ROUNDABOUT ....

SCHOOL - PRIVATE ....
SCHOOL - PUBLIC ....
SERVICE STATION ....
SHOPPING CENTRE ....
SWIMMING POOL..............
TELEPHONE ....

TERTIARY - PRIVATE ....
TERTIARY - PUBLIC ....
TOILETS ....
TRAFFIC LIGHT..................
WEIGHBRIDGE ....
WINERIES ....

LOCALITY
DIAGRAM
Key Map Coverage
Wollongong

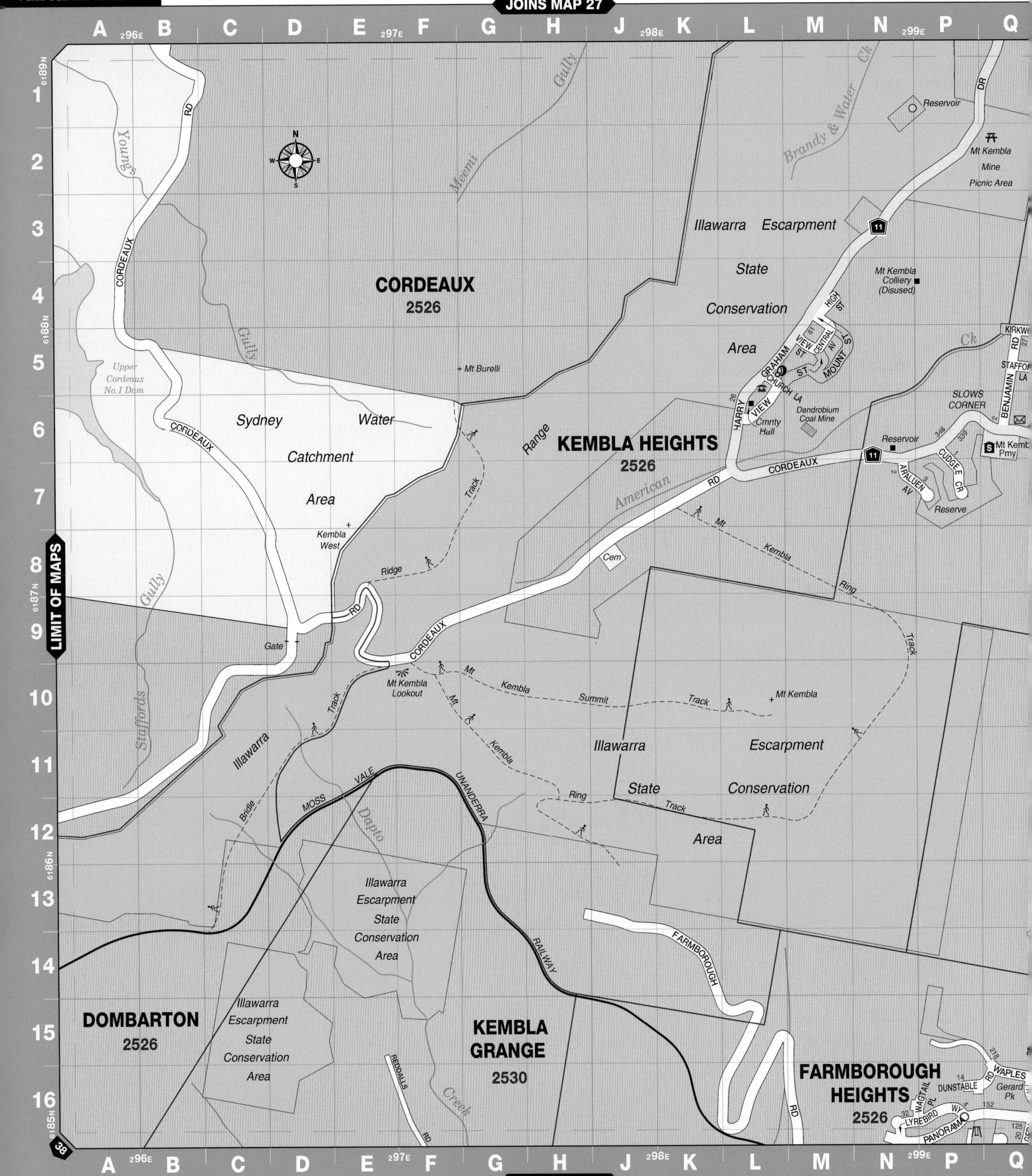

MAP
33
PREVIOUS MAP 30
4 GRID SQUARES MEASURE 1km

JOINS MAP 27

CORDEAUX
2526

KEMBLA HEIGHTS
2526

DOMBARTON
2526

KEMBLA
GRANGE
2530

FARMBOROUGH
HEIGHTS
2526

Illawarra Escarpment State Conservation Area

Sydney Water Catchment Area

Upper Cordeaux No.1 Dam

+ Mt Burelli

Kembla West

Mt Kembla Lookout

Mt Kembla

Mt Kembla Mine Picnic Area

Mt Kembla Colliery (Disused)

Dendrobium Coal Mine

Reservoir

Cmnty Hall

Slows Corner

Reserve

LIMIT OF MAPS

JOINS MAP 39

SCALE 1:19 000 1km
Metres 500 1000

FREEWAY
PROPOSED FREEWAY
HIGHWAY or MAIN ROUTE
ALTERNATE ROUTE
TRAFFICABLE ROAD
PROPOSED ROAD

PARK, RESERVE, OVAL
SCHOOL, HOSPITAL
MISCELLANEOUS AREA
MALL, PLAZA
SWAMP

AMBULANCE STATION
BARBECUE
BOAT RAMP
BOWLING CLUB/GREEN
CAMPING AREA
CARAVAN PARK

CAR PARK
CYCLEWAY
DISTANCE FROM GPO
EMERGENCY TELEPHONE
EXPRESS POST BOX
FIRE STATION

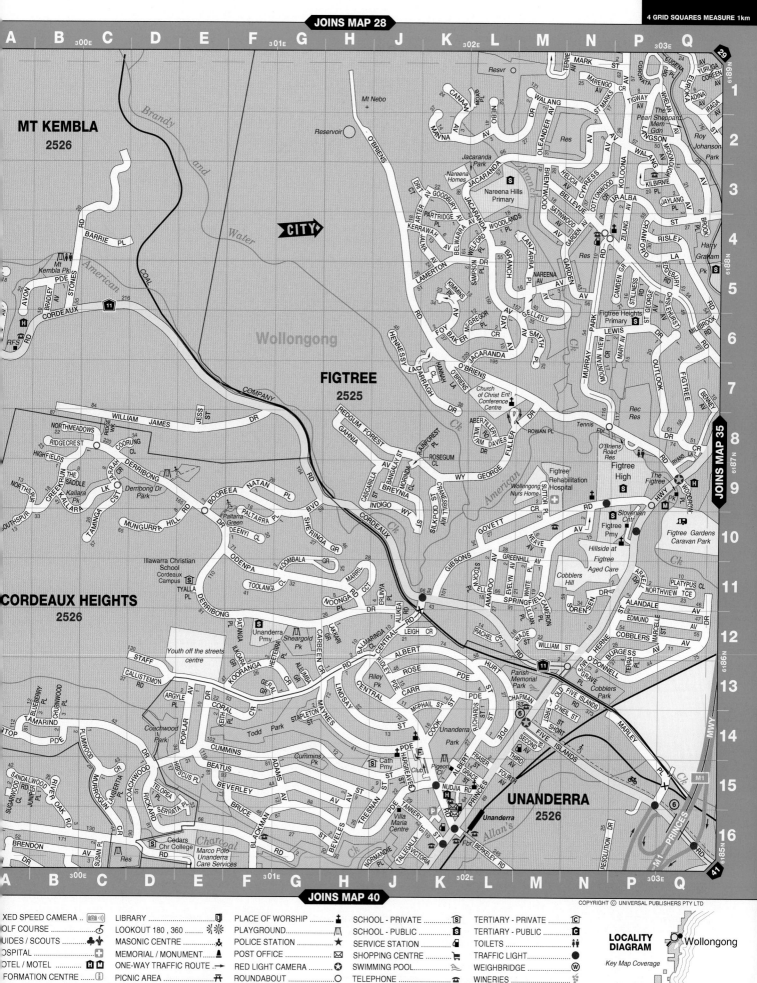

MAP 34

JOINS MAP 35

JOINS MAP 29

JOINS MAP 41

MT KEMBLA
2526

Wollongong

FIGTREE
2525

CORDEAUX HEIGHTS
2526

UNANDERRA
2526

CITY ▶

COPYRIGHT © UNIVERSAL PUBLISHERS PTY LTD

FIXED SPEED CAMERA .. 📷
GOLF COURSE ....
GUIDES / SCOUTS ....♣
HOSPITAL ....✚
MOTEL / MOTEL ......🅷 Ⓜ
INFORMATION CENTRE ...ⓘ

LIBRARY ....📖
LOOKOUT 180 , 360 .....
MASONIC CENTRE ....
MEMORIAL / MONUMENT.....▲
ONE-WAY TRAFFIC ROUTE .→
PICNIC AREA ....

PLACE OF WORSHIP ......♱
PLAYGROUND............
POLICE STATION ....★
POST OFFICE ....✉
RED LIGHT CAMERA ......✲
ROUNDABOUT ....○

SCHOOL - PRIVATE ....Ⓢ
SCHOOL - PUBLIC ....Ⓢ
SERVICE STATION ....
SHOPPING CENTRE ....🛒
SWIMMING POOL ....
TELEPHONE ....☎

TERTIARY - PRIVATE ....Ⓒ
TERTIARY - PUBLIC ....Ⓒ
TOILETS ....
TRAFFIC LIGHT...........●
WEIGHBRIDGE ....Ⓦ
WINERIES ....

LOCALITY DIAGRAM
Key Map Coverage

Wollongong

MAP 35

4 GRID SQUARES MEASURE 1km

JOINS MAP 29

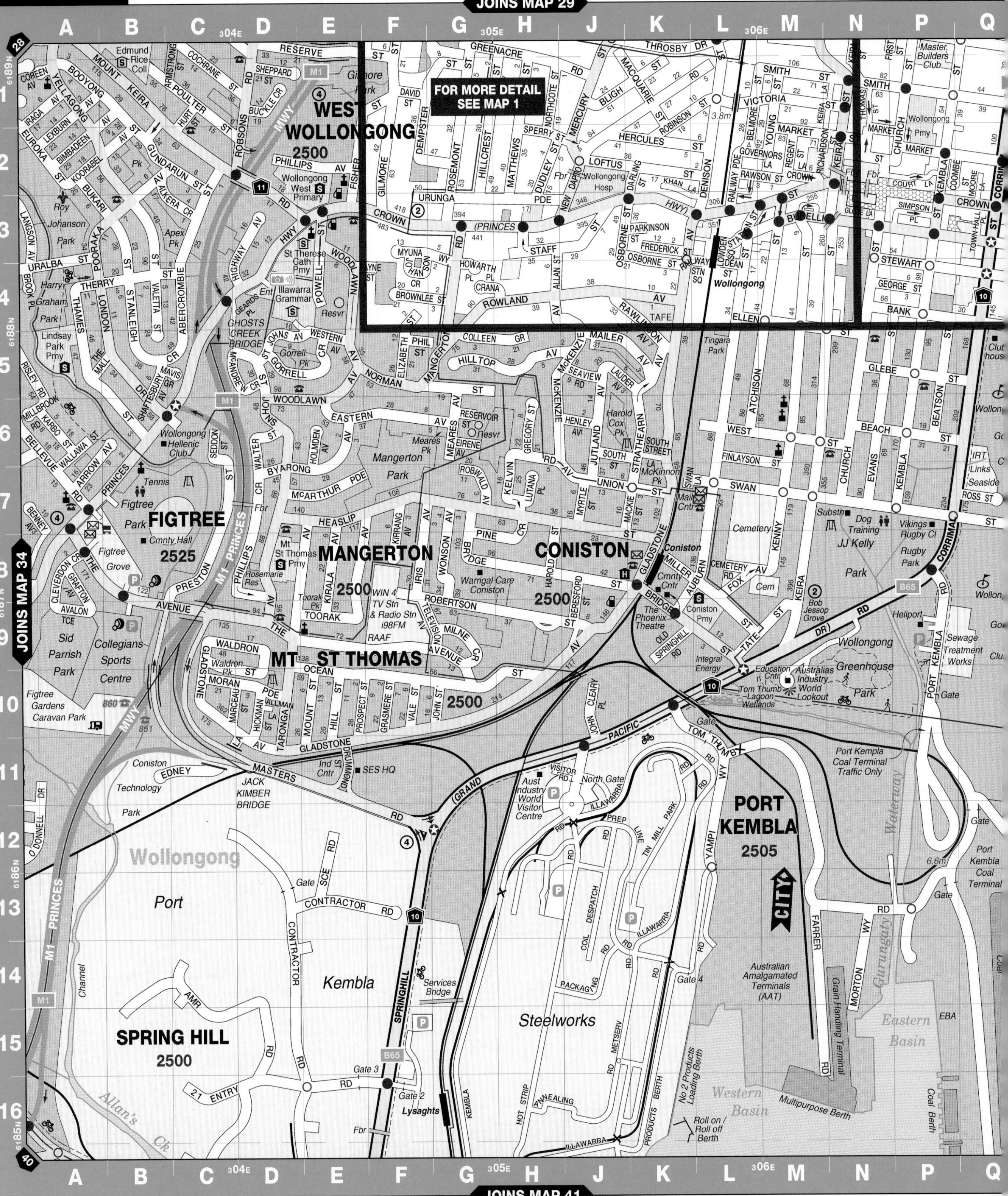

WEST WOLLONGONG 2500

FOR MORE DETAIL SEE MAP 1

FIGTREE 2525

MANGERTON 2500

MT ST THOMAS 2500

CONISTON 2500

PORT KEMBLA 2505

SPRING HILL 2500

Wollongong

Port Kembla

Kembla

Steelworks

Eastern Basin

Western Basin

Wollongong Hosp

Wollongong

SCALE 1:19 000

Metres 500 1000 1km

Legend	
FREEWAY	PARK, RESERVE, OVAL
PROPOSED FREEWAY	SCHOOL, HOSPITAL
HIGHWAY or MAIN ROUTE	MISCELLANEOUS AREA
ALTERNATE ROUTE	MALL, PLAZA
TRAFFICABLE ROAD	SWAMP
PROPOSED ROAD	

Symbols	
AMBULANCE STATION	CAR PARK
BARBECUE	CYCLEWAY
BOAT RAMP	DISTANCE FROM GPO
BOWLING CLUB/GREEN	EMERGENCY TELEPHONE
CAMPING AREA	EXPRESS POST BOX
CARAVAN PARK	FIRE STATION

A B C D 308E E F G H 309E J K L M 310E N P Q

6189N
1
2
3
4

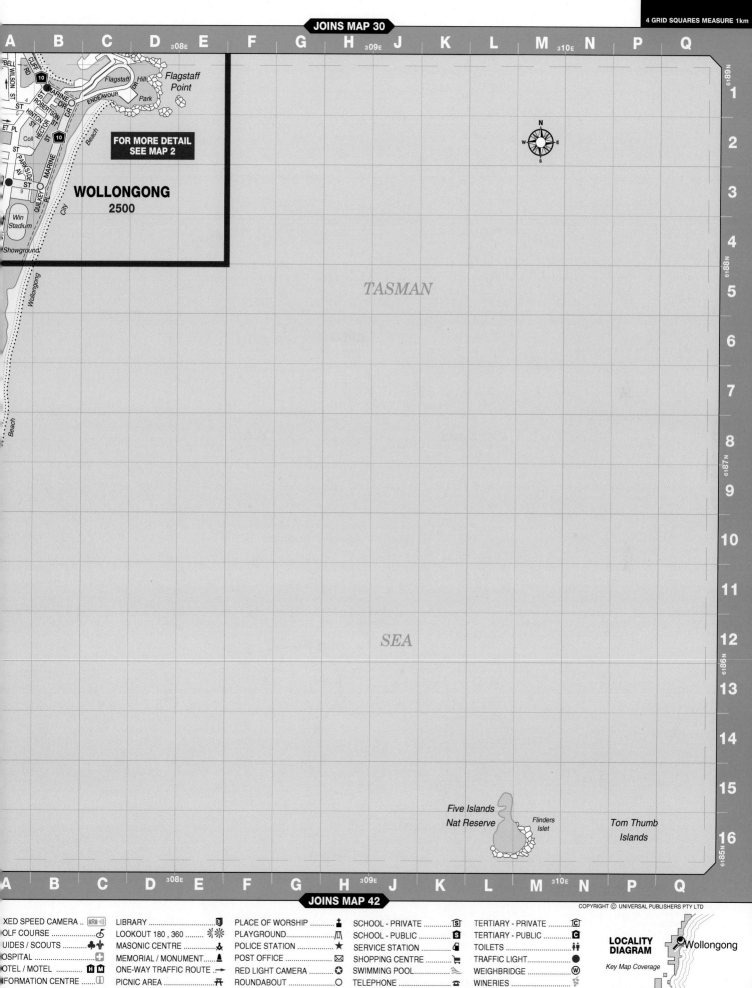

FOR MORE DETAIL
SEE MAP 2

WOLLONGONG
2500

Win Stadium
Showground

Flagstaff Hill
Flagstaff Point
Park

TASMAN

6188N
5

6187N

SEA

6186N

Five Islands
Nat Reserve
Flinders Islet

Tom Thumb
Islands

6185N

6
7
8
9
10
11
12
13
14
15
16

A B C D 308E E F G H 309E J K L M 310E N P Q

XED SPEED CAMERA ..
OLF COURSE ....
UIDES / SCOUTS ....
OSPITAL ....
OTEL / MOTEL ....
FORMATION CENTRE ...

LIBRARY ....
LOOKOUT 180 , 360 ....
MASONIC CENTRE ....
MEMORIAL / MONUMENT.....
ONE-WAY TRAFFIC ROUTE ..
PICNIC AREA ....

PLACE OF WORSHIP ....
PLAYGROUND....................
POLICE STATION ....
POST OFFICE ....
RED LIGHT CAMERA ....
ROUNDABOUT ....

SCHOOL - PRIVATE ....
SCHOOL - PUBLIC ....
SERVICE STATION ....
SHOPPING CENTRE ....
SWIMMING POOL ....
TELEPHONE ....

TERTIARY - PRIVATE ....
TERTIARY - PUBLIC ....
TOILETS ....
TRAFFIC LIGHT..................
WEIGHBRIDGE ....
WINERIES ....

LOCALITY
DIAGRAM
Key Map Coverage

Wollongong

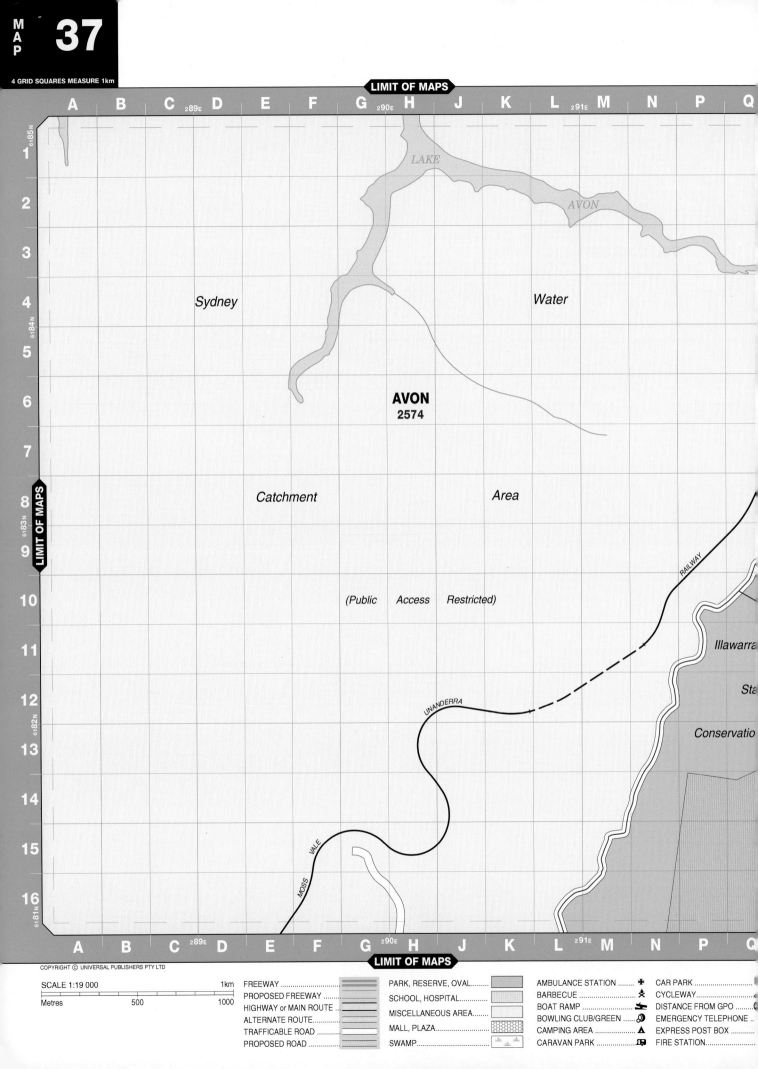

MAP 37

4 GRID SQUARES MEASURE 1km

LIMIT OF MAPS

A B C 289E D E F G 290E H J K L 291E M N P Q

1
2
3
4
5
6
7
8
9
10
11
12
13
14
15
16

6185N
6184N
6183N
6182N
6181N

LIMIT OF MAPS

Sydney

LAKE

AVON

Water

AVON
2574

Catchment   *Area*

(Public   Access   Restricted)

RAILWAY

Illawarra

Sta

Conservatio

UNANDERRA

VALE

MOSS

A B C 289E D E F G 290E H J K L 291E M N P Q

LIMIT OF MAPS

COPYRIGHT © UNIVERSAL PUBLISHERS PTY LTD

FREEWAY	PARK, RESERVE, OVAL..........	AMBULANCE STATION .... ✳	CAR PARK ....
PROPOSED FREEWAY	SCHOOL, HOSPITAL..............	BARBECUE .... 🔥	CYCLEWAY........................
HIGHWAY or MAIN ROUTE ...	MISCELLANEOUS AREA........	BOAT RAMP	DISTANCE FROM GPO ....
ALTERNATE ROUTE.............	MALL, PLAZA.......................	BOWLING CLUB/GREEN	EMERGENCY TELEPHONE ...
TRAFFICABLE ROAD	SWAMP...............................	CAMPING AREA .... ▲	EXPRESS POST BOX ....
PROPOSED ROAD		CARAVAN PARK	FIRE STATION....................

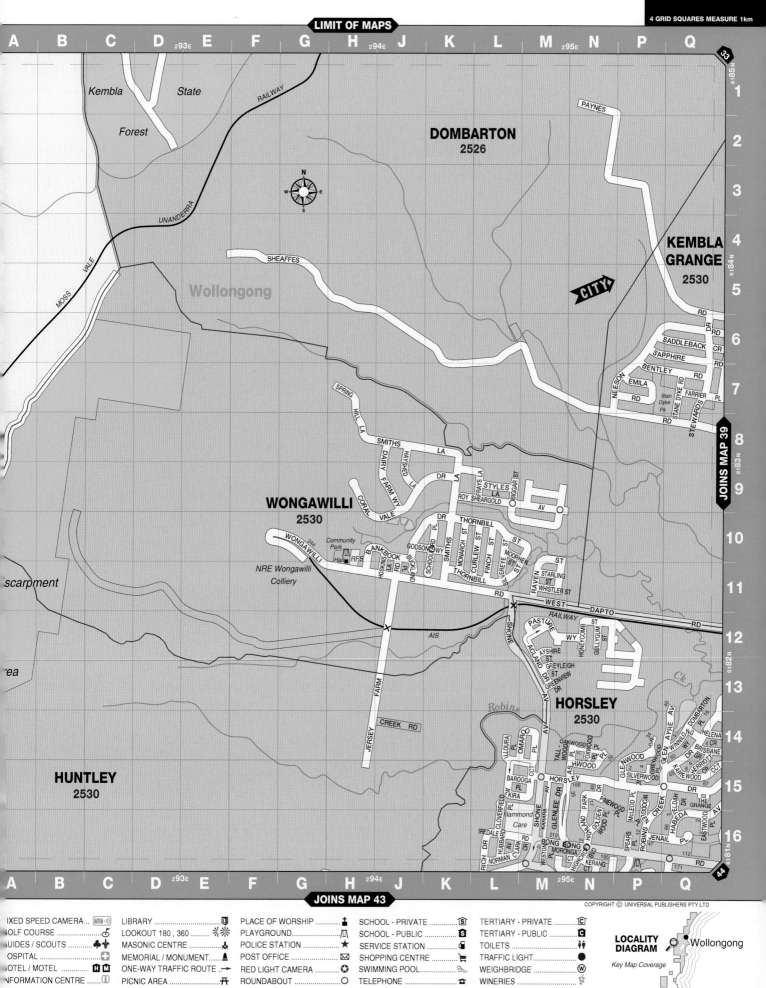

MAP 38
4 GRID SQUARES MEASURE 1km

LIMIT OF MAPS

Kembla State Forest

Railway

DOMBARTON
2526

PAYNES

UNANDERRA

KEMBLA
GRANGE
2530

MOSS VALE

SHEAFFES

CITY

Wollongong

RD
RD
SADDLEBACK
SAPPHIRE
BENTLEY
EMILA
NEESON
Stan Dyke Pk
STANE DYKE RD
FARRIER
STEWARDS
RD

SPRING
HILL LA
SMITHS
DAIRY FARM WY
HAYSHED LA
LA
DR
LA
FRAYS LA
STYLES LA
BIGGAR ST
ROY SHEARGOLD
AV

WONGAWILLI
2530

CORAL VALE

WONGAWILLI
244
Community Park
Hall
RFS
BANKBOOK
HOSKINS LA
GODSON
SCHOOL
SMITHS
MONARCH ST
CURLEW ST
FINCH ST
THORNBILL
ST
MOORHEN ST
VEREYE ST
STARLING ST
RAVEN ST
WHISTLER ST

NRE Wongawilli
Colliery

THORNBILL
RD
WEST DAPTO RD
RAILWAY

scarpment

AIS

SHONE
PASTURE
WY
ACLAND
AYSHIRE ST
GREYLEIGH
GREENVIEW DR
HONEYCOMB
GULLYGUM ST

Robins Ck

HORSLEY
2530

JERSEY FARM

CREEK RD

HUNTLEY
2530

LLOURA
OMARO PL
TALL-WOOD
OAKWOOD PL
ASHWOOD
FOXWOOD
GLENWOOD PL
SILVERWOOD
DOMBARTON
HELENA
BRISBANE
KAPTEWOOD
DR
THE GRANGE
EASTWOOD
HABEDA
JENAIL
BAROOGA PL
KIRA
HORSLEY
SHONE
KARARA
GLENLEE DR
PARK
PINEWOOD
GOLDEN
WOOD PL
IREDALE DR
HUBBARD
CLOVERFIELD
Hammond Care
SPEARS
ROBINS CREEK
EASTWOOD
WESTON
NORMAN
CLARK RD
BONG BONG
MORONGA
HIGHCROFT
KERANG
FOWOOD

IXED SPEED CAMERA ..
OLF COURSE
UIDES / SCOUTS
OSPITAL
OTEL / MOTEL
NFORMATION CENTRE

LIBRARY
LOOKOUT 180 , 360
MASONIC CENTRE
MEMORIAL / MONUMENT
ONE-WAY TRAFFIC ROUTE
PICNIC AREA

PLACE OF WORSHIP
PLAYGROUND
POLICE STATION
POST OFFICE
RED LIGHT CAMERA
ROUNDABOUT

SCHOOL - PRIVATE
SCHOOL - PUBLIC
SERVICE STATION
SHOPPING CENTRE
SWIMMING POOL
TELEPHONE

TERTIARY - PRIVATE
TERTIARY - PUBLIC
TOILETS
TRAFFIC LIGHT
WEIGHBRIDGE
WINERIES

LOCALITY DIAGRAM
Wollongong
Key Map Coverage

MAP 39

4 GRID SQUARES MEASURE 1km

A 296E B C D E 297E F G H J 298E K L M N 299E P Q

6185N
1
2
6184N
3
4
5
6183N
6
7

JOINS MAP 38

8
9
6182N
10
11
12
6181N
13
14
15
16

KEMBLA GRANGE
2530

HORSLEY
2530

DAPTO
2530

BROWNSVILLE
2530

Wollongong
Resource   Recovery
Park

Whytes Gully
Waste Disposal
Gate   Depot
Mon-Fri: 7:30am-4:30pm
Weekends &
Public Holidays: 8am-4pm
Closed Christmas Day

Glengarry
■ Cottage

Thiess

Keevers PL

War Cem

Substation

Kembla
Grange
Lawn
Cemetery

One Steel

WEST DAPTO RD

Wollongong
City Raceway ■

The Grange
Golf
Club

William
Beach

Clubhouse

Mullet

Ped U'pass

Integral Energy
Recreation Park

Hall

Proposed Indoor
Sports Shooters
Facility

The Australian
Motorlife Museum

Cath Cem

Gate

Creek

Kembla Grange PL

Keith
Nola
Stand

Gibsons

Karrara
Park

Robins

RAILWAY

Mullet

Ck

Ck

Robins Ck

Rocla

Kundle
Street
Reserve

Dandaloo
Oval

IRT
William
Beach
Gardens

Hayes
Park Pr

M1 - PRINCES

KANAHOOKA RD

PAYNES DR
STEWARDS
NEESON
SADDLEBACK CR
FARRIER
Mcphail Res
PAYNES PL

SHEAFFES RD

REDDALLS RD

FARM RD

DARKES RD

RAINBOW
FARMSTEAD
ELEVATION
CLAYTON
MALBOW
ACREAGE
SANCTUARY
PASTURELAND
DUFFY
CAPTAIN
ASPECT
YAD
SUMMIT
ABBEY
VIVIAN
VISTA
DAPTO RD

AIS

WEST DAPTO RD

FARMBOROUGH RD

LYREBIRD WY
PANORAMA
HIGHVIEW
CARLON
ROSELLA
KINGFISHER
HONEYEATER
PRIMROSE
GERARD
FAIRLOCH
LOCH LOMOND
LOCH CARRON
BEN NEVIS
BARDESS CR
MOSS VALE

Charles
Stimson
Park

Gate
RFS Reserve

WYLLIE

RD

RITCHIE
BALLANTINE
ELLAMATTA
MARIE
MEEHAN
CACHIA
SUNNY BANK
BARHAM
GOODMAN
CREEK
MELROSE
HELENA
BRISBANE
KARIEWOOD
HORSLEY
HABEDA
GREENBROOK
EASTWOOD
HOMESTEAD
BONG BONG
WOODRIDGE
PARKDALE
ELLENBOROUGH
COL-WY
HUXLEY
AMANDA
WOLLONY
CACHIA
FELIX
DABPETO
UH CR

PRINCE EDWARD DR
BROWNSVILLE AV
HORE ST
QUARTER SESSIONS DR
WINDSOR
REGAL ST
Park

St Lukes
St Lukes AV
Cem

PRINCES HWY
EDWARD
ARMSTRONG
JOHNSON
COOLABAH
YALUNGA
KUNDLE
KAPOOKA AV
BILLABONG
BARINGA
BUNDARRA
BARELLAN
MULDA
DOLAN
DULEY
KUNDLE
Lions AV

DARLY AV
KALANG AV
TARANA
MYEE
JINDALEE
EXMOUTH
VALLEY

Khan Pk

Gate
COVIN
GRN
UNARA RD
NORTH
STATION ST
HAMILTON
CLARKE ST
WEROWI
OSBORNE
SURREY

Dimond Bros Pk

COPYRIGHT © UNIVERSAL PUBLISHERS PTY LTD

JOINS MAP 44

SCALE 1:19 000

Metres   500   1000   1km

FREEWAY
PROPOSED FREEWAY
HIGHWAY or MAIN ROUTE
ALTERNATE ROUTE
TRAFFICABLE ROAD
PROPOSED ROAD

PARK, RESERVE, OVAL
SCHOOL, HOSPITAL
MISCELLANEOUS AREA
MALL, PLAZA
SWAMP

AMBULANCE STATION
BARBECUE
BOAT RAMP
BOWLING CLUB/GREEN
CAMPING AREA
CARAVAN PARK

CAR PARK
CYCLEWAY
DISTANCE FROM GPO
EMERGENCY TELEPHONE
EXPRESS POST BOX
FIRE STATION

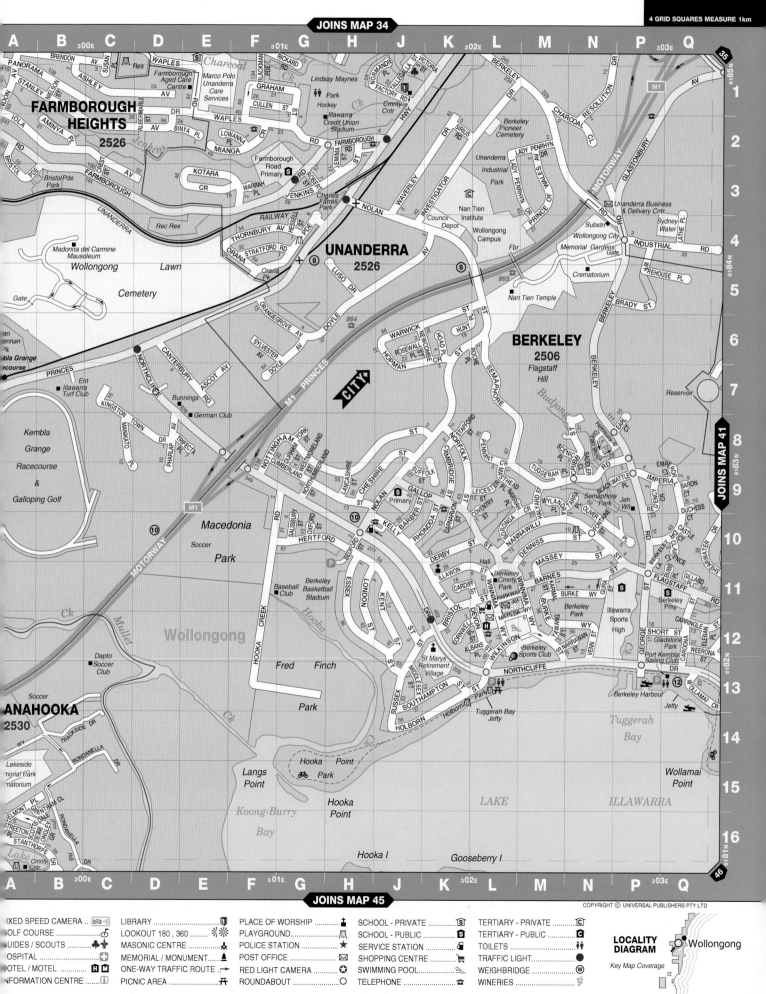

FARMBOROUGH
HEIGHTS
2526

UNANDERRA
2526

BERKELEY
2506
Flagstaff
Hill

Wollongong
Lawn
Cemetery

Kembla
Grange
Racecourse
&
Galloping Golf

Macedonia
Soccer
Park

Wollongong

Fred   Finch
Park

ANAHOOKA
2530

Langs
Point

Hooka   Point
Park

Hooka
Point

Koong-Burry
Bay

LAKE   ILLAWARRA

Tuggerah
Bay

Wollamai
Point

Hooka I   Gooseberry I

FIXED SPEED CAMERA ..
GOLF COURSE ....
GUIDES / SCOUTS ....
HOSPITAL ....
MOTEL / MOTEL ....
INFORMATION CENTRE ...

LIBRARY ....
LOOKOUT 180 , 360 ......
MASONIC CENTRE ....
MEMORIAL / MONUMENT ...
ONE-WAY TRAFFIC ROUTE ..
PICNIC AREA ....

PLACE OF WORSHIP ....
PLAYGROUND....................
POLICE STATION ....
POST OFFICE ....
RED LIGHT CAMERA ....
ROUNDABOUT ....

SCHOOL - PRIVATE ....
SCHOOL - PUBLIC ....
SERVICE STATION ....
SHOPPING CENTRE ....
SWIMMING POOL ....
TELEPHONE ....

TERTIARY - PRIVATE ....
TERTIARY - PUBLIC ....
TOILETS ....
TRAFFIC LIGHT..................
WEIGHBRIDGE ....
WINERIES ....

LOCALITY
DIAGRAM
Key Map Coverage

Wollongong

MAP 41

4 GRID SQUARES MEASURE 1km

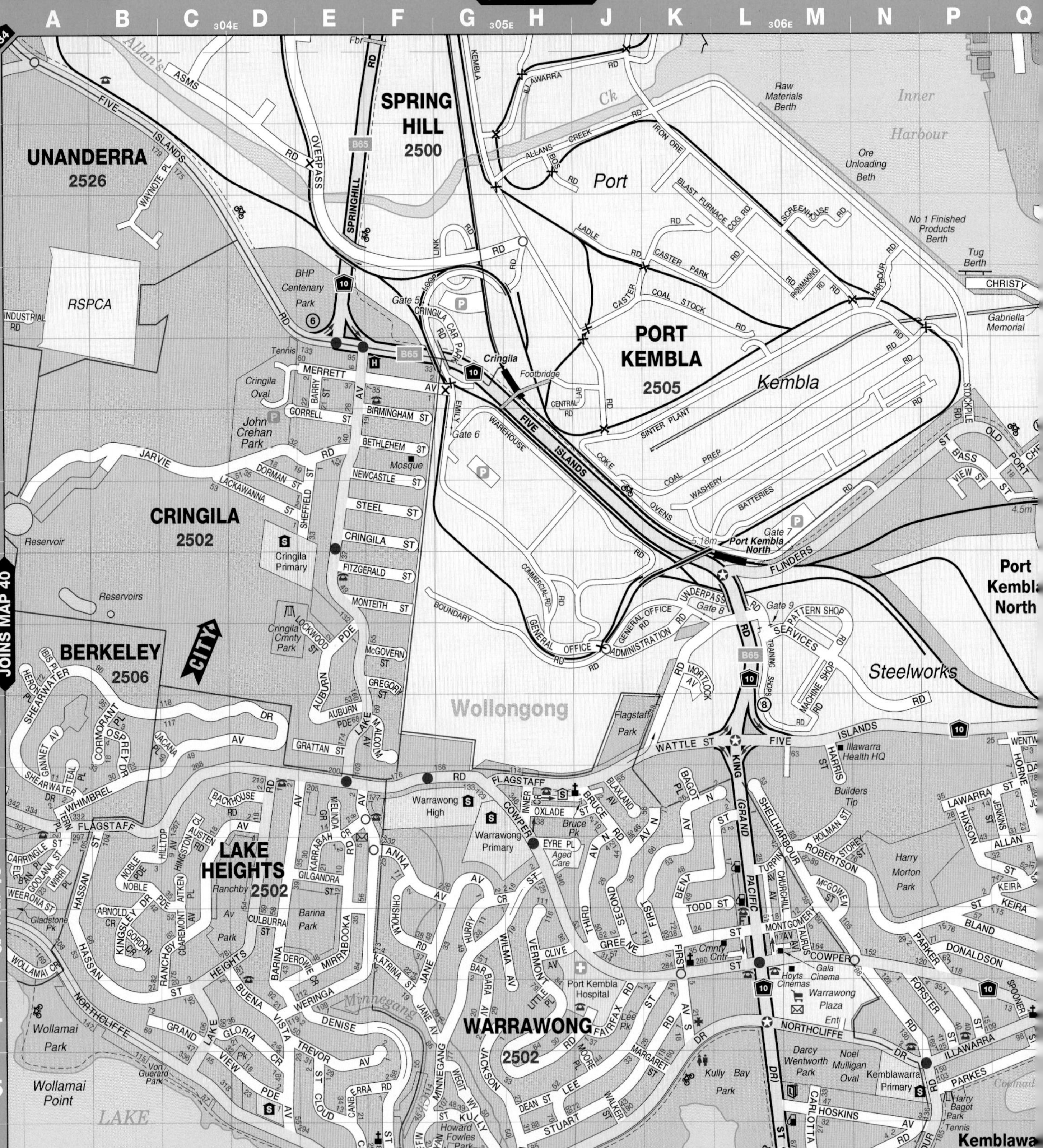

UNANDERRA 2526

SPRING HILL 2500

RSPCA

PORT KEMBLA 2505

Inner Harbour

Raw Materials Berth

Ore Unloading Beth

No 1 Finished Products Berth

Tug Berth

CHRISTY

Gabriella Memorial

Port

BHP Centenary Park

Cringila Car Park

Cringila

Footbridge

Kembla

CRINGILA 2502

Cringila Oval

John Crehan Park

Cringila Primary

Cringila Cmnty Park

Reservoir

Reservoirs

BERKELEY 2506

CITY

Wollongong

Steelworks

Flagstaff Park

Port Kembla North

Port Kembla North

LAKE HEIGHTS 2502

Warrawong High

Warrawong Primary

Aged Care

Port Kembla Hospital

WARRAWONG 2502

Illawarra Health HQ

Builders Tip

Harry Morton Park

Hoyts Cinemas

Gala Cinema Cinemas

Warrawong Plaza

Darcy Wentworth Park

Noel Mulligan Oval

Kemblawarra Primary

Harry Bagot Park

Kemblawa

Wollamai Park

Wollamai Point

LAKE ILLAWARRA

Kully Bay Park

Kully Bay

Bob Grabham Jetty

Howard Fowles Park

AFL

Barnes Park

The Illawarra Yacht Club

Lake Illawarra Cadet Facility

Illawarra Rowing Centre

Kemblawarra Portuguese Sports & Social Club

SCALE 1:19 000

Metres   500   1000   1km

Legend	
FREEWAY	PARK, RESERVE, OVAL	AMBULANCE STATION	CAR PARK
PROPOSED FREEWAY	SCHOOL, HOSPITAL	BARBECUE	CYCLEWAY
HIGHWAY or MAIN ROUTE	MISCELLANEOUS AREA	BOAT RAMP	DISTANCE FROM GPO
ALTERNATE ROUTE	MALL, PLAZA	BOWLING CLUB/GREEN	EMERGENCY TELEPHONE
TRAFFICABLE ROAD	SWAMP	CAMPING AREA	EXPRESS POST BOX
PROPOSED ROAD		CARAVAN PARK	FIRE STATION

MAP
42
4 GRID SQUARES MEASURE 1km

A B C D 308E E F G H 309E J K L M 310E N P Q

Flinders Islet

Tom Thumb Islands

1

2

3

TASMAN

4

Northern Breakwater

Inflammable Liquids Berth

Outer

5

Jetty No 6

Harbour

6

THE

7

N
W E
S

FIVE

8

Water Police

Jetty No 4

Port Kembla Heritage Park

Military Res

Museum

ISLANDS

9

FORESHORE RD

Port Kembla

AFL

Orica

Incitec

LANCE RD

GLOUCESTER RD

North

10

Customs House

Court House

RSL

Shipp

SEA

11

Military

Wentworth

Fitzwilliam

ELECTROLYTIC RESERVOIR ST

Rock Pool

12

Kembla

St Patricks Cath Pmy Cnr

MARNE ST

GALLIPOLI ST

Beach

Port Kembla Pmy

13

Charles

Church

AV

QUARRY ST

STANZAC

SOMME

WY

BROD

SUVLA

BVD

14

Railway

Fifth

Wentworth

THIRD

Perth

ROW

MATTHEWS

TOBRUK RD

CR

AV

King George V Park

10

Hill 60 Park

Fishermans

15

Sixth

COWPER

SURFSIDE DR

Five Islands Secondary College

Port Kembla Scenic Lookout

Rocky Islet

Parkyns Beach

Big Island

16

Coomaditchy Lagoon

Reserve

10

SLSC

OLYMPIC BVD

GRIFFITHS AV

DOVERS DR

HILL ST

Coast Guard

Military Reserve

Sewage Treatment Works

Red Point

(Five Islands Nat Res)

Martins Islet

Port Kembla Beach

A B C D 308E E F G H 309E J K L M 310E N P Q

KED SPEED CAMERA ..	LIBRARY	PLACE OF WORSHIP	SCHOOL - PRIVATE ....
OLF COURSE	LOOKOUT 180 , 360	PLAYGROUND	SCHOOL - PUBLIC ....
IDES / SCOUTS	MASONIC CENTRE	POLICE STATION	SERVICE STATION ....
OSPITAL	MEMORIAL / MONUMENT......	POST OFFICE	SHOPPING CENTRE ....
OTEL / MOTEL	ONE-WAY TRAFFIC ROUTE ..	RED LIGHT CAMERA	SWIMMING POOL ....
FORMATION CENTRE ...	PICNIC AREA	ROUNDABOUT	TELEPHONE ....

TERTIARY - PRIVATE	
TERTIARY - PUBLIC	
TOILETS	
TRAFFIC LIGHT....................	
WEIGHBRIDGE	
WINERIES	

LOCALITY DIAGRAM

Key Map Coverage

Wollongong

MAP
43
4 GRID SQUARES MEASURE 1km

JOINS MAP 38

A B C D E F G H J K L M N P Q

HORSLEY
2530

CLEVELAND
2530

HUNTLEY
2530

PENROSE
2530

AVONDALE
2530

LIMIT OF MAPS

Purrungully Woodland

Training Track

Reed

Mullet

BONG BONG

CLEVELAND RD

AVONDALE

SOUTH AVONDALE

CEDAR AV

MOUNTAIN VIEW TCE

Gate

HUNTLEY RD

TAFE
Illawarra
Yallah Ca...

JOINS MAP 47

A B C D E F G H J K L M N P Q

SCALE 1:19 000   1km

Metres   500   1000

FREEWAY ....
PROPOSED FREEWAY ....
HIGHWAY or MAIN ROUTE ...
ALTERNATE ROUTE.............
TRAFFICABLE ROAD ....
PROPOSED ROAD ....

PARK, RESERVE, OVAL..........
SCHOOL, HOSPITAL.............
MISCELLANEOUS AREA.........
MALL, PLAZA.....................
SWAMP...........................

AMBULANCE STATION ....
BARBECUE ....
BOAT RAMP ....
BOWLING CLUB/GREEN ....
CAMPING AREA ....
CARAVAN PARK ....

CAR PARK ....
CYCLEWAY............................
DISTANCE FROM GPO ....
EMERGENCY TELEPHONE ...
EXPRESS POST BOX ....
FIRE STATION......................

MAP 44

4 GRID SQUARES MEASURE 1km

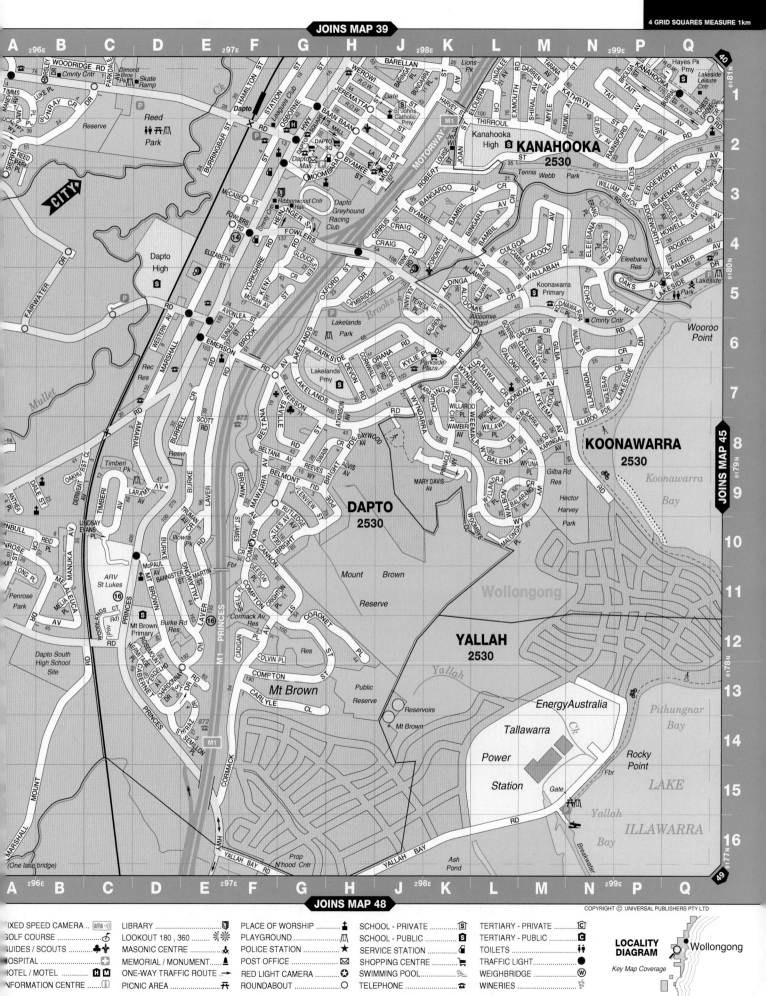

JOINS MAP 45

KANAHOOKA 2530

DAPTO 2530

KOONAWARRA 2530

YALLAH 2530

Wollongong

Mount Brown Reserve

EnergyAustralia
Tallawarra Power Station

LAKE ILLAWARRA

Yallah Bay

Pithungnar Bay

Rocky Point

Wooroo Point

Koonawarra Bay

COPYRIGHT © UNIVERSAL PUBLISHERS PTY LTD

FIXED SPEED CAMERA ..	LIBRARY	PLACE OF WORSHIP	SCHOOL - PRIVATE	TERTIARY - PRIVATE
GOLF COURSE	LOOKOUT 180 , 360	PLAYGROUND	SCHOOL - PUBLIC	TERTIARY - PUBLIC
GUIDES / SCOUTS	MASONIC CENTRE	POLICE STATION	SERVICE STATION	TOILETS
HOSPITAL	MEMORIAL / MONUMENT	POST OFFICE	SHOPPING CENTRE	TRAFFIC LIGHT
HOTEL / MOTEL	ONE-WAY TRAFFIC ROUTE	RED LIGHT CAMERA	SWIMMING POOL	WEIGHBRIDGE
INFORMATION CENTRE	PICNIC AREA	ROUNDABOUT	TELEPHONE	WINERIES

LOCALITY DIAGRAM

Wollongong

Key Map Coverage

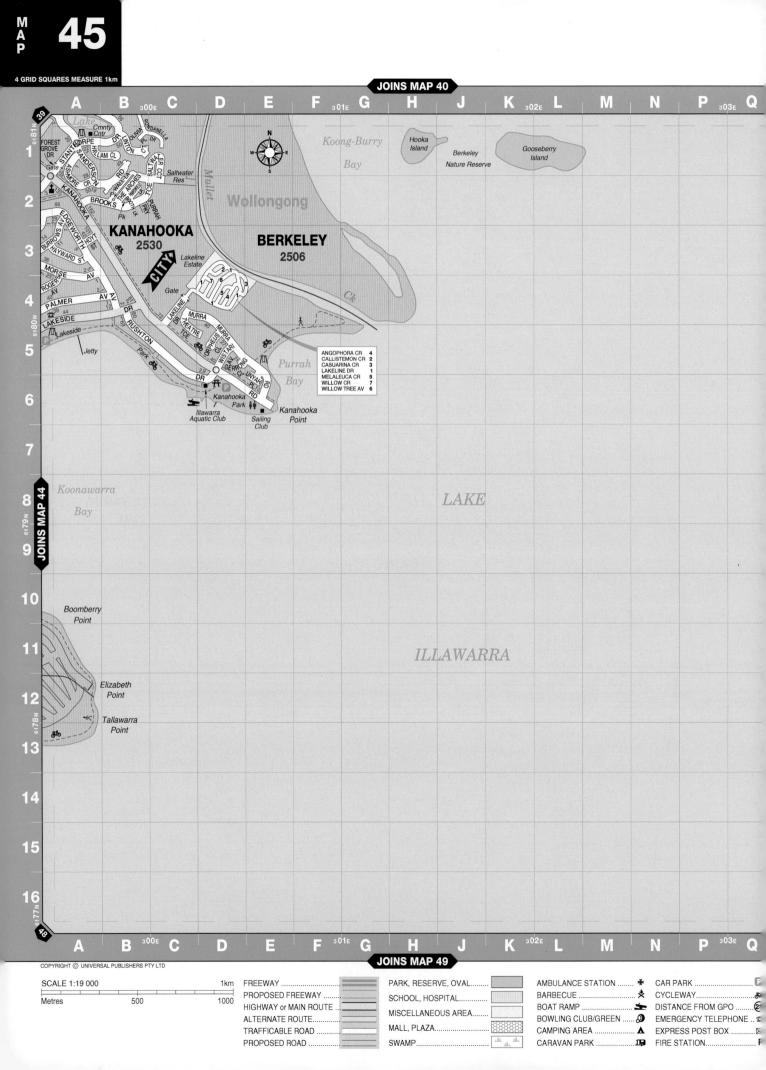

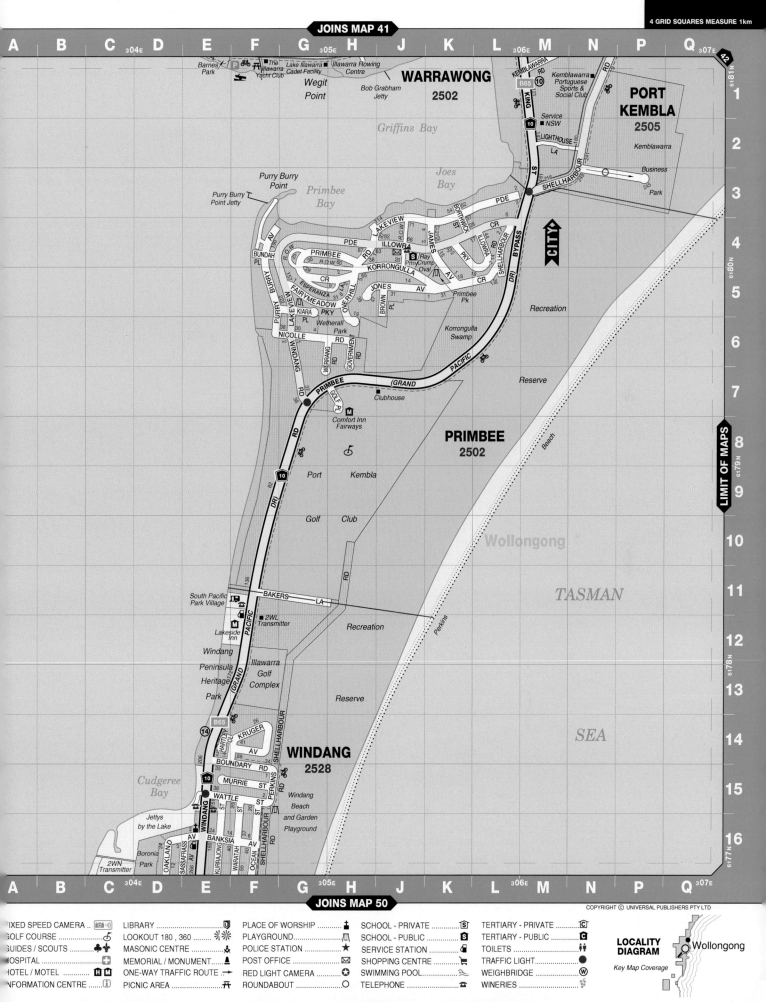

WARRAWONG 2502

PORT KEMBLA 2505

Kemblawarra

Kemblawarra Portuguese Sports & Social Club

Business Park

Griffins Bay

Joes Bay

Primbee Bay

Purry Burry Point

Purry Burry Point Jetty

Barnes Park

The Illawarra Yacht Club

Lake Illawarra Cadet Facility

Illawarra Rowing Centre

Wegit Point

Bob Grabham Jetty

LIGHTHOUSE

Service NSW

CITY

Recreation

Korrongulla Swamp

Primbee Pk

Ray Crump Oval

Illowra

Reserve

Beach

PRIMBEE 2502

Recreation Reserve

Comfort Inn Fairways

Clubhouse

Port Kembla Golf Club

Wollongong

TASMAN

South Pacific Park Village

2WL Transmitter

Recreation

Lakeside Inn

Windang Peninsula Heritage Park

Illawarra Golf Complex

Reserve

SEA

WINDANG 2528

Cudgeree Bay

Jettys by the Lake

Windang Beach and Garden Playground

Boronia Park

2WN Transmitter

LIMIT OF MAPS

FIXED SPEED CAMERA .. 📷📶
GOLF COURSE .... ⛳
GUIDES / SCOUTS .... ♣↯
HOSPITAL .... ✚
HOTEL / MOTEL .... 🏠Ⓜ
INFORMATION CENTRE ...... ℹ️
LIBRARY .... 📖
LOOKOUT 180 , 360 .... ❋❋
MASONIC CENTRE .... ⚒
MEMORIAL / MONUMENT..... ▲
ONE-WAY TRAFFIC ROUTE ...→
PICNIC AREA .... ⚏
PLACE OF WORSHIP .... ✝
PLAYGROUND .... ⚏
POLICE STATION .... ★
POST OFFICE .... ✉
RED LIGHT CAMERA .... ✪
ROUNDABOUT .... ○
SCHOOL - PRIVATE .... Ⓢ
SCHOOL - PUBLIC .... Ⓢ
SERVICE STATION .... ⛽
SHOPPING CENTRE .... 🛒
SWIMMING POOL .... 🏊
TELEPHONE .... ☎
TERTIARY - PRIVATE .... Ⓒ
TERTIARY - PUBLIC .... Ⓒ
TOILETS .... 🚻
TRAFFIC LIGHT........... ●
WEIGHBRIDGE .... Ⓦ
WINERIES .... 🍇

LOCALITY DIAGRAM
Key Map Coverage

Wollongong

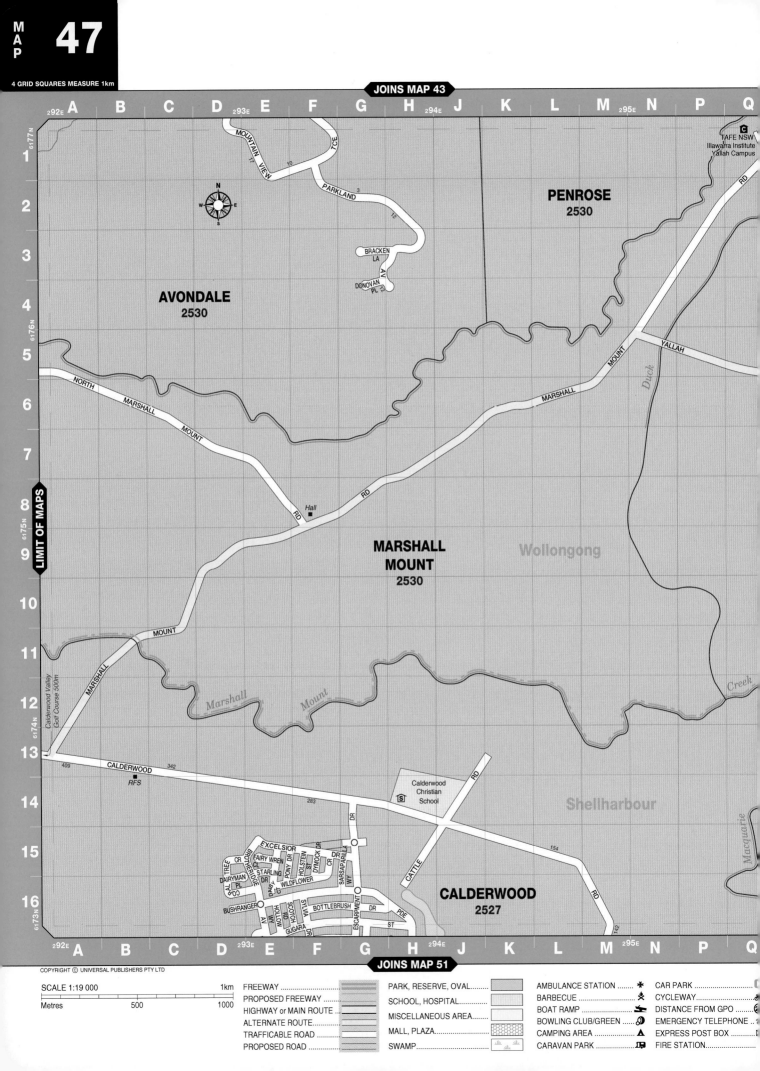

MAP 48

4 GRID SQUARES MEASURE 1km

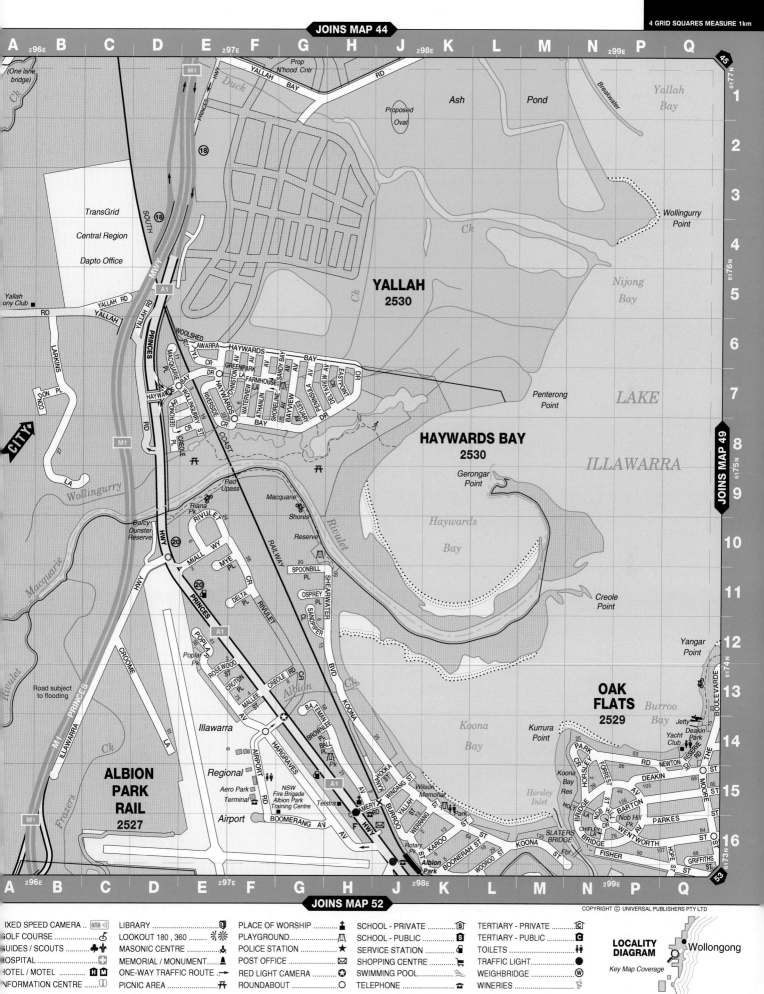

YALLAH
2530

HAYWARDS BAY
2530

OAK
FLATS
2529

ALBION
PARK
RAIL
2527

JOINS MAP 49

Wollingurry
Point

Nijong
Bay

LAKE

ILLAWARRA

Penterong
Point

Gerongar
Point

Haywards
Bay

Creole
Point

Yangar
Point

Burroo
Bay

Koona
Bay

Kurrura
Point

Horsley
Inlet

Yallah
Bay

Ash   Pond

Proposed
Oval

TransGrid
Central Region
Dapto Office

Road subject
to flooding

Regional

Airport

Aero Park
Terminal

NSW
Fire Brigade
Albion Park
Training Centre

Darcy
Dunster
Reserve

Macquarie
Shores

Macquarie
Reserve

Ped
Upass

Riana
Pk

Poplar
Pk

Rotary
Park

Albion
Park

COPYRIGHT © UNIVERSAL PUBLISHERS PTY LTD

MAP 49

4 GRID SQUARES MEASURE 1km

A B 300E C D E F 301E G H J K 302E L M N P 303E Q

6177N JOINS MAP 44

1 2 3 4 5 6 7 8 9 10 11 12 13 14 15 16

6176N
6175N JOINS MAP 48
6174N
6173N JOINS MAP 52

LAKE

ILLAWARRA

N W E S

Beva Island

Police & Cmnty Youth Club Road Safety Park
Cec Glenholmes Oval

Whyjuck Bay Lake Illawarra High

MT WARRIGAL
2528

Boonerah Point

Morley Park

KOTARI PDE STANLEY

REDDALL PDE

CHARLTON PDE

WARILLA
2528

Moureendah Bay

Burroo Point

Skiway Park
Jetty

Balarang

OAK FLATS
2529 **Balarang**

Karoo Point

Karoo Bay

Hennegar Bay

Yangar Point *Mogurah Point*

Central Pk

Shane Lee Field
Balarang Primary

Oak Flats High

TAFE NSW Illawarra Institute
Shellharbour Campus

Shellharbour Hospital

JN King Memorial Park

Warilla Primary

Jock Brown Oval

BARRACK HEIGHTS
2528

Oak Flats Pmy
Hall

Urban Park

Cinema
Stockland Shellharbour

Memorial Dr

A B 300E C D E F 301E G H J K 302E L M N P 303E Q

SCALE 1:19 000   1km
Metres   500   1000

Legend		Legend
FREEWAY		AMBULANCE STATION
PROPOSED FREEWAY		BARBECUE
HIGHWAY or MAIN ROUTE		BOAT RAMP
ALTERNATE ROUTE		BOWLING CLUB/GREEN
TRAFFICABLE ROAD		CAMPING AREA
PROPOSED ROAD		CARAVAN PARK
PARK, RESERVE, OVAL		CAR PARK
SCHOOL, HOSPITAL		CYCLEWAY
MISCELLANEOUS AREA		DISTANCE FROM GPO
MALL, PLAZA		EMERGENCY TELEPHONE
SWAMP		EXPRESS POST BOX
		FIRE STATION

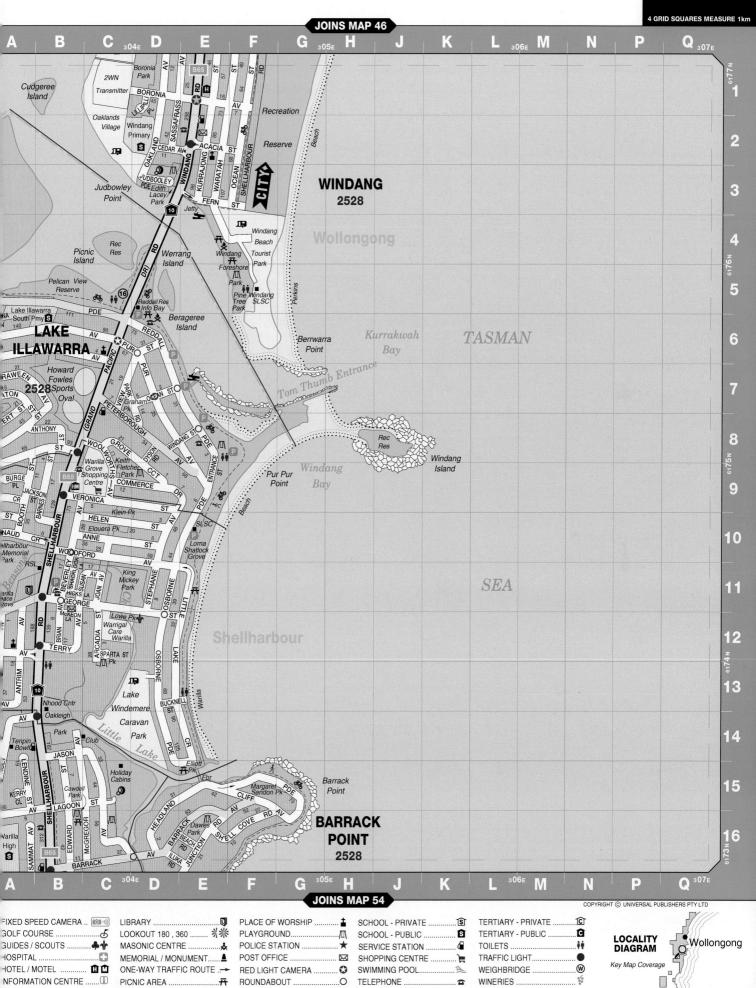

WINDANG
2528

Wollongong

LAKE
ILLAWARRA
2528

TASMAN

Kurrakwah
Bay

Berwarra
Point

Tom Thumb Entrance

Windang Island

Rec
Res

SEA

Windang
Bay

Pur Pur
Point

Shellharbour

Lake
Windemere
Caravan
Park

Little Lake

Barrack
Point

BARRACK
POINT
2528

FIXED SPEED CAMERA ..
GOLF COURSE ....
GUIDES / SCOUTS ....
HOSPITAL ....
HOTEL / MOTEL ....
INFORMATION CENTRE .....

LIBRARY ....
LOOKOUT 180 , 360 ....
MASONIC CENTRE ....
MEMORIAL / MONUMENT ...
ONE-WAY TRAFFIC ROUTE ...
PICNIC AREA ....

PLACE OF WORSHIP ....
PLAYGROUND...................
POLICE STATION ....
POST OFFICE ....
RED LIGHT CAMERA ....
ROUNDABOUT ....

SCHOOL - PRIVATE ....
SCHOOL - PUBLIC ....
SERVICE STATION ....
SHOPPING CENTRE ....
SWIMMING POOL ....
TELEPHONE ....

TERTIARY - PRIVATE ....
TERTIARY - PUBLIC ....
TOILETS ....
TRAFFIC LIGHT.................
WEIGHBRIDGE ....
WINERIES ....

LOCALITY
DIAGRAM
Key Map Coverage

Wollongong

MAP 51
4 GRID SQUARES MEASURE 1km
JOINS MAP 47

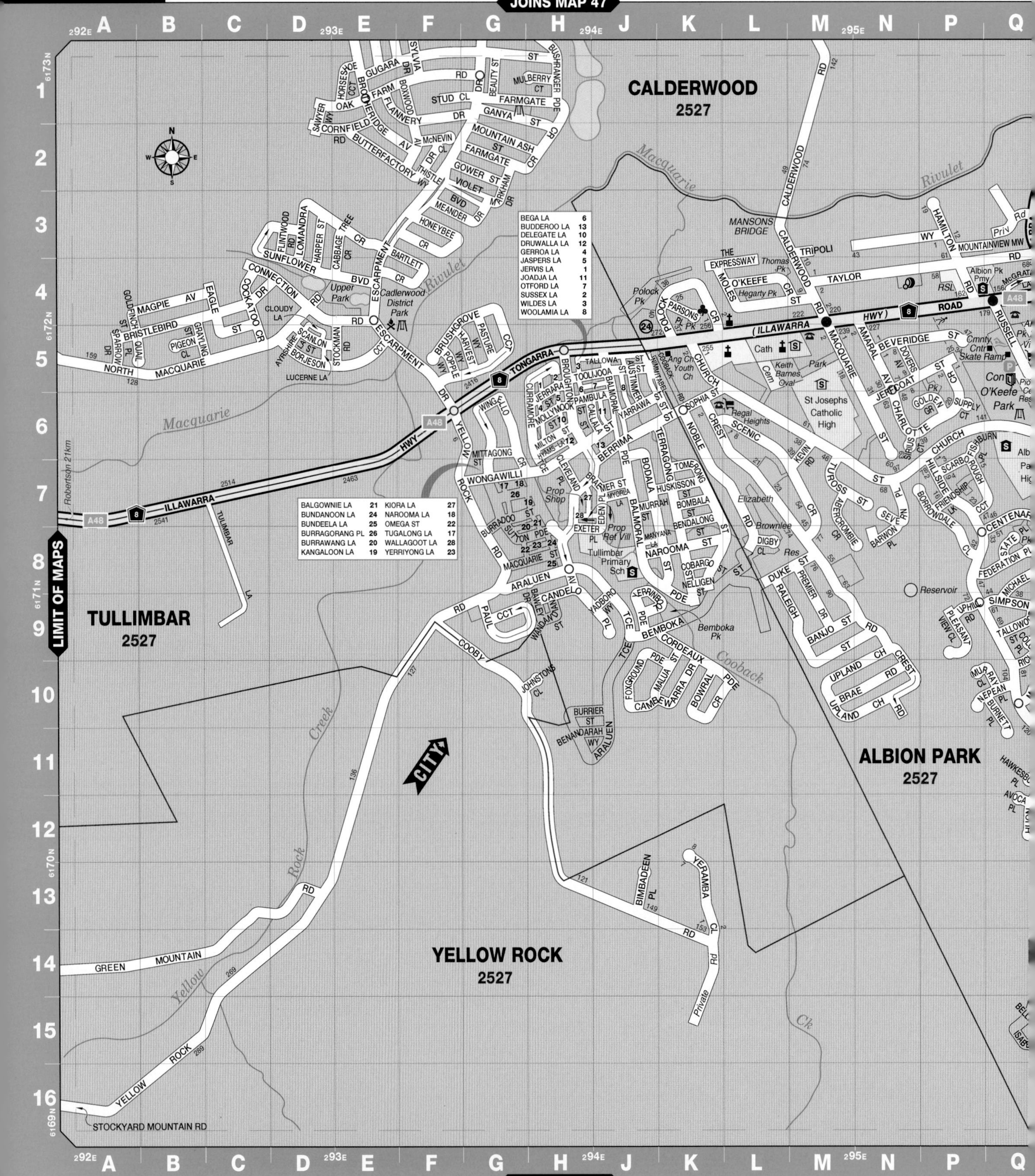

CALDERWOOD
2527

TULLIMBAR
2527

ALBION PARK
2527

YELLOW ROCK
2527

LIMIT OF MAPS

Street index (centre panel, upper):

BEGA LA	6
BUDDEROO LA	13
DELEGATE LA	10
DRUWALLA LA	12
GERROA LA	4
JASPERS LA	5
JERVIS LA	1
JOADJA LA	11
OTFORD LA	7
SUSSEX LA	2
WILDES LA	3
WOOLAMIA LA	8

Street index (centre panel, lower):

BALGOWNIE LA	21	KIORA LA	27
BUNDANOON LA	24	NAROOMA LA	18
BUNDEELA LA	25	OMEGA ST	22
BURRAGORANG PL	26	TUGALONG LA	17
BURRAWANG LA	20	WALLAGOOT LA	28
KANGALOON LA	19	YERRIYONG LA	23

Macquarie Rivulet

MANSONS BRIDGE

Cadlerwood District Park

ILLAWARRA HWY

A48

Green Mountain

Stockyard Mountain Rd

CITY

COPYRIGHT © UNIVERSAL PUBLISHERS PTY LTD

SCALE 1:19 000

Metres   500   1000   1km

Legend:

FREEWAY	PARK, RESERVE, OVAL	AMBULANCE STATION	CAR PARK
PROPOSED FREEWAY	SCHOOL, HOSPITAL	BARBECUE	TERTIARY - PRIVATE
HIGHWAY or MAIN ROUTE	MISCELLANEOUS AREA	BOAT RAMP	TERTIARY - PUBLIC
ALTERNATE ROUTE	MALL, PLAZA	BOWLING CLUB/GREEN	CYCLEWAY
TRAFFICABLE ROAD	SWAMP	CAMPING AREA	DISTANCE FROM GPO
PROPOSED ROAD		CARAVAN PARK	EMERGENCY TELEPHONE

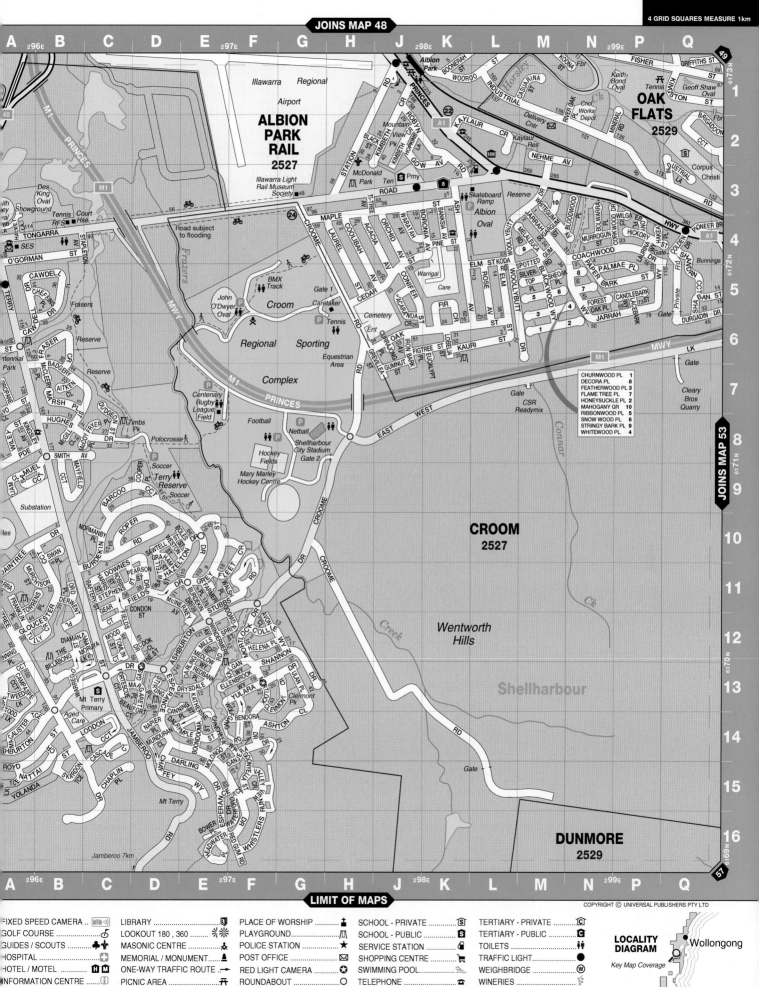

ALBION PARK RAIL 2527

OAK FLATS 2529

CROOM 2527

Wentworth Hills

Shellharbour

DUNMORE 2529

Illawarra Regional Airport

Croom Regional Sporting Complex

CHURNWOOD PL 1
DECORA PL 8
FEATHERWOOD PL 3
FLAME TREE PL 7
HONEYSUCKLE PL 2
MAHOGANY GR 10
RIBBONWOOD PL 5
SNOW WOOD PL 6
STRINGY BARK PL 9
WHITEWOOD PL 4

COPYRIGHT © UNIVERSAL PUBLISHERS PTY LTD

FIXED SPEED CAMERA ..
GOLF COURSE .....
GUIDES / SCOUTS ......
HOSPITAL ....
HOTEL / MOTEL .....
INFORMATION CENTRE ....

LIBRARY ....
LOOKOUT 180 , 360 ....
MASONIC CENTRE ....
MEMORIAL / MONUMENT...
ONE-WAY TRAFFIC ROUTE ..
PICNIC AREA .....

PLACE OF WORSHIP ......
PLAYGROUND....
POLICE STATION ....
POST OFFICE ....
RED LIGHT CAMERA .....
ROUNDABOUT .....

SCHOOL - PRIVATE ....
SCHOOL - PUBLIC ...
SERVICE STATION ....
SHOPPING CENTRE ....
SWIMMING POOL....
TELEPHONE .....

TERTIARY - PRIVATE ....
TERTIARY - PUBLIC ...
TOILETS ....
TRAFFIC LIGHT....
WEIGHBRIDGE ...
WINERIES .....

LOCALITY DIAGRAM
Key Map Coverage

Wollongong

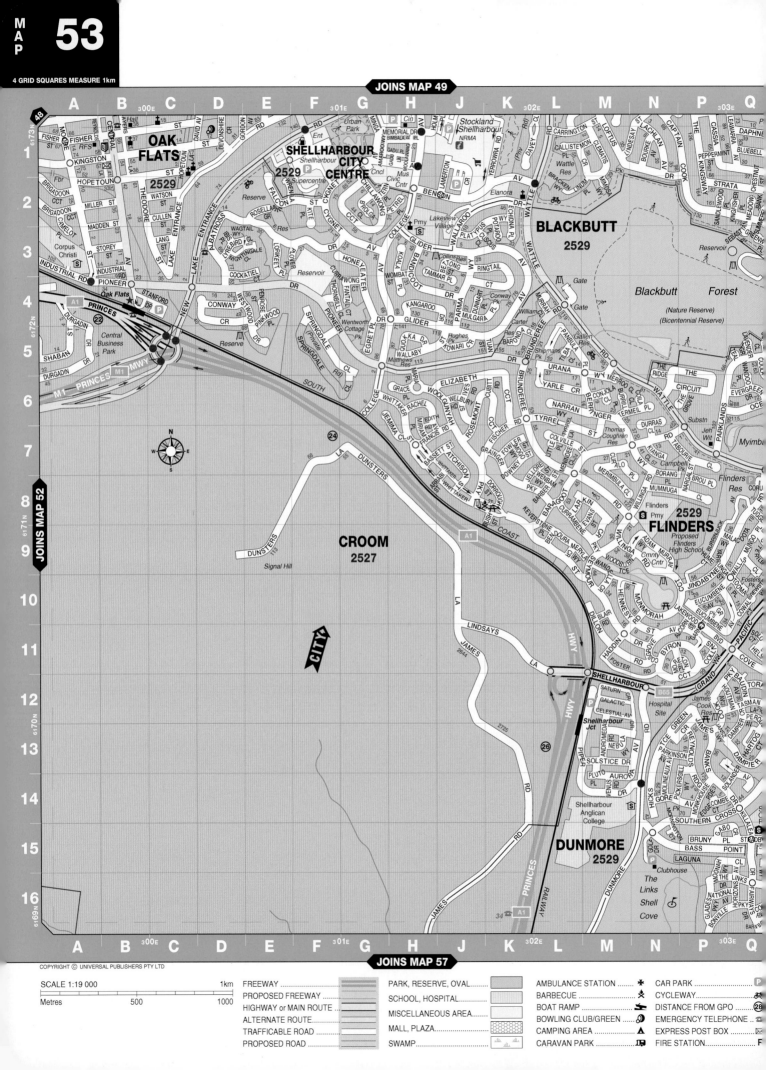

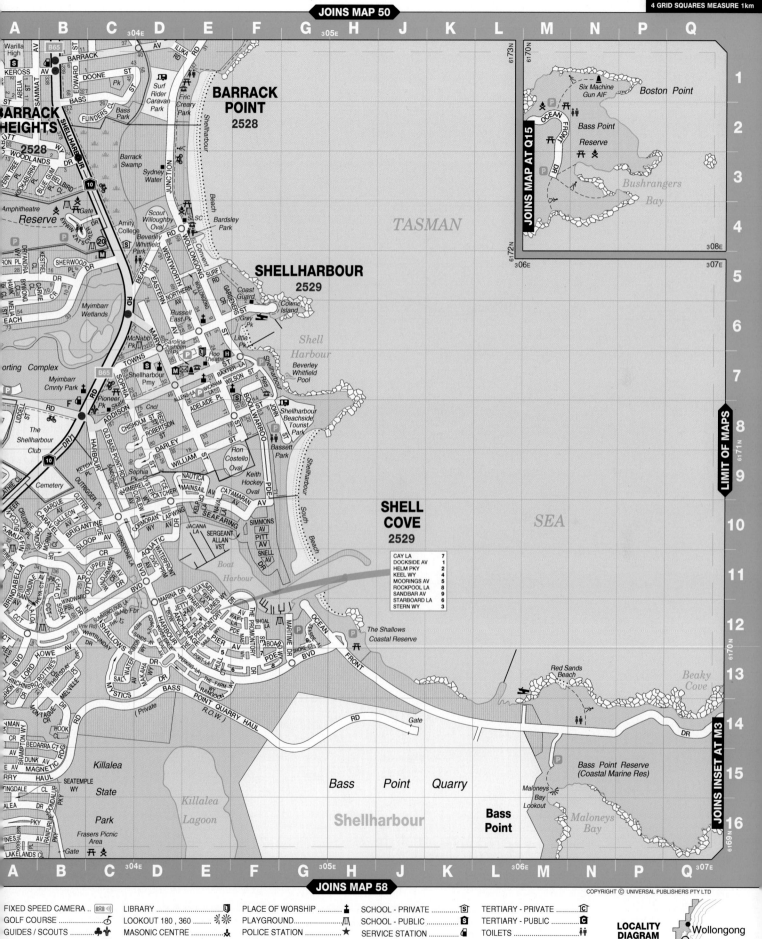

MAP 54

MAP 57 FOLLOWS

4 GRID SQUARES MEASURE 1km

JOINS MAP 50

A B C D E F G H J K L M N P Q

BARRACK HEIGHTS 2528

BARRACK POINT 2528

SHELLHARBOUR 2529

SHELL COVE 2529

TASMAN

SEA

Six Machine Gun AIF
Boston Point
Bass Point Reserve
Bushrangers Bay

JOINS MAP AT Q15

CAY LA	7
DOCKSIDE AV	1
HELM PKY	2
KEEL WY	4
MOORINGS AV	5
ROCKPOOL LA	8
SANDBAR AV	9
STARBOARD LA	6
STERN WY	3

The Shallows Coastal Reserve

Red Sands Beach
Beaky Cove

Bass Point Quarry

Shellharbour

Killalea State Park

Killalea Lagoon

Frasers Picnic Area

Bass Point Reserve (Coastal Marine Res)
Maloneys Bay Lookout
Maloneys Bay

LIMIT OF MAPS

JOINS INSET AT M3

A B C D E F G H J K L M N P Q

JOINS MAP 58

FIXED SPEED CAMERA	LIBRARY	PLACE OF WORSHIP	SCHOOL - PRIVATE	TERTIARY - PRIVATE	
GOLF COURSE	LOOKOUT 180, 360	PLAYGROUND	SCHOOL - PUBLIC	TERTIARY - PUBLIC	
GUIDES / SCOUTS	MASONIC CENTRE	POLICE STATION	SERVICE STATION	TOILETS	
HOSPITAL	MEMORIAL / MONUMENT	POST OFFICE	SHOPPING CENTRE	TRAFFIC LIGHT	
HOTEL / MOTEL	ONE-WAY TRAFFIC ROUTE	RED LIGHT CAMERA	SWIMMING POOL	WEIGHBRIDGE	
INFORMATION CENTRE	PICNIC AREA	ROUNDABOUT	TELEPHONE	WINERIES	

LOCALITY DIAGRAM
Key Map Coverage
Wollongong

MAP 58

4 GRID SQUARES MEASURE 1km

A B C 304E D E F G 305E H J K L 306E M N P Q 307E

Killalea
Lagoon

Bass

Bass
Point

Point

Quarry

N
W E
S

1

2

3

4

5

6

7

8

9

10

11

12

13

14

15

16

6169N
6168N
6167N
6166N
6165N

LAKELANDS
CL

Gate
Kiosk Killalea

State   Park

Killalea   Beach

SHELL
COVE
2529

Westringia
Point

TASMAN

SEA

Minnamurra

(Mystics)

Beach

Rangoon
Res

River

Minnamurra
Point

James Oates
Res
Tennis

MINNAMURRA
2533

Kiama

KIAMA
DOWNS
2533

Boyds
Beach

COPYRIGHT © UNIVERSAL PUBLISHERS PTY LTD

FIXED SPEED CAMERA ..	LIBRARY	PLACE OF WORSHIP	SCHOOL - PRIVATE
GOLF COURSE	LOOKOUT 180 , 360	PLAYGROUND	SCHOOL - PUBLIC
GUIDES / SCOUTS	MASONIC CENTRE	POLICE STATION	SERVICE STATION
HOSPITAL	MEMORIAL / MONUMENT	POST OFFICE	SHOPPING CENTRE
HOTEL / MOTEL	ONE-WAY TRAFFIC ROUTE	RED LIGHT CAMERA	SWIMMING POOL
INFORMATION CENTRE	PICNIC AREA	ROUNDABOUT	TELEPHONE

TERTIARY - PRIVATE
TERTIARY - PUBLIC
TOILETS
TRAFFIC LIGHT
WEIGHBRIDGE
WINERIES

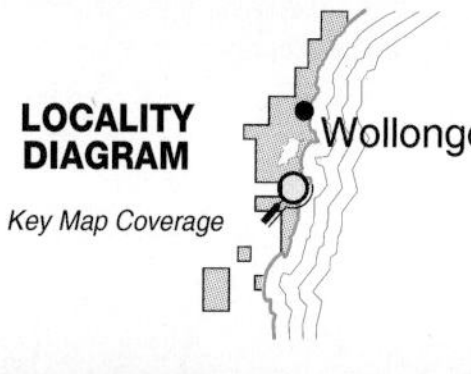

LOCALITY
DIAGRAM

Wollongong

Key Map Coverage

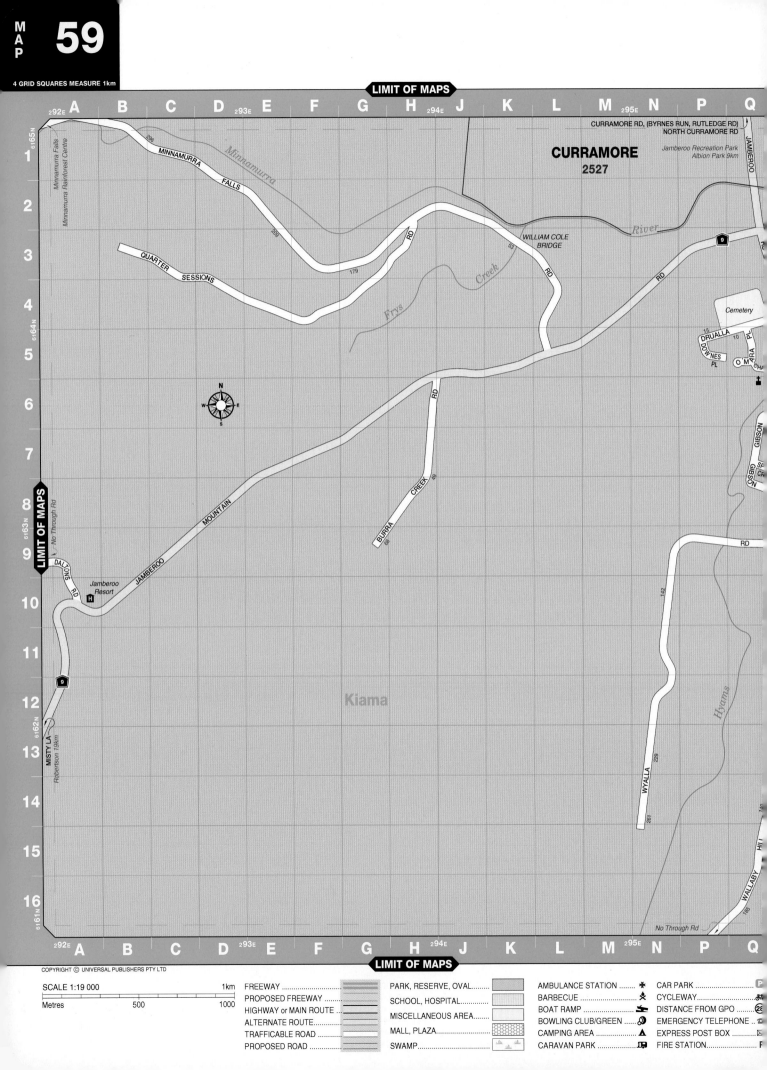

MAP 60

4 GRID SQUARES MEASURE 1km

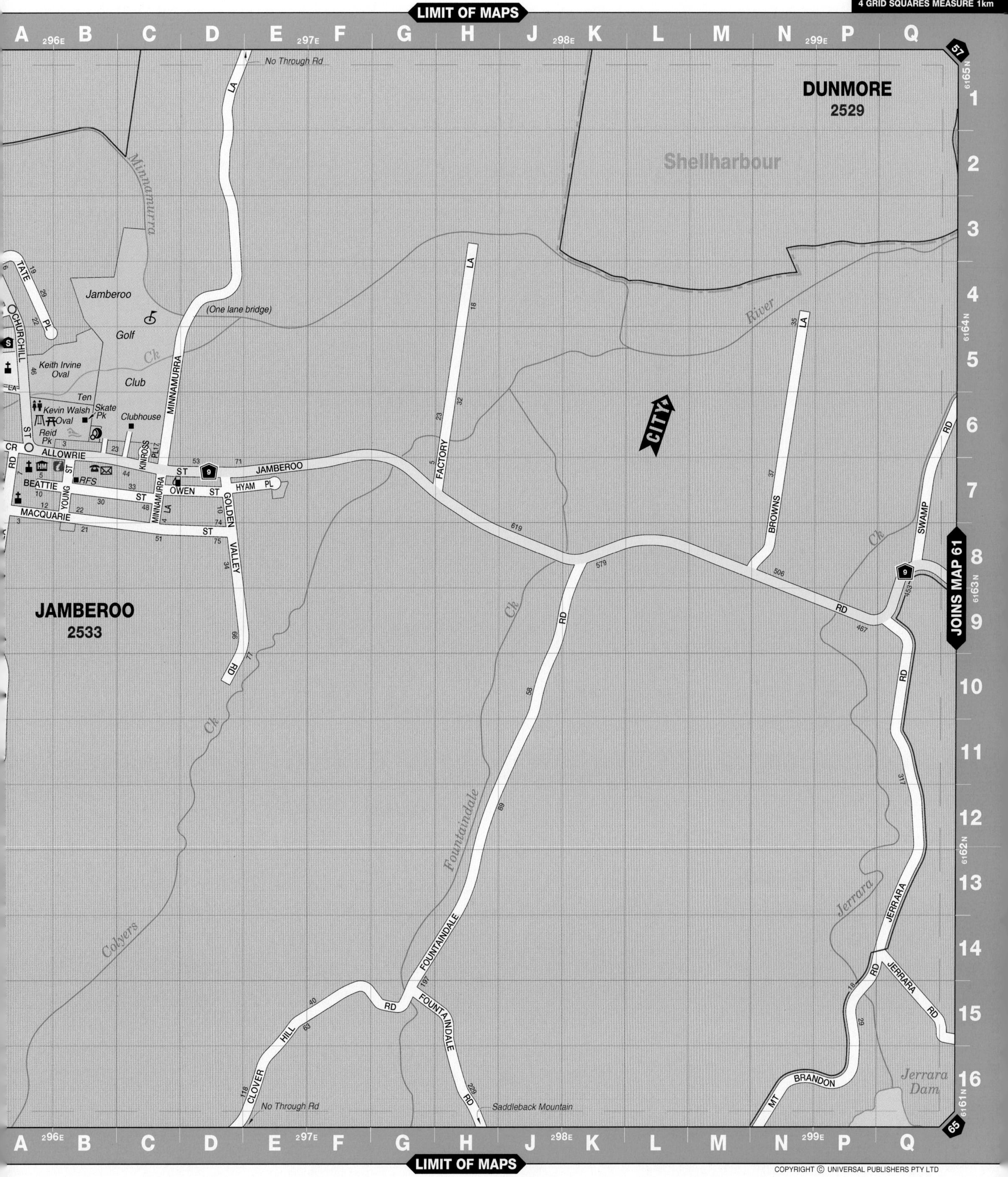

LIMIT OF MAPS

A 296E B C D E 297E F G H J 298E K L M N 299E P Q

DUNMORE
2529

Shellharbour

No Through Rd

Minnamurra

Jamberoo

Golf

(One lane bridge)

Keith Irvine
Oval

Club

Ten

Kevin Walsh
Oval

Skate
Pk

Clubhouse

Reid
Pk

CHURCHILL

TATE

PL

ST

CR

RD

Minnamurra

Ck

KINROSS PL

ALLOWRIE ST

BEATTIE ST

MACQUARIE ST

YOUNG LA

MINNAMURRA ST

OWEN ST

HYAM PL

GOLDEN VALLEY RD

JAMBEROO

RFS

River

LA

LA

FACTORY

BROWNS

SWAMP RD

CITY

RD

RD

RD

RD

JAMBEROO
2533

Ck

Colyers Ck

Fountaindale

Ck

RD

RD

FOUNTAINDALE

FOUNTAINDALE RD

CLOVER HILL RD

No Through Rd

Saddleback Mountain

MT BRANDON

JERRARA RD

JERRARA RD

Jerrara

Jerrara
Dam

JOINS MAP 61

57

6165N

6164N

6163N

6162N

6161N

65

1
2
3
4
5
6
7
8
9
10
11
12
13
14
15
16

LIMIT OF MAPS

A 296E B C D E 297E F G H J 298E K L M N 299E P Q

COPYRIGHT © UNIVERSAL PUBLISHERS PTY LTD

FIXED SPEED CAMERA
GOLF COURSE
GUIDES / SCOUTS
HOSPITAL
HOTEL / MOTEL
INFORMATION CENTRE

LIBRARY
LOOKOUT 180 , 360
MASONIC CENTRE
MEMORIAL / MONUMENT
ONE-WAY TRAFFIC ROUTE
PICNIC AREA

PLACE OF WORSHIP
PLAYGROUND
POLICE STATION
POST OFFICE
RED LIGHT CAMERA
ROUNDABOUT

SCHOOL - PRIVATE
SCHOOL - PUBLIC
SERVICE STATION
SHOPPING CENTRE
SWIMMING POOL
TELEPHONE

TERTIARY - PRIVATE
TERTIARY - PUBLIC
TOILETS
TRAFFIC LIGHT
WEIGHBRIDGE
WINERIES

**LOCALITY
DIAGRAM**
Key Map Coverage

Wollongong

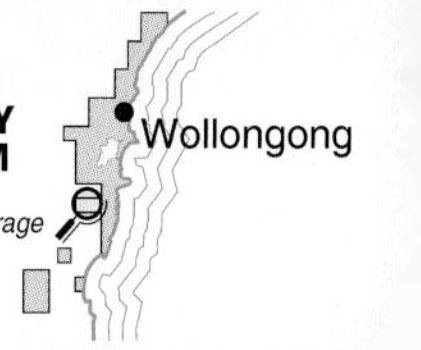

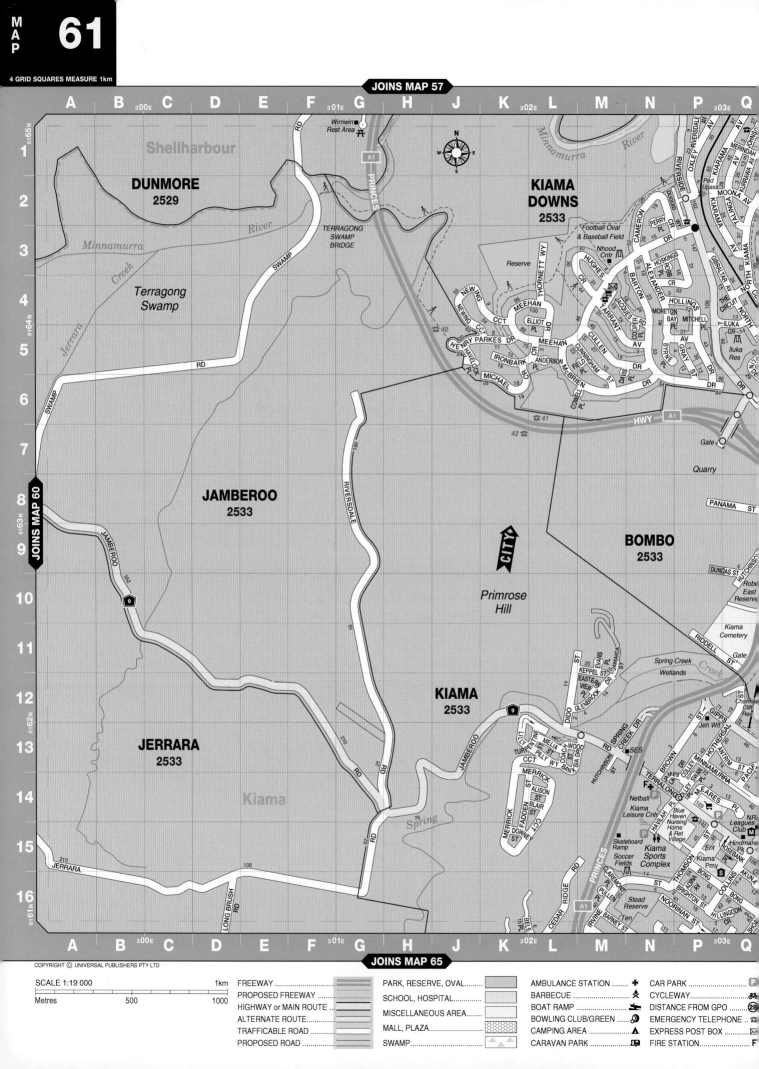

A B C 304E D E F G 305E H J K L 306E M N P Q 307E

6165N 1

2

3

4

Cathedral
Rocks 5

The
Boneyard 6

TASMAN 7

Bombo
Headland 8

SEA 9

10

11

12

6162N 13

Pheasant
Point 14

Rock
Pool 15

Kiama
Harbour

Helipad Rock
Pool

The Basin Cabins
Black Beach
Blowhole
Point 16

Pilots Cottage
Museum Kiama
Blowhole 6161N

A B C 304E D E F G 305E H J K L 306E M N P Q 307E

FIXED SPEED CAMERA ..
GOLF COURSE ....
GUIDES / SCOUTS ....
HOSPITAL ....
HOTEL / MOTEL ....
INFORMATION CENTRE ....

LIBRARY ....
LOOKOUT 180 , 360 ....
MASONIC CENTRE ....
MEMORIAL / MONUMENT...
ONE-WAY TRAFFIC ROUTE ..
PICNIC AREA ....

PLACE OF WORSHIP ....
PLAYGROUND....................
POLICE STATION ....
POST OFFICE ....
RED LIGHT CAMERA ....
ROUNDABOUT ....

SCHOOL - PRIVATE ....
SCHOOL - PUBLIC ....
SERVICE STATION ....
SHOPPING CENTRE ....
SWIMMING POOL...............
TELEPHONE ....

TERTIARY - PRIVATE ....
TERTIARY - PUBLIC ....
TOILETS ....
TRAFFIC LIGHT...................
WEIGHBRIDGE ....
WINERIES ....

LOCALITY
DIAGRAM
Key Map Coverage
Wollongong

MAP
65
PREVIOUS MAP 62
4 GRID SQUARES MEASURE 1km

JOINS MAP 61

KIAMA
2533

JERRARA
2533

LIMIT OF MAPS

Tootawallin
Gully

Munna

Munnora

Kiama

CITY

SADDLEBACK
MOUNTAIN
2533

KIAMA
HEIGHTS
2533

Truck
Parking

Easts Beach

Holiday Park

ROSE VALLEY
2534

GERRINGONG
2534

JOINS MAP 69

COPYRIGHT © UNIVERSAL PUBLISHERS PTY LTD

SCALE 1:19 000

Metres   500   1000

FREEWAY	
PROPOSED FREEWAY	
HIGHWAY or MAIN ROUTE	
ALTERNATE ROUTE	
TRAFFICABLE ROAD	
PROPOSED ROAD	
PARK, RESERVE, OVAL	
SCHOOL, HOSPITAL	
MISCELLANEOUS AREA	
MALL, PLAZA	
SWAMP	
AMBULANCE STATION	CAR PARK
BARBECUE	CYCLEWAY
BOAT RAMP	DISTANCE FROM GPO
BOWLING CLUB/GREEN	EMERGENCY TELEPHONE
CAMPING AREA	EXPRESS POST BOX
CARAVAN PARK	FIRE STATION

TASMAN

SEA

Church Point

Storm

Kendalls Point

Kendalls Point Res

Bay

Kaleula Point

Friars Cave

Little Blowhole

Little Blowhole Reserve

Marsden Head

TINGIRA

Loves Bay

Coronation Park

Showground Pav

Kiama

FIXED SPEED CAMERA .. 📷
GOLF COURSE .... ⛳
GUIDES / SCOUTS .... ♣
HOSPITAL .... ✚
HOTEL / MOTEL .... 🏨 Ⓜ
INFORMATION CENTRE .... ℹ

LIBRARY .... 📚
LOOKOUT 180 , 360 .... ❋ ❋
MASONIC CENTRE .... ⚒
MEMORIAL / MONUMENT.. ▲
ONE-WAY TRAFFIC ROUTE �
PICNIC AREA .... ⛲

PLACE OF WORSHIP .... ⛪
PLAYGROUND .... ⚏
POLICE STATION .... ★
POST OFFICE .... ✉
RED LIGHT CAMERA .... ✪
ROUNDABOUT .... ○

SCHOOL - PRIVATE .... Ⓢ
SCHOOL - PUBLIC .... Ⓢ
SERVICE STATION .... ⛽
SHOPPING CENTRE .... 🛒
SWIMMING POOL .... ⚊
TELEPHONE .... ☎

TERTIARY - PRIVATE .... Ⓒ
TERTIARY - PUBLIC .... Ⓒ
TOILETS .... 👫
TRAFFIC LIGHT.................. ●
WEIGHBRIDGE .... Ⓦ
WINERIES .... 🍷

LOCALITY DIAGRAM

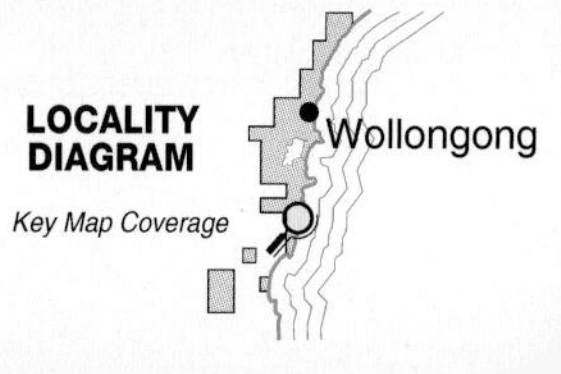

Key Map Coverage

Wollongong

MAP 69
PREVIOUS MAP 66
4 GRID SQUARES MEASURE 1km

JOINS MAP 65

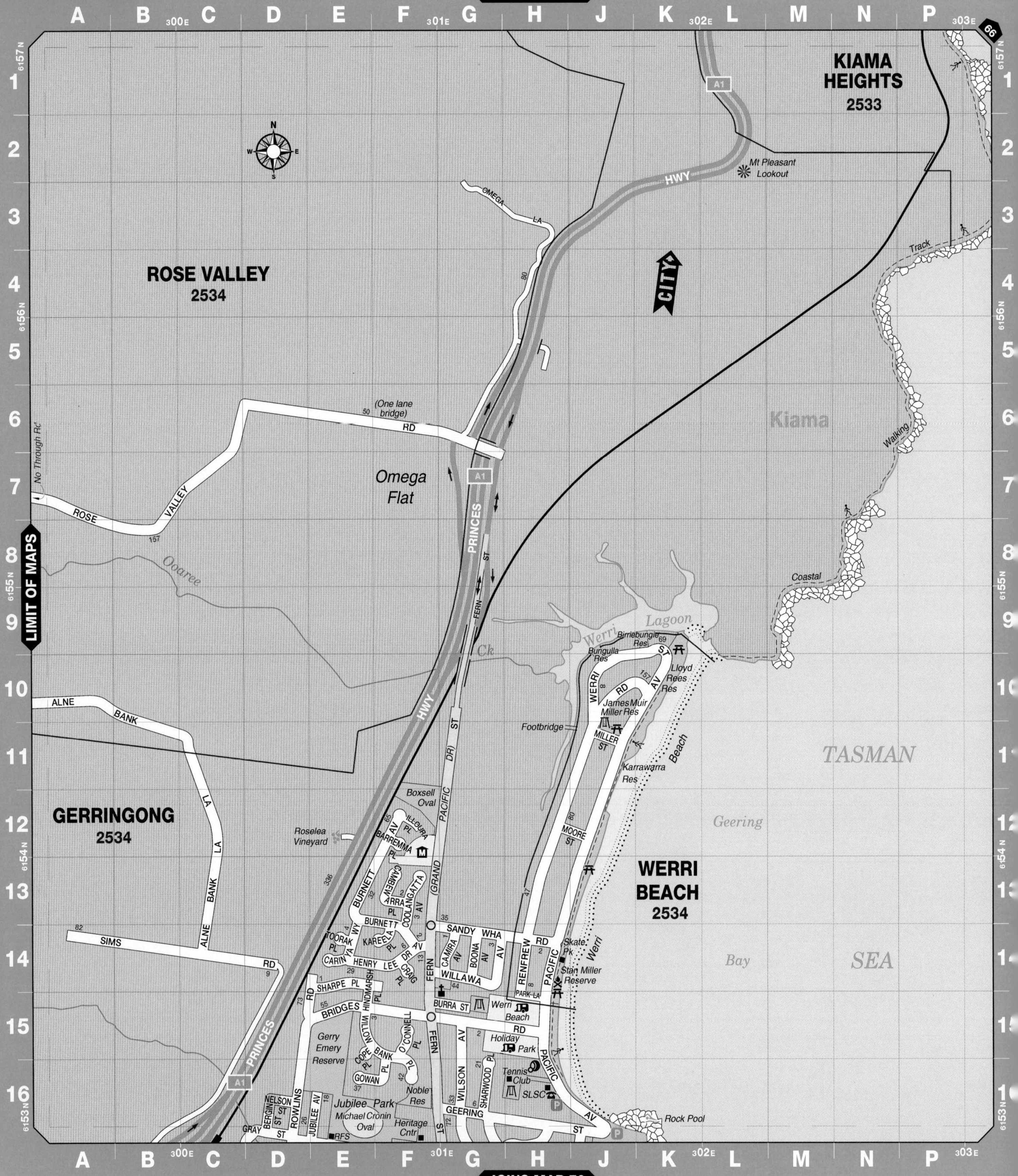

A B C 300E C D E F 301E G H J K 302E L M N P 303E 66

KIAMA HEIGHTS
2533

Mt Pleasant Lookout

HWY

OMEGA LA

CITY

ROSE VALLEY
2534

Kiama

Track

Walking

(One lane bridge)
50 RD

Omega Flat

No Through Rd

ROSE VALLEY

157

Ooaree

A1

PRINCES ST

FERN ST

Coastal

LIMIT OF MAPS

Werri Lagoon

Ck

ALNE BANK

ALNE BANK LA

GERRINGONG
2534

Birriebungie Res
Bungulla Res
Lloyd Rees Res
James Muir Miller Res
Footbridge
MILLER ST
Karrawarra Res

HWY

PACIFIC DRI ST

Boxsell Oval

Roselea Vineyard

TASMAN

Geering

MOORE ST

WERRI BEACH
2534

SIMS RD

82

ILLOURA PL
BARREMMA PL
BURNETT
CAMBEWARRA
COOLANGATTA
BURNETT

TOORAK PL
KAREELA PL
CARIN WY
HENRY LEE DR
CRAIG AV
SHARPE PL

Bay

SEA

SANDY WHA
CAMIRA AV
BOONA AV
WILLAWA AV

Skate Pk

RENFREW

PACIFIC

Stan Miller Reserve

BRIDGES RD
HINDMARSH

BURRA ST

Werri Beach RD

Gerry Emery Reserve

O'CONNELL
OOPE MOTUM BANK PL
GOWAN

Holiday Park

Tennis Club

WILSON AV

SHARWOOD AV

SLSC

PACIFIC AV

NELSON ST
BERGIN ST
ROWLINS
JUBILEE AV
GRAY ST

Jubilee Park
Michael Cronin Oval
RFS

Noble Res

Heritage Cntr

GEERING ST

Rock Pool

JOINS MAP 70

A B C 300E D E F 301E G H J K 302E L M N P 303E

COPYRIGHT © UNIVERSAL PUBLISHERS PTY LTD

SCALE 1:19 000
1km
Metres   500   1000

FREEWAY	PARK, RESERVE, OVAL
PROPOSED FREEWAY	SCHOOL, HOSPITAL
HIGHWAY or MAIN ROUTE	MISCELLANEOUS AREA
ALTERNATE ROUTE	MALL, PLAZA
TRAFFICABLE ROAD	SWAMP
PROPOSED ROAD	

AMBULANCE STATION
BARBECUE
BOAT RAMP
BOWLING CLUB/GREEN
CAMPING AREA
CARAVAN PARK

CAR PARK
CYCLEWAY
DISTANCE FROM GPO
EMERGENCY TELEPHONE
EXPRESS POST BOX
FIRE STATION

GERRINGONG
2534

GERROA
2534

Kiama

Gerringong
Golf
Club

Walkers Beach

TASMAN

SEA

Shoalhaven
Bight

Seven Mile Beach

Shelly
Beach

Black
Head

Kingsford - Smith
Lookout

Gerringong
Boat
Harbour

Crooked River Winery

PRINCES

LIMIT OF MAPS

LIMIT OF MAPS

COPYRIGHT © UNIVERSAL PUBLISHERS PTY LTD

FIXED SPEED CAMERA	LIBRARY	PLACE OF WORSHIP	SCHOOL - PRIVATE	TERTIARY - PRIVATE
GOLF COURSE	LOOKOUT 180 , 360	PLAYGROUND	SCHOOL - PUBLIC	TERTIARY - PUBLIC
GUIDES / SCOUTS	MASONIC CENTRE	POLICE STATION	SERVICE STATION	TOILETS
HOSPITAL	MEMORIAL / MONUMENT	POST OFFICE	SHOPPING CENTRE	TRAFFIC LIGHT
HOTEL / MOTEL	ONE-WAY TRAFFIC ROUTE	RED LIGHT CAMERA	SWIMMING POOL	WEIGHBRIDGE
INFORMATION CENTRE	PICNIC AREA	ROUNDABOUT	TELEPHONE	WINERIES

Wollongong

Shoalhaven River, Nowra. Destination NSW.

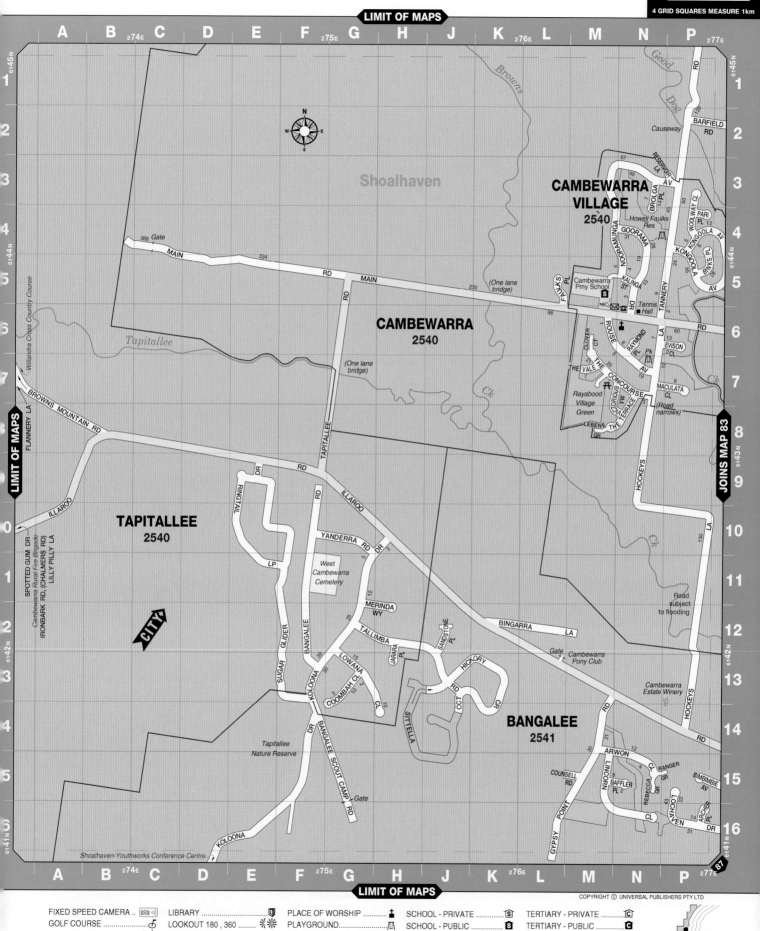

MAP 82
PREVIOUS MAP 70
4 GRID SQUARES MEASURE 1km

LIMIT OF MAPS

A B 274E C D E F 275E G H J K 276E L M N P 277E

Shoalhaven

CAMBEWARRA
VILLAGE
2540

Browns

Good Dog

BARFIELD RD

Causeway

RESERVOIR AV
BROLGA PL
NOORAMUNGA
GOORAMA
Howell Faulks Res
WOOLWAY CL
PARI
KONGOOLA AV
KONGOOLA
BINKS PL
AV

Gate
388
MAIN
334
MAIN RD
RD
230
(One lane bridge)
98
KALINGA ST
TANNERY
FAULKS PL
Cambewarra Pmy School
Tennis Hall

CAMBEWARRA
2540

(One lane bridge)

Browns Ck

CLOVER CT
ROUSE DR
RAYMOND PL
Pk
EVISON CL
THE CONCOURSE
THE VALE
GLORIOUS TERRACE
MACULATA CL
(Road narrows)
Rayabood Village Green
LEBENE GR
THE

JOINS MAP 83

BROWNS MOUNTAIN RD

FLANNERY LA

Willandra Cross Country Course
Tapitallee

Cambewarra Rural Fire Brigade
IRONBARK RD, (CHALMERS RD)
LILLY PILLY LA

SPOTTED GUM DR

ILLAROO

ILLAROO
RD
TAPITALLEE RD
RINGTAIL DR
LP
YANDERRA RD
DR
HOCKEYS
LA
130
Ck

TAPITALLEE
2540

West Cambewarra Cemetery

MERINDA WY
TALLIMBA
JARARA PL
SANDSTONE PL
BINGARRA LA
Road subject to flooding

SUGAR GLIDER
BANGALEE
KOLOONA
LOWANA
COOMBAH CL
CL
SITTELLA
HICKORY RD
CCT
CR
Gate
Cambewarra Pony Club

Cambewarra Estate Winery
HOCKEYS RD

CITY

BANGALEE
2541

Tapitallee Nature Reserve

DR
BANGALEE SCOUT CAMP RD
Gate

ARWON
COUNSELL RD
LINCOLN PL
BAFFLER PL
REBECCA
GR
BANGER
LOCHAN CL
BIMBIMBIE AV
ARCHER DR

KOLOONA

GYPSY POINT

Shoalhaven-Youthworks Conference Centre

LIMIT OF MAPS

A B 274E C D E F 275E G H J K 276E L M N P 277E

JOINS MAP 87

FIXED SPEED CAMERA
GOLF COURSE
GUIDES / SCOUTS
HOSPITAL
HOTEL / MOTEL
INFORMATION CENTRE
LIBRARY
LOOKOUT 180 , 360
MASONIC CENTRE
MEMORIAL / MONUMENT
ONE-WAY TRAFFIC ROUTE
PICNIC AREA
PLACE OF WORSHIP
PLAYGROUND
POLICE STATION
POST OFFICE
RED LIGHT CAMERA
ROUNDABOUT
SCHOOL - PRIVATE
SCHOOL - PUBLIC
SERVICE STATION
SHOPPING CENTRE
SWIMMING POOL
TELEPHONE
TERTIARY - PRIVATE
TERTIARY - PUBLIC
TOILETS
TRAFFIC LIGHT
WEIGHBRIDGE
WINERIES

Wollongong

LIMIT OF MAPS

A B C D 278E E F G H 279E J K L M 280E N P Q

CARRINGTON RD
Kangaroo Valley 13km
Moss Vale 50km

BARFIELD RD

PARI PL
BINKS PL
KONGOOLA AV

MAIN RD

MOSS VALE RD

CAMBEWARRA 2540

JOINS MAP 82

MOSS VALE RD

CAMBEWARRA

Western

TAYLORS

HOCKEYS LA

Good Dog Ck

Tapitallee Ck

Proposed

Bomaderry Ck

BANGALEE 2541

North Nowra Playing Fields

Bernie Regan Sporting Complex

ILLAROO

BIMBIMBIE
ARCHER
LOCHAVEN DR
WARRAH
MOONDARA AV
BURRANDOOL AV
WONGOONOO AV

TUSCAN PL
ARANA PL
TREVISO PL
CHITTICK AV
SOPER DR

Gordon Cook Apex Park

WEST CAMBEWARRA

NORTH NOWRA 2541

Bomaderry Creek Regional Park

NORTH NOWRA LINK RD

Abernethys

ABERNETHYS LA

ABERNETHYS LA

Bypass

CITY

BELLS RD

THEODORE PL
GLADIOLI
TARTARIAN
VST
TARTARIAN CR
PEACHEY CL
ELVIN CR

Reserve

MARIGOLD CR
GARDENIA
MAGNOLIA
WISTERIA
SHERATON
FRESIA CR
HIBISCUS PL
MAYFAIR
JASMINE
HAMILTON
PRINCETON
CRESTON
FERNTREE DR
REGAL PL
CAVALIER DR
CHESTNUT
AMBER PL
COCOS
PALM
HEL

Bomaderry Sporting Complex

Treehaven Tourist Park

PRINCES HWY

CAMBEWARRA RD

NARANG RD

Skateway

Tennis

Bomaderry Creek Bushland Reserve

Walking Track

SEAFORTH ST
CAMEL GR
WEST ST
BARWON ST
BIRRILEY ST
CHEBES
ROBEY ST

Ent Hall
Artie Smith Oval

Basketball Stadium

A1

A B C D 278E E F G H 279E J K L M 280E N P Q

COPYRIGHT © UNIVERSAL PUBLISHERS PTY LTD

SCALE 1:19 000

Metres 500 1000 1km

Legend	
FREEWAY	PARK, RESERVE, OVAL
PROPOSED FREEWAY	SCHOOL, HOSPITAL
HIGHWAY or MAIN ROUTE	MISCELLANEOUS AREA
ALTERNATE ROUTE	MALL, PLAZA
TRAFFICABLE ROAD	SWAMP
PROPOSED ROAD	

AMBULANCE STATION
BARBECUE
BOAT RAMP
BOWLING CLUB/GREEN
CAMPING AREA
CARAVAN PARK
CAR PARK
CYCLEWAY
DISTANCE FROM GPO
EMERGENCY TELEPHONE
EXPRESS POST BOX
FIRE STATION

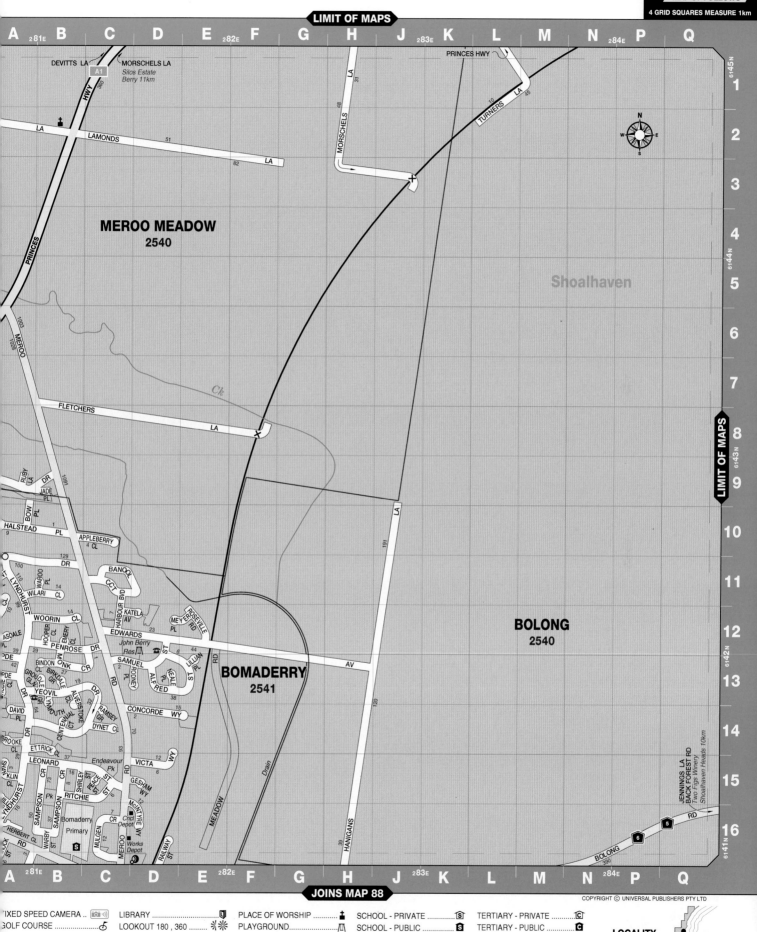

A 281E B C D E 282E F G H J 283E K L M N 284E P Q

DEVITTS LA
A1
MORSCHELS LA
Silos Estate
Berry 11km

PRINCES HWY

LA LAMONDS 51

LA 82

MEROO MEADOW
2540

Shoalhaven

MORSCHELS LA 37

TURNERS LA 45

PRINCES HWY

HWY

PRINCES

MEROO

1093

1028

Ck

FLETCHERS LA 1091

RUBY LA DR

JADE PL

BOW PL

HALSTEAD PL

APPLEBERRY CL

DR 129 100

BANOOL

CCT

LYNDHURST

WAROO PL

WILARI CL

WOORIN CL

HOOPER CL

EMERY CL

KATELA AV

HARBOUR BLVD

ROSEVILLE RD

MEYER PL

EDWARDS

PENROSE DR

John Berry Res

NEALE ST

LILLIAN PL

BOMADERRY
2541

AV

SAMUEL

ALFRED ST

ROONEY

BINDON CL

BIRKDALE GR

AVERSTOKE

RAMSEY GR

CONCORDE WY

YEOVIL

LYNMOUTH DR

DAVID PL

DYNET CL

ETTRICK CL

LEONARD

VICTA WY

CENTENNIAL CT

Endeavour Pk

GESHAM WY

SHIRLEY

PEACE ST

RITCHIE

McINTYRE WY

SAMPSON

WARBY CL

Bomaderry Primary

MULGEN CR

Cncl Depot

MEROO

RAILWAY ST

Works Depot

Drain

MEADOW

HANIGANS

191

120

39

LA

BOLONG
2540

JENNINGS LA
BACK FOREST RD
Two Figs Winery
Shoalhaven Heads 10km

6
5
BOLONG RD 390

A 281E B C D E 282E F G H J 283E K L M N 284E P Q

1
2
3
4
5
6
7
8
9
10
11
12
13
14
15
16

6145N
6144N
6143N
6142N
6141N

COPYRIGHT © UNIVERSAL PUBLISHERS PTY LTD

FIXED SPEED CAMERA .. 📷))
GOLF COURSE .... ⛳
GUIDES / SCOUTS .... ♣♣
HOSPITAL .... ✚
HOTEL / MOTEL .... H M
INFORMATION CENTRE ...... ℹ

LIBRARY .... 📖
LOOKOUT 180 , 360 ...... ☀☀
MASONIC CENTRE .... ⚒
MEMORIAL / MONUMENT.. ▲
ONE-WAY TRAFFIC ROUTE ..➜
PICNIC AREA .... ⛱

PLACE OF WORSHIP .... ✝
PLAYGROUND.................. 🎠
POLICE STATION .... ★
POST OFFICE .... ✉
RED LIGHT CAMERA .... ◈
ROUNDABOUT .... ○

SCHOOL - PRIVATE .... Ⓢ
SCHOOL - PUBLIC .... Ⓢ
SERVICE STATION .... ⛽
SHOPPING CENTRE .... 🛒
SWIMMING POOL............. 🏊
TELEPHONE .... ☎

TERTIARY - PRIVATE .... Ⓒ
TERTIARY - PUBLIC .... Ⓒ
TOILETS .... 🚻
TRAFFIC LIGHT............... ●
WEIGHBRIDGE .... Ⓦ
WINERIES .... 🍇

LOCALITY DIAGRAM
Key Map Coverage

Wollongong

MAP 87
PREVIOUS MAP 84
4 GRID SQUARES MEASURE 1km
JOINS MAP 83

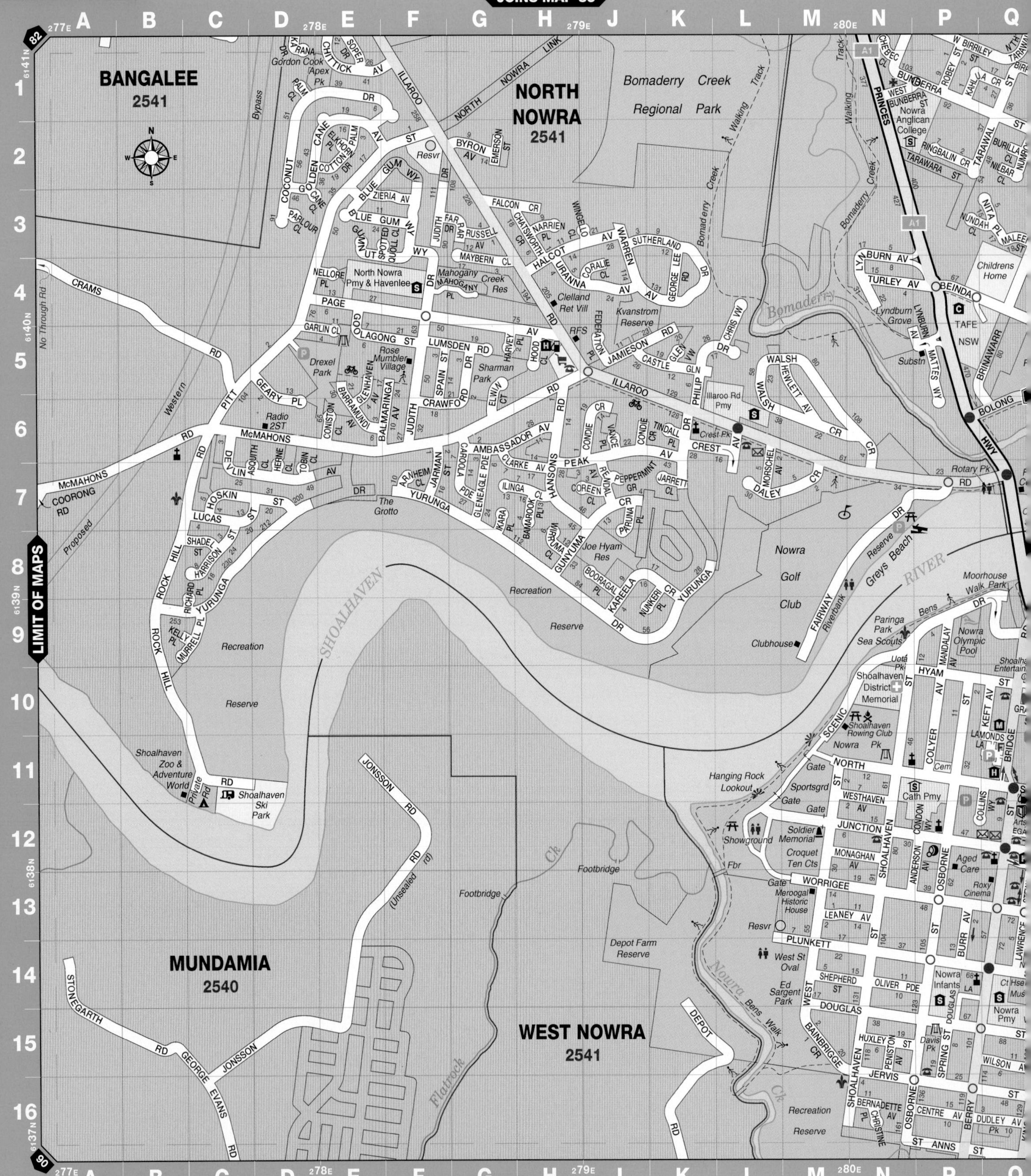

A B C D E F G H J K L M N P Q

BANGALEE
2541

NORTH NOWRA
2541

Bomaderry Creek Regional Park

Nowra Anglican College

Childrens Home

TAFE NSW

Nowra Golf Club

Greys Beach

RIVER

Moorhouse Walk Park

Nowra Olympic Pool

Shoalhaven District Memorial

Nowra Pk

Shoalhaven Rowing Club

LIMIT OF MAPS

SHOALHAVEN

Shoalhaven Zoo & Adventure World

Shoalhaven Ski Park

Hanging Rock Lookout

Sportsgrd

Showground

Soldier Memorial

Croquet Ten Cts

Meroogal Historic House

West St Oval

Ed Sargent Park

Nowra Infants

Roxy Cinema

Aged Care

MUNDAMIA
2540

WEST NOWRA
2541

Depot Farm Reserve

Recreation Reserve

SCALE 1:19 000   1km
Metres   500   1000

FREEWAY	
PROPOSED FREEWAY	
HIGHWAY or MAIN ROUTE	
ALTERNATE ROUTE	
TRAFFICABLE ROAD	
PROPOSED ROAD	
PARK, RESERVE, OVAL	
SCHOOL, HOSPITAL	
MISCELLANEOUS AREA	
MALL, PLAZA	
SWAMP	
AMBULANCE STATION	
BARBECUE	
BOAT RAMP	
BOWLING CLUB/GREEN	
CAMPING AREA	
CARAVAN PARK	
CAR PARK	
CYCLEWAY	
DISTANCE FROM GPO	
EMERGENCY TELEPHONE	
EXPRESS POST BOX	
FIRE STATION	

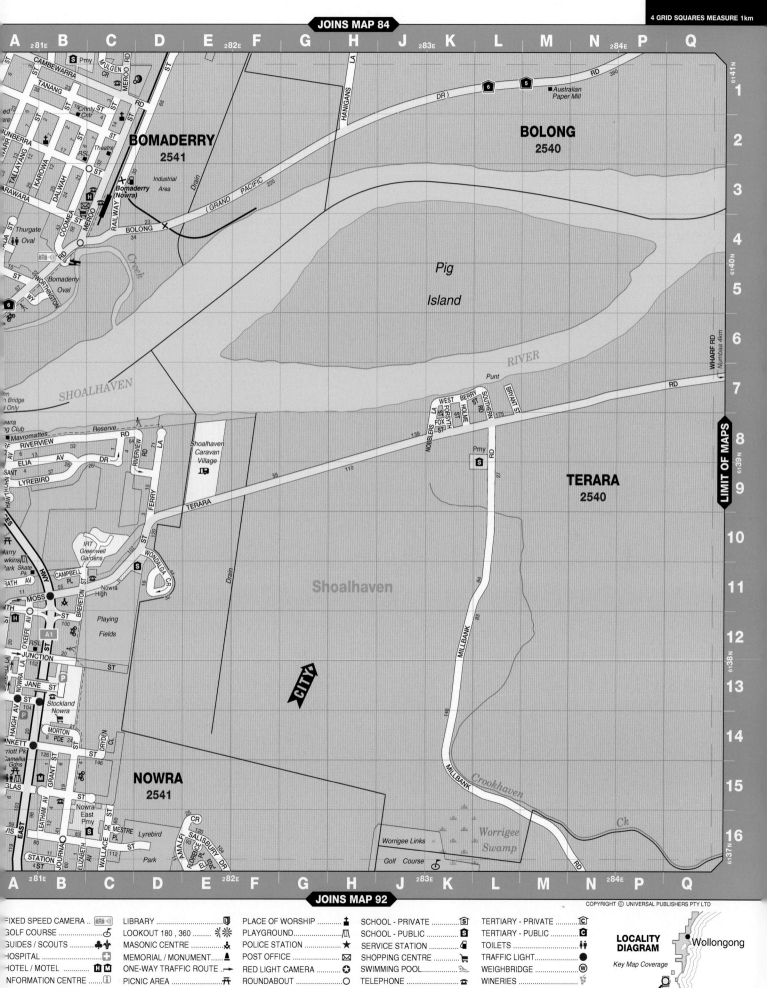

MAP 88

4 GRID SQUARES MEASURE 1km

JOINS MAP 84

BOMADERRY
2541

BOLONG
2540

Australian
Paper Mill

Industrial
Area

Pig
Island

SHOALHAVEN

RIVER

Punt

TERARA
2540

Shoalhaven

NOWRA
2541

Worrigee
Swamp

Worrigee Links

Golf Course

Crookhaven

Ck

LIMIT OF MAPS

CITY

FIXED SPEED CAMERA .. 📷))
GOLF COURSE ....
GUIDES / SCOUTS ....
HOSPITAL ....
HOTEL / MOTEL ....
INFORMATION CENTRE ....ℹ️

LIBRARY ....
LOOKOUT 180 , 360 ....
MASONIC CENTRE ....
MEMORIAL / MONUMENT....▲
ONE-WAY TRAFFIC ROUTE ..→
PICNIC AREA ....

PLACE OF WORSHIP ....
PLAYGROUND...................
POLICE STATION ....★
POST OFFICE ....✉️
RED LIGHT CAMERA ....✪
ROUNDABOUT ....○

SCHOOL - PRIVATE ....Ⓢ
SCHOOL - PUBLIC ....Ⓢ
SERVICE STATION ....
SHOPPING CENTRE ....
SWIMMING POOL.............
TELEPHONE ....☎

TERTIARY - PRIVATE ....Ⓒ
TERTIARY - PUBLIC ....Ⓒ
TOILETS ....
TRAFFIC LIGHT...................●
WEIGHBRIDGE ....Ⓦ
WINERIES ....

LOCALITY
DIAGRAM
Key Map Coverage

Wollongong

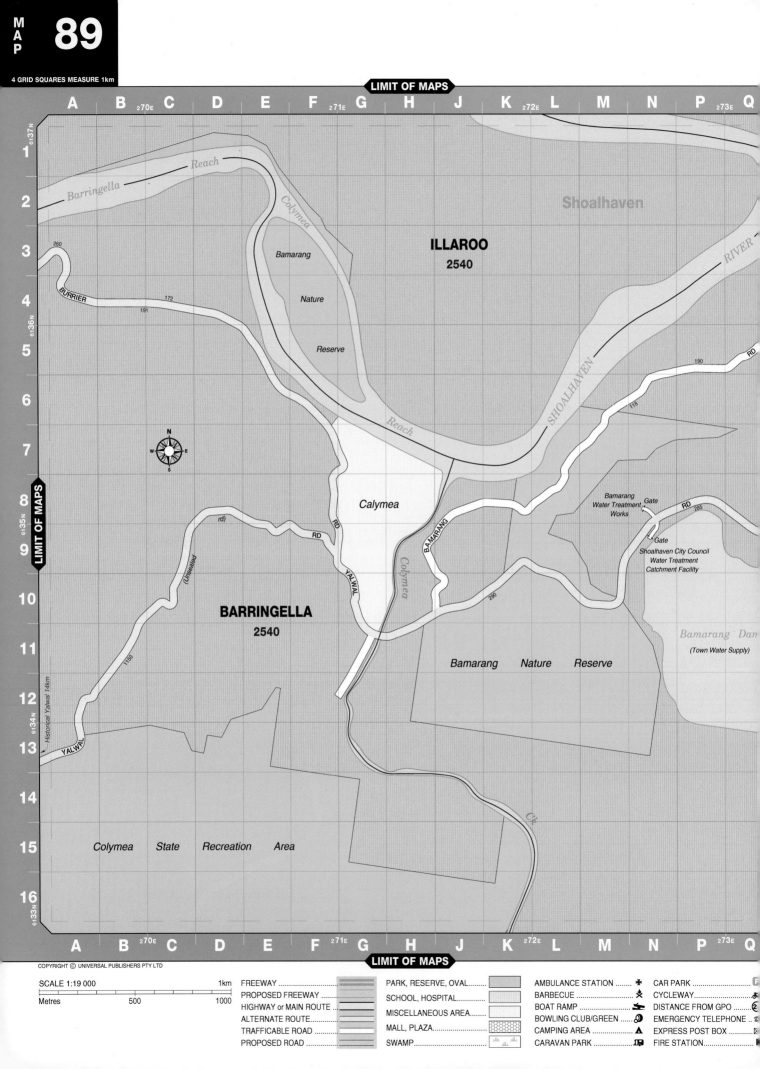

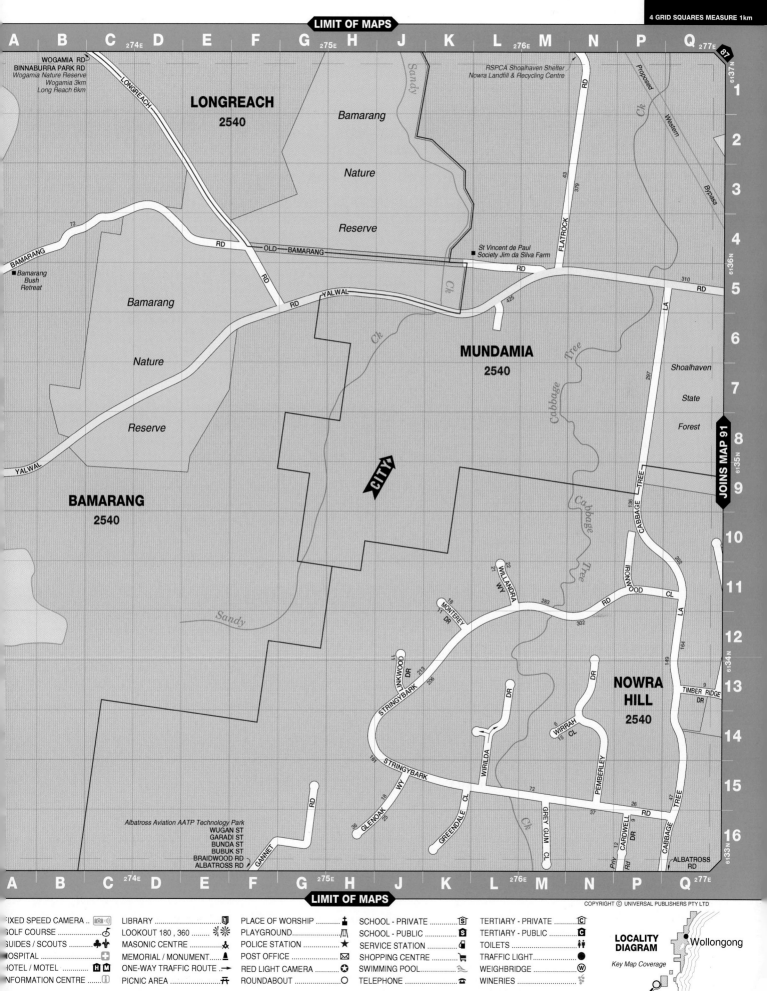

LIMIT OF MAPS

A B C 274E D E F G 275E H J K L 276E M N P Q 277E

WOGAMIA RD
BINNABURRA PARK RD
Wogamia Nature Reserve
Wogamia 3km
Long Reach 6km

LONGREACH
2540

Bamarang

Nature

Reserve

RSPCA Shoalhaven Shelter
Nowra Landfill & Recycling Centre

LONGREACH

72

BAMARANG

RD OLD — BAMARANG

RD

YALWAL

St Vincent de Paul
Society Jim da Silva Farm

RD

310 RD

Bamarang
Bush
Retreat

Bamarang

Nature

Reserve

YALWAL

425

MUNDAMIA
2540

Shoalhaven

State

Forest

297

CITY

BAMARANG
2540

136

Sandy

22
21 WILLANDRA WY

18
17 MONTEREY DR

283

202

NOWRA
HILL
2540

302

149

164

TIMBER RIDGE DR
9

LINKWOOD DR
213

STRINGYBARK 206

DR

6
15 WIRRAH CL

PEMBERLEY DR

72

26

47

STRINGYBARK WY
18
25

GLENOAK WY

36

GREENDALE CL

WIRILDA DR

GREY GUM CL

37

CARDWELL DR
12

CABBAGE TREE RD

Albatross Aviation AATP Technology Park
WUGAN ST
GARADI ST
BUNDA ST
BUBUK ST
BRAIDWOOD RD
ALBATROSS RD

GANNET RD

ALBATROSS
RD

1
2
3
4
5
6
7
8
9
10
11
12
13
14
15
16

6137N
6136N
6135N
6134N
6133N

87

JOINS MAP 91

LIMIT OF MAPS

A B C 274E D E F G 275E H J K L 276E M N P Q 277E

FIXED SPEED CAMERA ..
GOLF COURSE ....
GUIDES / SCOUTS ....
HOSPITAL ....
HOTEL / MOTEL ....
INFORMATION CENTRE ......

LIBRARY ....
LOOKOUT 180 , 360 ......
MASONIC CENTRE ....
MEMORIAL / MONUMENT. ..
ONE-WAY TRAFFIC ROUTE ..
PICNIC AREA ....

PLACE OF WORSHIP ....
PLAYGROUND..................
POLICE STATION ....
POST OFFICE ....
RED LIGHT CAMERA ....
ROUNDABOUT ....

SCHOOL - PRIVATE ....
SCHOOL - PUBLIC ....
SERVICE STATION ....
SHOPPING CENTRE ....
SWIMMING POOL ....
TELEPHONE ....

TERTIARY - PRIVATE ....
TERTIARY - PUBLIC ....
TOILETS ....
TRAFFIC LIGHT..................
WEIGHBRIDGE ....
WINERIES ....

LOCALITY
DIAGRAM
Key Map Coverage

Wollongong

MAP 91

4 GRID SQUARES MEASURE 1km

JOINS MAP 87

A B C D E F G H J K L M N P Q

277E 278E 279E 280E

1
2
3
4
5
6
7
8
9
10
11
12
13
14
15
16

6137N
6136N
6135N
6134N
6133N

JOINS MAP 90

University of Wollongong
Shoalhaven Campus

MUNDAMIA
2540

YALWAL

GEORGE EVANS

394

261

RD

Proposed

WEST NOWRA
2541

Ck

Flat

Rock

Shoalhaven

State

Forest

Shoalhaven Dam

Triplarina
Nature
Reserve

Western

N
W E
S

Flatrock

Timber Ridge

HAKEA CL
DR
40 87 118

Bypass

NOWRA HILL
2540

ALBATROSS
CALYMEA ST
136 36

Fleet Air Arm Museum   No Through Rd

RACEMOSA AV
CAVANAGH
STOCKLEY CL
BROMLEY CL
BENNEY CL
FILTER
GLEN
TUMMELL
CL
TAY GR
TULLA PL
RANNOCH
GARRY GLN
LEBARK
FOLIA
BEVERI
LYDON CR
DON
CHRIST CL
DOREEN GT
MAY BUSH WY
DEPOT
LANGSIDE AV
FLANNELFLOWER AV
ROKEN GLN
CAN
DR
IR
AV
38
21
17
5
25
32
7
79
6
10

BICE
RAINFORD
OLYMPIC DR
Smorgan Steel
Temp Access
LIGHTWOOD DR
DOBBIE CL
ISABEL CL
CORAL SEA DR
RD

RFS Training Centre
RFS & SES

NOWRA
2541

Substation
W

RD

Recreation Reserve

Nowra Creek Res

WESTBORNE CL
OSBORNE
ROSEWOOD CL
KERWICK CL
MACLEAN
ELYARD
ULRICK
McDONALD
REIBY
PURDUE CR
SCHREGE PL
PIONEER
ERNEST
ALBERT
MALEAN
132
173
9
49
24
22
94

ST ANNS
BERRY
KALANDAR
HALE
KINGHORNE
120
75

Shoalhaven State Forest

Nowra

ALBATROSS RD

FLINDERS RD

Pine Bowl Greyhound Course
Nowra Paceway
Nowra Speedway

Archer
Racecourse
(Shoalhaven City Turf Club)

Nowra
Raceway

RUGBY
Shoalhaven Rugby Park
Gate

FLINDERS RD
RD

Shoalhaven
Water

Flinders Industrial Estate

NORFOLK
TOM
TRIM
INVESTIGATOR ST
THUMB AV
SEXTANT ST
CUMBERLAND
NORFOLK AV
THE LINKS
AV
KINGS
PROSPERITY
CENTRAL
12
3
15
26
33
21
19
2

Telstra

SOUTH
NOWRA
2541

JELLICOE ST
BELLEVUE
OXFORD
CENTRAL
RD
17
20
23
92

Service NSW
Mannar
Min Ce

Nowra Correctional Facility

Delivery Dock

SCALE 1:19 000
Metres   500   1000   1km

FREEWAY
PROPOSED FREEWAY
HIGHWAY or MAIN ROUTE
ALTERNATE ROUTE
TRAFFICABLE ROAD
PROPOSED ROAD

PARK, RESERVE, OVAL
SCHOOL, HOSPITAL
MISCELLANEOUS AREA
MALL, PLAZA
SWAMP

AMBULANCE STATION
BARBECUE
BOAT RAMP
BOWLING CLUB/GREEN
CAMPING AREA
CARAVAN PARK

CAR PARK
CYCLEWAY
DISTANCE FROM GPO
EMERGENCY TELEPHONE
EXPRESS POST BOX
FIRE STATION

MAP 92
MAP 95 FOLLOWS
4 GRID SQUARES MEASURE 1km

JOINS MAP 88

WORRIGEE
2540

Worrigee Swamp

Worrigee Links Golf Course

Shoalhaven

Worrigee

Nature

Reserve

LIMIT OF MAPS

LIMIT OF MAPS

FIXED SPEED CAMERA ..
GOLF COURSE ....
GUIDES / SCOUTS ....
HOSPITAL ....
HOTEL / MOTEL ....
INFORMATION CENTRE ......

LIBRARY ....
LOOKOUT 180 , 360 ....
MASONIC CENTRE ....
MEMORIAL / MONUMENT...
ONE-WAY TRAFFIC ROUTE
PICNIC AREA ....

PLACE OF WORSHIP ....
PLAYGROUND............
POLICE STATION ....
POST OFFICE ....
RED LIGHT CAMERA ......
ROUNDABOUT ....

SCHOOL - PRIVATE ....
SCHOOL - PUBLIC ....
SERVICE STATION ....
SHOPPING CENTRE ......
SWIMMING POOL........
TELEPHONE ....

TERTIARY - PRIVATE ......
TERTIARY - PUBLIC ....
TOILETS ....
TRAFFIC LIGHT..........
WEIGHBRIDGE ....
WINERIES ....

LOCALITY DIAGRAM
Key Map Coverage

Wollongong

LIMIT OF MAPS

A B C D E F G H J K L M N P

BRYCES RD
AGARS LA
Berry 9km

COOLANGATTA

Gerroa 11km
Gerringong 14km

The Winery Barn

Shoalhaven

BERRY
2535

Seven   Mile   Beach

National

Park

Mountain Ridge Wines

COOLANGATTA
2535

Waste Water Treatment Plant

Shoalhaven Heads

LOVEGROVE

BOYD ST
HANLON ST
HEARD AV
McJAY AV

Golf

Pepper Res

NIMROD ST

Club

DISCOVERY PL
GERROA ST
TOWERS
NOAKES ST
RYGATE PL
MEEHAN AV
DAVIDSON DR
AMUNDSEN
MAWSON RD
SHACKLETON
BASS RD

The Shack

Clubhouse

SCOTT ARLEY
SCOTT OVAL

TALLIA ST

The Shack

Reserve

Ingenia Holidays

WELLS PL
GRAY PL
EXPLORER BVD

Shoalhaven Heads Sporting Complex

Vic Zealand Memorial Reserve

BOOKER DR

ST

THROSBY ST

STAPLES ST

TASMAN

SHOALHAVEN
HEADS
2535

SHOALHAVEN
HEADS

Mountain View Caravan & Mobile Home Village

Coastal Palms Holiday Park

MOUNTAIN VIEW PL
TRENTHAM
INGESTRE AV

SILVER SPUR CL
STAFFORD RD
CHELTENHAM DR

Cmnty Centre

WAGIN
ASPINALL
WOOLSTENCRAFT
LLOYD ST
DAVID ST
BERRY ST

Jerry Bailey Oval

Shoalhaven Heads Mem Pk

SLSC
CH
Gumley Res

DAVENPORT
BRAMALL RD
BAWDEN AV
RAVENSCLIFFE
RENOWN AV

BAILEY
GOLDEN HILL

Shoalhaven Heads Pmy

MATHEWS
McINTOSH
BOLT ST

Ent

Holiday Haven Shoalhaven Heads

CITY

Coolangatta Estate Resort Winery

EDWARD WOLLSTONECRAFT LA
Coolangatta Estate Resort Entrance
Two Figs Winery Nowra 13km

NORTHVIEW CL
PACIFIC
GRAND
BOLONG RD

CELIA PDE
JERRY AV
RIVER

Curtis Res

HAY
WHARF RD

Wharf

Shoalhaven   *River*

SEA

Bevan Island

Comerong Island

COMERONG ISLAND

COMERONG
ISLAND
2540

RD

LIMIT OF MAPS

A B C D E F G H J K L M N P

SCALE 1:19 000

1km

Metres   500   1000

FREEWAY	
PROPOSED FREEWAY	
HIGHWAY or MAIN ROUTE	
ALTERNATE ROUTE	
TRAFFICABLE ROAD	
PROPOSED ROAD	

PARK, RESERVE, OVAL	
SCHOOL, HOSPITAL	
MISCELLANEOUS AREA	
MALL, PLAZA	
SWAMP	

AMBULANCE STATION	✳
BARBECUE	
BOAT RAMP	
BOWLING CLUB/GREEN	
CAMPING AREA	▲
CARAVAN PARK	

CAR PARK	
CYCLEWAY	
DISTANCE FROM GPO	
EMERGENCY TELEPHONE	
EXPRESS POST BOX	
FIRE STATION	

MAP 96

4 GRID SQUARES MEASURE 1km

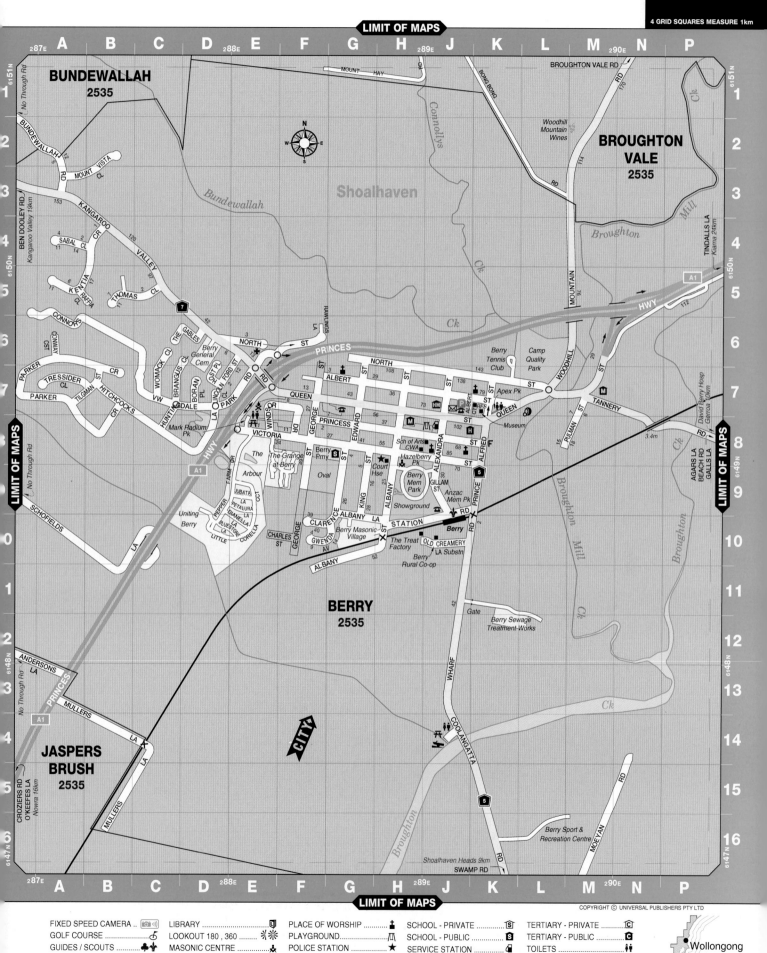

LIMIT OF MAPS

BUNDEWALLAH
2535

BROUGHTON VALE
2535

Shoalhaven

BERRY
2535

JASPERS BRUSH
2535

CITY

Wollongong

FIXED SPEED CAMERA	LIBRARY	PLACE OF WORSHIP
GOLF COURSE	LOOKOUT 180 , 360	PLAYGROUND
GUIDES / SCOUTS	MASONIC CENTRE	POLICE STATION
HOSPITAL	MEMORIAL / MONUMENT	POST OFFICE
HOTEL / MOTEL	ONE-WAY TRAFFIC ROUTE	RED LIGHT CAMERA
INFORMATION CENTRE	PICNIC AREA	ROUNDABOUT

SCHOOL - PRIVATE	TERTIARY - PRIVATE
SCHOOL - PUBLIC	TERTIARY - PUBLIC
SERVICE STATION	TOILETS
SHOPPING CENTRE	TRAFFIC LIGHT
SWIMMING POOL	WEIGHBRIDGE
TELEPHONE	WINERIES

UNIVERSITY OF WOLLONGONG

P5a

PARKING

31C

31B

31

P4

23

25

WESTERN CARPARK

ROBSONS RD ENTRY

58

59 60

57

47 46 45

50

51

21
UNDER CONSTRUCTION

22

67

56

52 53

54

38

49

55

48

30

POND

70

71

BLOCK A

POND

BLOCK B

40

POND

68

SOUTH WESTERN

BLOCK C

CARPARK P3

POND

ROBSONS

ROAD

POND

POND

PARRY LANE

63

37

NORTHFIELDS

WESTE

Scale 1:3000   0 10   50   100m

UNIVERSITY OF
WOLLONGONG

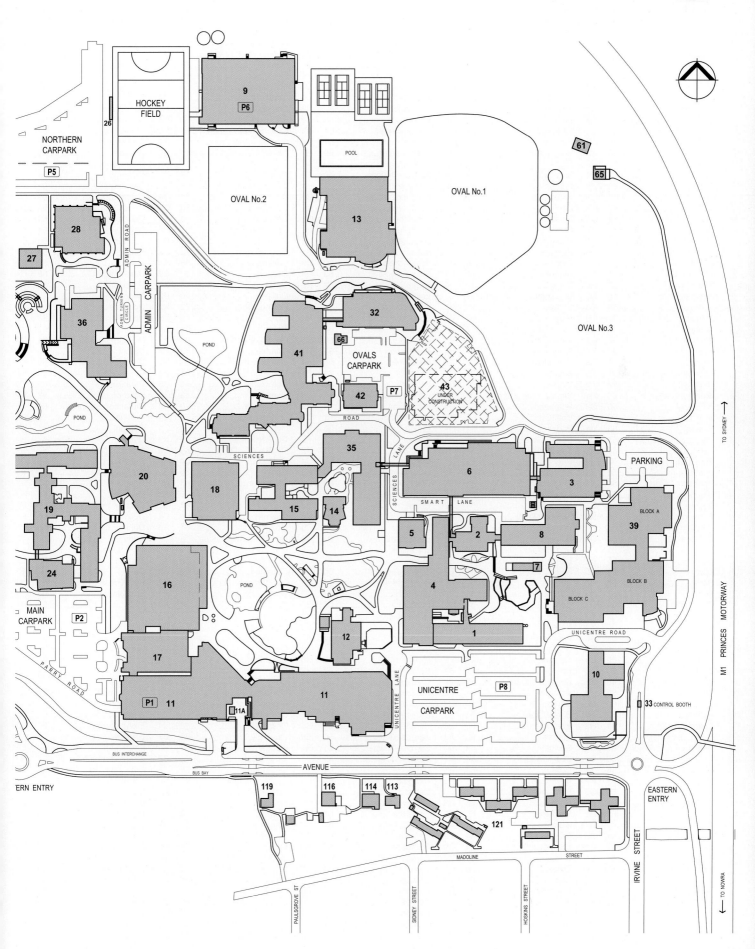

HOCKEY FIELD

NORTHERN CARPARK

P5

26

9

P6

POOL

OVAL No.1

61

65

28

27

36

ADMIN ROAD

ADMIN CARPARK

ADMIN TURNING CIRCLE

POND

POND

32

66

OVALS CARPARK

41

42

P7

43
UNDER CONSTRUCTION

OVAL No.3

ROAD

SCIENCES

35

20

18

15

14

SCIENCES LANE

6

3

PARKING

BLOCK A

19

5

SMART LANE

2

8

39

24

16

MAIN CARPARK

P2

POND

17

12

4

7

1

BLOCK B

BLOCK C

UNICENTRE ROAD

10

PARRY ROAD

P1

11

11A

UNICENTRE LANE

UNICENTRE CARPARK

P8

33 CONTROL BOOTH

M1   PRINCES MOTORWAY

TO SYDNEY →

BUS INTERCHANGE

AVENUE

BUS BAY

ERN ENTRY

EASTERN ENTRY

119

116

114

113

121

IRVINE STREET

PAULSGROVE ST

SIDNEY STREET

HOSKINS STREET

MADOLINE   STREET

TO NOWRA

State Atlas Index

Name	Page	Grid
Aberdeen	61	G2
Aberfoyle	57	F4
Abington	56	E4
Adaminaby	64	B4
Adelong	64	A3
Albert	60	B3
Albury	63	J4
Alectown	60	C4
Alfred Town	63	K2
Alice	57	G2
Alison	61	H3
Alleena	60	A5
Alstonville	57	J2
Amosfield	57	G2
Ando	64	C5
Angledool	55	J2
Angourie	57	J3
Anna Bay	61	J4
Appin	61	G6
Arajoel	63	J2
Arakoon	57	H5
Araluen	64	D3
Ardglen	61	G2
Ardlethan	63	J1
Ariah Park	60	B6
Armatree	60	D1
Armidale	57	F5
Arrawarra	57	H4
Arthurville	60	D3
Ashford	56	E3
Ashley	56	C3
Attunga	56	E5
Baan Baa	56	C5
Backwater	57	F4
Baerami	61	G3
Baerami Creek	61	F3
Bald Knob	57	F3
Baldry	60	D4
Balladoran	60	D2
Ballbank	62	E3
Balldale	63	J4
Ballina	57	J2
Balranald	62	D2
Bangalow	57	J2
Baradine	56	B5
Barellan	59	K6
Bargo	61	G6
Barham	62	E3
Barmedman	60	B6
Barooga	63	H4
Barraba	56	D4
Barrington	61	J2
Barringun	55	F2
Barry	60	E5
Barry	61	H2
Baryulgil	57	H3
Batehaven	64	D3
Batemans Bay	64	D3
Bathurst	60	E4
Batlow	64	A3
Bawley Point	64	E3
Beargamil	60	C4
Beckom	60	A6
Bedgerebong	60	B4
Beelbangera	59	J6
Bega	64	D5
Beilpajah	59	F4
Belford	61	H3
Bell	61	F5
Bellangry	61	K1
Bellarwi	60	B6
Bellata	56	C4
Bellbird	61	H4
Bellbrook	57	G5
Bellingen	57	H5
Belltrees	61	H2
Belmont	61	H4
Beloka	64	B5
Bemboka	64	C5
Ben Bullen	61	F4
Ben Lomond	57	F4
Benarca	63	F4
Bendalong	64	E3
Bendemeer	56	E5
Bendick Murrell	60	C6
Bendolba	61	H3
Bengerang	56	C2
Bentley	57	H2
Berendebba	60	B5
Bergallia	64	D4
Bermagui	64	D4
Bermagui South	64	D5
Berowra	61	G5
Berridale	64	B4
Berrigan	63	H3
Berrima	64	E1
Berry	64	E2
Bethungra	64	A2
Bevendale	64	C1
Biala	64	C2
Bibbenluke	64	C5
Biddon	60	D1
Bidgeemia	63	J3
Bigga	60	D6
Billeroy	56	A5
Billimari	60	D5
Bilpin	61	F5
Bimbi	60	C5
Binalong	64	B2
Binda	60	E6
Binda	64	C1
Bingara	56	D4
Biniguy	56	D3
Binnaway	60	E1
Binya	59	J6
Birdwood	61	J1
Birrego	63	J2
Birriwa	60	E2
Black Mountain	57	F4
Black Springs	60	E5
Blackheath	61	F5
Blackville	61	F2
Blandford	61	G2
Blayney	60	E5
Blighty	63	G3
Boambee	57	H4
Bobadah	59	K3
Bodalla	64	D4
Bogan Gate	60	B4
Bogangar	57	J1
Bogee	61	F4
Boggabilla	56	D1
Boggabri	56	C5
Bogolong Creek	60	C5
Bomaderry	64	E2
Bombah Point	61	J3
Bombala	64	C5
Bomera	61	F1
Bonalbo	57	H2
Bonny Hills	61	K2
Bonshaw	56	E2
Bonville	57	H5
Bookham	64	B2
Booligal	59	G5
Boomi	56	C2
Boomley	60	D2
Boonoo Boonoo	57	G2
Booral	61	J3
Booroorban	63	F2
Boorowa	64	B1
Boppy Mountain	59	J1
Borambil	61	F2
Boree	60	D4
Boree Creek	63	J2
Borenore	60	D4
Bourke	55	F4
Bowna	63	K4
Bowning	64	B2
Bowral	64	E1
Bowraville	57	H5
Brackendale	57	F6
Braidwood	64	D3
Branxton	61	H3
Brawlin	64	A2
Brayton	64	D2
Breadalbane	64	C2
Bredbo	64	C4
Breeza	56	D6
Bretti	61	J2
Brewarrina	55	H4
Bribbaree	60	C6
Brindabella	64	B3
Broadwater	57	J2
Brocklehurst	60	D2
Brocklesby	63	J3
Brogo	64	D5
Broke	61	G3
Broken Hill	58	B2
Brolgan	60	C4
Brooman	64	D3
Brooms Head	57	J3
Broula	60	D5
Broulee	64	D4
Bruinbun	60	E4
Brundah	60	C5
Brunswick Heads	57	J2
Brushwood	63	K2
Buckenderra	64	B4
Bucketty	61	G4
Buddabadah	60	B2
Buddigower	60	A5
Budgee Budgee	60	E3
Budgewoi	61	H4
Bugaldie	56	B6
Bugilbone	56	A4
Bukalong	64	C5
Bukkulla	56	E3
Bulahdelah	61	J3
Bulga	61	G3
Bulgandramine	60	C3
Bulgandry	63	J3
Bulgary	63	K2
Bullarah	56	B3
Bullenbung	63	J2
Bullocks Flat	64	B4
Bumberry	60	C4
Bundaburrah	60	B5
Bundanoon	64	E2
Bundarra	56	E4
Bundella	61	F1
Bundure	63	H2
Bungendore	64	C3
Bungonia	64	D2
Bungwahl	61	J3
Bunna Bunna	56	B3
Bunnaloo	63	F3
Bunnan	61	G2
Bunyan	64	C4
Buralyang	59	K5
Burcher	60	B5
Burgooney	59	K4
Burraboi	63	F3
Burraga	60	E5
Burragate	64	C5
Burrandana	63	K3
Burrapine	57	G5
Burrell Creek	61	J2
Burren Junction	56	B4
Burrill Lake	64	E3
Burringbar	57	J1
Burrinjuck	64	B2
Burrumbuttock	63	J3
Buxton	61	F6
Byabarra	61	K2
Bylong	61	F3
Byrock	55	G5
Byron Bay	57	J2
Cabramurra	64	B4
Cal Lal	58	B6
Caldwell	63	F3
Camberwell	61	G3
Camden	61	G6
Campbells River	60	E5
Campbelltown	61	G6
Canbelego	59	J1
Canberra	64	C3
Candelo	64	D5
Canonba	55	H6
Canowindra	60	D5
Capertee	61	F4
Captains Flat	64	C3
Carabost	64	A3
Caragabal	60	B5
Carcoar	60	D5
Cargo	60	D4
Carinda	55	J4
Carlachy	60	B4
Caroda	56	D4
Caroona	60	G1
Carrathool	63	G1
Carroll	56	D5
Casino	57	H2
Cassilis	61	F2
Castle Rock	61	G3
Cathcart	64	C5
Cawongla	57	H2
Cedar Point	57	H2
Central Mangrove	61	H4
Central Tilba	64	D4
Cessnock	61	H4
Charleyong	64	D3
Charlotte Pass	64	B4
Clandulla	61	F4
Clarence Town	61	H3
Clear Ridge	60	B5
Clouds Creek	57	G4
Clunes	57	J2
Clybucca	57	H5
Coaldale	57	H3
Cobar	59	J1
Cobargo	64	D4
Cobbadah	56	D4
Cobbora	60	E2
Coffs Harbour	57	H4
Coila	64	D4
Coleambally	63	H2
Collarenebri	56	A3
Collector	64	C2
Collerina	55	G3
Collie	60	C2
Collingullie	63	K2
Colo	61	G5
Comara	57	G5
Combaning	64	A1
Combara	55	K6
Comboyne	61	K2
Come By Chance	56	A4
Comobella	60	D3
Conargo	63	G3
Condobolin	60	A4
Connemarra	60	E1
Conoble	59	G4
Cookardinia	63	K3
Coolabah	55	G5
Coolac	64	A2
Coolah	60	E2
Coolamon	63	K2
Coolatai	56	E3
Coolongolook	61	J3
Cooma	64	C4
Coomba	61	K3
Coombah Roadhouse	58	B4
Coonabarabran	56	B6
Coonamble	55	K5
Coonong	63	H2
Coopernook	61	K2
Cooranbong	61	H4
Cootamundra	64	A2
Copmanhurst	57	H3
Coppabella	64	A3
Coradgery	60	C4
Coraki	57	J2
Coramba	57	H4
Coree South	63	G3
Coreen	63	J3
Corindi	57	H4
Corindi Beach	57	H4
Corobimilla	63	J2
Corowa	63	J4
Corringle	60	B5
Cougal	57	H1
Countegany	64	C4
Couradda	56	C4
Coutts Crossing	57	H4
Cowabbie	63	K1
Cowper	57	H3
Cowra	60	D5
Craigie	64	C6
Craven	61	J3
Creeper Gate	60	A2
Crescent Head	57	H6
Cronulla	61	G6
Crooble	56	D3
Crookwell	64	C1
Croppa Creek	56	D2
Crowdy Head	61	K2
Crowther	60	D6
Cryon	56	A4
Cubbaroo	56	B4
Cudal	60	D4
Culburra Beach	64	E2
Culcairn	63	K3
Culgoora	56	C4
Cullen Bullen	61	F4
Cullulla	64	D2
Cumborah	55	J3
Cumnock	60	D4
Cundumbul	60	D3
Curban	60	D1
Curlewis	56	D6
Currabubula	56	D6
Currarong	64	E2
Currawarna	63	K2
Cuttabri	56	B4
Dahwilly	63	F3
Dalgety	64	B5
Dalmeny	64	D4
Dalmorton	57	G4
Dalton	64	C2
Dandaloo	60	B3
Dapto	64	E1
Dareton	58	C6
Darlington Point	63	H1
Darnick	58	E4
Daroobalgie	60	C4
Daysdale	63	J3
Deepwater	57	F3
Delegate	64	B5
Delungra	56	E3
Deniliquin	63	G3
Denman	61	G3
Derain	63	K2
Deringulla	60	E1
Derriwong	60	B4
Dhuragoon	62	E3
Dilpurra	62	E2
Dirnaseer	64	A2
Dirrung	59	H5
Dorrigo	57	H4
Doubtful Creek	57	H2
Drake	57	G2
Dubbo	60	D3
Dundee	57	F3
Dunedoo	60	E2
Dungog	61	H3
Dungowan	56	E6
Dunkeld	60	E4
Dunmore	60	C3
Dunoon	57	J2
Duramana	60	E4
Duri	56	E6
Durras	64	E3
East Gresford	61	H3
East Jindabyne	64	B4
Ebor	57	G5
Eccleston	61	H3
Eden	64	D6
Eden Creek	57	H2
Edgeroi	56	C4
Edith	61	F5
Elands	61	J2
Elderslie	61	H3
Elizabeth Beach	61	K3
Ellenborough	61	K1
Ellerston	61	H2
Elong Elong	60	D2
Elsmore	56	E3
Emden Vale	60	E6
Emerald Beach	57	H4
Emerald Hill	56	C5
Emmaville	57	F3
Emmdale Roadhouse	59	F2
Enmore	57	F5
Enngonia	55	F2
Eribung	60	B3
Erigolia	59	J5
Euabalong	59	K4
Euabalong West	59	K4
Euchareena	60	D4
Eucumbene	64	B4
Eugowra	60	C4
Eumungerie	60	D2
Eungai Creek	57	H5
Eurabba	60	B5
Euratha	59	K5

State Atlas Index

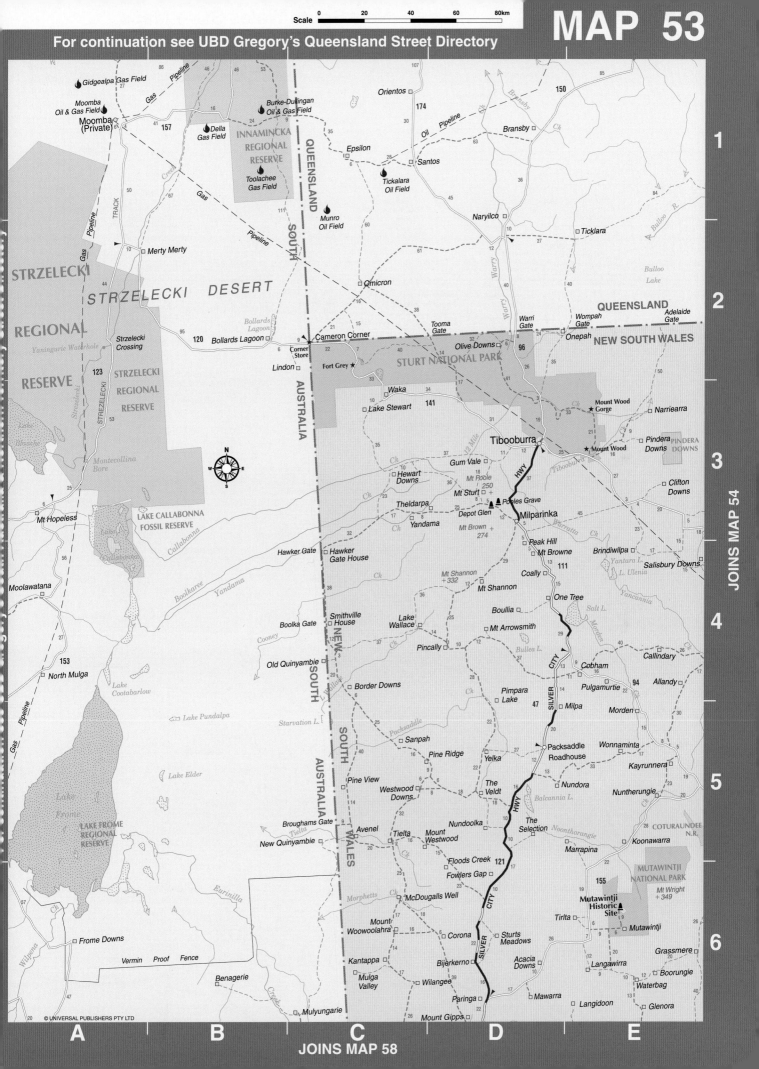

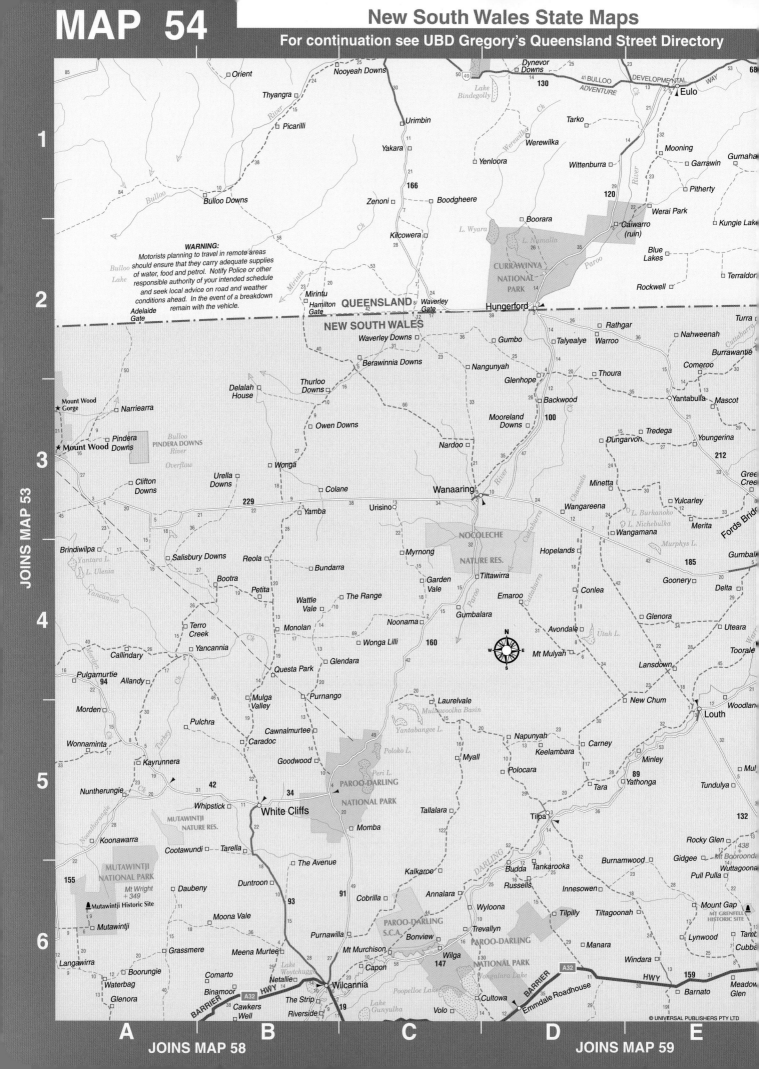

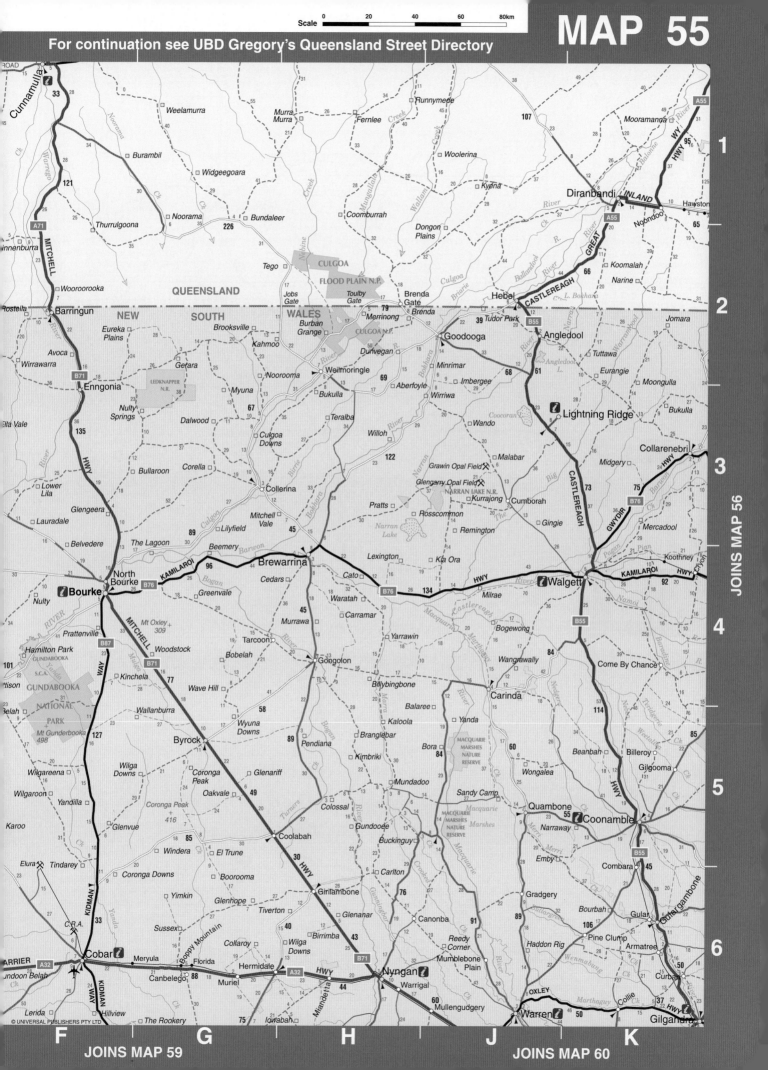

Scale 0 20 40 60 80km

Map labels (placenames and features)

Row 1 / area
Cunnamulla 33
Weelamurra
Murra Murra
Fernlee
Runnymede
Mooramanna
107
95
Burambil
Widgeegoara
Woolerina
Kyena
Diranbandi
INLAND
Hawston
121
Thurrulgoona
Noorama
Bundaleer 226
Coomburrah
Dongon Plains
Wando
Noondoo 65
MITCHELL
Wooroorooka
Tego
CULGOA FLOOD PLAIN N.P.
Koomalah
Narine 66
QUEENSLAND
Jobs Gate
Toulby Gate
Brenda Gate
Hebel
CASTLEREAGH

NEW SOUTH WALES
Barringun
Brooksville
Burban Grange
Merrinong
Brenda
Tudor Park
Goodooga
Angledool
Jomara
Eureka Plains
Kahmoo
CULGOA N.P.
Minirmar
Tuttawa
Eurangie
Avoca
Getara
Norooma
Weilmoringle
Aberfoyle
Imbergee
Moongulla
Wirrawarra
Myuna
Dunvegan
Wirriwa
Bukulla
Enngonia
LEDKNAPPER N.R.
Bukulla
Lightning Ridge
Nulty Springs
Dalwood
Culgoa Downs
Teralba
Wando
Malabar
Collarenebri
Ella Vale
Bullaroon
Corella
Willoh
Grawin Opal Field
Midgery
122
Lower Lila
Glengeera
Lilyfield
Mitchell Vale
Collerina
Glengarry Opal Field
NARRAN LAKE N.R.
Kurrajong
Cumborah
Mercadool
Lauradale
Belvedere
The Lagoon
Beemery
Pratts
Rosscommon
Gingie
Remington
Koothney
North Bourke
Brewarrina
Lexington
Kia Ora
Walgett
Bourke
KAMILAROI
Cedars
Cato
Milrae
Nulty
Greenvale
Waratah
Bogewong
Come By Chance
Prattenville
Murrawa
Carramar
Yarrawin
Wangrawally
Mt Oxley 309
Woodstock
Tarcoon
Bobelah
Gongolon
Billybingbone
Carinda
Hamilton Park
Kinchela
Wave Hill
Wyuna Downs
Branglebar
Balaree
Yanda
Billeroy
GUNDABOOKA NATIONAL PARK
Wallanburra
Byrock
Pendiana
Kaloola
Bora
Gilgooma
Mt Gunderbooka 498
Wilga Downs
Glenariff
Kimbriki
MACQUARIE MARSHES NATURE RESERVE
Wongalea
Beanbah
Wilgareena
Coronga Peak
Oakvale
Mundadoo
Quambone
Billeroy
Wilgaroon
Yandilla
Glenvue
Coronga Peak 416
Colossal
Sandy Camp
Coonamble
Karoo
Windera
El Trune
Gundooee
Narraway
Combara
Elura
Tindarey
Coronga Downs
Booroma
Buckinguy
Carlton
Emby
Gradgery
Cobar
Meryula
Florida
Yimkin
Glenhope
Tiverton
Girilambone
Glenanar
Canonba
Bourbah
Gular
Canbelego
Muriel
Wilga Downs
Birrimba
Reedy Corner
Pine Clump
Armatree
Hermidale
Nyngan
Mumblebone Plain
Haddon Rig
Curban
Lerida
Hillview
The Rookery
Iowabah
Mullengudgery
Warren
OXLEY
Collie
Gilgandra

© UNIVERSAL PUBLISHERS PTY LTD

CUNNINGHAM HWY

Mt Emlyn
Leyburn
Ellinthorp
Allora
Goomburra F.R.
Fassifern
Kalbar
Nth Tamborine
Southport
Surfers Paradise
Pratten
Hendon
Boonah
Nerang
Burleigh Heads
Massie
Mt Alford
Mudgeeraba
Beechmont
Coolangatta
Karara
Thane
Yangan
Rathdowney
Hillview
Binna Burra
Springbrook
Tweed Heads
Yuraraba
Graysholme
Warwick
Killarney
Mt Barney N.P.
Kingscliff
Gore
Loch Lomond
Elbow Valley
Legume
Mt Lindesay
Murwillumbah
Bogangar
Hastings Point
Pottsville Beach
QUEENSLAND
Cottonvale
Dalveen
Urbenville
Woodenbong
Grevillia
Wiangaree
Cawonga
Mullumbimby
Nimbin
Ocean Shores
Brunswick Heads
Burringbar
Bapaume
Thulimbah
Upper Tooloom
Eden Ck
Kyogle
Larnook
Cedar Point
Dunoon
Bangalow
Byron Bay
Pikedale
Stanthorpe
Amosfield
Old Bonalbo
Bonalbo
Doubtful Ck
Bentley
Clunes
Suffolk Park
Glen Aplin
Eukey
Theresa Ck
Mummulgum
Piora
Lismore
Alstonville
Lennox Head
Ballandean
Wyerba
Boonoo Boonoo
Drake
Tabulam
Casino
Ballina
Wallangarra
Mallanganee
Tatham
Coraki
Tenterfield
Steinbrook
Alice
Wyan
Rappville
Bungawalbin
Broadwater
Torrington
Stannum
Baryulgil
Whiporie
Woodburn
Evans Head
Strathbogie
Emmaville
Deepwater
Dundee
Coaldale
Harwood
Maclean
Iluka
Yamba
Wellingrove
Glen Innes
Bald Knob
Jackadgery
Copmanhurst
Lawrence
Cowper
Gulmarrad
Brooms Head
Sandon
Red Range
Newton Boyd
Grafton
South Grafton
Ulmarra
Tucabia
Glencoe
Dalmorton
Coutts Crossing
Pillar Valley
Minnie Water
Ben Lomond
Wandsworth
Nymboida
Kungala
Halfway Ck
Wooli
Llangothlin
Backwater
Kookabookra
Glenreagh
Corindi
Red Rock
Corindi Beach
Guyra
Aberfoyle
Clouds Ck
Nana Glen
Arrawarra
Woolgoolga
Black Mountain
Tyringham
Paddys Plain
Coramba
Emerald Beach
Moonee Beach
Sapphire Beach
North Dorrigo
Megan
Boambee
Coffs Harbour
Sawtell
Mitchells Flat
Dorrigo
Bonville
Armidale
Ebor
Wollomombi
Bellingen
Raleigh
Urunga
Jeogla
Kalang
Valla
Valla Beach
Uralla
Missabotti
Bowraville
Kentucky
Enmore
Comara
Burrapine
Macksville
Scotts Head
Eastlake
Taylors Arm
Warrell Ck
Stuarts Point
Bellbrook
Eungai Ck
South West Rocks
Walcha
Millbank
Willawarrin
Arakoon Trial Bay Gaol
Jerseyville
Moona Plains
Clybucca
Smithtown
Smoky Cape
Kangaroo Flat
Frederickton
Gladstone
Hat Head
Sherwood
Kempsey
Brackendale
Yarrowitch
Myrtle Scrub
Birdwood
Bellangry
Crescent Head
Kundabung
Pappinbarra
Pembrooke
Telegraph Point
Mt Seaview
Yarras
Long Flat
Port Macquarie
Nowendoc
Ellenborough
Byabarra
Wauchope
Lake Cathie
Comb80yne
Bonny Hills

NEW SOUTH WALES

CORAL SEA

TASMAN SEA

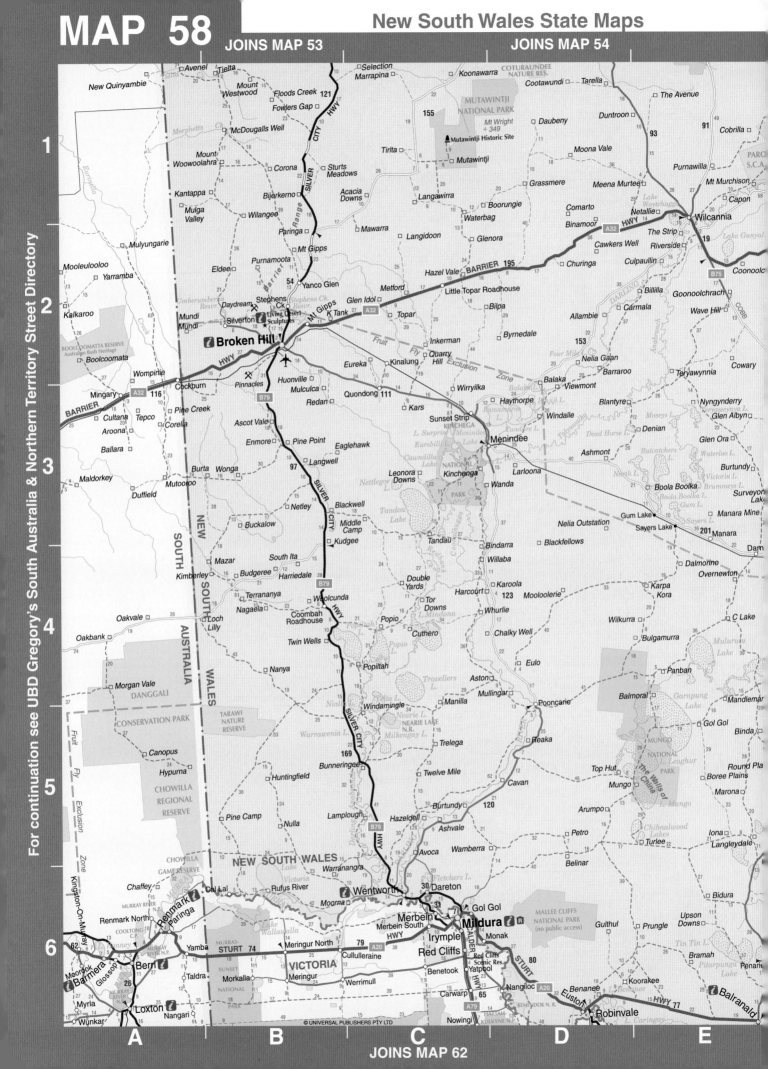

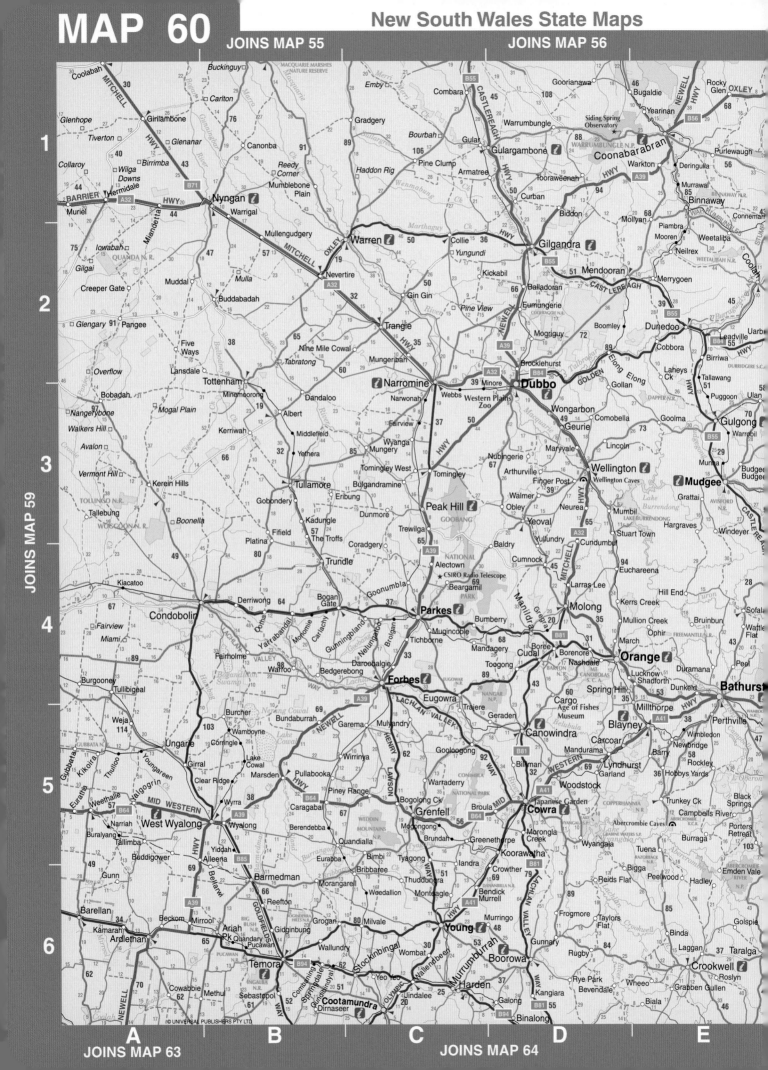

Scale 0 20 40 60 80km

1

2

3

4

5

6

F G H J K

© UNIVERSAL PUBLISHERS PTY LTD

Gunnedah, Mullaley, Curlewis, Carroll, Somerton, Moore, Woolbrook, Walcha, Willawarrin, Clybucca, Smithtown, Kempsey, Crescent Head, Kundabung, Gladstone, Frederickton, Sherwood, Bellangry, Pembrooke, Port Macquarie, Wauchope, Lake Cathie, Bonny Hills, North Haven, Laurieton, Kew, Lorne, Kendall, Johns River, Diamond Head, Moorland, Coopernook, Harrington, Manning Point, Crowdy Head, Old Bar, Taree, Wingham, Lansdowne, Tuncurry, Forster, Cape Hawke, Coomba, Elizabeth Beach, Bungwahl, Seal Rocks, Bulahdelah, Myall Lakes N.P., Port Stephens, Nelson Bay, Hawks Nest, Tea Gardens, Karuah, Raymond Terrace, Newcastle, Belmont, Swansea, Toronto, Morisset, Wyee, Budgewoi, Toukley, The Entrance, Wyong, Gosford, Woy Woy, Australian Reptile Park, Berowra, Hornsby, Mona Vale, Manly, SYDNEY, Parramatta, Liverpool, Penrith, Richmond, Windsor, Katoomba, Lithgow, Wallerawang, Portland, Blackheath, Springwood, Camden, Campbelltown, Appin, Picton, Mittagong, Bowral, Moss Vale, Wollongong, Port Kembla, Dapto, Shellharbour, Thirroul, Robertson, Exeter

Tamworth, Werris Ck, Quirindi, Murrurundi, Scone, Muswellbrook, Aberdeen, Denman, Merriwa, Singleton, Cessnock, Kurri Kurri, Maitland, Dungog, Gloucester, Stroud, Nabiac, Gresford, Clarence Town, Paterson

MAP 62

New South Wales State Maps

JOINS MAP 58

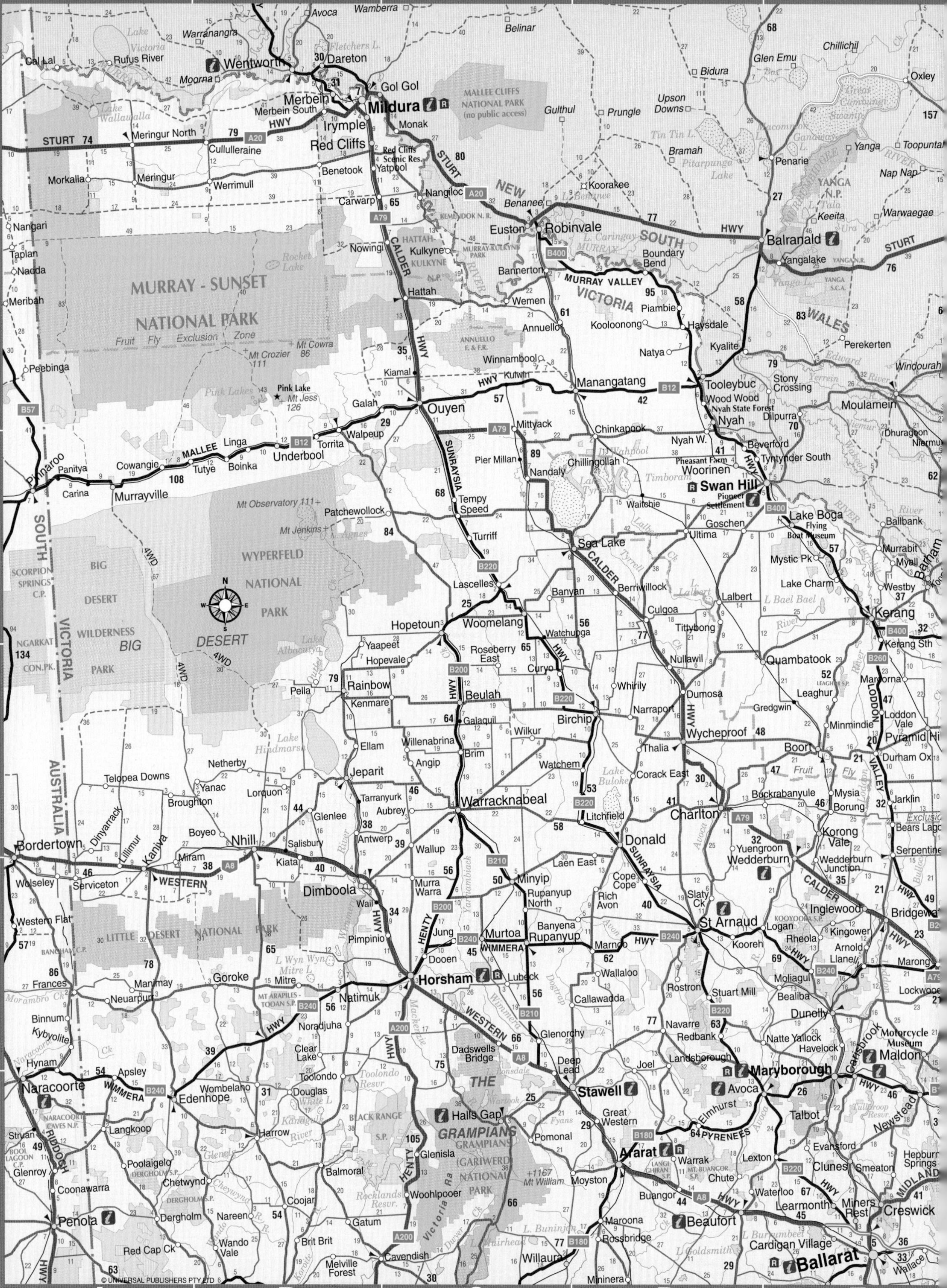

For continuation see UBD Gregory's South Australia & Northern Territory Street Directory

MURRAY - SUNSET NATIONAL PARK
Fruit Fly Exclusion Zone

WYPERFELD NATIONAL PARK

BIG DESERT WILDERNESS PARK

BIG DESERT

SCORPION SPRINGS C.P.

NGARKAT CON. PK.

LITTLE DESERT NATIONAL PARK

VICTORIA

SOUTH AUSTRALIA

NEW SOUTH WALES

MALLEE CLIFFS NATIONAL PARK (no public access)

MURRAY-KULKYNE PARK

YANGA N.P.

YANGA S.C.A.

THE GRAMPIANS (GARIWERD) NATIONAL PARK

NARACOORTE CAVES N.P.

Places (selection): Cal Lal, Rufus River, Warranangra, Avoca, Wamberra, Belinar, Glen Emu, Chillichil, Oxley, Wentworth, Dareton, Gol Gol, Bidura, Upson Downs, Penarie, Yanga, Nap Nap, Toopunta, Meringur North, Merbein, Merbein South, Irymple, Mildura, Monak, Red Cliffs, Yatpool, Benetook, Carwarp, Nangiloc, Koorakee, Prungle, Nangari, Taplan, Nadda, Meribah, Euston, Robinvale, Benanee, Boundary Bend, Balranald, Yangalake, Morkalla, Meringur, Werrimull, Nowingi, Hattah, Bannerton, Wemen, Piambie, Haysdale, Kyalite, Perekerten, Windourah, Peebinga, Annuello, Kooloonong, Natya, Manangatang, Tooleybuc, Stony Crossing, Moulamein, Kiamal, Kulwin, Wood Wood, Nyah, Dilpurra, Dhuragoon, Niermu, Galah, Ouyen, Mittyack, Chinkapook, Nyah W., Beverford, Tyntynder South, Woorinen, Pinnaroo, Cowangie, Linga, Underbool, Torrita, Walpeup, Pier Millan, Nandaly, Chillingollah, Swan Hill, Lake Boga, Ballbank, Murrabit, Myall, Westby, Murrayville, Carina, Panitya, Tutye, Boinka, Tempy, Speed, Waitchie, Goschen, Ultima, Mystic Pk, Lake Charm, Kerang, Patchewollock, Turriff, Sea Lake, Berriwillock, Lalbert, Quambatook, Kerang Sth, Hopetoun, Woomelang, Banyan, Watchupga, Culgoa, Tittybong, Leaghur, Marorna, Yaapeet, Roseberry East, Curyo, Whirily, Narraport, Dumosa, Gredgwin, Minmindie, Loddon Vale, Pyramid Hill, Hopevale, Rainbow, Kenmare, Beulah, Galaquil, Wilkur, Birchip, Wycheproof, Boort, Durham Ox, Pella, Ellam, Willenabrina, Brim, Watchem, Thalia, Corack East, Buckrabanyule, Mysia, Borung, Jarklin, Netherby, Telopea Downs, Yanac, Lorquon, Jeparit, Tarranyurk, Aubrey, Warracknabeal, Litchfield, Charlton, Korong Vale, Serpentine, Broughton, Boyeo, Glenlee, Antwerp, Wallup, Laen East, Donald, Wedderburn, Yuengroon, Wedderburn Junction, Bordertown, Dinyarrack, Lillimur, Kaniva, Miram, Kiata, Nhill, Salisbury, Murra Warra, Minyip, Rupanyup North, Rich Avon, Cope Cope, Slaty Ck, Inglewood, Bridgewa, Wolseley, Serviceton, WESTERN HWY, Dimboola, Wail, Jung, Murtoa, Rupanyup, Marnoo, St Arnaud, Kooreh, Rheola, Arnold, Llanelly, Marong, Western Flat, BANGHAM C.P., Pimpinio, Dooen, Lubeck, Wallaloo, Rostron, Stuart Mill, Moliagul, Lockwoo, Frances, Manimay, Goroke, Mitre, Horsham, Callawadda, Navarre, Redbank, Bealiba, Dunolly, Binnum, Kybybolite, Neuarpur, Natimuk, Noradjuha, Glenorchy, Landsborough, Natte Yallock, Havelock, Maldon, Hynam, Apsley, Wombelano, Douglas, Clear Lake, Dadswells Bridge, Deep Lead, Joel, Elmhurst, Avoca, Talbot, Naracoorte, Edenhope, Harrow, Toolondo, Stawell, Great Western, Pomonal, Amphitheatre, Maryborough, Clunes, Smeaton, Struan, Langkoop, Chetwynd, Nareen, Balmoral, Halls Gap, Glenisla, Ararat, Warrak, Moyston, Buangor, Waterloo, Learmonth, Miners Rest, Creswick, Penola, Coonawarra, Glenroy, Dergholm, Coojar, Gatum, Woohlpooer, Mininera, Beaufort, Cardigan Village, Ballarat, Red Cap Ck, Wando Vale, Brit Brit, Melville Forest, Cavendish, Willaura, Maroona, Rossbridge

© UNIVERSAL PUBLISHERS PTY LTD

Grid columns: A B C D E
Grid rows: 1 2 3 4 5 6

Scale
0   20   40   60   80km

1

2

3

4

5

6

F   G   H   J   K

© UNIVERSAL PUBLISHERS PTY LTD

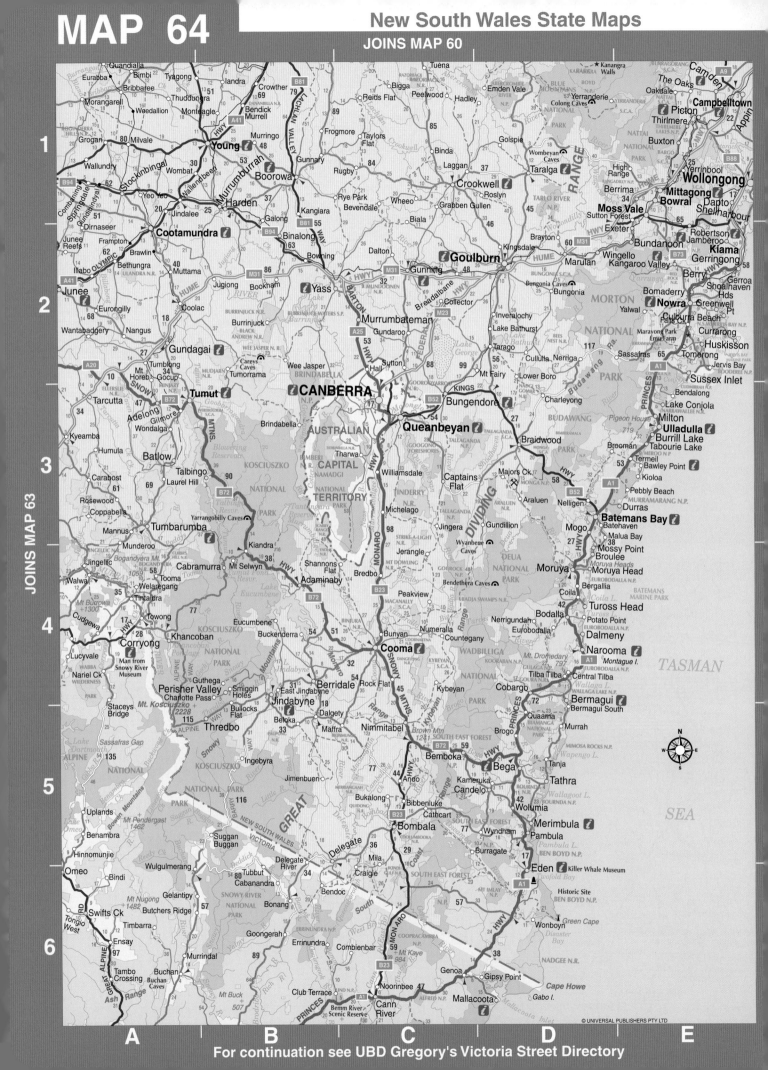

MAP 64
New South Wales State Maps
JOINS MAP 60

Blue Mile Pathway, Wollongong. Destination NSW.

BATEMANS BAY

LOCATION
On the Princes Hwy, 280km south of Sydney

POPULATION
11 300

NRMA ROAD SERVICE
Ph: 13 11 22

A bustling and vibrant holiday resort, Batemans Bay lies at the mouth of the Clyde River in the centre of the New South Wales south coast. It is a favourite spot for holiday makers from across New South Wales, including Canberra; despite being 152 kilometres away, it is the closest beach to the national capital. Families flock to Batemans Bay for its clean uncrowded beaches with views of small tree-covered islands and for the rivers, lakes, fishing and fossicking. South of Batemans Bay, the old gold-mining region of Mogo has many attractions, including Mogo Zoo and The Original Gold Rush Colony, which recreates a 19th century gold town.

ACCOMMODATION GUIDE

Abel Tasman Motel 2 **G2**
Araluen Motor Lodge 2 **G2**
Argyle Terrace Motor Inn 1 **G11**
Batemans Bay Marina Resort 1 **K13**
Bay Breeze Motel 1 **E9**
Bayside Motel 1 **H12**
Bayview Hotel 1 **E9**
Beach Drive Motel 1 **G11**
BIG4 Batemans Bay at Easts Riverside Holiday Park 1 **G7**
BIG4 Batemans Bay Beach Resort 1 **M17**
Bridge Motel 1 **D7**
Caseys Beach Holiday Park 2 **M6**
Clyde View Holiday Park 2 **J3**
Coachhouse Marina Resort 1 **K14**
Country Comfort 1 **G6**
Del Costa Motel 1 **G11**
Edgewater Gardens Motel 2 **L5**
Esplanade Motel 1 **F9**
Lakesea Caravan Park 1 **N1**
Lincoln Downs Resort 1 **H5**
Mariners On The Waterfront 1 **E9**
Pleasurelea Tourist Resort 2 **M7**
Rio Rita Caravan Park 1 **G7**
Shady Willows Holiday Park 1 **E13**
Sunseeker Motor Inn 1 **D13**

FACILITIES & ATTRACTIONS

Albert Ryan Park 1 **E10**
Batehaven Post Office 2 **H3**
Batemans Bay Post Office 1 **E9**
Batemans Bay Sailing Club 1 **M15**
Batemans Bay Service Centre 1 **D10**
Batemans Bay Soldiers RSL Club 1 **E10**
Birdland Animal Park 1 **L16**
Bowling Club 1 **D9**
Catalina Country Club Golf Course 1 **J14**
Corrigans Beach Reserve 2 **G1**
Eurobodalla Regional Botanic Gardens 1 **A18**
Firegaze Lookout 1 **B18**
Fishing Charters 1 **J12**
Folders Hill Lookout 1 **E4**
Holmes Lookout 1 **F1**
Hospital 1 **F12**
Keith & Mavis Smith Park 1 **J15**
Korner Park 1 **F7**
Mackay Park 1 **C9**
Merinda River Cruises 1 **E8**
Mini Golf 1 **C9**
Mogo Zoo 2 **E15**
Murramarang Aboriginal Area 1 **N1**
NRMA 1 **E10**
Observation Head Lookout 2 **L2**
Oyster Shed 1 **E4**
Rotary Park 1 **H11**
Stockland Batemans Bay 1 **D8**
Swimming Pool 1 **C10**
ZZ7UR

STREETS

Albatross Rd 1 E18
Angophora Pl 2 D3
Anne St 2 J5
Annett St 2 D14
Apple Berry Pl 1 H4
Ascension Wy 2 H8
Avalon St 1 L14
Banks Pl 2 L10
Barbara Cr 2 N11
Bass St 2 K15
Batehaven Rd 2 K4
Bateman St 2 D14
Batemans Rd 1 H1
Batman Pl 2 K9
Bavarde Av 1 F13
Bayridge Dr 1 F1
Bay View St 2 N16
Bayview St 1 K6
Beach Rd
  Batehaven 2 G2
  Batemans Bay 1 F10
  Catalina 1 J13
  Denhams Beach 2 N7
  Sunshine Bay 2 N7
  Surf Beach 2 M14
Beauty Cr 1 K4
Beechwood Ct 2 N7
Bellbird Cl 1 L4
Bent St 1 D10
Bernadette Bvd 2 H4
Berrima Pde 1 K3
Berrima St 2 D1
Berry Pl 2 K13
Billabong Pl 2 N15
Bimbimbie Pl 2 B18
Blaxland Cr 2 L9
Blaxland Ct 2 L9
Bligh St 2 J14
Bluemoor Rd 1 J1
Braidwood Rd 1 F2
Bronte Cr 2 M5
Brooke Wy 2 K11
Brushbox Pl 2 E7
Buckenboura Rd 2 A17
Burkes La 2 C13
Burkes Wy
  Denhams Beach 2 L12
  Surf Beach 2 L12
Burrawang Cr 2 N8
Burri Palm Wy 1 M1
Caley Pl 2 L9
Calga Cr 2 E2
Calton Rd 2 K5
Camp St 1 D11
Canning Cr 2 K8
Cassia Pl 2 D3
Catalina Dr 2 E2
Catlin Av 1 K15
Charles St 2 D15
Christopher Cr 2 G5
Church St 2 B16
Clare Cr 2 G5
Clyde Rd 1 J1
Clyde St 1 D7
Clyde River Bridge 1 E6
Commercial La 1 D10
Cook Av 2 K14
Correa Pl 2 C4

Corrigan Cr 2 H3
Cors Pde 1 N1
Country Club Dr
  Catalina 1 G18
  Catalina 2 A1
Cox Pl 2 L11
Crag Rd 2 H3
Cranbrook Rd 1 B16
Crane Ct 2 B1
Crinum Pl 2 D4
Crosby Dr
  Batehaven 2 E8
  Batehaven 2 H9
Crown St 1 D12
Crystal La 1 H1
Cullendulla Dr 1 N1
Cunningham Cl 2 K7
Cunningham Cr 2 K7
Curtis Rd 2 D8
Dampier Pl 2 K8
David Av 2 K5
Denham Av 2 M11
Denise Dr 2 P17
Derribong Av 1 K18
Dhurga Wy 2 C16
Dilkira Cl 1 L6
Dog Trap Rd 2 E13
Dolphin Av 1 K14
Domonic Dr 2 H4
Drinnan Cl 2 J15
Dunns Creek Rd 2 H18
Edgewood Cl 2 M13
Edgewood Pl 2 M13
Edward Rd
  Batehaven 2 G5
  Sunshine Bay 2 G5
Enterprise La 2 E8
Eric Fenning Dr 2 J13
Explorers Wy 2 L13
Eyre Pl 2 L8
Fairway Vw 1 H16
Figtree Cl 2 H16
Flinders Wy 2 L14
Flora Cr 1 E10
Flora Ct 1 E10
Foam St 1 K7
Freycinet Dr
  Sunshine Bay 2 J12
  Sunshine Bay 2 K11
Gannet Pl 2 A3
George Bass Dr
  Batehaven 2 F6
  Sunshine Bay 2 F6
  Surf Beach 2 J13
  Surf Beach 2 N17
Gibson Pl 2 J7
Giles Pl 2 L9
Glenella Rd
  Batehaven 2 A6
  Batemans Bay 1 B17
  Catalina 2 A6
Golf Links Dr 1 H12
Gosse Pl 2 K9
Grandfathers
  Gully Rd 2 P17
Grantham Rd 2 J6
Gray Pl 2 L8
Graydon Av 2 M12

Greendale Cl 2 G10
Gregory St 1 E14
Gull Cl 1 H17
Guy La 1 D11
Guy St 1 D11
Hakea Pl 2 D3
Hanging Rock Pl 1 K15
Hanna Pl 1 G1
Hartog Pl 2 J9
Haven Pl 2 H6
Hawks Nest Pl 1 L5
Heradale Pde 1 G12
Herarde St 1 G11
Heron Rd 1 F18
High St 1 F12
Highland Av 2 G14
High View Av 2 N16
Hill St 1 D10
Hilltop Cr 2 L16
Hillview Pl 2 M8
Hoya Pl 2 D4
Hughes St 1 E14
Hume Ct 2 M9
Hume Rd
  Denhams Beach 2 L12
  Sunshine Bay 2 L7
  Surf Beach 2 L12
Hunter Pl 2 K10
Iandra Rd 1 M5
Ibis Pl 2 B1
Irene Av 2 H4
Ison St 2 B16
James St
  Batehaven 2 J1
  Mogo 2 E15
Jamie Cr 2 J1
Janet Bvd 2 J1
Jardine Rd 2 K10
Jedel Dr 2 B8
Jenny Tce 2 J2
Jerupa Cl 2 M17
John St
  Batehaven 2 L5
  Mogo 2 D14
John Forrest Pl 2 K9
John Oxley Cr 2 K7
Johnson Pl 2 L13
Johny Esp 2 J2
Joseph St 2 H4
Joy Cr 2 J2
Julia Rd 2 J2
Karoola Cr 1 K3
Kauzal Cr 2 H16
Kennedy Cr 2 N10
Kerang St 1 K2
Kings Hwy 1 F1
Kylie Cr 1 C13
Lattas Point Rd
  Batemans Bay 1 A7
  Batemans Bay 1 B17
Law La 2 F9
Lawson Pl 2 L11
Leichardt Pl 2 K8
Leigh St 1 F13
Leslie Pl 2 L7
Lincoln Cr 1 G6
Lisa Pl 2 L6
Lockyersleigh Av 2 J3

Lord Pl 1 G6
Luks Wy 2 H7
Mcleod St
  North Batemans Bay 1 H7
  Surfside 1 H7
Marina Av 1 K3
Marjorie Cr 2 K4
Marlin Av 1 K14
Matthew Pde 2 G3
Maulbrooks Rd 2 B18
Mawson Pl 2 K10
Melaleuca Cr 2 C4
Miller St 1 H12
Milton Rd 1 K1
Mogo St
  Mogo 2 A16
  Mogo 2 A17
Mogo Trig Rd 2 C13
Mundarra Wy
  North Batemans Bay 1 J7
  Surfside 1 J7
Museum Pl 1 E11
Myamba Pde 1 K7
Newth Pl 2 N17
North St 1 D8
Northside Cl 1 J1
Oakwood Wy 2 E5
Observation Av 2 K2
Ocean Av 2 L16
Ocean Cl 2 L16
Ocean Rd 2 J4
Old Grandfathers
  Pit Rd 2 P18
Old Mossy
  Point Rd 2 C18
Old Princes Hwy 1 E13
Old Punt Rd 1 E6
Orient St 1 D11
Osprey Pl 1 L4
Oxley Pl 2 K8
Pacific Rd 2 K15
Pacific St 1 F13
Palana St 1 K5
Palm Pl 1 K3
Park St 2 B17
Parker Av 2 M15
Paul Pl 2 H5
Pelsart Av 2 K12
Penguin Pl 2 A2
Peninsula Dr
  North Batemans Bay 1 G6
  Surfside 1 G6
Penthouse Pl 1 F5
Perry La 1 E8
Perry St 1 D9
Peter Cr 2 K5
Picnic Rd 1 N1
Pine St 2 J4
Pleasurelea Dr 2 N8
Poole Pl 2 L10
Princes Hwy
  Batemans Bay 1 C11
  Batemans Bay 1 C17
  Mogo 2 B18
  North Batemans Bay 1 F6
  Surfside 1 F6
Protea Pl 2 C4
Queen St 2 B17

Ridge Av 2 G18
Ridge St 1 J18
Riverview Cr 1 J17
Runnyford Rd 2 C13
Russell La 1 E14
Russell St 1 E14
Sanctuary Pl 1 K17
Sandpiper Pl 2 B2
Sawmill Rd 2 L18
Sea St 1 J17
Sharon Rd 1 C14
Sheila St 2 J5
Short St
  Batemans Bay 1 F11
  Mogo 2 A14
Silverdell Pl 2 H13
Sorrel Pl 2 E4
South St 1 E13
Spotted Gum Pl 1 G4
Stuart Pl 2 K8
Sturt Pl 2 M9
Sunset St 1 K4
Sunshine Bay Rd 2 J8
Tallgums Wy 2 H18
Tasman St 2 K14
Tench St 2 K4
The Outlook Rd 1 K2
The Ridge Rd
  Batemans Bay 2 A11
  Mogo 2 A11
  Surf Beach 2 F15
The Vista 1 K7
Thomas Mitchell Cr 2 L8
Throsby Cr 2 K11
Timbara Cr 1 J7
Timber Wy
  Surf Beach 2 K16
  Surf Beach 2 M16
Tomakin Rd 2 D16
Towrang Av 2 H14
Tuna St 1 L14
Valley Rd
  Denhams Beach 2 M9
  Sunshine Bay 2 M9
Vesper St 1 D13
Vetich St 2 C15
Victor Cct 2 F8
View St 2 J4
Vista Av 2 B3
Wagtail Cr 2 H6
Wallarah St 1 L5
Wallaringa St 1 K7
Waterson Dr 2 G12
Wattle Cr 2 J4
Wentworth Av 2 K10
Wharf Rd 1 F7
White Sands Pl
  Denhams Beach 2 M13
  Surf Beach 2 M13
Wills Cr 2 L11
Wimbie St 2 N16
Woodlot Pl 2 E7
Woodrush Rd 1 K1
Wray St 1 E5
Yarrabee Dr 2 B5

MAP 1 BATEMANS BAY

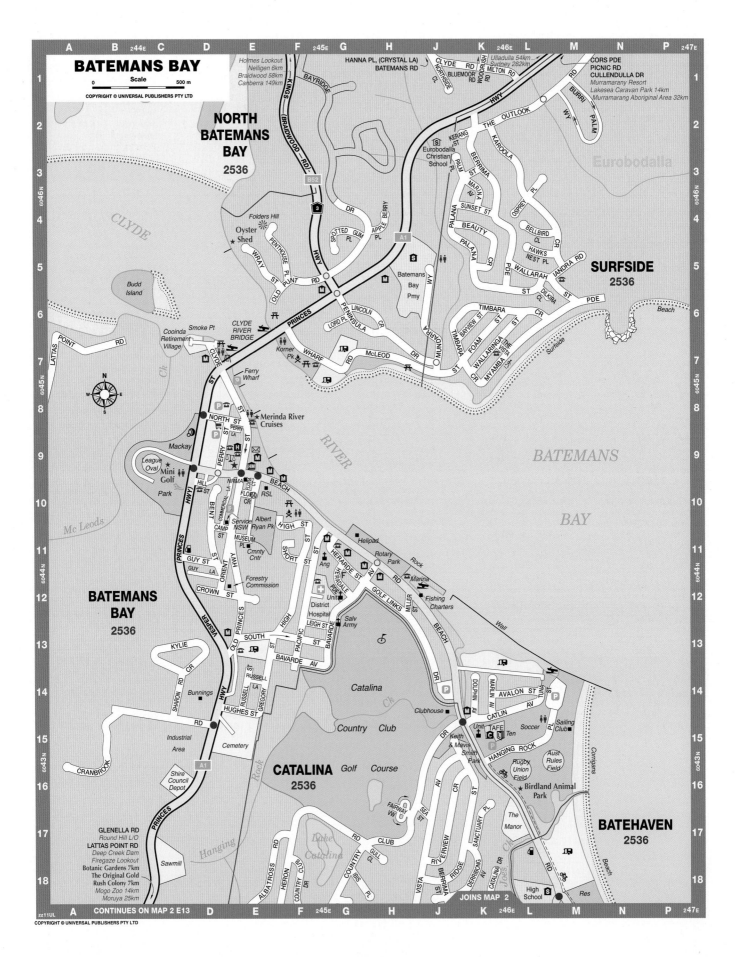

BATEMANS BAY

Scale 0 — 500 m

COPYRIGHT © UNIVERSAL PUBLISHERS PTY LTD

NORTH BATEMANS BAY 2536

SURFSIDE 2536

Eurobodalla

BATEMANS BAY

BAY

BATEMANS BAY 2536

CATALINA 2536

BATEHAVEN 2536

GLENELLA RD
Round Hill L/O
LATTAS POINT RD
Deep Creek Dam
Firegaze Lookout
Botanic Gardens 7km
The Original Gold
Rush Colony 7km
Mogo Zoo 14km
Moruya 25km

HANNA PL, (CRYSTAL LA)
BATEMANS RD

Holmes Lookout
Nelligen 6km
Braidwood 58km
Canberra 149km

Ulladulla 54km
Sydney 282km

CORS PDE
PICNIC RD
CULLENDULLA DR
Murramarang Resort
Lakesea Caravan Park 14km
Murramarang Aboriginal Area 32km

CONTINUES ON MAP 2 E13

JOINS MAP 2

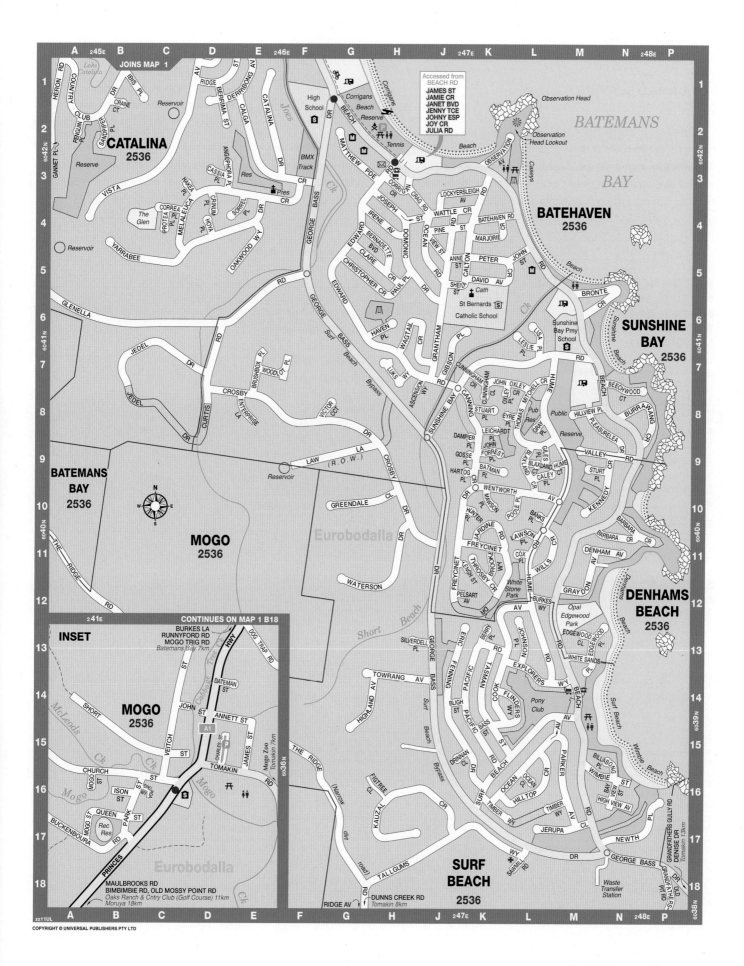

BEGA

LOCATION
On the Princes Hwy
431km south of Sydney
POPULATION
4500
NRMA ROAD SERVICE
Ph: 13 11 22

VISITOR INFORMATION
Bega Tourist Information Centre
Bega Cheese Heritage Centre
Lagoon St,
Ph: (02) 6491 7645
www.sapphirecoast.com.au
www.begacheese.com.au

This picturesque town is strategically placed approximately 18 kilometres inland on the Bega River, and 7 kilometres south of the junction of the Princes and Snowy Mountains Highways linking Sydney, Canberra and Melbourne. Surf and snow enthusiasts may like to test the claim that when staying in Bega it is possible to snow ski and ride the waves on the same day. First settled by farmers and timber-cutters in the 1830's, the rich dairying land of the Bega Valley has long been famous for producing fine quality cheeses.

ACCOMMODATION GUIDE
Bank Hotel **H8**
Bega Caravan Park **G14**
Bega Downs Motel **H10**
Bega Motel **G12**
Bega South Town Motor Inn **G14**
Bega Village Motor Inn **H9**
Commercial Hotel **H8**
Grand Hotel **G8**

FACILITIES & ATTRACTIONS
Apex Park **E8**
Bega Cheese Heritage Centre **D5**
Bega Country Club **P7**
Bega Park **J10**
Bega Pioneers Museum **H7**
Bega RSL Club **H9**

Bega Showground **K10**
Bega Sportsground **D8**
Bega Tourist Information Centre **D5**
Bega Valley Regional Art Gallery **H9**
Bowling Club **J8**
Council Office **H9**
Hospital **N15**
Lions Park **E11**
Littleton Gardens **H9**
Littleton House **K8**
NRMA **H9**
Post Office **H8**
Racecourse **M6**
Riverside Park **C6**
Sapphire Marketplace **H9**
Swimming Pool **J10**
Valley Field Sportsground **C7**
ZZ7UR

STREETS

Albert St **J11**
Anderson Dr **C4**
Angle St **B9**
Angledale Rd **G3**
Applegum Cl **E17**
Auckland St **F15**
Auckland St **G13**
Baker St **F8**
Ballima Ct **F14**
Barrack St **H12**
Bega St **B6**
Bega St **D7**
Belmore St **H11**
Bishops La **H8**
Blacket La **L12**
Blomfield Av **E12**
Bodalla Rd **G4**
Boundary Rd **H17**
Boundary St **A16**
Bridge St **C4**
Bridge St **J5**
Bridle Pl **L15**
Brogo St **D10**
Broulee St **G4**
Buckajo Rd **A8**
Buckajo Rd **A12**
Bunyarra Dr **K13**
Burgess Pl **M13**
Canning St **J8**
Carp St **G8**
Carp St **J8**

Charlotte St **C14**
Charlotte St **F15**
Charlotte St **H15**
Church St **H8**
Cloverdale La **A3**
Coopers Gully Rd **A2**
Corridgeree Rd **L2**
Cross St **G12**
Daisy Hill Rd **A12**
Dandar Rd **L13**
Deborah Cr **G14**
Denison Cl **M15**
Douglas St **J10**
Dowling St **E9**
Drain St **E4**
East St **J17**
East St **L9**
Eden St **F11**
Elbe St **F14**
Elliot La **K8**
Fairview St **C10**
Finucanes La **F18**
Game Cr **H13**
Garnet St **J12**
Gipps St **H10**
Girraween Cr **G11**
Glebe Av **L12**
Glen Mia Dr **K15**
Gloucester St **K9**
Goldberg Pl **G14**
Gordon St **K9**

Gowing Av **E11**
Gowing La **H8**
Gregory Wy **G14**
Harry Scanes Av **M15**
Hart Cr **G13**
Healy St **C4**
Heath St **F9**
Hergenhans La **G1**
High St **C9**
Hill St **F8**
Howard Av **K14**
Jasper St **C4**
John St **B4**
Kielpa Pl **K14**
Kirkland Av **E8**
Kirkland Cr **D9**
Koma Cct **K16**
Koolgarra Dr **F12**
Kooringal Pl **A8**
Kooringal Pl **C8**
Lagoon St **C5**
Lagoon St **D6**
Lagoon St **H6**
Laws Dr **H13**
Little Bega La **D7**
Little Bega St **K8**
Little Church St **H10**
Loftus St **H11**
Lucas La **H8**
Lynjohn Dr **G14**
Mckee Dr **F11**

Maher St **E13**
Manam Rd **P3**
Manning St **H12**
Mecklenberg St **F14**
Meringo St **E12**
Millbank Wy **J13**
Millowine La **K7**
Miners Cl **A2**
Minyama Pde **F13**
Moore Wren Rd **P7**
Mount Pleasant Rd **A4**
Nelson St **F10**
Newtown Rd **F13**
Norman Av **C9**
Nullica Rd **P3**
Old Princes Hwy **A2**
Parbery Cr **D8**
Park La **J11**
Park St **J13**
Parker St **J10**
Parrabel St **C3**
Peden St **G9**
Poplar Av **C7**
Princes Hwy **B3**
Princes Hwy **D11**
Prospect St **E13**
Ravenswood St **D15**
Rawlinson St **C12**
Rawlinson St **G13**
Redgum Cl **F15**
Ridge St **A4**

Rose St **L12**
Salway Cl **K14**
Sattler St **J9**
Spindler St **F12**
Springvale Cl **A12**
Stevenson St **E10**
Swan St **F8**
Taronga Cr **M13**
Tarraganda La **M9**
Tarraganda La **P3**
Tathra Rd **L11**
Thawa Cl **H13**
Union St **J9**
Upper St **F9**
Valley St **C11**
Valley St **D4**
Victoria St **G12**
Virginia Dr **N14**
Walker St **F9**
Wallace St **F10**
Watson St **F10**
Weerona Cr **F14**
West St **B3**
West St **B5**
Willow Ct **H14**
Wumbara Cl **J14**
Yuin Pl **L16**
Zingel Pl **H9**

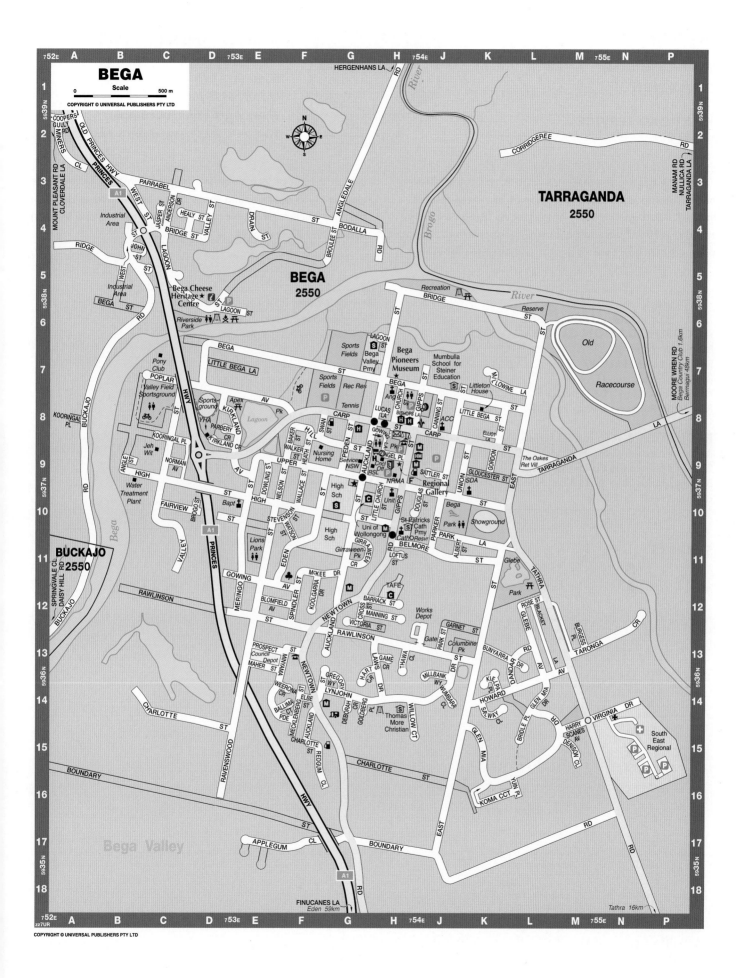

BERMAGUI

LOCATION
Off the Princes Hwy
378km south of Sydney

POPULATION
1550

NRMA ROAD SERVICE
Ph: 13 11 22

VISITOR INFORMATION

Bermagui Visitor Information Centre
Bunga St
Ph: (02) 6493 3054
www.visitbermagui.com.au

Water activities are the main drawcard at this coastal New South Wales town, located nine kilometres off the Princes Highway. Bermagui has been famous for its big game fishing since the 1930's when author Zane Grey popularised the sport. Today, charter boats take big game and deep sea fishermen out in pursuit of black marlin and yellow fin tuna. Diving boat charters also operate, and shore diving is a well-rewarded pastime. Surfers have several beaches to choose from, including Beares and Mooreheads.

ACCOMMODATION GUIDE

Beachview Motel **J6**
Bermagui Beach Hotel **K6**
Bermagui Motor Inn **J7**
Harbourview Motel **G6**
Reflections Bermagui Holiday Park **K6**

FACILITIES & ATTRACTIONS

Bermagui Country Club **H7**
Bermagui Fishermans Co-op **G6**
Bermagui Indoor Sports Stadium **H7**
Bermagui River Park **D5**

Bermagui Visitor Information Centre **J7**
Bermagui War Memorial **L5**
Blue Swimming Pool **L7**
Bowling Club **H7**
Bruce Steer Swimming Pool **G5**
Dickinson Park **J6**
Dickinson Recreation Reserve **H7**
Edgar Jaggers Reserve **G12**
Library **J7**
Old River Wharf Reserve **D5**
Post Office **J6**
Spooner Park **K7**
ZZ7UR

STREETS

Alexander Dr **B13**
Barragoot La **K7**
Barragoot St **K7**
Beare St **K8**
Bent St **F7**
Bleakley St **G10**
Blue Wren Pl **E7**
Bridge St **E6**
Bunga St **H10**
Callow Pl **K8**
Carnago St **G7**
Cobargo St **E4**
Corunna St **K7**
Dickinson Av **J9**
Dromedary Ct **E8**
Engstrom Cl **D14**
Fairway Ct **D12**
George La **C2**
George St **C2**
Ginn St **D5**
Golf Rd **G9**
Guboo Pl **D7**
Hart St **D8**
Hay St **E7**
Henry St **D3**
Hill St **D6**
Jerimbut St **K8**
Jones La **E6**
Keating Dr **D1**
Koerber St **H10**
Lagoon St **C2**
Lakeview Ct **C11**
Lamont St **E6**
Lamont St **J6**
Lindo St **D4**
Main Rd **H8**

Mill St **J8**
Monarch St **D8**
Montague St **K6**
Moorhead St **K7**
Mumbulla St **G10**
Murrah St **C7**
Murrah St **J7**
Murunna St **L7**
Narira St **E4**
Nutleys Creek Rd **B12**
Ocean View Dr **B12**
Pacific St **L7**
Paraboon Dr **J9**
Parbery Av **C8**
Pine Dr **E14**
River Rd **B3**
Scenic Dr **K8**
Scenic Dr **L6**
Sea View Ct **C12**
Sherwood Rd **F14**
Sinclair St **G10**
Songlark St **C8**
South River Rd **B5**
Strudwicks Rd **H14**
Tathra Bermagui Rd **G13**
Tuross La **G7**
Tuross St **H7**
Wagonga St **E4**
Wallaga St **J7**
Wallaga Lake Rd **D2**
Wapengo St **E4**
Wattle St **E7**
Welsh St **G9**
West St **D8**
Wills St **C2**
Young St **J7**

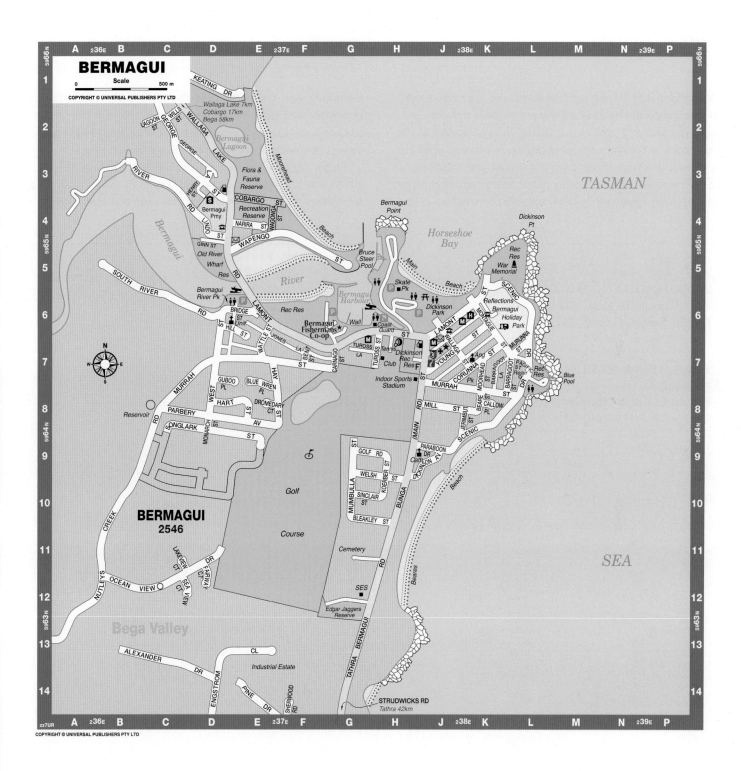

BERMAGUI

Scale
0 — 500 m

COPYRIGHT © UNIVERSAL PUBLISHERS PTY LTD

TASMAN

SEA

BERMAGUI
2546

Bega Valley

Golf
Course

Horseshoe
Bay

Bermagui
Lagoon

Bermagui
Harbour

Dickinson
Pt

Wallaga Lake 7km
Cobargo 17km
Bega 58km

Flora &
Fauna
Reserve

Bermagui
Point

Bruce
Steer
Pool

Dickinson Park

Rec
Res

War
Memorial

Reflections
Bermagui
Holiday
Park

Blue
Pool

Skate
Pk

Coast
Guard

Bermagui
Fishermans
Co-op

Wall

Tennis
Club

Dickinson
Rec
Res

Indoor Sports
Stadium

Bermagui
River Pk

Rec Res

Old River
Wharf Res

Bermagui Pmy

COBARGO

Recreation
Reserve

SES

Cemetery

Edgar Jaggers
Reserve

Industrial Estate

STRUDWICKS RD
Tathra 42km

KEATING DR

Reservoir

LAGOON ST
GEORGE
GE WILLS ST
WALLAGA LAKE
GEORGE
HENRY RD
LINDO
RIVER
SOUTH RIVER RD
MURRAH RD
PARBERY
SONGLARK
WEST ST
MONARCH
HART
GUBOO PL
BLUE WREN PL
DROMEDARY CT
AV
SEA VIEW CT
FAIRWAY
LAKEVIEW CT
OCEAN VIEW
NUTLEYS
CREEK RD
ALEXANDER DR
ENGSTROM
PINE DR
SHERWOOD RD
CL

GINN ST
NARIRA ST
WAPENGO
WAGONGA ST
Moorhead
Beach
LAMONT ST
BRIDGE ST
HILL ST
WATTLE ST
JONES
BENT ST
CARNAGO
TUROSS ST
TUROSS LA
MUMBULLA ST
GOLF RD
WELSH ST
SINCLAIR ST
BLEAKLEY ST
KOERBER ST
BUNGA ST
MILL
MAIN RD
MURRAH ST
PARABOON DR
CATKINSON A
Catti.on
SCENIC
JERIMBUT
BEARE ST
CALLOW PL
MOORHEAD ST
Beares
Beach
Beach
TATHRA BERMAGUI RD

St Unit

LAMONT ST
YOUNG ST
WALLAGA
MONTAGUE ST
CORUNNA ST
Ang
Pk
BARRAGOOT LA
BARRAGOOT
MURUNNA
PACIFIC DR
Rec
Res
Reservr
SCENIC DR

Bermagui

Bega Valley

Main

Beach

COPYRIGHT © UNIVERSAL PUBLISHERS PTY LTD
zz7UR

BERRIMA

LOCATION
Off the Hume Hwy, 118km south of Sydney
POPULATION
600
NRMA ROAD SERVICE
Ph: 13 11 22

VISITOR INFORMATION
Berrima Courthouse Museum
Wilshire St
Ph: (02) 4877 1505
www.southern-highlands.com.au

Watered by the Wingecarribee River, the Berrima region of the Southern Highlands attracted settlers moving up from the Sydney Plains in the 1820's. In expectation of the new town becoming a regional centre, it was equipped with an impressive sandstone courthouse and matching gaol as well as other imposing public and private buildings. The first inn appeared in 1834, followed by the Surveyor

General a year later – by 1843 there were six public houses. However, when the railway bypassed Berrima in the 1860's the town stopped growing and became a sleepy backwater, almost perfectly preserved as a village of that time.

Today, the courthouse, gaol and Surveyor General Inn are all still there, as well as plenty of quaint craft shops, just waiting for visitors to explore, relive the past and relax over a meal.

ACCOMMODATION GUIDE
Berrima Bakehouse Motel **G8**
Berrima Camping Ground **E6**
Surveyor General Inn **F8**

FACILITIES & ATTRACTIONS
Berrima Courthouse **G7**
Berrima Courthouse Museum **F7**
Berrima District Museum **E8**

Berrima Old Gaol **F7**
Berrima Sportsground **D6**
Harpers Mansion **H6**
Information Centre Berrima Courthouse Museum **G7**
Joadja Winery **J1**
Makin Reserve **F8**
Ostrich & Emu Farm **H1**
Post Office **F8**
Saint Deryckes Wood Winery **H1**
The Berrima Cemetery **J13**
Wombeyan Caves **H1**
ZZ7UR

STREETS

Adelaide St **G15**	Brookdale Rd **L18**	M31 Hume Mwy	Perth St **G16**
Apple St **F5**	Bryan St **E8**	Berrima **A12**	Quarry St **H7**
Argyle St	Burwan St **D12**	Berrima **A2**	Raglan St **D10**
Berrima **F12**	Carribee Cl **D2**	New Berrima **A14**	Schotts La **H7**
Berrima **F8**	Centennial Rd **L2**	Market Pl **F8**	Shelley Rd **C9**
Berrima **G7**	Countess St **G9**	Medway Rd **A12**	Stockade St **E11**
New Berrima **E15**	Douglas Rd **L18**	Melbourne St **F14**	Surrey St **E7**
Australia Av	Ennis Av **E13**	Mortimer Rd **J7**	Sutton St **D9**
Berrima **B12**	Fountain St **E6**	Nathan St **A8**	Sydney St **F14**
New Berrima **B12**	Greenhills Rd **J4**	Nicholson St **E10**	Taylor Av **B13**
Bedford Pl **F5**	Hoskins Av **E15**	Odessa St **C11**	Taylor St **H7**
Berrima Dr **D2**	Howard St **E14**	Oldbury St **E9**	Vincent Rd **G1**
Berrima Rd	Iran St **G8**	Old Hume Hwy	Wilkinson St
Berrima **G10**	Jellore St	Berrima **A13**	Berrima **G11**
Moss Vale **J17**	Berrima **C8**	Berrima **G8**	Berrima **H6**
New Berrima **J16**	Berrima **E8**	Old Mandemar Rd **F2**	Wilshire St **F7**
Berrima Bridge **E9**	Berrima **F8**	Oxley St	Wingecarribee St
Bowen St **G10**	John Cr **B9**	Berrima **F6**	Berrima **D7**
Brisbane St **G14**	Lennox Rd **J7**	Berrima **H6**	Berrima **F7**
		Oxleys Hill Rd **L3**	Berrima **G7**

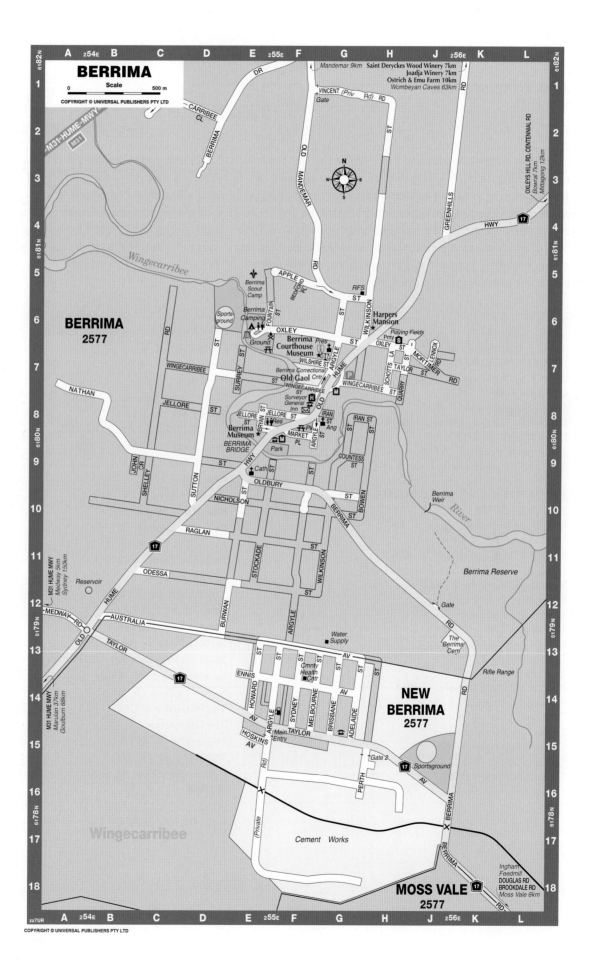

BERRIMA

Scale
0 — 500 m

COPYRIGHT © UNIVERSAL PUBLISHERS PTY LTD

BERRIMA
2577

NEW BERRIMA
2577

MOSS VALE
2577

Mandemar 9km   Saint Deryckes Wood Winery 7km
Joadja Winery 7km
Ostrich & Emu Farm 10km
Wombeyan Caves 63km

M31 HUME MWY
Medway 5km
Sydney 150km

M31 HUME MWY
Marulan 37km
Goulburn 68km

OXLEYS HILL RD, CENTENNIAL RD
Bowral 7km
Mittagong 12km

Ingham
Feedmill
DOUGLAS RD
BROOKDALE RD
Moss Vale 6km

Wingecarribee

Wingecarribee

Berrima Reserve

Berrima Weir

Berrima Cem

Rifle Range

Cement Works

Berrima Scout Camp

Berrima Camping Ground

Sportsground

Berrima Courthouse Museum

Old Gaol

Berrima Correctional Cntr

Surveyor General Inn

Berrima Museum

Harpers Mansion

Playing Fields

Reservoir

Water Supply

Cmnty Health Cntr

BOWRAL

LOCATION
5km off the Hume Hwy
115km south-west of Sydney

POPULATION
12 155

NRMA ROAD SERVICE
Ph: 13 11 22

VISITOR INFORMATION
Mittagong Visitor Information Centre
62 Main St (Old Hume Hwy)
Mittagong
Ph: (02) 4871 2888
Toll free: 1300 657 559
www.southern-highlands.com.au

Bowral is a thriving tourist and health resort in the beautiful Southern Highlands. This stylish town and its surroundings offer country resorts and weekend getaways renowned for their excellent cuisine. Bowral's beautiful gardens and trees attract many visitors, and a highlight of Bowral's year is Tulip Time. This annual spring celebration sees thousands of spring flowers blooming in public and private gardens, with some spectacular private gardens open for viewing at this time.

Celebrated as the home of Sir Donald Bradman, cricket fans will want to see the display of cricket memorabilia in the Bradman Museum which has been transformed into the International Cricket Hall of Fame. As well as highlighting Sir Donald's achievements, this amazing museum reveals the origins of the game, its growth in Australia, the history of the Ashes and the Bradman era.

ACCOMMODATION GUIDE
Briars Country Lodge 3 B10
Golf View Lodge 1 H2
Grand Mecure Hotel 1 K11
Milton Park Country House Hotel 4 L16
Oxley Motel 1 H13
The Imperial Hotel 2 A7
The Sebel Bowral Heritage Park 1 K11

FACILITIES & ATTRACTIONS
Apex Park 3 G2
Bong Bong Picnic Race Club 4 C18
Bowling Club 2 C8
Bowral & District Hospital 2 B10
Bowral Country Club Golf Course 1 H2
Bowral Golf Course 1 K12
Bowral Lookout 2 E3
Bowral Railway Station 1 K7
Bowral RSL Club 1 H2
Bowral Vietnam War Memorial 2 B5
Bradman Oval 2 C9
Burradoo Park 3 G2
Burradoo Railway Station 1 D14
Burradoo Sportsground 3 F7
Centennial Park 1 K4
Centennial Vineyards 1 C2
Cherry Tree Walk 2 B5
Coates Oval 3 H3
Corbett Gardens 2 B7
Craigieburn Golf Course 1 F2

David Wood Sporting Fields 2 L11
Eridge Park 3 F7
Fire Station 2 A7
Foley Park 2 C6
Gibberguyah Reserve 1 G1
Glebe Park 2 C9
Greenbrier Park Vineyard 4 D5
Inner Bowl Picnic Area 2 E3
Loseby Park 2 B11
Main Oval 3 J4
Mansfield Reserve 4 F12
Maynard Park 1 K9
Mittagong Lookout 2 F1
Mount Gibraltar Reserve 2 E1
Mt Jellore Lookout 2 C1
NRMA 1 L8
Oxley Lookout 2 D2
Post Office 1 L7
Sadlier Oval 3 J3
Settlers Park 2 A5
Southern Highlands Botanic Gardens 2 F16
Southern Highlands Private Hospital 2 C10
Swimming Pool 2 B5
The International Cricket Hall of Fame 2 C9
The Intersection 1 J9
Velodrome 3 G7
Venables Park 2 D8
Wyeera Bong Bong Picnic Race Club 4 D18
ZZ7UR

STREETS

Aberdeen Pl 2 K17
Acacia St 2 J1
Acer Ct 2 G16
Aitken Rd 2 C13
Al Av 1 J14
Albert St
  Bowral 2 F10
  Bowral 2 F11
  Bowral 2 F8
Alcorn St 1 H12
Alder Pl 2 E15
Alexandra Cr 1 E5
Alfreda St 1 G3
Alice Av 2 F15
Anglewood Dr 1 F14
Annesley Av 2 C14
Arborea Pl 2 F13
Argyle La 1 K9
Argyle St 4 G1
Arthur Smith Av 1 E14
Ascot Rd 2 C10
Aspen Gr 2 J13
Ayrshire Pde 2 K11
Balliol Cl 2 K10
Banksia St 2 C6
Banyette St 1 K9
Beavan Pl 1 J12
Bedford Pl 3 F5
Belmore St 1 J10
Bendooley St 1 L11
Betty Cl 4 A10
Bill O'reilly Cl 2 D14
Blackett Pl 2 K13
Bloomfield Cl 4 F17
Boardman Rd
  Bowral 2 J17
  Bowral 2 K11
  Bowral 2 J18
Bong Bong Rd 4 K1
Bong Bong St 1 K9
Bonnie Glen Rd 4 B16
Boolwey St 1 K8
Boronia St 1 H1
Bowral St 1 J9
Bracken St 2 J1
Bradman Av 2 D9
Braeside Rd 2 D14
Bren Pl 2 K14
Bronwyn Pl 2 J14
Bruce St 1 K16
Bundaroo St 2 A6
Burns Pl 1 G13
Burradoo Rd
  Bowral 2 A16
  Burradoo 1 D15
Burton Pl 1 H6

Caley St 2 K13
Camellia Pl 2 J11
Campbell Av 1 J14
Campbell St 1 G10
Carisbrooke Row 4 C16
Carlisle St 2 G7
Caroline Av 2 L11
Carrington St 1 J11
Cassandra Pl 2 H11
Centennial Rd
  Bowral 1 D2
  Bowral 1 F3
Charlotte St 3 G3
Charlton Cl 2 B11
Cherry La 2 H16
Chip Chase Ct 2 F13
Church St 2 B9
Clarke St 2 B4
Clearview St 2 F7
Cliff St 2 B3
Cluff Cr 2 J8
College Pl 2 E12
Copplestone La 1 E4
Cowpastures Rd 4 D14
Crabapple Cl 2 G17
Cutter Pl
  Bowral 2 L15
  Bowral 4 A15
Cypress Pde 2 E15
Daphne St 2 E9
David St 1 K12
Denbigh Dr 4 B14
Derby St 2 F13
Duke St
  Bowral 2 F2
  Mittagong 2 F2
Dumfries Pl 2 K16
Dundee Pl 2 L17
Earl St
  Bowral 2 G3
  Mittagong 2 G1
Edith Ct 2 H14
Edward St 2 B9
Edward Riley Dr 4 E13
Elizabeth St 3 D6
Ellen St 2 D5
Ellis Ct 2 H11
Elm St 2 E9
Emily Cct 2 H13
Eridge Park Rd
  Burradoo 2 D18
  Burradoo 3 F8
Evans La 2 A1
Fairway Dr 1 G5
Farmborough Cl 2 F10
Foldgarth Wy 1 J17
Forest La 1 K6

Funston St 1 J10
Gibraltar Rd
  Bowral 2 H3
  Mittagong 2 H3
Ginahgulla Dr 2 K10
Gladstone Rd 2 F6
Glebe St 2 C9
Glenquarry Cr
  Bowral 2 L14
  Bowral 4 A13
Glenrowan Gr 2 J13
Gloucester Pde 1 F12
Gordon Rd 2 D11
Government Rd 2 L1
Greyleaves Av 2 C18
Hamilton Av 2 D6
Hammock Hill Ri 4 C15
Hansen St 2 G12
Harby Av 2 C18
Harley St 4 D14
Harnett La 2 K3
Herald St 4 E12
Highland Dr
  Bowral 2 K16
  Bowral 4 A16
Holly Rd 1 C16
Holly St 2 D8
Holmhale St 1 L10
Hopewood Rd 1 E5
Horderns Rd 4 E18
Hudson St 1 B15
Hurlingham Av 3 C4
Inverness Pl 2 K17
Isabel St 2 F8
Isabella Wy 2 K17
Ivy St 2 F8
Jasmine St 2 D7
Jonathan St 4 B14
Kangaloon Rd
  Bowral 1 K11
  Bowral 4 A17
  Burradoo 2 F17
Kiama St 1 H10
Kiameron Pl 4 B15
Kimberley Dr 4 G14
Kims Pl 4 L14
King St 2 E5
King Ranch Dr 2 H15
Kings Cr 1 F15
Kingsbury Cct 2 J14
Kirkham Rd
  Bowral 1 J8
  Bowral 1 L3
Kokoda Pl 2 K14
Kyeema Cl 1 J17
Lavis Rd 2 H15

Lilac Av 2 J13
Linden Wy 2 H13
Links Rd
  Bowral 1 J13
  Burradoo 1 J13
Loftus St 1 H12
Lord St 1 G3
Loris St 4 C14
Loseby St 2 C11
Mcdonald St
  Bowral 2 H10
  Bowral 2 H8
Macquarie Gr 4 B14
Mairinger Cr 2 J15
Manor Ri 4 G14
Mansfield Rd
  Bowral 4 F14
  Bowral 4 F15
Maple Gr 2 F15
Marney Cl
  Bowral 2 L16
  Bowral 4 A16
Martha St 1 K10
Mary St 4 G2
Matavia Pl 4 B14
Merilbah Rd 1 G5
Merrigang St 2 A7
Meryla Rd 1 H12
Milton St 2 G13
Minnows Dr 1 A7
Miro Cr 2 J12
Mittagong Rd 2 B3
Mona Rd 2 C10
Morts La 2 J1
Moss Vale Rd
  Bowral 1 G17
  Burradoo 1 G17
  Burradoo 3 D10
Mount Rd 1 G6
Moynoe Cl 1 F15
Myosotis St 1 G3
Myrtle St 2 E9
Nannas La 4 L5
Nerang St 1 G15
Nero St 2 K1
Norton La 4 B15
Oak La 2 F8
Old Bong Bong Wy 3 D7
Old Hume Hwy 1 B2
Old South Rd
  Bowral 2 E16
  Mittagong 4 A8
Orchard Rd 1 D10
Osborne Rd
  Burradoo 3 C1
  Burradoo 3 J2

Oxley Dr
  Bowral 2 B5
  Bowral 2 D1
  Bowral 2 E2
  Mittagong 2 F1
Oxleys Hill Rd 1 B8
Park Rd 2 B11
Parmenter Ct 2 J17
Parry Dr 1 F11
Patchway Pl 3 D2
Pauline Pl 2 J12
Phillip St 3 C5
Plane Tree Cl 2 H16
Price St 2 E14
Prince St 2 J1
Prunus Pl 2 G16
Purcell St 2 E14
Pyrus Pl 2 J16
Queen St 2 E7
Queensmead Pl 1 E14
Railway Pde
  Bowral 1 H12
  Burradoo 1 A16
Rain Tree Wy 2 H17
Ranelagh Rd 3 E3
Range Rd 4 G1
Reflections Wy 2 G15
Retford Rd 2 F12
Rex La 3 H3
Riversdale Av 3 C3
Robinia Dr 2 H16
Robinson St 4 B1
Romney Pl 1 F13
Rose St 2 C7
Rosemary Cr 2 G14
Rouse Rd 4 C13
Rowan Pl 2 H17
Rowland Rd
  Bowral 4 B13
  Bowral 4 B14
Roycroft St 2 J15
St Clair St 1 H1
St Denis Cl 1 C18
St James Cl 3 E5
St Judes St 2 C9
St Martins Gr 4 C16
Sandra Ct 2 J11
Sheaffe St 2 E14
Sheffield Rd 2 B11
Shepherd St
  Bowral 2 C8
  Bowral 2 H8
Sherwood Av 1 K6
Short St 2 B8
Sir Don
  Bradman Dr 2 D14

Sir James
  Fairfax Cct 2 K10
Soma Av 2 C3
Songline Pl 3 D8
Sproules La 4 F18
Stan Mccabe Pl 2 D14
Station St 1 J9
Stephens Pl 2 G13
Stirling Dr 2 L16
Stratford Wy 1 K17
Sullivan Rd 3 B2
Sunninghill Av 1 J16
Sutherland Park Dr 3 L4
Sweeny Pl 2 E12
The Avenue 1 C15
The Highlands Wy
  Bowral 1 L6
  Burradoo 1 H15
  Burradoo 3 F6
Thompson St 2 F13
Tillia Pl 2 H16
Tirrikee La 3 P2
Toongoon Rd 3 K1
Tourist Rd 4 F18
Tulip Cl 2 H16
Tulloona Av 2 B1
Tynedale Cr 2 H11
Una St 2 C8
Victoria St 2 B6
Walker St 1 K10
Warburton Rd
  Bowral 1 E1
  Bowral 1 F1
Warby St 2 L12
Warenda St 2 A10
Warwick Cl 2 K9
Wattle La 1 K8
Webb St 4 F1
Werrington St 3 C2
Westbrook Cr 2 K12
Westminster Pl 3 H5
Westwood Dr 2 D12
Wheen Cl 2 D13
William St 2 D4
Willow Rd 1 J8
Wingecarribee St 1 L7
Wirreanda Rd 3 G7
Wiseman Rd
  Bowral 2 F18
  Bowral 2 K18
  Burradoo 2 F18
Woodbine St 2 C7
Woodbury Ct 1 F5
Yean St 1 E14
Youngingbill Cl 4 C13

MAP 1 BOWRAL

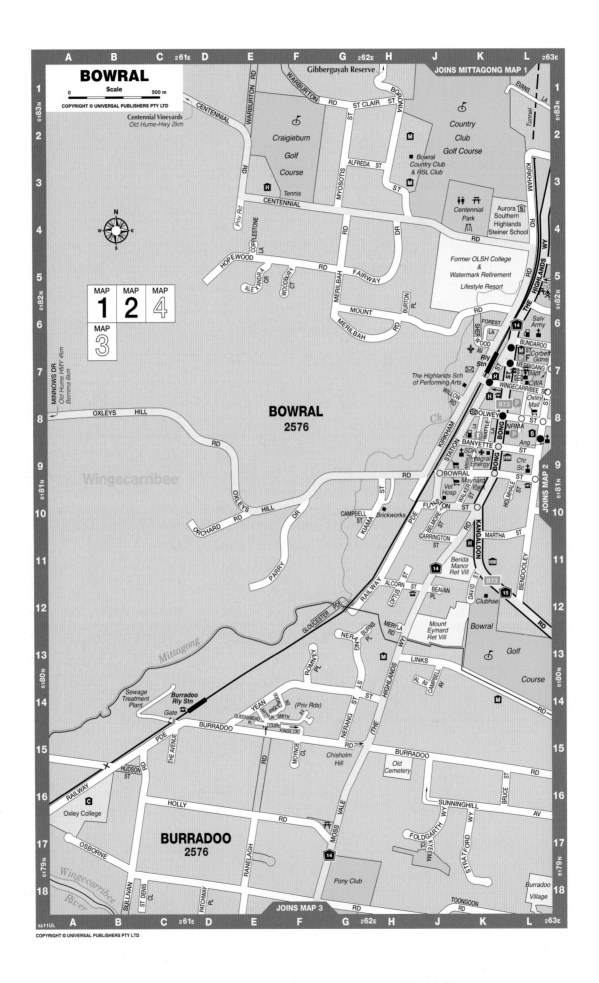

BOWRAL

Scale
0   500 m

COPYRIGHT © UNIVERSAL PUBLISHERS PTY LTD

BOWRAL
2576

BURRADOO
2576

MAP 1	MAP 2	MAP 4
MAP 3		

JOINS MITTAGONG MAP 1

JOINS MAP 2

JOINS MAP 3

COPYRIGHT © UNIVERSAL PUBLISHERS PTY LTD

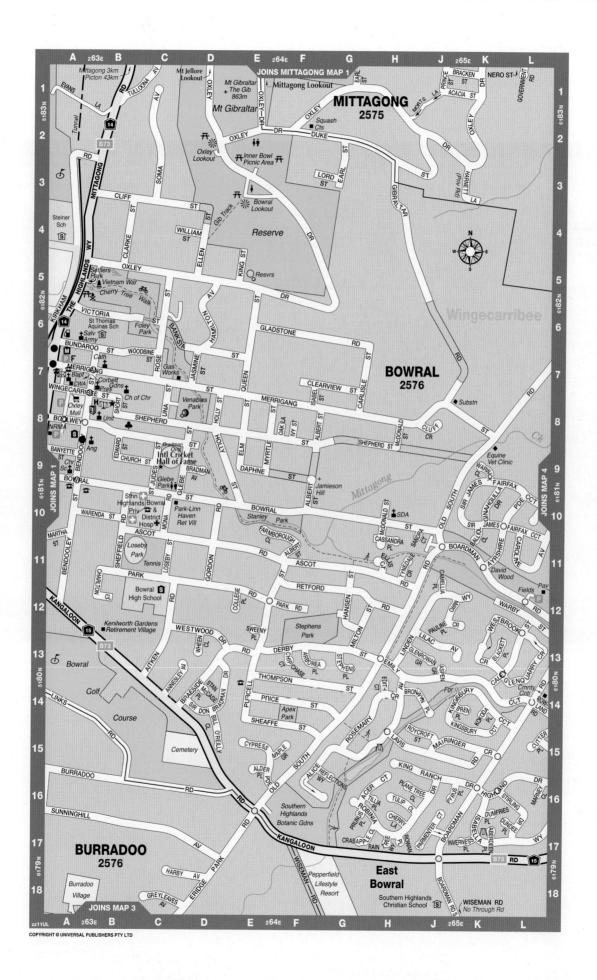

MAP 3 BOWRAL

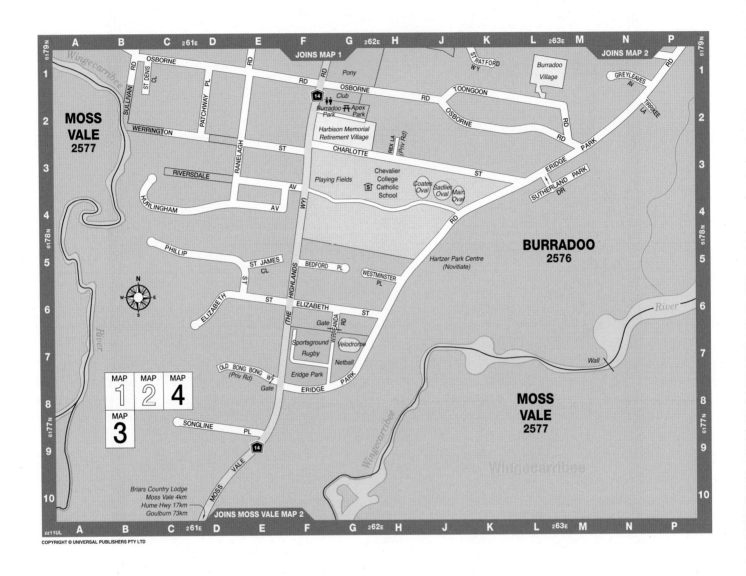

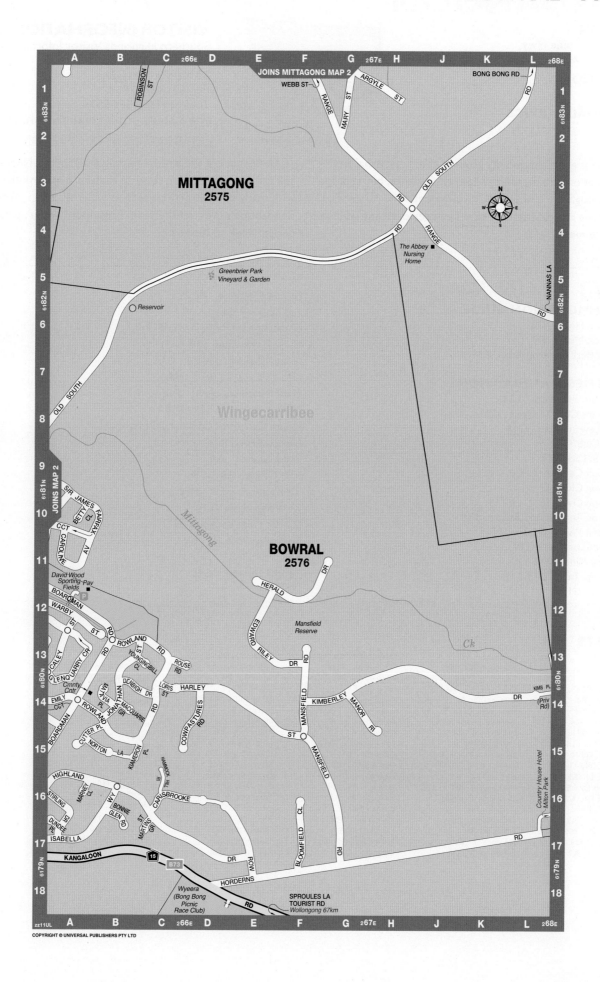

BUNDANOON

LOCATION
13km off the Hume Hwy
143km south-west of Sydney

POPULATION
2420

NRMA ROAD SERVICE
Ph: 13 11 22

VISITOR INFORMATION
Southern Highlands Visitor Information
Centre
62 Main St Mittagong
Ph: (02) 4871 2888
Tollfree: 1300 657 559
www.southern-highlands.com.au

Bundanoon is a vibrant, rapidly growing community that has managed not only to retain its village atmosphere, but improve upon it through the enthusiastic involvement of its residents. Several of the old guesthouses have been restored and welcome guests once more.

The beauty of the natural bush in the Morton National Park still attracts visitors and tourism remains a major industry with many new attractions such as wineries, open gardens and Bundanoon's event of the year, 'Brigadoon', when up to 20,000 people flock to the town.

ACCOMMODATION GUIDE
Bundanoon Hotel **G8**
Bundanoon Motel **F9**
Gambells Rest Camping Area **F14**

FACILITIES & ATTRACTIONS
Amphitheatre Lookout **L14**
Beauchamps Cliffs Lookout **G13**
Bonnie View Lookout **G13**
Bowling Club **J7**
Broughton Park **K7**
Bundanoon Cemetery **C6**
Bundanoon Club **J7**
Bundanoon Oval **J6**
Bundanoon Recreation Reserve **F14**
Bundanoon Visitor Centre **F9**
Echo Point Lookout **G14**
Erith Coal Mine **G12**
Fairy Bower Falls **G13**
Fern Glen **G13**
Fern Tree Gully **P14**
Ferndale Reserve **B6**
Fire Station **G8**
Gambells Rest Picnic Area **F14**
Glow Worm Glen **P8**
Grand Canyon Lookout **G13**
Jordans Crossing Park **H5**
Mark Morton Lookout **P14**
Morton National Park **P10**
Mount Carnarvon Lookout **G14**
Nicholas Pass **L14**
Police Station **G8**
Post Office **G8**
Riverview Lookout **P14**
Riverview Walk **L14**
Sunrise Point Lookout **G13**
Swimming Pool **J7**
The Old Library **J8**
Tooths Lookout **G13**
ZZ7UR

STREETS

Amos La **J8**	Burgess St **H8**	Garland Rd **L9**	Lorna Cl **H5**	Ringwood La **G1**
Amphitheatre Tr **N14**	Cambourn Cl **N4**	Garland Rd **M10**	Lower Gullies Rd **F11**	River View Rd **G12**
Amy St **F8**	Church St **G10**	Garnida Cl **M5**	Lucas St **D9**	Robbie Burns Pl **M6**
Anzac Pde **F9**	Coalmines Rd **A14**	Glen Cl **E5**	Lynne Cl **J4**	Rochester Dr **D7**
Ardross Av **P4**	Curringa Pl **J6**	Glow Worm Glen Tr **M8**	Mangold La **K7**	Rosenthal Av **L7**
Ashgrove Pl **F4**	Dimmocks Creek Tr **P12**	Glow Worm Glen Wk **P11**	Morgans Rd **G1**	Ross St **C11**
Bamburgh Pl **C4**	Dorothy Friend Pl **L7**	Governors St **G11**	Morris Ct **C9**	Rumsey Pl **L4**
Barnett Av **G7**	Durham Rd **A4**	Greasons Rd **C5**	Nerrim St **E6**	Skye Pl **M7**
Ben Nevis Cct **L10**	Ebury St **F8**	Grey Gum La **D10**	Nicholas Av **F9**	Talisker Wy **E6**
Betula Gr **G5**	Echo Point Rd **F14**	Grice Dr **L4**	Old Wingello Rd **A6**	The Gullies Rd **F10**
Bindar Cr **H6**	Ella St **B10**	Harriet Wk **E8**	Osborn Av **H8**	The Gullies Rd **F13**
Birch Park Rd **E5**	Ellsmore Rd **G1**	Hawthorne St **J8**	Osborne St **H8**	Tobin Pl **N4**
Birch Ponds Dr **E6**	Ellsmore Rd **G7**	Haymans Rd **A4**	Panorama Rd **K10**	Tooth St **E9**
Birchwood Dr **L2**	Elmswood Ct **G5**	Heritage Dr **F3**	Penola St **C7**	Victoria St **H9**
Birriga Av **F5**	Erith St **F8**	Hill St **F8**	Penrose Rd **A12**	Viewland St **K8**
Blue Gum Rd **H3**	Ferndale Rd **A5**	Kin Tyre Cl **M7**	Phillip St **G9**	William St **K8**
Brigadoon Dr **M6**	Fidelis St **D9**	Larkin Cl **D5**	Quarry Rd **A11**	Willis St **B11**
Bromhall Rd **D9**	Florence St **B10**	Leaver Park Rd **A11**	Quarry Rd **A7**	Yuille Av **P5**
Broughton St **K7**	Forwood Cr **C8**	Lodge La **C7**	Railway Av **G8**	

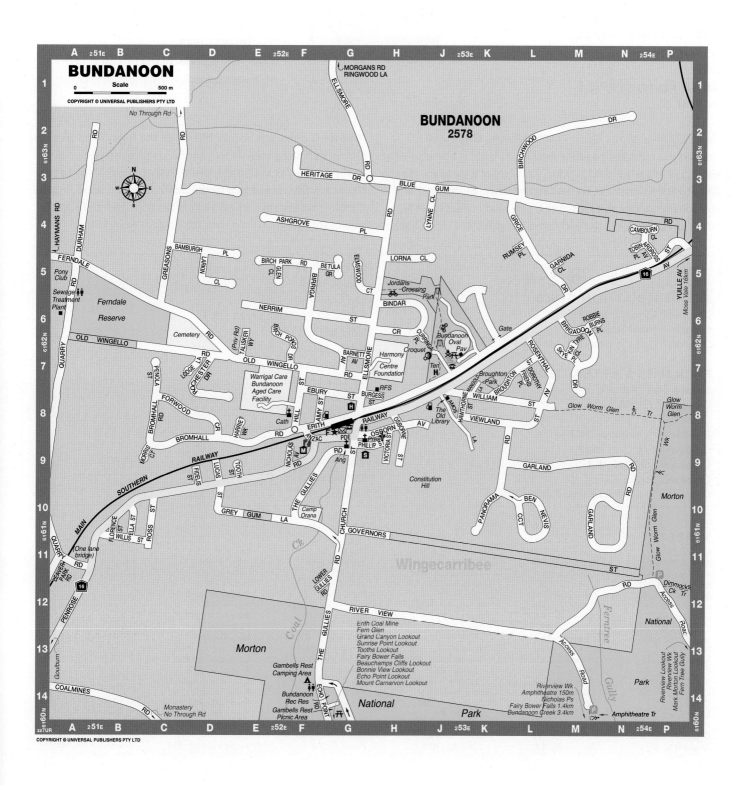

BUNDANOON

Scale

0   500 m

COPYRIGHT © UNIVERSAL PUBLISHERS PTY LTD

BUNDANOON
2578

Erith Coal Mine
Fern Glen
Grand Canyon Lookout
Sunrise Point Lookout
Tooths Lookout
Fairy Bower Falls
Beauchamps Cliffs Lookout
Bonnie View Lookout
Echo Point Lookout
Mount Carnarvon Lookout

Riverview Wk
Amphitheatre 150m
Nicholas Ps
Fairy Bower Falls 1.4km
Bundanoon Creek 3.4km

CROOKWELL

LOCATION
Off the Hume Highway
(North west from Goulburn)
230km south west of Sydney

POPULATION
2000

NRMA ROAD SERVICE
Ph: 13 11 22

VISITOR INFORMATION
Crookwell Visitor Information Centre
36 Goulburn St
Ph: (02) 4832 1988
www.visitupperlachlan.com.au

Situated high atop the Great Dividing Range, Crookwell is situated in a naturally beautiful area. Crookwell is home to what was NSW's first wind farm, which consists of 8 turbines. It's the first attraction one sees on nearing the town. Bushranger and gold mining history abounds in this area, and many old stone buildings remain from the early days of settlement. The Sheck

Webster Lookout at Snowy Mount on the Bigga Road gives the visitor a stunning view of the surrounding countryside north to Mt Canobolas at Orange, while further afield, Wombeyan Caves has five caves open to the public. Lindner Socks, a small factory that attracts repeat visitors from all over the state is one of the last remaining sock factories in Australia.

ACCOMMODATION GUIDE
Crookwell Caravan Park **H5**
Crookwell Hotel Motel **J7**
Crookwell Upland Pastures Motor Inn **H5**

FACILITIES & ATTRACTIONS
Bowling Club **K8**
Coleman Park **K8**
Council Office **J7**
Crookwell Aerodrome **H14**
Crookwell Golf Club **M12**
Crookwell RSL Club **K8**
Crookwell Service Centre **J7**
Crookwell Visitor Information Centre **H6**

Fire Station **J8**
Hospital **G10**
Jean Todkill Park **N11**
Lin Cooper Recreation Area **M11**
Memorial Oval **K7**
NRMA **J7**
Pat Cullen Reserve **H6**
Post Office **H7**
Sheck Webster Lookout **A3**
Showground **L10**
State Emergency Service **J3**
Swimming Pool **K9**
Wind Farm **P13**
Wombeyan Caves **P2**
ZZ7UR

STREETS

Adoni Pl **E7**	Clements St **D7**	Goulburn La **J8**	King Rd **G5**	Parkes St **F7**	Somerset Pl **G13**
Allambie Pl **D7**	Clements St **E7**	Goulburn Rd **N11**	Laggan Rd **H5**	Philip St **H4**	Soudan Rd **L2**
Anderson Rd **A8**	Clifton St **J3**	Goulburn St **H6**	Laver Pl **F4**	Picker St **H10**	Spring La **H9**
Barry Pl **G11**	Colyer St **H9**	Grabben Gullen Rd **A9**	Leila Mayo Cl **F4**	Pine Av **M3**	Spring St **H8**
Bessie Ford Cl **F4**	Corcoran Pl **E5**	Graham Cr **K4**	McDonald St **B9**	Pleasant St **L10**	Stephenson St **C7**
Bigga Rd **F7**	Cowper La **H8**	Grange Rd **M14**	McGeechan St **L3**	Prell St **L5**	Tait St **D9**
Binda Rd **A4**	Cowper St **H8**	Hall Cr **F5**	McGraw Rd **P6**	Prospect St **M9**	Tulloh St **G14**
Boongarra Rd **N1**	Croker Pl **P4**	Harley Rd **L9**	McInnes St **G5**	Railway St **K6**	Valley Rd **B14**
Boorowa Rd **A5**	Crown St **F4**	Hay St **K5**	McIntosh Rd **F2**	Redground Rd **J2**	Wade La **G9**
Bray St **J5**	Cullen St **J13**	Henderson St **D7**	Marsden La **J6**	Reservoir Rd **P8**	Wade St **G8**
Broderick St **M2**	Denham St **K10**	Henderson St **E8**	Marsden St **J6**	Richardson St **K3**	Warne La **K9**
Brooklands La **F6**	Denison La **H8**	High St **F4**	Memory Av **L3**	Roberts St **H7**	Warne St **J9**
Brooklands St **D6**	Denison St **H7**	Holborrow St **E8**	North St **K1**	Robertson St **J6**	White St **F5**
Brooklands St **F6**	Derwent St **F4**	Iron Mine Rd **J1**	Northcott St **E6**	Roslyn La **E7**	Willis St **C6**
Carr St **J4**	East St **K13**	Jamieson St **J5**	Old Binda Rd **A5**	Roslyn Rd **P13**	Wolseley Rd **K2**
Carrington La **D6**	Elizabeth St **H4**	John St **B8**	Old Binda Rd **A6**	Rosyln St **F7**	Woodville St **F8**
Carrington St **D5**	Findhorn La **K6**	Kennedy St **E5**	Oram St **H5**	Saleyards Rd **K4**	Woodward La **M2**
Charles St **G4**	Findhorn St **K6**	Kensit St **F4**	Park St **K8**	Short St **F7**	Woodward Rd **N3**
Churchill St **H12**	Gordon St **K2**	Kialla Rd **H10**	Parker St **F4**	Showground La **L10**	

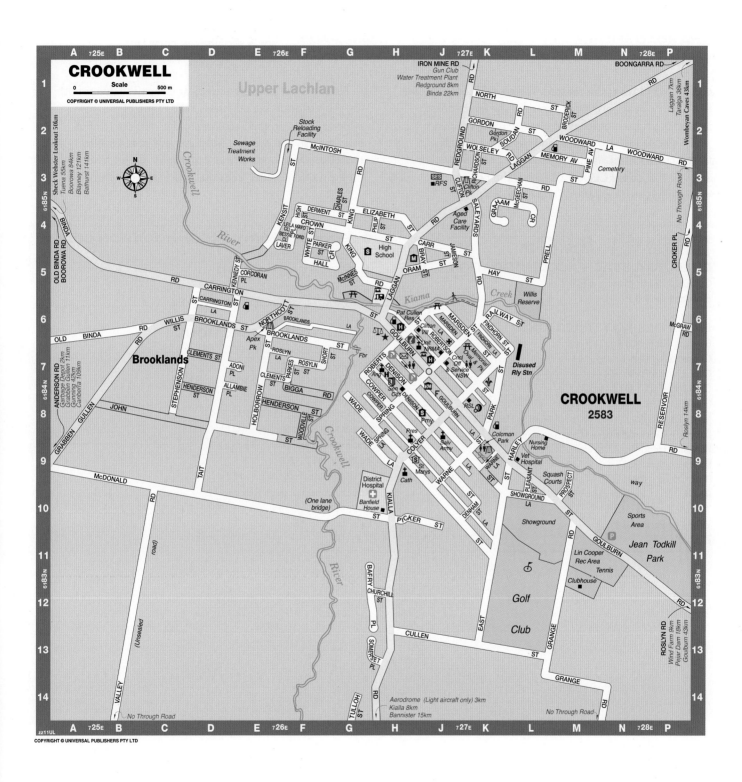

CROOKWELL

Scale
0 — 500 m

COPYRIGHT © UNIVERSAL PUBLISHERS PTY LTD

Upper Lachlan

Brooklands

CROOKWELL
2583

COPYRIGHT © UNIVERSAL PUBLISHERS PTY LTD

CULBURRA BEACH/GREENWELL POINT

LOCATION
Off the Princes Hwy
182km south of Sydney

POPULATION
Culburra Beach 3000   Greenwell Point 1200

NRMA ROAD SERVICE
Ph: 13 11 22

VISITOR INFORMATION
Shoalhaven Visitors Centre
Bridge Rd
Ph: (02) 4421 0778
Ph: 1300 662 808
www.shoalhaven.com.au

Accessed via Nowra, the coastal villages of Greenwell Point and Culburra Beach are hidden gems of the south coast. Boasting the closest beaches to Nowra, Culburra Beach is the larger of the two villages and has a well-established infrastructure for tourists. Originally designed by Walter Burley Griffin, today Culburra Beach is the perfect destination for swimming, surfing, general relaxing and fishing.

Fishing is the primary activity at Greenwell Point, both for professionals and amateurs alike. One of the main seafood ports on the Shoalhaven, the village is famous both for fish and oysters. Boats are available for hire, charters take groups offshore and game fishing, and fishing is also popular from the riverbank and wharf.

CULBURRA BEACH ACCOMMODATION GUIDE
Culburra Beach Motel   **E13**
Holiday Haven   **F4**

FACILITIES & ATTRACTIONS
Bowling Club   **C14**
Crookhaven Lighthouse   **H1**
Crookhaven Park   **E4**
Culburra Park   **D13**
Fred Evans Park   **F13**
Jervis Bay National Park Lake Wollumboola   **G16**
Lakeside Park   **K18**
Penguins Head Road Reserve   **P14**
Police Station   **C15**
Post Office   **C14**
Roseby Bay Cemetery Jerrinja Trible Clans   **C4**
Tilbury Reserve   **L14**
Wheeler Park   **L14**
ZZ7UR

GREENWELL POINT ACCOMMODATION GUIDE
Anchor Bay Motel   **H4**
Anglers Rest Caravan Park   **H3**
Coral Tree Lodge   **H8**
Pine Park Tourist Grounds & Marina   **E2**

FACILITIES & ATTRACTIONS
Adelaide Street Reserve   **H2**
Bowling Club   **G8**
Comerong Island Nature Reserve   **J1**
Gordon Ravell Park   **F5**
Greenwell Point Post Office   **G4**
Greenwell Point Reserve   **G1**
Haiser Road Reserve   **G6**
Jindyandy Mill   **A4**
Orient Point Post Office   **N4**
Robert Lonesborough Reserve   **L5**
Swimming Pool   **H4**
Titania Park   **J3**
ZZ7UR

CULBURRA BEACH STREETS

Addison Rd **E9**
Albacore Rd **H3**
Allerton Av
  Culburra Beach **G13**
  Culburra Beach **J14**
Allerton La **G13**
Araluen Wy **H16**
Bay St **F14**
Belgrave St **E9**
Black Swan Wy **E15**
Bream Rd **H3**
Brighton Pde **C13**
Broadview Av **J15**
Canal St E **C14**
Carlton Cr **E14**
Crookhaven Lighthouse Tr **F1**
Cross St **D15**
Culburra Rd **A14**
Duke St **L15**
East Cr **H16**
Eastbourne Av **L17**
Eastwood Av **F11**
Fairlands St
  Culburra Beach **D13**
  Culburra Beach **G15**
Fairlight Wy **K15**
Farrant Av **L15**
Fern Wy **F8**
First St **A4**
Flora St **C6**
Fourth St **A5**
Fred Evans La **B15**
Glenholme Wy **F11**
Greenbank Gr **D15**

Haven St **K15**
Hope St **K16**
Ingle Ring **E14**
Jay St **C5**
Jopejija Cr **J16**
Kiah La **F16**
Kingfish Rd **H3**
Kookaburra Rd **H3**
Lee St **H17**
Lighthouse Lp **H1**
Marlin Rd **H4**
Mia Wy **F10**
Mona St **K16**
Mowbray Rd **F13**
Mullaway Rd **H4**
North Cr **H14**
Ocean St **J14**
Orient Point Rd **C6**
Orsova Pde **A6**
Palm Wy **F9**
Park Row
  Culburra Beach **B5**
  Orient Point **B5**
Park St **F14**
Penguins Head Rd
  Culburra Beach **F12**
  Culburra Beach **J15**
Platform Lp **G2**
Plimsoll Pl **J16**
Prince Edward Av
  Culburra Beach **C14**
  Culburra Beach **E7**
Raglan St **D6**
Redbank La **C14**

River Lp **F2**
Rosella Rd **H4**
Seagull St **C4**
Second St **A4**
Silvermere St **H16**
Snapper Rd **H4**
Sunshine St **E7**
Tern St **B5**
The Bowery **F12**
The Lake Cct
  Culburra Beach **E14**
  Culburra Beach **J15**
The Mall **E10**
The Marina
  Culburra Beach **F8**
  Culburra Beach **G10**
  Culburra Beach **H13**
The Retreat **G12**
The Strand **F8**
The Triangle **F13**
Tuna Rd **H4**
Vivian Wy **E7**
Wattle Rd **H4**
Wentworth St **F12**
West Cr
  Culburra Beach **C15**
  Culburra Beach **F16**
  Culburra Beach **H15**
Weston St **C14**
Whistler St **E11**
Wollumboola La **F15**
Woodland St **G13**
Wren St **C5**

GREENWELL POINT STREETS

Adelaide St **F2**
Albert Av **G2**
Bailey Av **F8**
Bartlett Dr **G8**
Berellan St **F3**
Bindaree St **E4**
Bournes La **A6**
Bream Rd **H7**
Church St **F2**
Comarong St **F3**
Coonemia Rd
  Wollumboola **A18**
  Wollumboola **B17**
Crookhaven Dr **F9**
Culburra Rd
  Culburra Beach **H18**
  Wollumboola **C18**
Dory Dr **H7**
First St **P4**
Flathead Cl **H7**
Flounder Pl **H7**
Fourth St **P5**
Fraser Av **F7**
Greens Rd **F5**
Greenwell Point Rd
  Greenwell Point **A5**
  Pyree **A5**
Haiser Rd **F5**
Higgins Pl **G8**
Hume St **F6**

Jervis St **G4**
Keith Av **F6**
Leonore Av **F7**
Marlin Dr **H8**
Morrissey Wy **F8**
Ophir St **N5**
Orama Cr **L4**
Orient Av **M5**
Ormonde Cr **M5**
Orontes St **L5**
Orsova Pde **P6**
Osterley Av **N6**
Otranto Av **M6**
Otway St **N5**
Park Row **P5**
Pyree La **A6**
Pyree St **F4**
Ravells Rd **H9**
Regmoore Cl **N14**
Reg Wilson Wy **H4**
Ryans La **A6**
Snapper St **H7**
South St **F5**
Spies Av **G9**
Strathstone St **N14**
Terrara St **G4**
West St **E4**
Whiting Wy **H7**
Wilkins St **H4**

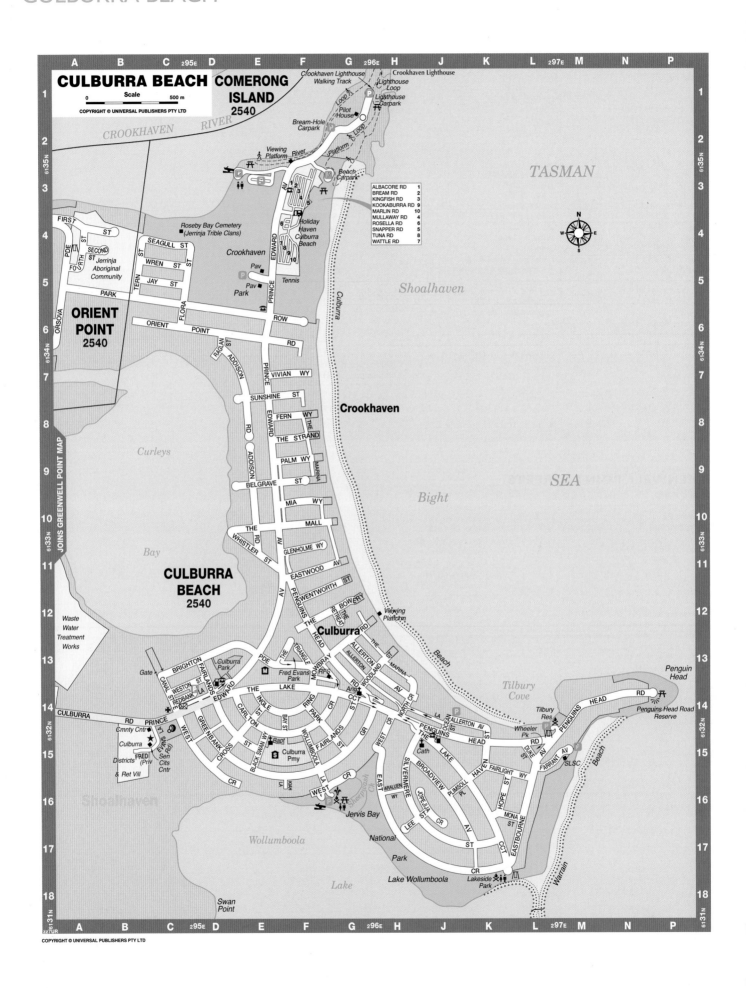

CULBURRA BEACH

COMERONG ISLAND 2540

Scale
0   500 m

COPYRIGHT © UNIVERSAL PUBLISHERS PTY LTD

ALBACORE RD	1
BREAM RD	2
KINGFISH RD	3
KOOKABURRA RD	9
MARLIN RD	10
MULLAWAY RD	4
ROSELLA RD	6
SNAPPER RD	5
TUNA RD	8
WATTLE RD	7

ORIENT POINT 2540

CULBURRA BEACH 2540

COPYRIGHT © UNIVERSAL PUBLISHERS PTY LTD

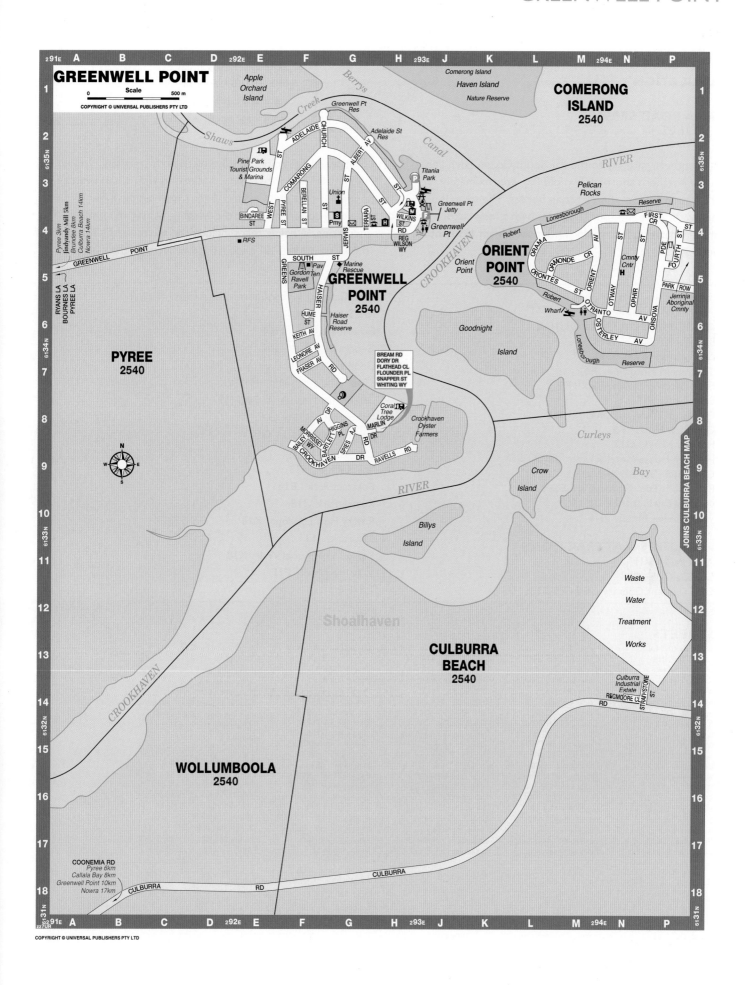

GREENWELL POINT

Scale
0   500 m

COPYRIGHT © UNIVERSAL PUBLISHERS PTY LTD

Apple Orchard Island

Comerong Island
Haven Island
Nature Reserve

COMERONG ISLAND 2540

Greenwell Pt Res

Adelaide St Res

Titania Park

Greenwell Pt Jetty

Greenwell Pt

Pelican Rocks

Reserve

ORIENT POINT 2540

Orient Point

GREENWELL POINT 2540

Marine Rescue

Haiser Road Reserve

BREAM RD
DORY DR
FLATHEAD CL
FLOUNDER PL
SNAPPER ST
WHITING WY

Coral Tree Lodge

Crookhaven Oyster Farmers

Goodnight Island

Curleys Bay

Jerrinja Aboriginal Cmnty

Reserve

Pine Park Tourist Grounds & Marina

BINDAREE ST

Gordon Ten Ravell Park

Pyree 3km
Jindyandy Mill 5km
Briundee 8km
Culburra Beach 14km
Nowra 14km

RYANS LA
BOURNES LA
PYREE LA

PYREE 2540

Crow Island

Billys Island

Shoalhaven

CULBURRA BEACH 2540

Waste Water Treatment Works

Culburra Industrial Estate

WOLLUMBOOLA 2540

CROOKHAVEN

RIVER

COONEMIA RD
Pyree 6km
Callala Bay 8km
Greenwell Point 10km
Nowra 17km

CULBURRA RD

EDEN

LOCATION
On the Princes Hwy
493km south of Sydney

POPULATION
3000

NRMA ROAD SERVICE
Ph: 13 11 22

VISITOR INFORMATION
Eden Gateway Visitor Information Centre
cnr Mitchell & Imlay Sts
Ph: (02) 6496 1953
www.visiteden.com.au

The southern gateway to the Far South Coast, Eden lies on the northern shore of Twofold Bay, approximately 50 kilometres from the Victorian border. The town is a deepwater port and tourist centre, with a long history founded on the whaling industry which flourished from 1818 until the 1930's.

Sightseeing cruises and fishing trips operate on Twofold Bay and whales are once again a fascination with whale-watching a popular pastime. On land, Eden's memorable Killer Whale Museum commemorates the whaling, fishing and timber industries. Whaling relics include the skeleton of 'Old Tom', the killer whale who once guided whalers to their prey.

ACCOMMODATION GUIDE
Bayview Motor Inn **D13**
Centretown Motel **G13**
Coachmans Motor Inn **F6**
Eden Gateway Holiday Park **F8**
Eden Motel **F7**
Garden of Eden Caravan Park **G9**
Golf View Motel **F5**
Halfway Motel **G12**
Heritage House Motel & Units **H15**
Quarantine Bay Beach Cottages **A17**
Reflections Eden Holiday Park Eden **L7**
Twofold Bay Motor Inn **H14**
Whale Fisher Motel **H15**

FACILITIES & ATTRACTIONS
Apex Park **H11**
Bowling Club **E5**
Eden Gardens Country Club Golf Club **D5**

Eden Gateway Visitor Information Centre **G12**
Fire Station **E4**
Fishermans Club **H14**
George Bass Park **J14**
George Brown Sportsground **F5**
Killer Whale Museum **H15**
Les Sheffield Memorial Oval **J9**
Lighthouse **K18**
Martha Kebby Park **G10**
Peisley Park **J11**
Post Office **H13**
Rotaract Park **E16**
Rotary Park **J18**
Rotary Park Lookout **K18**
RSL Park **J13**
Seamens Memorial Wall **K18**
Swimming Pool **F11**
ZZ7UR

STREETS

Albacore Cr **L4**	By St **J17**	George Brown St **F5**	Linton St **G8**	Strickland La **G14**
Albert Tce **J15**	Calle Calle St **H11**	Government Rd **F2**	Logan Ct **E6**	The Mews **D14**
Allira La **A14**	Cattle Bay Rd **F14**	Hollydale Pl **F8**	Love St **F2**	Towamba St **F1**
Alms St **D13**	Chandos St **G14**	Hopkins St **E3**	Maling St **F11**	Trumpeter Av **L2**
Andrea St **D15**	Clare Cr **D6**	Hosies Rd **H12**	Marlin Av **L3**	Tuna Wy **L2**
Aslings Beach Rd **J11**	Cocks La **H12**	Hume St **H3**	Melrose St **F12**	Twofold Ct **G15**
Banks St **D7**	Cocora St **G15**	Ida Rodd Dr **C15**	Mitchell St **E13**	Victoria Tce **H16**
Barclay St **G9**	Cook Dr **D7**	Ida Rodd Dr **D14**	Moorhead St **E6**	View St **E15**
Bass St **G13**	Cosham Cl **C16**	Imlay St **F7**	Museum St **J15**	Wahoo Ct **G11**
Bay St **E15**	Curalo St **F11**	Imlay St **J16**	Nethercote Rd **A13**	Weecoon St **K17**
Bellbird Ct **D15**	Curalo St **G10**	Ireland Timms La **B13**	Nicholson St **E7**	Wellings Ct **E7**
Bellevue Pl **C13**	Dolphin Cr **H10**	Irene Cr **F6**	Phillipps St **E14**	West St **F6**
Ben Boyd Dr **D3**	Egan Ct **F13**	K B Timms **Dr K3**	Princes Hwy **A17**	West St **F7**
Bimmil St **D12**	Emblen St **G7**	Kiah Ct **C16**	Princes Hwy **E2**	Whale Cove Cct **C15**
Blue Marlin Ct **F7**	Endeavour Ct **D7**	King Pl **G7**	Quarantine Bay Rd **A18**	William St **E3**
Bonito Pl **L2**	Evans Wy **L3**	Kingfisher Cct **K4**	Reservoir St **F8**	Wirriga St **E10**
Botany St **E7**	Fishermans Ct **G15**	Komirra Dr **H2**	Rodd St **E13**	Wykes La **E12**
Boyd St **D13**	Flinders St **F12**	Lake St **H10**	Rose Court Pl **G11**	Young St **E7**
Bramble St **K17**	Flinders St **G15**	Lake St N **H10**	Stanley St **E12**	Yule St **K17**
Bungo St **E12**	Flora St **J14**	Lakeside Dr **G6**	Storey Av **C4**	

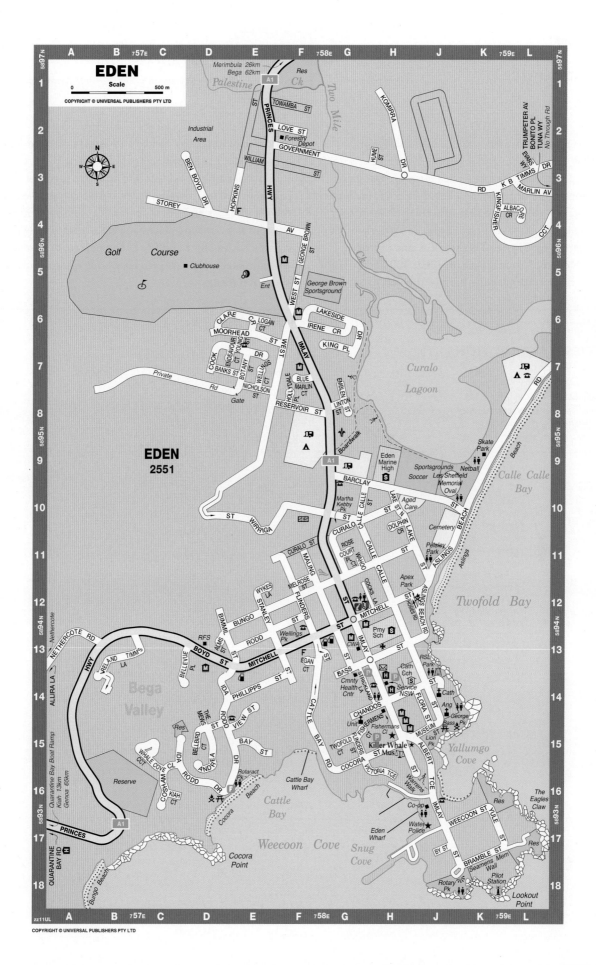

EDEN

Scale

0   500 m

COPYRIGHT © UNIVERSAL PUBLISHERS PTY LTD

EDEN
2551

Merimbula 26km
Bega 62km

Palestine   Ck

Two Mile

Industrial
Area

Golf   Course

Clubhouse

Curalo
Lagoon

Calle Calle
Bay

Twofold Bay

Bega
Valley

Reserve

Cattle
Bay

Killer Whale
St Mus

Yallumgo
Cove

The
Eagles
Claw

Cocora
Point

Weecoon Cove

Snug
Cove

Bungo Beach

Lookout
Point

Pilot
Station

zz11UL

COPYRIGHT © UNIVERSAL PUBLISHERS PTY LTD

FITZROY FALLS

LOCATION
137km south west of Sydney

POPULATION
215

NRMA ROAD SERVICE
Ph: 13 11 22

VISITOR INFORMATION
Fitzroy Falls Visitors Centre
1301 Nowra Rd
Ph: (02) 4887 7270

Fitzroy Falls is a village located in the Southern Highlands region of New South Wales and is best known for the waterfall that plunges spectacularly into the thick eucalypt forests of the valley beneath the escarpment. Fitzroy Falls has become a popular stopping point for tourists travelling towards the Southern Highlands. Discovered by European settlers in the early 19th century by Charles Throsby, It is one of many waterfalls in Morton National Park. In 1882, 4000 acres were set aside as a reserve forming the basis of the vast national park that exists today. While a town was planned for the area in the 1860s, little development occurred. The area provides substantial parking and catering facilities, together with pathways and boardwalks which enable able-bodied visitors to view the falls and other spectacular natural features. There are stairways, resting places and signs strategically placed to identify native fauna and flora. The nearest bushwalking trail is a 1.6 kilometres round trip to a lookout where you'll see the full glory of the falls

FACILITIES & ATTRACTIONS

Fitzroy Falls **G9**
Fitzroy Falls Dam **J6**
Fitzroy Falls Dam Picnic Area **K11**
Fitzroy Falls Reservoir Water Activity Area **K10**
Fitzroy Falls Visitors Centre **G8**
Lady Hordern Falls **F9**

Mimosa Gardens **F8**
Morton National Park **B9**
Renown Lookout **D11**
Twin Falls **C9**
Twin Falls Lookout **E9**
Valley View Lookout **G14**
Warragong Lookout **G11**
ZZ7UR

STREETS

Belimbla Rd **E6**
Bodycotts La **F3**
Bresnahans La **F1**
Casuarina Cr **F8**
East Rim Tr **H10**
Gwen Rd **F9**
Manning Lookout Rd **K14**
Myra Vale Rd
  Fitzroy Falls **K12**
  Wildes Meadow **K12**
Nowra Rd
  Fitzroy Falls **A2**
  Fitzroy Falls **F6**

Oxley Rd **D6**
Redhill Fire Trl **D11**
Redhills Rd **A2**
Ryans La **P13**
Sheepwash Rd
  Avoca **E4**
  Fitzroy Falls **E4**
Somerset Rd **A6**
Throsby Rd **D7**
Vermont Rd **F5**
West Rim Tr **D9**

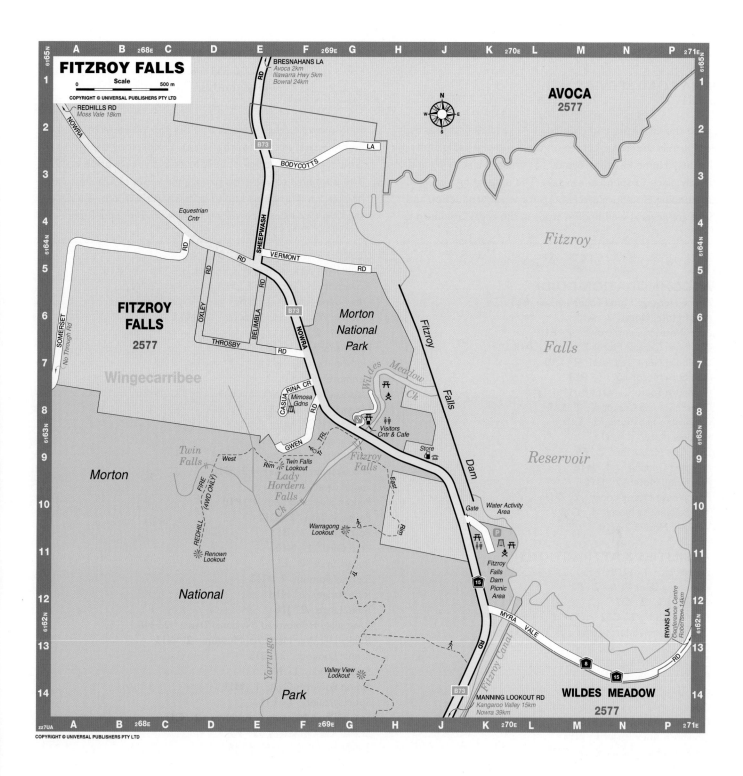

FITZROY FALLS

Scale
0   500 m

COPYRIGHT © UNIVERSAL PUBLISHERS PTY LTD

REDHILLS RD
Moss Vale 18km

BRESNAHANS LA
Avoca 2km
Illawarra Hwy 5km
Bowral 24km

AVOCA
2577

NOWRA

B73

BODYCOTTS   LA

Equestrian
Cntr

SHEEPWASH

VERMONT   RD

Fitzroy

FITZROY
FALLS
2577

OXLEY   RD

BELIMBLA   RD

RD

NOWRA

B73

Morton
National
Park

Falls

SOMERSET

No Through Rd

THROSBY   RD

Wingecarribee

CASUA   RINA   CR

Mimosa
Gdns

Wildes   *Meadow*   *Ck*

Reservoir

GWEN

RD

TRL

TF

Visitors
Cntr & Cafe

Store

Twin
Falls

West

Rim

Twin Falls
Lookout

Fitzroy

Falls

Morton

FIRE

(4WD ONLY)

Lady
Hordern
Falls

Ck

East

Fitzroy

Falls

Dam

Gate

Water Activity
Area

REDHILL

Renown
Lookout

Warragong
Lookout

Rim

P

Fitzroy
Falls
Dam
Picnic
Area

National

15

RYANS LA
Conference Centre
Robertson 14km

Yarrunga

Valley View
Lookout

MYRA   VALE

RD

Fitzroy Canal

8

15

Park

B73

MANNING LOOKOUT RD
Kangaroo Valley 15km
Nowra 39km

WILDES MEADOW
2577

GOULBURN

LOCATION
Just off the Hume Hwy
196km south-west of Sydney

POPULATION
21 500

NRMA ROAD SERVICE
Ph: 13 11 22

VISITOR INFORMATION
Goulburn Visitor Information Centre
201 Sloane St
Ph: (02) 4823 4492
Ph: 1800 353 646
www.goulburnaustralia.com.au

Called the Lilac City and claimed as Australia's first inland city, Goulburn is the major centre on the Southern Tablelands. The busy Hume Highway bypass has created a relaxing and friendly place to spend a few days. The undulating tablelands surrounding Goulburn are famous for wool production and there are several well-known studs in the area. Goulburn is well-known as the home of the 'Big Merino', now located on Hume Street near Sowerby Street. Dominating the city is the Goulburn War Memorial built by public subscription in 1923. The 20m high tower gives panoramic views of Goulburn and houses a military museum in its base. Also worth visiting is the Old Goulburn Brewery complex on Bungonia Road.

ACCOMMODATION GUIDE
Alpine Heritage Motel Goulburn 2 **B13**
Astor Hotel Motel 2 **A13**
Best Western Centretown 2 **E10**
Goulburn Central Motor Lodge 2 **A13**
Goulburn Heritage Motel 2 **L10**
Goulburn Motor Inn 1 **P13**
Goulburn South Caravan Park 1 **J18**
Governors Hill Carapark 2 **L10**
Governors Hill Motel 2 **L10**
Hillview Motel 1 **M14**
Lilac City Motor Inn 2 **F9**
Mercure Goulburn 1 **H18**
Parkhaven Motel 2 **D10**
Post House Motor Lodge 2 **D11**
The Bakehouse Motel 1 **G18**
Willows Motel 2 **J10**

FACILITIES & ATTRACTIONS
Big Merino 1 **H18**
Black Stag Deer Park 2 **P2**
BMX Track 2 **D7**
Bowling Club 2 **C12**
Cookbundoon Sports Fields 2 **K1**
Council Office 2 **B11**
Eastgrove Park South 2 **D15**
Fire Station 2 **B11**
Garroorigang Historic Home 1 **P18**
Goulburn & District Racing Club 2 **L1**
Goulburn Airport 2 **F18**
Goulburn Apex Park 1 **N14**
Goulburn Base Hospital 1 **P10**
Goulburn City Speedway 2 **P10**
Goulburn Golf Course 2 **D12**
Goulburn Rail Heritage Centre 1 **N18**
Goulburn Recreation Area & Showground 2 **B17**
Goulburn Service Centre 2 **C11**
Goulburn Soldiers Club 2 **C12**
Goulburn Visitor Information Centre 2 **C13**
Goulburn War Memorial 2 **G13**

Goulburn Workers Club 2 **B12**
Goulburn Workers Sports & Recreation Club 1 **K18**
Governors Hill Mt Gray Bushland Reserve 2 **N7**
Greyhound Racing 2 **B18**
Historic Waterworks Museum 1 **M6**
Hospital 2 **B10**
Hovells Grave 2 **J8**
Hudson Park 2 **H3**
Kenmore Hospital 2 **M1**
Lansdowne Park Historic Homestead 2 **D18**
Leggett Park 2 **C6**
Marsden Weir Park 1 **M6**
Memorial Park 2 **F13**
Mortis Street Cemetery 2 **G9**
Old Goulburn Brewery 2 **B16**
Peden Oval 1 **M9**
Pelican Sheep Station 1 **P18**
Police Station 2 **C12**
Post Office 2 **B13**
Prell Oval 1 **N10**
Racecourse 2 **L1**
Railway Station 2 **C13**
Rifle Range 2 **H18**
Rifle Range 2 **J18**
Riversdale Homestead (National Trust) 2 **H6**
Rocky Hill War Memorial Museum 2 **G13**
Scenic Lookout 2 **G13**
Seiffert Oval 1 **N11**
Simon Poidevin Oval 1 **H11**
Sportsground 1 **L11**
St Clair Folk Museum & Archives 2 **C11**
St Patricts Cemetery 2 **F2**
St Saviours Cemetery 2 **J8**
Swimming Pool 1 **N10**
Thoroughgood Park 2 **F2**
Tully Park Golf Course 2 **G6**
Victoria Park 1 **N10**
Wakefield Park Motor Racing Circuit 1 **P18**
Wombeyan Caves 2 **L2**
Workers Club Sports Arena 1 **K17**
ZZ7UR

STREETS

Abbey Rd 1 H16
Academy Dr 2 E5
Ada St 2 F16
Adam St 1 K14
Addison La 1 P14
Addison St 1 G11
Albert St 1 N10
Albion St 2 D7
Alice St 1 M18
Allen Wy 2 M2
Allison St 2 F8
Amaroo Pl 2 G2
Amber Ct 2 K2
Angela Pl 1 L8
Apex Cir 1 K10
Arcade La 2 B13
Argyle St 2 B9
Arnheim St 2 B10
Arthur St 2 H12
Ash Cl 1 N4
Aston Martin Dr
  Goulburn 1 P3
  Goulburn 2 A2
Atkinson Cr 2 G4
Auburn St
  Goulburn 1 N15
  Goulburn 2 D10
Audubon Cr 2 B7
Australia St 1 N14
Avoca St 2 D8
Ball Pl 2 G3
Ballanya Av 2 D5
Ballina St
  Goulburn 1 N14
Banksia Wy 2 E17
Baptiste Pl 2 L3
Barber St 1 M9
Barlow Pl 1 P12
Barry Cr 2 D3
Bathurst St 2 E14
Baxter Dr 1 N5
Baxter Pl 1 M5
Beckett St 2 F14
Bellevue St 2 D8
Belmore St 2 C9
Ben St 2 C3
Benbullen Pl 2 G2
Benjamin Pl 1 N4
Benlin Ct 2 H1
Bennett St 1 L17
Bent St 2 F9
Beppo St 2 C10
Betts St 1 L12
Beverly Cl 1 M7
Bigwood Pl 1 L3
Bishop St 2 E10
Bishopthorpe La 1 H9
Blackshaw Rd 2 B14
Bladwell Pl 1 A17
Bolong Pl 2 C5
Bonnett Dr 1 D17
Bonneville Bvd
  Goulburn 1 P2
  Goulburn 2 A2
Boomerang Dr 1 H14
Bourke St 1 N14
Bowerman Rd 1 A14
Box Av 1 L4
Bradford Dr 2 G2
Bradley St 2 B10
Braidwood Rd 1 N18
Brendas Dr 1 M8
Brennan Dr 2 B4
Brewer St 2 G5
Brisbane Grove Rd 1 P17
Brooklands Cct
  Goulburn 1 P2
  Goulburn 2 A2
Broughton St 2 N16
Brownhill St 2 E9
Bruce St 2 D10
Bryant St 1 M10
Budawang Wy 1 L5
Buffalo Cr 2 C7
Bungonia Rd 2 B16
Burge St 1 G14
Bushs La 1 F14
Butler Pl 2 G3
Cahill Pl 2 D3
Calasanctius St 2 L3
Campbell La 2 G1
Caoura Cr 2 D5
Caoura Pl 2 D5
Capri Pl 1 E12
Carmella St 2 K3
Carr St 1 G17
Carramar Wy 1 H13
Carroll Pl 2 D4
Cartwright Pl 2 B12
Cathcart St
  Goulburn 1 H15
  Goulburn 1 H16

Cemetery St 2 H9
Centenary Dr 2 M1
Chalker Rdg 1 A15
Chantilly Ct 1 J14
Chantry St
  Goulburn 2 G8
Chatsbury St 2 F9
Chinamans La
  Baw Baw 1 D2
  Kingsdale 1 D2
Chisholm St 1 K15
Chiswick St
  Goulburn 2 F13
  Goulburn 2 H13
Church St
  Goulburn 1 P12
  Goulburn 2 A12
  Goulburn 2 F5
Churchill St 1 K17
Citizen St 2 C9
Clancy Pl 2 E3
Clifford Ct 1 P11
Clifford St
  Goulburn 1 M10
  Goulburn 1 P10
Clinton La 2 B13
Clinton St 1 L11
Clure Cl 2 B4
Clyde St
  Goulburn 1 J7
  Goulburn 1 K8
Cohen Pl 2 B4
Cole St 2 E10
College St 1 L12
Combermere St 1 K13
Common St 2 K12
Confoy Pl 2 K5
Constantina Cct 1 M7
Constitution St 2 L10
Cooinda Cl 1 L12
Cooma Av 2 A16
Coopers La 1 A5
Copford Rd 2 K4
Coromandel St 1 L13
Cottonwood Av 1 K7
Cove St 2 E10
Cowper Av 1 N12
Cowper St 1 M14
Cowrang St 1 D18
Craig St 2 D11
Cressy St 1 K13
Crestwood Dr 2 B5
Crookwell Rd
  Goulburn 1 L2
  Kingsdale 1 L2
Crundwell St 2 H10
Cullerin Cir 1 K5
Dalley St 2 J7
Dandarbong Cr 2 G2
Darcy Cr 1 K17
Davies St 1 L17
Deccan St 1 L12
Deniehy La 2 C12
Denison St 2 C10
Derwent St 2 D7
Dewhirst St
  Goulburn 2 H1
  Goulburn 2 K1
Dianella Pl 2 E17
Dimitri St 2 B5
Dixon St 1 L8
Donnelly Cr 1 N4
Dossie St 1 M18
Drinkwater Dr 1 M3
Duchess Pl 1 P4
Duck Av 2 D11
Ducks La
  Goulburn 1 B18
  Run-O-Waters 1 B18
Duke St 1 K12
Dunne Cl 2 B4
East St 2 F12
Edward St 1 K13
Eldon St 1 N16
Eleanor St 2 E16
Elizabeth St 1 J14
Ellesmere St 2 B11
Elms St 1 P8
Emma St 2 E16
Emmerson St 1 K13
Endeavour Av 2 B5
Erith St 2 B10
Evangelista St 2 K2
Evans St 1 L11
Faithfull St 1 M14
Farm Rd 2 C15
Fenwick Cr 2 D11
Fife Pl 1 F18
Finlay St 1 J17
Fitzpatrick St 2 C4
Fitzroy St 1 N6

Fitzroy Bridge 2 H9
Foord Rd 1 F12
Forbes St 2 C17
Foster St 1 N9
Fox Cl 1 M4
Francis St 1 L13
Franklin St 1 M4
Fraser Cl 2 D2
Furner St 1 L15
Gale Pl 1 M7
Gallaher Pl 2 K1
Gannon St 2 C12
Gardiner Rd 1 M4
Garfield Av 1 K13
Garroorigang Rd
  Goulburn 1 G17
  Goulburn 1 L18
Geoghegan Dr 2 B4
George St 2 D9
Gerathy St 2 B7
Gertrude St 2 K3
Gibson St
  Goulburn 2 B8
  Goulburn 2 C6
Giddings St 2 D8
Gilmore St 1 L10
Glebe Av 2 A4
Glebe St 1 N15
Glendare Cr 2 G3
Glenelg St 2 D15
Godfrey St 1 P9
Goldsmith St 1 P10
Gorman Rd 2 M8
Gourock Av
  Goulburn 2 C4
  Goulburn 2 E7
Grafton St 2 E11
Grant Pde 2 H2
Gray Av 1 L16
Greenaway Pl 1 K9
Greendale Cr 1 A18
Green Valley Rd 2 A6
Grimston Cct 1 N7
Grunsell Cr 2 G3
Gulson St 2 K4
Gundary St 2 C6
Gurrundah Rd
  Baw Baw 1 A10
  Run-O-Waters 1 A10
Hampden St 2 H2
Hampshire La 2 C11
Harris St 2 L9
Hawthorne St 1 N7
Hazelwood Pl 1 N4
Healey St 2 J2
Heath St 1 N5
Henderson St 1 H12
Henry St 2 F12
Hercules St 2 D16
Hetherington St 2 G14
High St 2 F16
Hill St 1 L17
Hillview Rd 1 N13
Hinchcliffe Cl 1 L7
Hoddle Av 1 L9
Hogg Pl 1 M3
Holland St 1 P11
Hollis Av 1 M16
Hops Pl 1 A15
Hoskins St 1 P8
Hovell St 1 M17
Howard Bvd 2 C5
Hume Hwy
  Goulburn 1 H17
  Goulburn 1 N18
  Goulburn 2 P8
  Gundary 2 N18
Hume St 1 H17
Hunter St 1 M4
Hurrell St 2 H4
Hurst St 2 B9
Huxtable Pl 2 L2
Ibis Rd 1 H7
Ivy Lea Pl 2 H1
Jacqua Av 2 C6
James Pl 1 L16
Joanna Pl 2 B5
John St 1 M12
Joshua St 2 F9
Jubilee Av 1 L17
Kadwell St
  Goulburn 1 P8
  Goulburn 2 A8
Kavanagh St 2 B3
Keating Rd 1 A11
Kelly Pl 2 C4
Kelso St 1 L16
Kenmore St 2 E8
Kenmore Bridge 2 G6
Kent St 1 M12
Kerr Pl 2 B7

Kidd Cct 2 E2
King St 1 P15
Kingfisher Rd 1 H6
Kinghorne St 1 P8
Kings Wy 1 L15
Kirke Pl 2 G3
Knowlman Rd 1 A16
Knox St 2 J15
Komungla Cr 2 G4
Lagoon St 2 D10
Lamarra Pl 1 M7
Lambert Dr 1 M4
Lanigan La
  Goulburn 1 P13
  Goulburn 2 A13
Lansdowne Pl 1 K16
Lansdowne St
  Goulburn 1 J16
  Goulburn 1 L16
Lansdowne Bridge 2 D17
Lawrenny Av 2 C9
Ledger St 1 N5
Leeson St 2 E16
Leonard Ri 1 M3
Liguori Pl 2 K3
Lillkar Rd
  Goulburn 1 D18
  Goulburn 1 G18
Lions Pl 1 K10
Lisgar St 1 L16
Lithgow Cr 2 M1
Lithgow St 2 C10
Little Cl 1 D16
Little Addison St 1 N13
Llewellyn Av 1 M10
Lockyer St 1 H18
Loder St 1 G12
Loloma Pl 1 A18
Long St
  Goulburn 2 H18
  Goulburn 2 J10
  Goulburn 2 J13
Lorne St 2 B9
Lovet St 2 C3
Lower Sterne St 2 F11
Lucas Cl 2 D2
Macalister Dr 1 M9
Mcalroy Pl
  Goulburn 2 B3
  Goulburn 2 B4
McDermott Dr 2 D5
McGrath Pl 2 C3
McGuire Dr 2 D4
McKell Pl 2 B12
McNaught St 2 B12
MacQuarie St 1 L9
Madelaine Dr 2 L2
Major Pl 1 L9
Major St 1 M11
Malvern Rd 2 H2
Manar St 2 C5
Manchester La 1 M13
Manfred Pl 1 L13
Manion St 2 D9
Mannifera Pl 2 F16
Manning Dr 2 M2
Market St 2 C12
Marsden St 2 E10
Marsden Bridge 1 M6
Martyr St 1 M15
Mary St
  Goulburn 1 G14
  Goulburn 1 N15
Mary Martin Dr 1 L5
Marys Mount Rd
  Goulburn 1 M5
  Goulburn 2 B3
Matchless Av 2 B2
Maud St 2 G9
May St 2 E16
Mazamet Rd 1 G17
Meehan St 2 B7
Melliodora Dr 2 E17
Memorial Rd
  Goulburn 2 E17
  Goulburn 2 G15
Mewburn Dr 1 M5
Meyer St 2 K1
Middle Arm Rd 2 F3
Mill St 2 M7
Mistful Park Rd 1 M4
Mitchell St
  Goulburn 1 L4
  Goulburn 2 E7
Moffitt Av 2 L2
Monastery Dr 2 D4
Montague St
  Goulburn 1 P11
  Goulburn 2 B12
Moore Pl 1 M7
Mortis St 2 G9

Mount St 1 M9
Mt Baw Baw Rd 1 A2
Mullen St 1 M9
Mulwarree St 2 E11
Mundoonen Dr 1 K5
Mundy St 1 L13
Murac St 2 G7
Murphy Pl 2 C4
Murray St 2 C9
Naughten Av 2 M1
Nell Wy 2 B2
Nelson Pl 1 M7
Neville St 2 C7
New St 2 F10
Newton St 1 N8
Nichols St 2 G3
Nicholson St 1 P9
Nicole Pl 1 H16
North St 2 B10
Oakwood Av 2 C5
O Allen Dr 2 E6
O'brien St 1 M12
Oliver St 2 C10
Onslow Rd 1 K1
Opal St 2 C8
O'sullivan Pl 2 J4
Ottiwell St 1 N16
Oxley Cr 1 L5
Oxley St 1 J16
Paradise Pl 2 J2
Park Cl 1 F16
Park Rd
  Goulburn 2 C14
  Goulburn 2 E6
Park St 2 D9
Parkside Pl 2 B6
Paton Pl 1 L8
Pejar Pl 2 E6
Peppertree Pl 1 L7
Phillip St 2 E11
Pitt St 1 P9
Platypus Cct 1 H7
Plover Pl 1 H8
Pockley Rd 1 C17
Poidevin Pl 2 D3
Post Office La 2 B13
Prell St 2 A10
Prince St
  Goulburn 2 B9
  Goulburn 2 E6
Princes Av 1 J14
Princess St 2 L1
Progress St 2 H2
Pursehouse Pl 2 K4
Quadrant Pl 1 P3
Queen St 2 G4
Quiberon Wy
  Goulburn 1 P3
  Goulburn 2 A4
Racecourse Dr 2 L1
Range Rd
  Baw Baw 1 A4
  Goulburn 1 A4
Record St 2 H3
Redgum Pl 2 E17
Redman Cct 1 N5
Registration Av 2 F6
Reign St 2 H3
Renshaw St 1 P7
Rex St 2 K1
Reynolds St 2 F10
Rhoda St 1 J13
Ridge St 1 G13
Rifle Range Rd 2 F17
River St 1 K9
Rivergum Pl 1 K6
Riverview Pl 2 E8
Robert St 2 F11
Robinson Cl 1 J16
Robinson St 1 J16
Roebuck St 2 B2
Rosarii Pl 2 L3
Rose St 1 J13
Rosedale Ct 1 K14
Rosemont Rd 2 F18
Ross Av 2 M1
Ross Pl
  Goulburn 2 E6
Ross St
  Goulburn 2 H3
  Goulburn 2 J4
Rossi Pl 1 M7
Rossi Bridge 1 D5
Rossiville Rd 1 H11
Rossiville Wy 2 M1
Rotary Dr 1 K10
Rowallan La 1 M15
Ruby St 2 C8
Run-O-Waters Dr
  Run-O-Waters 1 A16
  Run-O-Waters 1 A18

Ruse St 1 M5
Ryan Pl 2 J1
St Aubyn Rd 1 N5
St Michaels Cl 2 E8
Salford St 1 M13
Samuel Pl 2 G2
Sanctuary Dr
  Goulburn 1 J6
  Goulburn 1 K9
Sanita St 1 L12
Sellors St 2 B9
Shannon Dr 1 F15
Shepherd St 2 D9
Shepherds Ct
  Goulburn 1 N12
Short St 2 G4
Show St 2 A9
Sinclair St 2 K11
Sloane St
  Goulburn 1 N18
  Goulburn 1 P15
Slocombe St 1 H14
Snowgums Dr 1 L8
Soares La 2 E10
Soho St 2 G9
Sowerby St 1 H18
Spadacini Pl 2 B4
Stalker St 1 M12
Stewart St 1 G13
Stombuco Pl 2 B4
Straker Rd 2 E2
Strathaird La
  Goulburn 2 F9
Strathallan Cr 2 F4
Success Pl 1 P4
Swan Lp 2 D2
Sydney Rd
  Goulburn 2 G10
  Goulburn 2 J10
Tait Cr 1 K18
Tallowwood St 1 K7
Tall Timbers Dr 1 A18
Tara Pl 2 B9
Taralga Rd 2 G4
Tarlo St 2 G5
Taylor St 2 C10
Teece Pl 2 G4
Theatre Dr 1 J16
The Avenue 1 N6
Therry Av 2 C8
Thomas Pl 1 L7
Thorne Av 1 N13
Thurbon Dr 1 N7
Towrang Av 2 C5
Trifecta Dr 2 L1
Turner St 1 L8
Tweedie St 2 D2
Twynam Dr 2 H6
Union La 2 F9
Union St 2 F9
Upper Sterne St 2 E10
Usshers La 2 E9
Vendetta St 1 P3
Verner St 1 L11
Vernon Rd 2 M2
Victoria Av 2 C11
Victoria Pde 1 N12
Victoria St 2 C9
Victoria St Bridge 2 D6
View St 1 M10
Village Rd 1 M8
Village High Rd 1 N8
Vincent Av 2 K2
Voyager Av 1 P3
Walker St 2 A14
Walsh Dr 2 C4
Waterfront Pl 1 J5
Waterlily Fy 1 H6
Waterview Rd 1 C18
Wayo St 2 G9
Werriwa St 2 E8
Wheatley Av 2 E10
Wheeo Rd 1 H9
William St 2 A7
William Alfred Pl 2 H1
Willow Grove Pl 2 G5
Wilmot St 2 F8
Windellama Rd 2 F18
Wollondilly Av 2 L2
Woodward St 2 F3
Workers Av 1 L10
Wran St 2 J1
Wright Pl 2 C4
Wyatt St 1 K12
Yarrowlow St 2 F3

MAP 1 GOULBURN

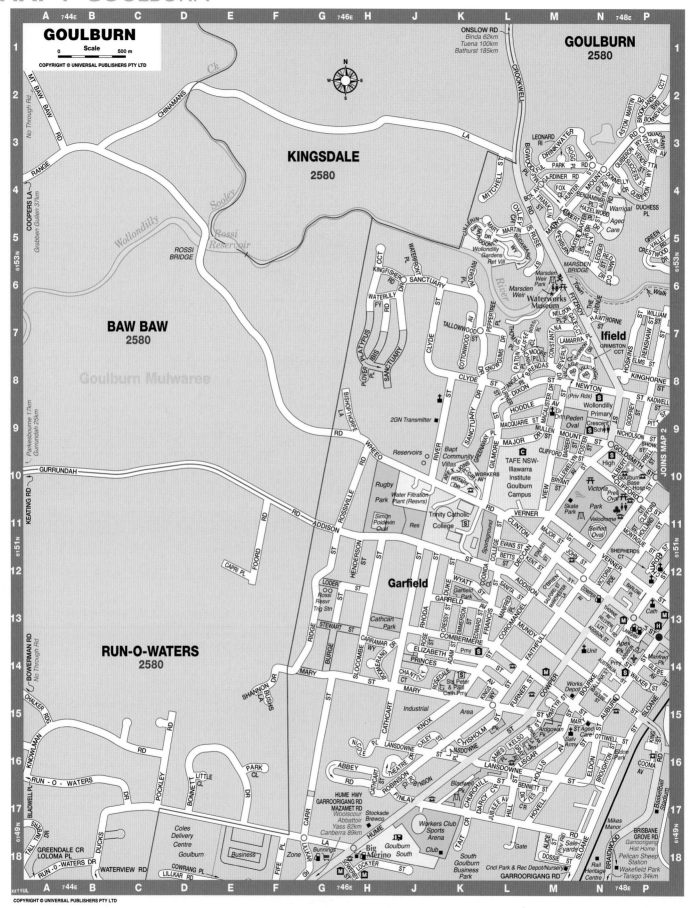

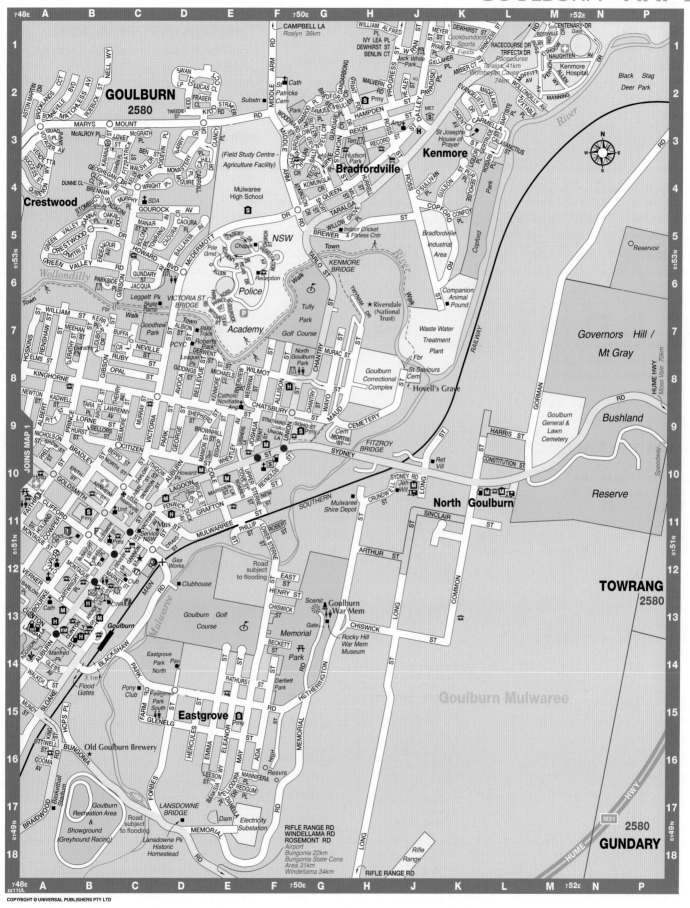

HUSKISSON/VINCENTIA

LOCATION
185km south of Sydney

POPULATION
3400

NRMA ROAD SERVICE
Ph: 13 11 22

VISITOR INFORMATION
Shoalhaven Visitor Information Centre
cnr Princes Highway & Pleasant Way
Nowra
Ph: (02) 4421 0778
www.shoalhavenholidays.com.au

Huskisson is a thriving tourist and fishing town lying in the curve of Jervis Bay. It is the main shopping and accommodation centre on the bay, just 24 kilometres south-east of Nowra. A popular destination for families, catamaran sailors, windsurfers, fishers and divers, Huskisson provides easy access to the beautiful clear waters of the Bay and all facilities. To the south, the clear water and brilliant white sands of Vincentia's beaches provide idyllic places for total relaxation.

Those interested in the history of boat-building should visit the Lady Denman Heritage Complex in Huskisson. The Lady Denman, a Sydney Harbour ferry built at Huskisson and launched in 1911, has returned to her birthplace as the centrepiece of the museum.

HUSKISSON ACCOMMODATION GUIDE
Holiday Haven Huskisson Beach **G8**
Holiday Haven Huskisson White Sands **G6**
Huskisson Bayside Motel **F6**
Huskisson Beach Motel **F5**
Jervis Bay Motel **E4**

FACILITIES & ATTRACTIONS
Bowling Club **C3**
Fleet Air Museum **A4**
Huskisson RSL Club **E4**
Husky Ferry **E2**
Jervis Bay Maritime Museum **D2**
Jervis Bay Visitor Information Centre **D2**
Marayong Park Emu Farm Emu Shop **A5**
Post Office **E5**
Showground **C3**
Swimming Pool **F4**

Theatre **D4**
Voyager Memorial Park **F4**
White Sands Park **F5**
ZZ7UR

VINCENTIA ACCOMMODATION GUIDE
Dolphin Shores Motor Inn **D9**

FACILITIES & ATTRACTIONS
Jervis Bay Maritime Park **G9**
Jervis Bay National Park **A6**
Post Office **E10**
Stuart King Reserve **L13**
Swimming Pool **A12**
Vincentia Golf Club **H14**
Vincentia Sailing Club **M10**
Violet Clark Reserve **G10**
Violet Clark Reserve **F10**
ZZ7UR

HUSKISSON STREETS

Admiralty Cr **E3**	Jervis Bay Rd **A4**
Beach St **G7**	Kent La **F6**
Beach St **G9**	Keppel St **E7**
Beecroft St **E6**	Kiola St **C3**
Berry St **E8**	Moona St **E9**
Bolten Rd **B2**	Morton St **E5**
Bowen St **E5**	Murdoch St **F10**
Burrill St **F9**	Nowra St **E6**
Calala St **D5**	Owen St **C4**
Clyde St **F8**	Park St **D3**
Currambene St **E9**	Scallop Rd **B2**
Dent St **D3**	Snapper Rd **A2**
Duncan St **F8**	Sydney St **D5**
Duranbah Dr **B2**	Tapalla Av **G9**
Erina Rd **B2**	Termeil St **C5**
Fegen St **G7**	Tomerong St **D3**
Field St **E4**	Waddell St **E6**
Frank Lewis Wy **D2**	Watt St **D4**
Hawke St **F7**	Winnima La **G7**
Huskisson Rd **A3**	Wood Cr **D3**
Illfracombe Av **G10**	Woollamia Rd **C2**
Jervis St **F8**	

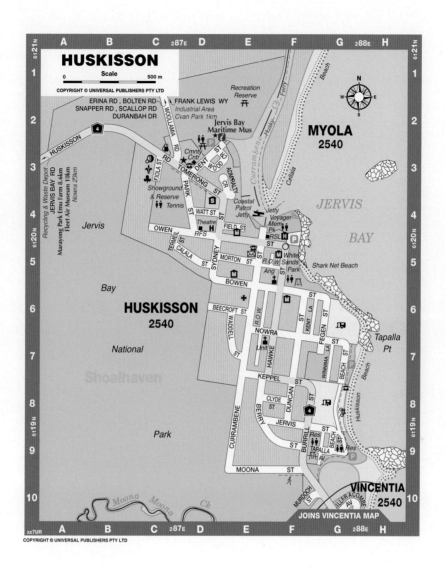

Murrays Beach Jervis Bay Shoalhaven

VINCENTIA STREETS

Ada St **F11**	Burton St **E10**	Egmont Pl **G11**	Irwin Pl **F12**	Montague St **C5**	Saumarez St **J12**
Albion St **D3**	Calder Cl **K14**	Elizabeth Dr **D7**	Jervis St **L12**	Murdoch St **D1**	Susan St **D7**
Anne St **G10**	Caroline St **G10**	Emmeline Pl **D10**	Knowles St **H12**	Murray St **J14**	Tharwa Rd **L13**
Anne St **H10**	Church St **E9**	Excellent St **E10**	Lambs Cr **L11**	Namur St **E11**	The Wool Rd **A12**
Argyle St **C9**	Cockbourne Pl **G13**	Foley St **J11**	Lanyon Rd **K12**	Naval College Rd **A14**	Towry Cr **J12**
Banksia St **E2**	Colloden Av **E10**	Frederick St **K14**	Linsay St **H12**	Niger St **E11**	Troubridge Dr **F12**
Barnett St **L11**	Dacres St **K12**	Garlies Cl **D9**	Louisa Gr **H13**	Omega Pl **H14**	Twyford St **H9**
Bayswater St **D4**	Deas Thomson St **M11**	George Caley Pl **C11**	Mcnamara Ct **C5**	Plantation Point Pde **L10**	Vincent St **G9**
Beach St **D9**	Diadem Av **F12**	Grey Pl **H11**	Miller St **H11**	Prowse Cl **H14**	Waldegrave Cr **J11**
Berry St **C5**	Duncan St **C9**	Hawke St **B8**	Minerva Av **H10**	Raven Cl **J13**	Wally Ct **C5**
Bess St **H11**	Duncan St **D6**	Holden St **G9**	Minerva Av **J12**	Roper St **J11**	Whitshed Pl **F12**
Bourke Cl **C9**	Edward St **C7**	Illfracombe Av **E2**	Mona St **J13**	St George Av **D10**	Wirrillko Wy **A13**
				Saumarez St **H12**	Woden St **D4**

KANGAROO VALLEY

LOCATION
On Moss Vale Road
140km south-west of Sydney
POPULATION
879
NRMA ROAD SERVICE
Ph: 13 11 22

VISITOR INFORMATION
Shoalhaven Visitors Centre
Bridge Rd
Nowra
Ph: (02) 4421 0778
Ph: 1300 662 808
www.shoalhavenholidays.com.au

Kangaroo Valley's climate offers the best of both worlds. Long, sunny summer days, just right for swimming in the river; and crisp winter nights, perfect for relaxing in front of a log-fire.

Kangaroo Valley is an extremely gorgeous valley surrounded by steep escarpments and is reputed to be one of only seven fully enclosed valleys in the world.

It is difficult to do justice to the beauty of Kangaroo Valley.

In fact the valley's first European explorer, George Evans, described a view that "no painter could beautify".

The famous sandstone Hampden Bridge, built in the 1890's, is Australia's oldest suspension bridge and is a most impressive and attractive structure well worth the visit when in the region. There is a good selection of cafes, restaurants and country style shops. A pioneer farm museum also welcomes visitors.

ACCOMMODATION GUIDE
Holiday Haven Kangaroo Valley **E9**
Kangaroo Valley Glenmack Caravan Park **L13**
Kangaroo Valley Golf & Country Resort **A14**
Pioneer Motel Kangaroo Valley **J13**

FACILITIES & ATTRACTIONS
Bendeela Picnic Area **A6**
Hampden Bridge **C9**
Hampden Bridge Park **E9**
Kangaroo River Nature Reserve **A8**
Kangaroo Valley Cemetery **P14**

Kangaroo Valley Golf & Country Resort **A14**
Kangaroo Valley Showground **K12**
Osbourne Park **K12**
Pioneer Museum Park **D8**
Pioneer Village Museum **D9**
Police Station **J13**
Post Office **H13**
Riverside Park **F11**
Swimming Pool **J12**
Tallowa Dam Picnic Area **A14**
War Memorial **J13**
ZZ7UR

STREETS

Bendeela Rd
  Barrengarry **A6**
  Kangaroo Valley **A6**
Bowlers Cl **F12**
Brooks La **G12**
Broughton St **G12**
Cavan Rd **D2**
Cedar Springs Rd **A6**
Cullen Cr **E10**
Grahams Rd **G1**
Gum Tree La **B15**
Hampden Bridge **C9**
Jarretts La **L17**
Jenanter Dr **C10**
Kangaroo Valley Rd **P14**
Kellys Rd **P7**

Mackays Rd **P7**
Marden La **A15**
Marshall St **F12**
Merchants Rd **P15**
Moss Vale Rd
  Barrengarry **D7**
  Kangaroo Valley **D9**
Mount Scanzi Rd **A14**
Murray St **G12**
Nugents Creek Rd **N17**
Paddington La **G1**
Quirk St **F13**
Rectory Park Wy **E11**
Rendga Ct **E12**
Upper Kangaroo River Rd **F6**

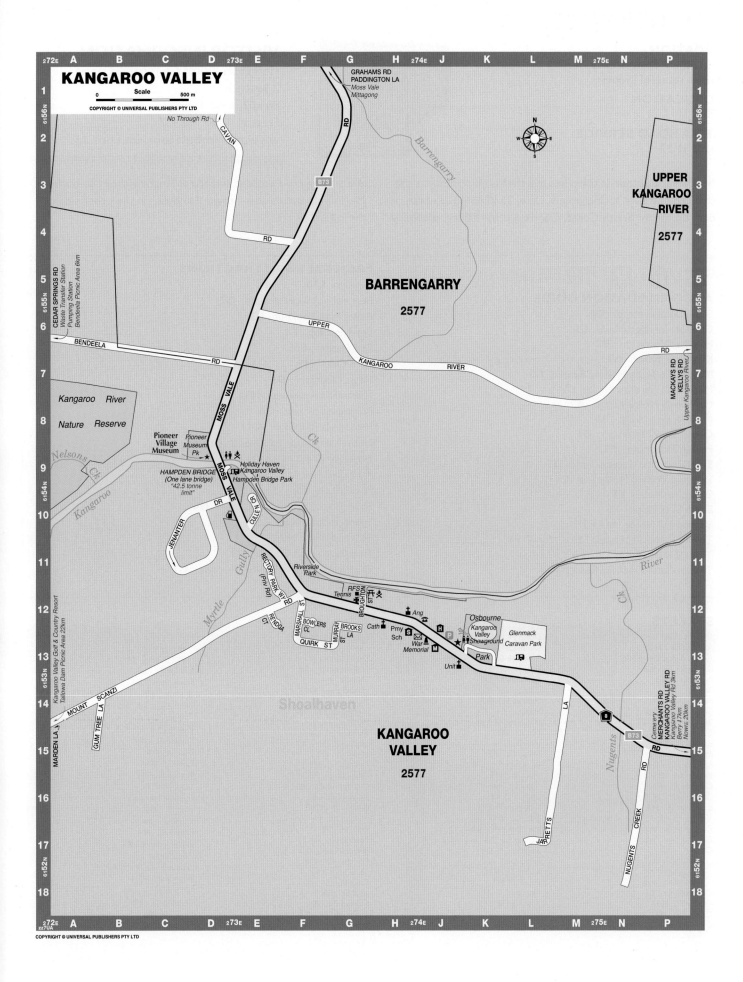

KANGAROO VALLEY

Scale
0 — 500 m

GRAHAMS RD
PADDINGTON LA
Moss Vale
Mittagong

No Through Rd

CAVAN

RD

B73

UPPER

KANGAROO   RIVER

BARRENGARRY

2577

UPPER
KANGAROO
RIVER

2577

MACKAYS RD
KELLYS RD
Upper Kangaroo River

RD

BENDEELA

RD

MOSS VALE

Kangaroo   River

Nature   Reserve

Pioneer
Village
Museum

Pioneer
Museum
Pk

Ck

Nelsons   Ck

Kangaroo

MOSS VALE

HAMPDEN BRIDGE
(One lane bridge)
"42.5 tonne
limit"

Holiday Haven
Kangaroo Valley
Hampden Bridge Park

JENANTER

DR

CULLEN DR

RECTORY PARK WY
(Priv Rd)

RENOGA CT

Myrtle   Gully

Riverside
Park

River

Ck

RFS
Tennis

BROUGHTON ST

Ang

MARSHALL ST

BOWLERS
CL

MURRAY ST

BROOKS
LA

Cath

QUIRK   ST

Pmy
Sch

War
Memorial

Osbourne
Kangaroo
Valley
Showground

H

P

Glenmack
Caravan Park

Park

Unit

Kangaroo Valley Golf & Country Resort
Tallowa Dam Picnic Area 22km

MOUNT   SCANZI

GUM TREE LA

MARDEN LA

Shoalhaven

KANGAROO
VALLEY

2577

JARRETTS

LA

Nugents

Ck

B73

RD

Cemetery
MERCHANTS RD
KANGAROO VALLEY RD
Kangaroo Valley Rd 3km
Berry 17km
Nowra 20km

NUGENTS   CREEK   RD

MERIMBULA

LOCATION
7km off the Princes Hwy
467km south of Sydney

POPULATION
6900

NRMA ROAD SERVICE
Ph: 13 11 22

VISITOR INFORMATION
Merimbula Visitor Information Centre
2 Beach St
Ph: (02) 6495 1129
Freecall: 1800 150 457
www.merimbulatourism.com.au

This fishing and tourist town lies in a sheltered position at the northern entrance to Merimbula Lake, 25 kilometres north of Eden, on the far South Coast. Conditions for fishing, prawning and surfing are excellent and attract many visitors to both Merimbula and its sister town Pambula, on the other side of the lake.

ACCOMMODATION GUIDE

Black Dolphin Motel **G9**
Comfort Inn Merimbula **E5**
Hillcrest Motor Inn **B4**
Kingfisher Motel **A3**
Merimbula Beach Holiday Resort **N5**
Merimbula Gardens Motel **E5**
Merimbula Motor Lodge **A2**
Norfolk Pine Motel **B5**
Ocean View Motor Inn **D6**
Pelican Motor Inn **F5**
Sapphire Valley Caravan Park **D3**
Sapphire Waters Motor Inn **E5**
Sea Spray Motel **E5**
South Seas Motel **F5**
Summerhill Motor Inn **F5**
The Merimbula Lakeview Hotel Motel **F6**
Town Centre Motor Inn **F5**
Tween Waters Holiday Resort **G9**

FACILITIES & ATTRACTIONS

Airport **E10**
Berrambool Sportsground **G2**
Boller Park Lookout **B3**
Bowling Club **F4**
Fire Station **F6**
Ford Oval **H9**
Magic Mountain **D1**
Merimbula Aquarium **M10**
Merimbula Marina **G6**
Merimbula RSL Club **G4**
Merimbula Visitor Information Centre **G5**
Museum **G4**
Pambula-Merimbula Golf Club **E10**
Post Office **F5**
Short Point Recreation Reserve **N4**
Spencer Park **K5**
Sportsground **H9**
Tura Beach Golf Course **D1**
Whale Watching & Fishing Charters **G7**
ZZ7UR

STREETS

Alice St **G5**
Apoona Rd **M6**
Arthur Kaine Dr **F10**
Bar Beach Rd **L8**
Beach St **G5**
Bega St **F7**
Bellbird Cr **B7**
Benandra Av **D8**
Berrambool Dr **F3**
Beverley St **C5**
Bodalla Pl **D8**
Brodribb Ct **F2**
Bronwyn Cl **D6**
Burton Av **H8**
Cabarita Pl **F6**
Calendo Ct **J8**
Cameron St **H4**
Camilla Ct **J1**
Carolynne St **E7**
Chapman Av **H8**
Cliff St
  Merimbula **L5**
  Merimbula **M7**
  Merimbula **N6**
Cockatoo Ct **L1**
Collins St **K4**
Curlew Cl **K1**
Currawong Cl **J1**

Doyle Pl **B7**
Dunns La **G9**
Elizabeth St **G8**
Fishpen Rd **H7**
Gannet Ct **L1**
Garden Cir **G2**
George St **M7**
Harbour Ct **C4**
Henwood St **J4**
Hill St **M7**
Hillmeads St **A7**
Hollis Ct **E2**
Illawong Hts **D4**
Illuka St **M6**
Imlay St **A8**
Jabiru Pl **K1**
Jacaranda Pl **K1**
John Cl **D7**
John Penn Av **C7**
Kalinda St **E4**
Katrina Ct **C5**
Kembla Cl **C7**
Kiama Pl **B8**
King St **M8**
Kowara Cr **D5**
Kyeamba St **F5**
Lake St **L6**
Lakeview Av **K4**

Lakewood Dr **A6**
Lisa Ct **D7**
Lorikeet Cl **J1**
Ludericks Ct **A5**
Main St **F4**
Marine Pde **G8**
Market St **G5**
Merimbula Dr **B4**
Mirador Dr **J1**
Monaro St **B6**
Mulloway Cct **A7**
Munn St **H3**
Ocean Dr **H9**
Ocean View Av **F7**
Old Tathra Rd **E1**
Oriole Ct **L1**
Otway Cl **C8**
Palmer La **F5**
Park St **E5**
Patrick Ct **D7**
Princes Hwy **A2**
Princess La **M9**
Queen St **M8**
Randolph St **J4**
Reid St **E6**
Salmon Ct **A6**
Sandpiper La **C7**
Sapphire Cr **B4**

Sapphire Coast Dr
  Berrambool **E1**
  Merimbula **E1**
Schafer Tr **L6**
Seaview Av **D6**
Short St **F7**
Short Point Rd **N5**
Snapper Ct **A5**
Tantawanglo St **C8**
Tasman St **M9**
Teal Ct **A6**
Tern Cl **A7**
The Crest **K1**
Tilba Pl **C8**
Trevally Tce **A5**
View St **D6**
Warn Cl **B6**
Wharf St **M9**
Whipbird Wy **K2**
Whistler Cl **L1**
Wildewoods Ct **C5**
Wonga St **F5**
Woodland Dr **B3**
Wyeebo St **M6**
Yarai St **M8**
Yarrawood Av **E2**

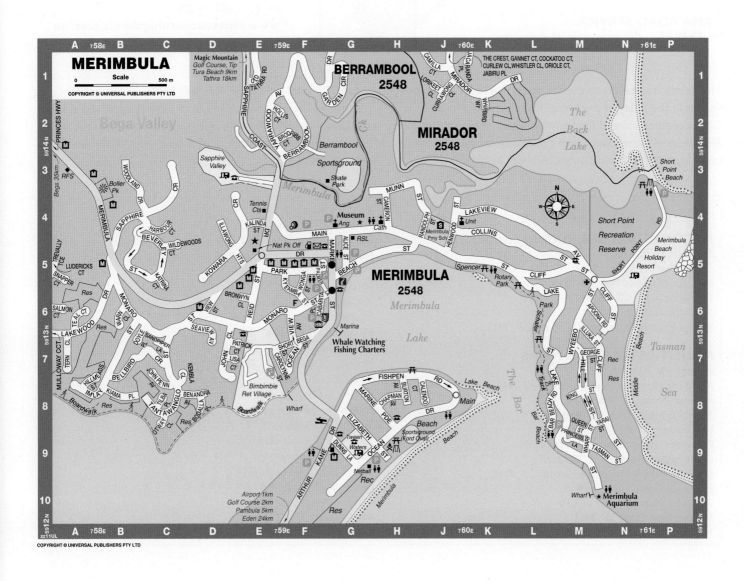

MERIMBULA

Scale
0 — 500 m

COPYRIGHT © UNIVERSAL PUBLISHERS PTY LTD

Magic Mountain
Golf Course, Tip
Tura Beach 9km
Tathra 18km

BERRAMBOOL 2548

MIRADOR 2548

THE CREST, GANNET CT, COCKATOO CT,
CURLEW CL, WHISTLER CL, ORIOLE CT,
JABIRU PL

Bega Valley

The Back Lake

Short Point Beach

Short Point Recreation Reserve

Merimbula Beach Holiday Resort

MERIMBULA 2548

Merimbula Lake

Whale Watching Fishing Charters

Tasman Sea

The Bar

Bimbimbie Ret Village

Bega 35km
Princes Hwy
Res

Airport 1km
Golf Course 2km
Pambula 5km
Eden 24km

Merimbula Aquarium

MITTAGONG

LOCATION
Off the Hume Hwy
109km south-west of Sydney
POPULATION
5780
NRMA ROAD SERVICE
Ph: 13 11 22

VISITOR INFORMATION
Mittagong Visitor Information Centre
62 Main St
(Old Hume Hwy)
Ph: (02) 4871 2888
www.visitsouthernhighlands.com.au

The northern gateway to the Southern Highlands, Mittagong nestles in the valley of the Nattai River beneath Mount Gibraltar (the Gib) and the wooded slopes of Mount Alexandra. An attractive town, Mittagong has many homes, both large and small, and public buildings built from the beautiful local sandstone. It is well known for its gardens, art, craft and antique shops. One of Mittagong's greatest assets is Lake Alexandra Reserve. Just three blocks from the main street, this popular picnic spot is home to a profusion of friendly bird life.

ACCOMMODATION GUIDE
Fitzroy Inn **2 F10**
Grand Country Lodge Motel **2 C11**
Mittagong Caravan Park **2 E10**
Mittagong Motel **2 D10**
Motel Melrose **2 C11**
Springs Resorts Mittagong RSL Motel **1 M12**

FACILITIES & ATTRACTIONS
Airport **2 P13**
All Aboard Braemar Model Railways **2 N3**
Artemis Wines **1 A6**
Bowral Country Club **1 B18**
Fire Station **1 P12**
Frensham Games Fields **2 D14**
Gibbergunyah Reserve **1 A12**
Greenbrier Park Vineyard & Garden **2 D18**
Highlands Golf Club **2 F9**
Highlands Marketplace **1 L10**
Historic Iron Cairn **1 M11**
Howards Lane Vineyard **1 A9**

Ironmines Oval **1 M10**
Katoomba Lookout **2 B5**
Lake Alexandra Reserve **1 P9**
Marist Brothers Wines **2 P15**
Mittagong Lookout **1 H17**
Mittagong RSL Club **1 M11**
Mittagong Sportsfield **2 E9**
Mittagong Visitor Information Centre **2 C11**
Mt Alexandra Reserve **2 A6**
Mt Gibraltar Reserve **1 H16**
Mt Jellore Lookout **1 G17**
Post Office **2 B11**
Railway Station **2 B12**
Rowes Hill Cemetery **2 P13**
Sir Charles Moses Park **1 A10**
Sixty Foot Falls **2 D4**
State Emergency Service **1 J11**
Sturt Craft Centre **2 B14**
Swimming Pool **2 F9**
Victoria House **2 B11**
Welby Oval **1 E7**
ZZ7UR

STREETS

MAP I MITTAGONG

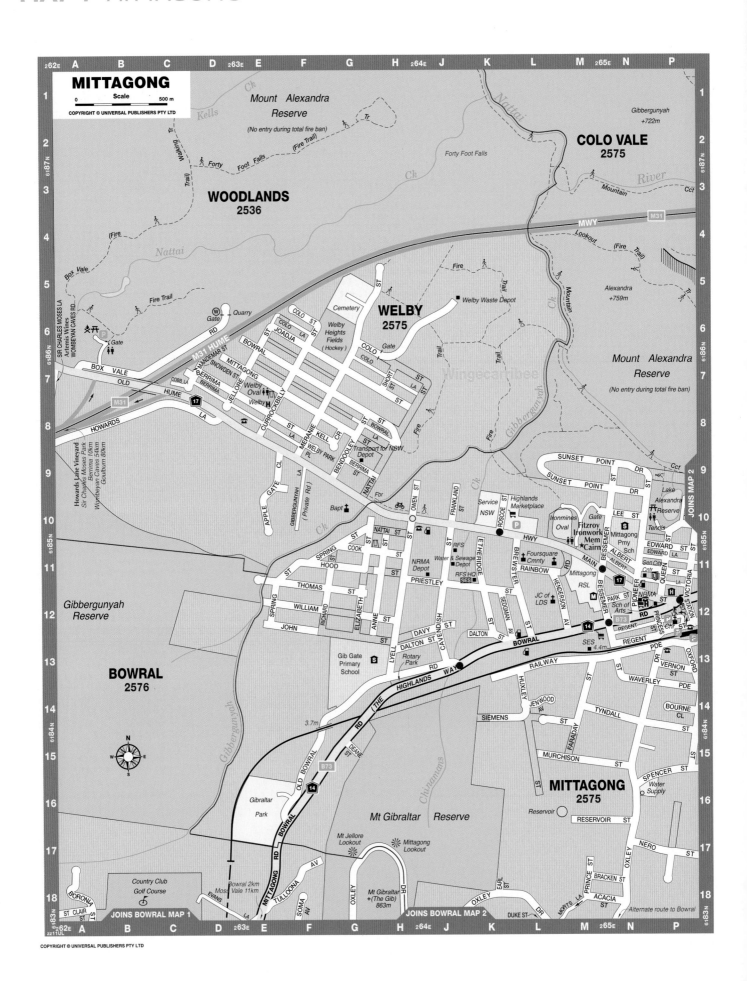

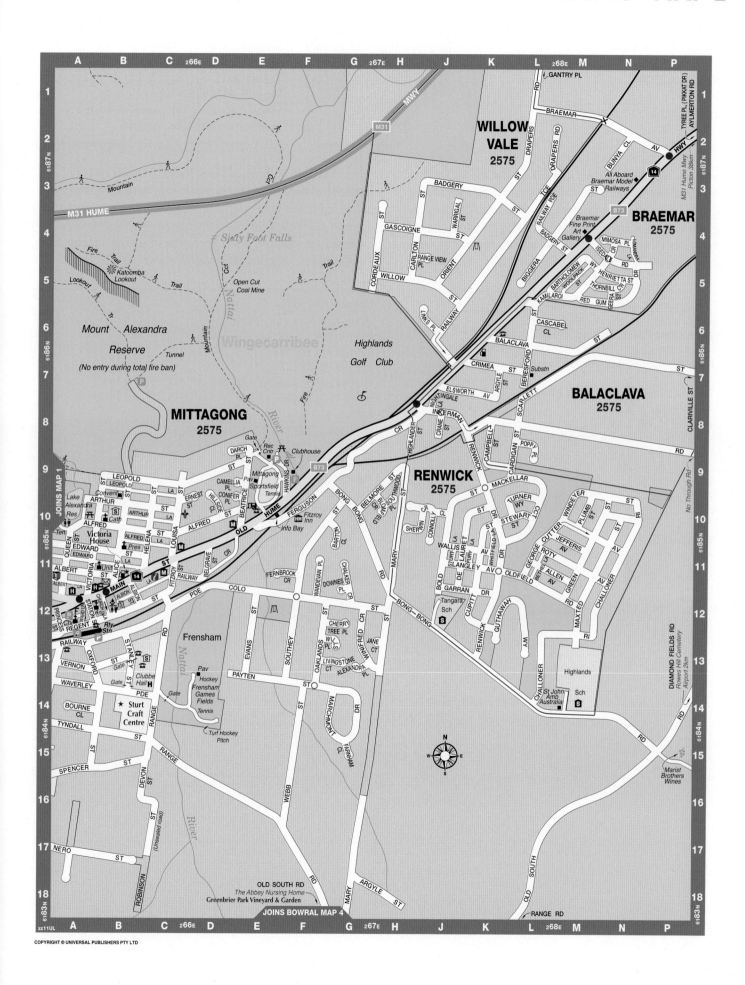

MORUYA

LOCATION
On the Princes Hwy
307km south of Sydney
POPULATION
2500
NRMA ROAD SERVICE
Ph: 13 11 22

VISITOR INFORMATION
Moruya Information Service
Shire Library
Vulcan St
Ph: (02) 4474 1333
www.naturecoast-tourism.com.au
www.eurobodalla.com.au

Lying six kilometres inland, this quiet rural centre services dairy and beef country and also has a small fishing industry. The river – with its mangroves, oyster leases, channels and mud banks – is a good fishing spot. Along its banks there are pretty picnic spots. Clustered in the centre of town are some beautiful old buildings; the courthouse, post office, churches and old Bank of New South Wales are all fine examples of mid-19th century public architecture. Moruya Museum preserves regional history, including that of the gold period at Mogo. Outside of the township, Deua National Park, inland from Moruya, is a rugged area of special interest to bushwalkers, canoeists and caving enthusiasts.

ACCOMMODATION GUIDE
Motel Luhana **J5**
River Breeze Tourist Park **H1**

FACILITIES & ATTRACTIONS
Ack Weyman Oval **J7**
Apex Park **H5**
Australias Bush Orchestra **A9**
Bowling Club **F2**
Council Office **H5**
Fire Station **J4**
Golf Club **G6**

Gundary Park **F3**
Hospital **E1**
Moruya **J4**
Moruya Airport **L2**
Moruya Heads **L7**
Moruya Information Service **H6**
Motor Club Racetrack **L2**
NRMA **J4**
Post Office **H3**
Rotary Park **J3**
Showground **H7**
Swimming Pool **J3**
ZZ7UR

STREETS

Albert St **C7**	Ford St **J5**	Mollee Rd **L8**	Riverwood Pl **A3**
Albert St **F7**	Ford St **K2**	Moruya St **G9**	Rose St **G10**
Anderson St **J9**	Foreman St **G4**	Moruya River Bridge **H2**	Ryan Pl **F5**
Araluen Rd **A7**	Francis St **J10**	Murray St **A5**	Ryley Cl **E8**
Behringers Point La **D1**	Gundary St **C6**	Murray St **C5**	Shore St **D2**
Bergalia St **G9**	Guthrie St **J1**	Murray St **K6**	Shore St **J3**
Braemar Dr **K7**	Haslingden St **G9**	Noads Rd **L8**	South Head Rd **L7**
Campbell St **D4**	Hawdon St **C8**	North Head Dr **J2**	Spencer St **E10**
Carrie Cr **K9**	Heffernan Pl **D3**	Otton St **F9**	Swan Ridge Pl **E9**
Cheddar St **C4**	Jeffery Pl **F8**	Page St **G5**	Ted Hunt Tce **A5**
Church St **G3**	Jersey Rd **C3**	Panorama Pde **E8**	Thomas St **E5**
Cobbers La **B4**	John St **J9**	Park La **H5**	Toose St **J1**
Congo Rd **L7**	John St **K4**	Parkland Ct **J10**	Turnbulls La **B9**
Costin St **H10**	John St **K8**	Patterson Cl **E9**	Vulcan St **H10**
Craig Mostyn Pl **C2**	Joy Pl **K7**	Pioneer Av **E8**	Vulcan St **H4**
Dr King Cl **K7**	Keightley St **L7**	Princes Hwy **J1**	Wamban Rd **A8**
Dwyer Creek Rd **F10**	Lagoon St **E7**	Princes Hwy **K7**	Wattlebark Pl **C3**
Emmott St **B6**	Luck St **B5**	Princes Hwy **K9**	Woodbridge Av **F8**
Evans St **F8**	Maluka Av **J10**	Queen St **D3**	Yaccaba Dr **E10**
Fitzroy St **F6**	Maunsell St **L7**	Queen St **H4**	Yarimup Pl **E10**
Flanagan Pl **F5**	Mirrabooka Av **H4**	Red Tree Pl **B3**	Yarragee Rd **A6**
Ford La **J4**		River St **D2**	Yarragee St **C6**

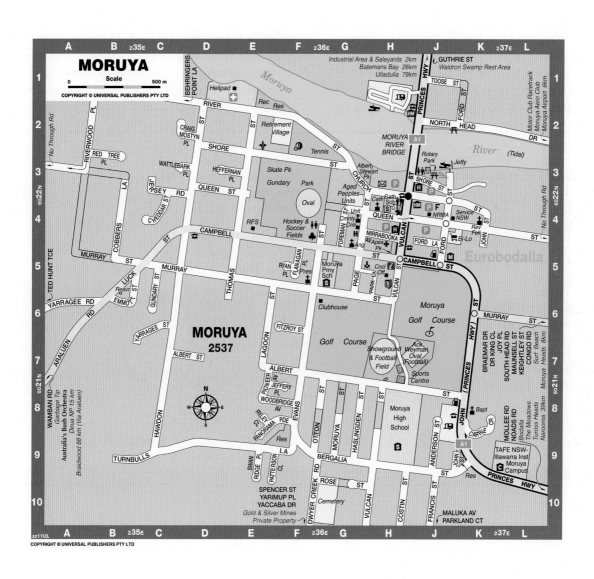

MORUYA

Scale

0 ━━━━━━ 500 m

COPYRIGHT © UNIVERSAL PUBLISHERS PTY LTD

MORUYA 2537

Eurobodalla

Industrial Area & Saleyards 2km
Batemans Bay 26km
Ulladulla 79km

GUTHRIE ST
Waldron Swamp Rest Area

Motor Club Racetrack
Moruya Aero Club
Moruya Airport 6km

Moruya (River)

MORUYA RIVER BRIDGE

BEHRINGERS POINT LA

No Through Rd

Riverwood PL
RED TREE PL

CRAIG MOSTYN PL
WATTLEBARK PL
HEFFERNAN PL

JERSEY RD
CHEDDAR ST

COBBERS LA

Retirement Village

Tennis

Skate Pk
Gundary Park

Oval

RFS
Hockey & Soccer Fields

Aged Peoples Units

Albert Stewart Pk

CHURCH ST

Rotary Park
Jetty

Cath Sch
Queen

NRMA
Service NSW

Rev Fell
Bi-Lo
John

MURRAY ST
CAMPBELL ST

QUEEN ST
SHORE ST

LUCK ST
EMMOT ST
Resvr
GUNDARY ST

YARRAGEE RD
YARRAGEE ST

TED HUNT TCE

WAMBAN RD
Garbage Tip
Australia's Bush Orchestra
Deua NP 15 km
Braidwood 88 km (Via Araluen)

ARALUEN RD

ALBERT ST

THOMAS ST

Mirrabooka AV
Apex Pk

Moruya Pmy Sch
PAGE ST

Cncl Off
PARK LA
VULCAN ST

Clubhouse

FITZROY ST

LAGOON ST

ALBERT ST

PIONEER AV
JEFFERY PL
WOODBRIDGE AV

PANORAMA
Res

RIVLEY CL

TURNBULLS

HAWDON ST

SWAN RIDGE PL
PATERSON CL

DWYER CREEK RD

SPENCER ST
YARIMUP PL
YACCABA DR
Gold & Silver Mines
Private Property

Golf Course

Moruya Golf Course

Showground & Football Field

Ack Weyman Oval (Football)

Sports Centre

EVANS ST
OTTON ST

MORUYA ST
HASLINGDEN ST

BERGALIA ST
ROSE ST

Cemetery

VULCAN ST

Moruya High School

COSTIN ST

FRANCIS ST

ANDERSON ST

MURRAY ST

PRINCES HWY

BRAEMAR DR
DR KING CL
JOY PL
SOUTH HEAD RD
MAUNSELL ST
KEIGHTLEY ST
CONGO RD
Surf Beach

MOLLEE RD
NOADS RD
The Meadows
Bodalla
Tuross Heads
Narooma 39km
Moruya Heads 8km

JOHN ST
CARTILE CR
Bapt

JOHN ST
Res

TAFE NSW-Illawarra Inst
Moruya Campus

PRINCES HWY

MALUKA AV
PARKLAND CT

TOOSE ST
FORD ST
NORTH HEAD DR

PRINCES HWY

No Through Rd

River (Tidal)

zz11UL

COPYRIGHT © UNIVERSAL PUBLISHERS PTY LTD

MOSS VALE

LOCATION
On the Illawarra Hwy
124km south-west of Sydney
POPULATION
7300
NRMA ROAD SERVICE
Ph: 13 11 22

VISITOR INFORMATION
Mittagong Visitor Information Centre
62 Main St (Old Hume Hwy)
Mittagong
Ph: (02) 4871 2888
Toll free: 1300 657 559
www.southern-highlands.com.au

Sheep, cattle, horses and goats feed on the lush pastures surrounding this pleasant Southern Highlands market and tourist town, the first major town in the region when arriving from the south. Leighton Gardens, in the centre of Moss Vale, is the place to stop for a break. The landscaped gardens are beautiful at any time of the year but particularly so in spring and then again in the autumn when the deciduous trees display their colours. Throsby Park Historic Site is home to Throsby Park Homestead, a fine Georgian home of sandstone and cedar built in 1834. It may be visited upon request, and open days are held.

ACCOMMODATION GUIDE
Allens Motel 1 **M14**
Briars Country Lodge 2 **G3**
Moss Vale Village Park 1 **H14**
Peppers Manor House Southern Highlands 1 **B18**

FACILITIES & ATTRACTIONS
Acacia Park 1 **H15**
Apex Park 2 **D10**
Bong Bong Cemetery 2 **F7**
Bong Bong Common 2 **F5**
Broulee Park 1 **J13**
Cecil Hoskins Nature Reserve 2 **L3**
Church Road Soccer Fields 2 **F11**
Community Oval 1 **P13**
Cosgrove Park 1 **J11**
Council Office 1 **N13**
Fire Station 1 **N12**
Greyhound Track 2 **D11**
Henderson Park 2 **C12**
Lackey Park 1 **N8**

Leighton Gardens 1 **M12**
Moss Vale Cemetery 1 **G6**
Moss Vale Golf Club 1 **N15**
Moss Vale Golf Club 1 **P17**
Moss Vale Services Club 1 **K14**
Mt Broughton Golf & Country Club 1 **B18**
NRMA 1 **N13**
Post Office 1 **N12**
Railway Station 1 **M11**
Regional Gallery 1 **N11**
Rotaract Club Park 1 **K18**
Rotary Parkway 1 **N13**
Roxburgh Park 2 **F11**
Seymour Park 1 **N17**
Showground 2 **C10**
Southern Highland Wines 1 **B16**
Strode Park 1 **H14**
Swimming Pool 1 **N13**
Thwaites Park 2 **D7**
Trosby Park Historic Site 2 **H12**
Whites Creek Reserve 1 **N14**
ZZ7UR

STREETS

Abattoir Rd 1 D4
Albany Rd 1 K17
Alkina Cr 1 L9
Amarina Av 1 L9
Anembo St 1 K9
Anulka St 1 J9
Argyle St
  Moss Vale 1 D15
  Moss Vale 1 J14
  Moss Vale 1 M12
  Moss Vale 2 C10
  Sutton Forest 1 D15
Arthur St 1 M13
Ashley Ct 1 G15
Attunga Pl 1 K9
Baker St 1 G17
Ball St 2 C9
Beaconsfield Rd 1 M8
Beatty St 2 C12
Bellevue Av 1 L16
Berrima Rd 1 E1
Black Wattle Cl 2 G10
Bong Bong Bridge 2 G5
Bowman Rd 1 F6
Brookdale Rd 1 F3
Broughton St 1 F17
Browley St 1 K13
Brown Barrel Rdg 2 M12
Bulwer Rd 1 J7
Caber St 1 G16
Camaroo La 1 C16
Campbell Cr 1 J12
Cecil Hoskins Access Rd 2 G4
Chapman St 1 M15
Cherry Tree Cl 1 G14
Chippendale Cl 2 C8
Church Rd
  Moss Vale 2 F12
  Moss Vale 2 F7
Clarence St 1 N12
Collins Pl 1 H12
Collins Rd 1 P1
Cooke Pl 2 F8
Coral Cl 2 C15
Corbett Wky 2 B14
Coromandel Pl 2 G9
Craig St 1 L18
Creek St 1 H14
Dalys Wy 1 N11
Dangar St 1 J13
Darraby Dr
  Moss Vale 1 G17
  Moss Vale 1 H18

Darran Rd 1 K17
Daylesford Dr 1 M18
Dengate Cr 2 B15
Denham Cl 2 D8
Dixon St 1 K14
Donkin Av 1 N13
Dormie Pl 2 B15
Dyson Pl 2 E7
East St 1 J15
Eliza St 1 H18
Elizabeth St 1 N12
Eloura La 1 K6
Endeavour Cct 1 J18
Eridge Park Rd 2 G1
Farmers Pl 1 M10
Farnborough Dr 2 L17
Fitzroy Rd 2 F15
Francis St 1 G18
Garrett St 1 M9
Gibbons Rd 1 H9
Hampton Ct 2 L14
Hawkins St 1 P10
Hazelton Dr 2 H15
Headlam Rd 2 G6
Hercules St 2 C14
Highlands Cl 2 C14
Hill Rd 2 C15
Hoskins St 1 P10
Hutchinson Rd 1 F8
Illawarra Hwy
  Moss Vale 1 A18
  Moss Vale 1 G15
  Moss Vale 1 P11
  Moss Vale 2 A11
  Moss Vale 2 C12
  Moss Vale 2 F13
  Sutton Forest 1 A18
Innes Rd 1 L11
Iona Park Rd 2 N18
James St 2 D12
James Taunton Dr 2 B14
Janice Cr 1 H15
Jopling Wy 1 K6
Joseph Hollins St 1 H17
Joyce St 1 G17
Kater Rd 1 A18
Keighley Pl 2 N14
Kennedy Cl 1 H12
Kewarra Pl 2 F9
Kings Rd 2 E9
Kirkham St 1 N13
Koyong Cl 1 P9
Kybeans Pl 1 M8

Kylie Pl 2 D7
Lackey Rd
  Moss Vale 1 M12
  Moss Vale 1 N9
Laconia Cr 2 D10
Lansdown Pl 1 L17
Lapwing Pl 1 J9
Lennox Cr 1 H15
Lindsay Rd 2 F15
Lisa Ct 1 H16
Lovelle St 1 M16
Lytton Rd 1 J7
McCleery Av 2 A10
McCourt Rd 1 P8
Mack St 1 N14
Mann Cr 1 J13
Mawson Tce 2 D8
Meehan Pl 2 F15
Merrett Dr 1 G16
Mitchell Pl 1 J12
Montery Av 1 K17
Montgomery Wy 1 H18
Morrice Ct 1 H9
Moss Vale Rd 2 G4
Mt Broughton Rd 1 K18
Napper Cl 1 K6
Narellan Rd 2 D14
Nari Cct 2 K16
North St 1 J15
Northcott Pl 2 N14
Nowra Rd 2 N18
Oldbury Rd 1 A13
Old Dairy Cl 1 G7
Old Oak Pl 2 K16
Parkes Rd 1 J8
Patuna Av 1 K18
Paul Cr 1 H16
Peppermint Dr 2 M11
Pine St 2 B12
Pleasant Av 1 K17
Price St 1 J11
Queen St 1 L13
Railway St 1 L15
Ralfe St 1 J13
Rebecca Pl 2 C9
Reeyana Pl 1 K7
Robertson Rd 2 B11
Roche Cl 1 L7
Roe St 1 H12
Rytina Pl 2 C7
Sagewick Pl 1 N7
Salamander Pl 1 H15

Semkin St
  Moss Vale 2 C8
  Moss Vale 2 D9
Simon Pl 2 C9
Snowy Gum Ri 2 L11
Songline Pl 2 G1
Spencer St 1 L17
Spring La 1 L14
Spring St 1 L14
Stables Pl 1 L7
Stanley Tce 1 K10
Suttor Rd 2 B10
The Highlands Wy 1 K14
Throsby St 1 L16
Throsby Park Rd 2 G14
Thwaites Dr 2 E7
Tomley St 2 E12
Torulosa Dr 2 E13
Trelm Pl 2 C9
Trotters La 1 L6
Tudor Cl 2 N14
Twickenham Pl 2 D7
Vale Rd 1 P8
Valetta St 1 P11
Vale View Rd 1 H17
Vanessa Pl 2 C9
Victor Cr 2 G8
Villiers Rd 2 C15
Waite St 1 L12
Walton Pl 1 K17
Warrawong Dr 2 F14
Watkins Dr 2 K15
Watson Rd 1 K10
Wembley Rd 2 E11
White La 1 M13
White St 1 M12
Whitton Cl 1 H17
Wiles Pl 1 H17
Willow Dr 1 H13
Wilson St 1 H13
Windella Rd 1 A12
Windsor Cr 2 L12
Woodside Dr 2 M14
Woodville Rd 2 C13
Wyatt St 1 J13
Yarrawa Rd 1 L17
Yarrawa St 1 J14
Young Rd
  Moss Vale 2 E13
  Moss Vale 2 F10
Yvonne Pl 2 D9

MAP I MOSS VALE

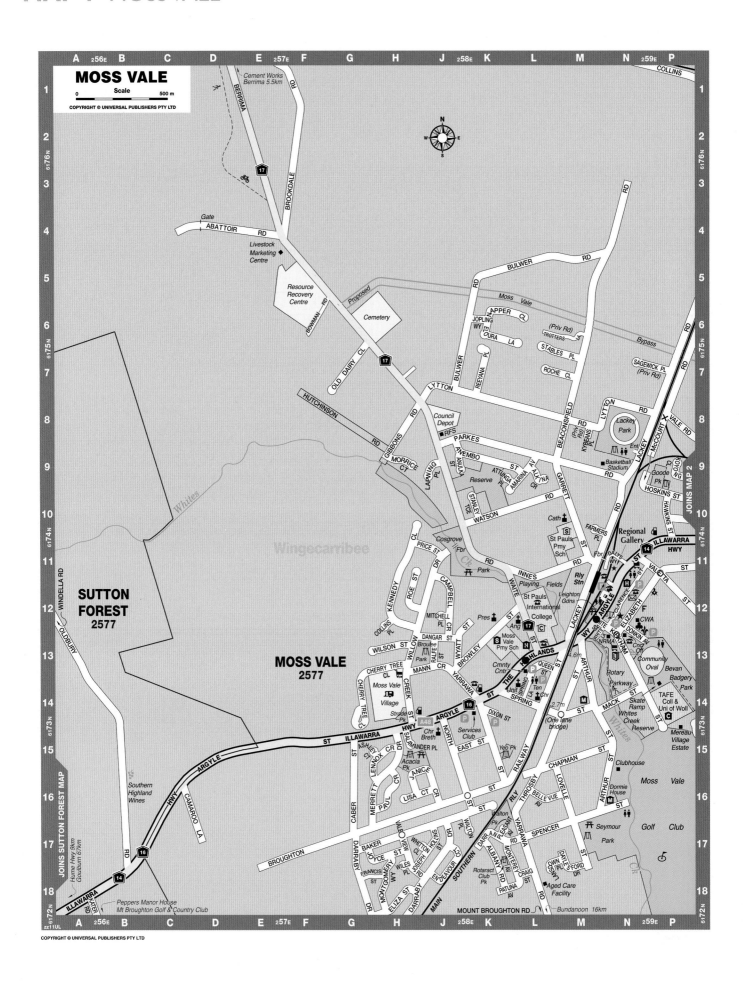

MOSS VALE

Scale
0   500 m

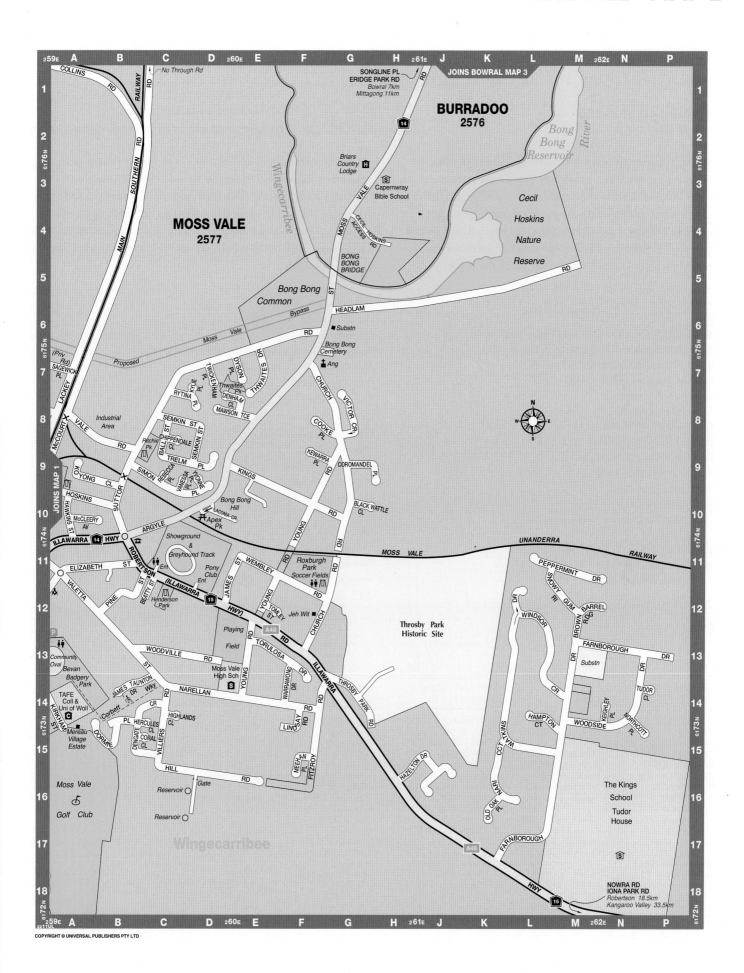

NAROOMA

LOCATION
345km south of Sydney
On the Princes Hwy
POPULATION
3100
NRMA ROAD SERVICE
Ph: 13 11 22

VISITOR INFORMATION
Narooma Visitor Information Centre
76 Princes Hwy
Ph: (02) 4476 2881
Freecall: 1800 802 528
www.eurobodalla.com.au

Narooma is a small town overlooking Wagonga Inlet, 70 kilometres south of Batemans Bay. Local attractions are mostly natural with surfing and family beaches, waterways and the surrounding State forest making the town such an appealing holiday destination. South of Main Beach lie the intriguing Glasshouse Rocks; Australia Rock is another interesting rock located below Bar Rock Lookout.

A hole the shape of Australia weathered into it gave the rock its name. Montague Island Nature Reserve is located nine kilometres south-east of Narooma, and tours operate from Narooma daily. The island is managed by the National Parks and Wildlife Service and protects Australian and New Zealand fur seals, which bask in the sun on the smooth rocks.

ACCOMMODATION GUIDE
Amooran Oceanside Apartments & Motel **K13**
BIG 4 Narooma Easts Holiday Park **F11**
Coastal Comfort Motel **H13**
Easts Van Village **E12**
Ecotel Narooma **C5**
Farnboro Motel **E17**
Holiday Lodge Motor Inn **H13**
Narooma Motel YHA **E16**
Surf Beach Holiday Park **L14**
The Tree Motel **F15**
The Whale Motor Inn **H12**
Top of the Town Motel **H13**

FACILITIES & ATTRACTIONS
Bar Rock Lookout **J9**
Bill Robinson Park **G15**
Bill Smyth Memorial Oval **F13**
Bowling Club **G12**
Ferry Crossing Park **D8**
Fire Station **J13**
Foxglove Spire Gardens (Tilba Tilba) **E18**
Glasshouse Rocks Lookout **L17**
Golf Club **K12**
Ken Rose Park **E9**
Lighthouse Museum **F11**
Narooma Lookout **C7**
Narooma Plaza **F15**
Narooma Sporting & Services RSL Club **G12**
Narooma Visitor Information Centre **F11**
Police Station **H12**
Post Office **H12**
Quota Park **D12**
Surf Life Saving Club **L14**
Swimming Pool **G11**
Wagonga Inlet Cruises **D13**
ZZ7UR

STREETS

Alexander Pl **B7**
Angle Pl **J12**
Angle St **H12**
Baldwin Av **E3**
Ballingalla St **J15**
Barker Pde **E12**
Bar Rock Rd **H11**
Bay La **J12**
Bay St **J12**
Beachview Cl **F5**
Bellbird La **D7**
Bettini La **E14**
Bluewater Dr **G11**
Bowen St **G12**
Brice St **E12**
Burrawang La **E11**
Burrawang St **E11**
Campbell St **G11**
Canty St **G13**
Carvan St **H13**
Cemetery Rd **L16**
Centenary Dr **E7**
Chisholm Pl **G15**
Clarke St **J13**
Cole Cr **D18**
Collins Cr **H14**

Corunna St **K13**
Costin St **F15**
Cove Ct **A7**
Creighton Pde **E5**
Curt La **E16**
Dalmeny Dr
  Kianga **C4**
  North Narooma **C4**
Davidson St **E14**
Dawn Pde **D3**
Dorothy Dr **D17**
Dudleys La **E13**
Eastway Av **E6**
Farncomb Av **H14**
Field St **E12**
Fifth Av **C11**
Fishermans Cr **A7**
Forsters Bay Rd **E13**
Foster St **J13**
Fourth Av **C11**
Gareth Av **D17**
Garvan La **H13**
Gem Cr **D17**
Gina Ct **D16**
Glasshouse Rocks Rd **F18**
Golf La **J11**

Graham St **E11**
Harper Cr **J15**
Harrington Rd **G14**
Hillcrest Av **A6**
Hillcrest La **D8**
Hillside Cr **F3**
Hopkins Pl **G18**
Hyland Av **E12**
Inlet Pl **A8**
Isabel St **F16**
John Pl **D5**
Kanga Commercial La **G3**
Kianga Pde **G3**
Kianga Bridge **G1**
Lakeside Dr **F1**
Lake View Dr **D15**
Lavender Point Rd **A8**
Loader Pde **G15**
Lynch St **E12**
McMillan Rd **E13**
Marine Dr **H14**
Mitchell Pl **J14**
Montague Av **F4**
Montague La **K13**
Montague St **J13**
Morris St **J15**

Murphy Pl **H18**
Nichelsen St **E12**
Noorooma Cr **H12**
Old Hwy **D18**
Old Coast Rd **E18**
Pacific Av **F1**
Payne St **E16**
Perkins Pde **C6**
Pilot St **J12**
Princes Hwy
  Kianga **A4**
  Narooma **E16**
  North Narooma **A4**
Raymond St **D7**
Rifle Range Pit Rd **A6**
Riley La **J15**
Riley St **H15**
Riverside Dr **D10**
Riverview Rd **A8**
Ross St **J14**
Second Av **C11**
Sesame St **C11**
Sheaffe St **J13**
Sunnyside Cr **F3**
Sunset Bvd **F3**
Surf Beach Rd **F2**

Taylor La **F13**
Taylor St
  Narooma **F13**
  Narooma **F14**
The Circle **C11**
The Loop **E15**
The Slipway **A18**
Third Av **C11**
Thompsens Wky **F14**
Thompson La **F13**
Tilba La **J13**
Tilba St **H13**
Tower La **C6**
Viewhill Rd **F3**
Wagonga St **H13**
Wagonga Inlet Bridge **E8**
Warbler Cr **D5**
Water Cr **C8**
Wharf St **G11**
Willcocks Av **G14**
Williamson Dr **D5**
Willis Bvd **G16**
Woodbury Rd **A8**
Woods Pl **E5**

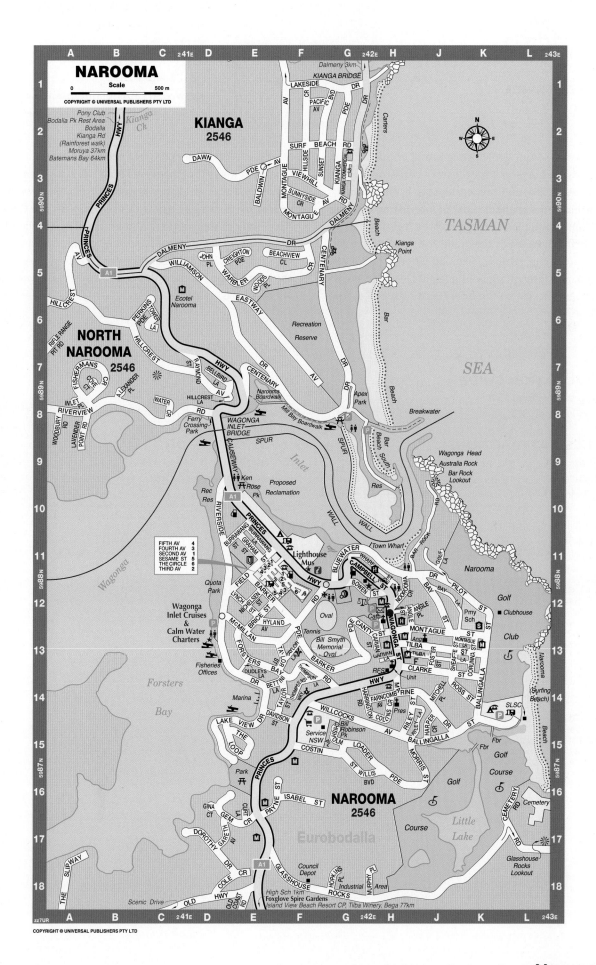

NAROOMA

Scale
0 — 500 m

Pony Club
Bodalla Pk Rest Area
Bodalla
Kianga Rd
(Rainforest walk)
Moruya 37km
Batemans Bay 64km

KIANGA
2546

Dalmeny 3km
KIANGA BRIDGE
LAKESIDE
PACIFIC AV
SURF BEACH
VIEWHILL
SUNNYSIDE CR
MONTAGU

TASMAN

Kianga Point

NORTH NAROOMA
2546

Ecotel Narooma

RIFLE RANGE PIT RD
FISHERMANS COVE
A.ALEXANDER PL
WATER CR
HILLCREST LA
INLET
RIVERVIEW
WOODBURY RD
LAVENDER
POINT RD

HILLCREST
PERKINS PDE
TOWER LA
RAYMOND
BELLBIRD LA
AV
HWY
CENTENARY DR

DALMENY
WILLIAMSON
JOHN PL
CREIGHTON PDE
WARBLER
WOODS PL
BEACHVIEW CL
EASTWAY
CENTENARY
DR

Recreation
Reserve

SEA

Bar
Beach

Narooma Boardwalk
WAGONGA INLET BRIDGE
SPUR
CAUSEWAY
Ferry Crossing Park

Mill Bay Boardwalk
Apex Park
SPUR

Breakwater
Wagonga Head
Australia Rock
Bar Rock Lookout

Inlet

Ken Rose Pk
Rec Res

Proposed
Reclamation

WALL
WALL
Beach South
Res

Bar Rock
GOLF LA

Town Wharf

FIFTH AV — 4
FOURTH AV — 3
SECOND AV — 1
SESAME ST — 5
THE CIRCLE — 6
THIRD AV — 2

RIVERSIDE
PRINCES
BURRAWANG
BURRAWANG
GRAHAM ST
FIELD
BARKER
LYNCH
McMILLAN
FORSTERS
BRICE ST
HYLAND AV

Lighthouse Mus
BLUEWATER
WHARF
CAMPBELL ST
BOWEN ST
Café
CANTY
PDE
Oval

Narooma
Golf
Clubhouse
Club

Wagonga Inlet Cruises & Calm Water Charters

Quota Park

Fisheries Offices

Forsters
Bay

NICHELSON
TATE
TAYLOR
TATE
Bill Smyth Memorial Oval
Tennis
BARKER RD

NOOROOMA
ANGLE PL
MONTAGUE ST
TILBA
MONTAGUE ST
CORINNA ST
SHEAFE ST
FOSTER ST
ROSS ST
BALLINGALLA

Pmy Sch

DUDLEYS
BETTINI LA
THOMPSON RD
THOMPSON RD
CLARKE
RES
Unit
HWY
HARRINGTON
FARNCOMB
CANTY
GARVAN
MARINE
LATWAN
TILBA

Marina

LAKE VIEW
THE LOOP
DAVIDSON ST
TAYLOR DR

WILLCOCKS
Bill Robinson Pk
Service NSW
COSTIN

RIVINE
RILEY ST
HARPER
MITCHELL
BALLINGALLA
SLSC
Fbr
Fbr

Narooma
(Surfing Beach)

Park

GINA CT
GEM
GARETH
CURT
PAYNE ST
ISABEL ST

COLE CR
DOROTHY DR

NAROOMA
2546

Eurobodalla

LOADER ST
WILLIS
MORRIS ST
BVD

Golf
Course

Little
Lake

Golf
Course

Cemetery
CEMETERY RD

PRINCES
GLASSHOUSE ROCKS
OLD COAST
HWY

Council Depot
HOPKINS PL
Industrial Area
MURPHY PL

Glasshouse Rocks Lookout

Scenic Drive
High Sch 1km
Foxglove Spire Gardens
Island View Beach Resort CP, Tilba Winery, Bega 77km

ROBERTSON

LOCATION
On the Illawarra Hwy
144km south-west of Sydney

POPULATION
1350

NRMA ROAD SERVICE
Ph: 13 11 22

VISITOR INFORMATION
Mittagong Visitor Information Centre
62 Main St
(Old Hume Hwy)
Ph: (02) 4871 2888
www.visitsouthernhighlands.com.au

If you are travelling from Wollongong inland up scenic Macquarie Pass, Robertson is a necessary rest stop. People from all over Australia, and the world, stop at the famous Pie Shop: picnic in the grounds. Lots of interesting antiques and craft shops, boutiques strung along the highway, not just in the town. Have tea in the grand rooms of Ranelagh House, then stroll the gardens. The Old Cheese Factory has refreshments, and interesting boutique gifts – not to mention of course cheese! A visit to the Robertson Nature Reserve is a must – heritage rainforest enclave. A picnic area on the Common (near the railway station) has signs leading to a number of interesting heritage walks around town. For a real adventure take a day trip with the family on the Cockatoo Run – one of the great train journeys of Australia. Robertson is famous for it's potatoes and now equally as famous for the film 'Babe'. It is a cosy country village with a great community spirit and once a month there are markets and bush dances to which all are welcome.

ACCOMMODATION GUIDE
Robertson Country Motel **E8**
The Robertson Hotel **K8**

FACILITIES & ATTRACTIONS
Belmore Falls **B14**
Bowling Club **D8**
Hampden Park **D7**
Heritage Railway Station & Museum **D9**
Old Cheese Factory **G8**
Old Potato Shed **F8**
Pinkwood Park **G8**
Police Station **D8**
Post Office **F8**
Robertson Cemetery **D14**
Robertson Nature Reserve **E9**
Robertson Sportsground **E4**
ZZ7UR

STREETS

Alcorn La **B8**	Cottee Cl **G6**	Kirkland Rd **E1**	Pearsons La **A7**
Armstrong Cr **C9**	Crown St **A9**	Lawn Av **K9**	Potters La **G7**
Arney St **C9**	Devonshire Rd **E5**	Lemmons Rd **F4**	Ranelagh St **K7**
Barrengarry St **C5**	East St **H7**	Mcevilly Rd **B14**	Rossgoll Rd **A7**
Bells Hill Rd **K14**	East St **H11**	Mackeys La **M5**	Sassafras Wy **B8**
Belmore Falls Rd **A13**	Fountaindale Rd **K12**	Main St **F8**	Shackleton St **H5**
Blackwood Pl **H6**	Hanrahan Pl **F6**	Maldon St **B9**	South St **A8**
Burrawang La **C7**	High St **B4**	Maugers Rd **K14**	South St **D9**
Burrawang St **B7**	High St **E4**	May St **C5**	Swan St **F6**
Burrawang St **F7**	Hindmarsh La **F3**	May St **F6**	The Old Rd **M7**
Caalong St **C10**	Hoddle La **G8**	Meryla St **E8**	Vaughan Av **K8**
Caalong St **C7**	Hoddle St **A7**	Meryla St **E11**	Victor Cr **D9**
Camp St **G7**	Illawarra Hwy **B7**	Missingham Pde **E13**	Wallangunda St **C7**
Camp St **G9**	Illawarra Hwy **J8**	Muasdale La **P13**	Waters Edge Rd **F5**
Charlotte St **B9**	Ingram St **A9**	North St **B6**	West St **A10**
Coachwood Pl **G6**	Jamberoo Mountain Rd **P5**	North St **E6**	West St **B7**
Congewoi St **C8**	Kangaloon Rd **D1**	Old Kangaloon Rd **A6**	Yarranga St **D8**
Congewoi St **F8**			

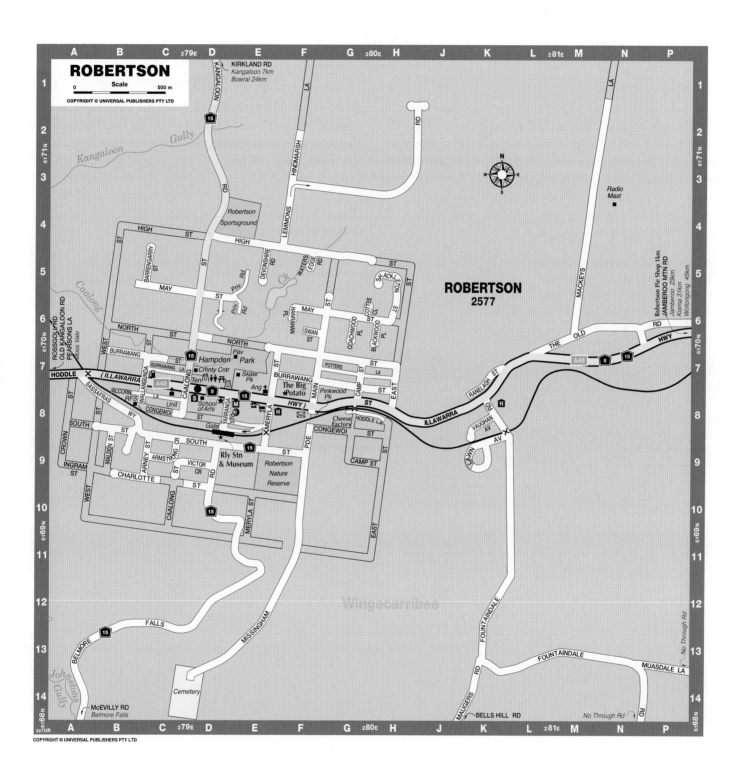

ROBERTSON

Scale
0   500 m

COPYRIGHT © UNIVERSAL PUBLISHERS PTY LTD

KIRKLAND RD
Kangaloon 7km
Bowral 24km

ROBERTSON
2577

Robertson Pie Shop 1km
JAMBEROO MTN RD
Jamberoo 23km
Kiama 31km
Wollongong 45km

Radio Mast

Wingecarribee

McEVILLY RD
Belmore Falls

ST GEORGES BASIN/SANCTUARY POINT

LOCATION
191km south of Sydney

POPULATION
St Georges Basin 2900
Sanctuary Point 7225

NRMA ROAD SERVICE
Ph: 13 11 22

VISITOR INFORMATION
Shoalhaven Visitor Information Centre
Bridge Rd
Nowra
Ph: (02) 4421 0778
Ph: 1300 662 808
www.shoalhaven.com.au

An easy drive south from Sydney are the picturesque villages of St Georges Basin and Sanctuary Point, which offer the visitor a variety of recreational and sporting facilities including picnic areas, sporting clubs and caravan park, cabin, and motel accommodation. The Minka Japanese Garden at Sanctuary Point contains nine different areas, each with its own theme and includes orientally pruned Ne Warke trees, water features with magnificent Koi and stunning views of St Georges Basin. It is open most public holidays.

ACCOMMODATION GUIDE
Aloha Caravan Park **2 G10**
Palm Beach Caravan Park **3 K16**
St Georges Basin Golf View Motel **3 H11**
The Sanctuary Motel **3 H12**
Worrowing Jervis Bay Eco Resort **3 M5**

FACILITIES & ATTRACTIONS
Basin View Reserve **1 C11**
Blue Wrens Retreat Reserve **2 H7**
Boobook Reserve **3 M12**
Bowling Club **3 G12**
Clifton Park **3 G14**
Firetail Creek Reserve **2 J12**
Francis Ryan Reserve Sports Field **3 H12**
Grass Tree Reserve **2 H9**
Hewitt Avenue Reserve **3 A8**
John Williams Reserve **3 M17**
Kingfisher Park **2 F14**
NRMA **2 G10**
Paradise Beach Reserve **3 E16**
Paul Bland Reserve **3 E13**
Post Office **3 G13**
Sanctuary Point Oval **3 K8**
St Georges Basin **1 L8**
St Georges Basin Country Club **3 G12**
St Georges Basin Shopping Centre **2 G9**
The Grange Reserve **2 D9**
Wool Lane Sporting Complex **3 B8**
Yellow Bellied Glider Reserve **3 E8**
ZZ7UR

STREETS

Aelous Pl 3 M2
Agnes Cr 3 M2
Albion St 3 H13
Allen St 3 J12
Anabel Pl 3 B8
Andrews Rd 1 A3
Anson St
  St Georges Basin 2 H10
  St Georges Basin 3 A7
  Sanctuary Point 3 C10
Ash Ct 3 L9
Atherton St 1 F6
Atkins Pl 2 H11
Attunga Av 3 G17
Audrey Av 1 C10
Auster Cr 3 L11
Avro Av 3 K12
Azalea Av 3 J9
Bader Rd 3 K14
Ball Cl 3 B7
Banksia Av 3 G10
Basin View Pde 1 D10
Bayly Rd 2 F3
Beaver Av 3 K12
Belpitt Pl 3 C8
Blackbird Gr 3 M2
Blacket Rd 2 E4
Boathaven Av 1 B13
Boomerang St 3 L16
Boronia Av 3 J9
Brompton Rd 1 F8
Bruce St 2 G9
Cammaray Dr
  St Georges Basin 2 J12
  St Georges Basin 3 A8
  Sanctuary Point 3 A8
Capeland Av 3 E8
Carmel Dr 3 F8
Carol Av 1 C11
Carver Ct 2 K10
Centaur Av 3 H13
Cessna Av 3 K12
Chessell Rd 2 K7
Chipmunk Av 3 K11
Clarendon Cr
  Basin View 1 G10
  St Georges Basin 1 H6
Claylands Dr 2 J11
Clifton St 3 H16
Collett Pl 2 G10
Collingwood St 1 D10
Corella Cr 3 E10
Cross St 3 E12
Curlew St 3 L13
Deane St 2 D8
Decora Av 3 F8
Dorothy Av 1 C10
Doyle Pl 2 H11
Dunisla St 3 J16
Durnford Pl 2 J10
Eagle Pl 3 J13
Eden Pl 3 M2
Edmund St
  Sanctuary Point 3 L16
  Sanctuary Point 3 M13
Elanora Pde 1 D10

Emu Av 3 L13
Endeavour St 3 H14
Ethel St 3 G16
Fairway Dr 3 H9
Firman Gln
  St Georges Basin 2 L10
  St Georges Basin 3 A7
Fisherman Rd 1 J7
Flamingo St 3 L15
Flora St 3 G16
Forrester Ct 3 C8
Frances Cst 2 J9
Frederick St 3 G15
Gibson Cr 3 J12
Goshawk St 3 L13
Graham Av 2 F10
Grange Rd
  Basin View 1 H6
  St Georges Basin 1 H6
  Tomerong 1 H6
Greville Av 3 D17
Gull Av 3 K12
Gumden La
  St Georges Basin 2 H6
  Tomerong 2 H6
Gymea Av 3 H9
Harper Rd 1 B13
Harriss Av 1 B12
Hawken Rd 1 H1
Heron Av 3 L13
Hewitt Av
  St Georges Basin 2 L11
  St Georges Basin 3 A8
Hilda St 3 M2
Hive Pl 3 M2
Hogbin Cr 3 B7
Hurst Pl 2 K12
Idlewild Av 3 H14
Irene St 3 G17
Island Point Rd
  St Georges Basin 1 H1
  St Georges Basin 2 G13
  Tomerong 1 H1
Jackson Cl 2 J11
Jean St 3 E11
Jervis Bay Rd 3 P3
John St 1 B10
June Av 1 C10
Karne St 3 M15
Kean Av 3 C10
Keevil Brae 2 K9
Keldie Cl 2 L11
Kells Rd 1 F1
Kenneth Av 3 B9
Kerry St 3 B9
Kestrel Av 3 L14
Kevin Cr 2 F9
Kingfisher Av 3 K14
Kingsford Smith Cr 3 J12
Kirkham Wy 3 D9
Kurraba Pl 2 K11
Lachlan Cr 2 G11
Larmer Av
  Sanctuary Point 3 K10
  Worrowing Heights 3 K10
Lawson Wy 3 B9

Leumeah St 3 G15
Links Av 3 D10
Loralyn Av
  St Georges Basin 2 G13
  St Georges Basin 3 A10
  Sanctuary Point 3 A10
Macleans Point Rd
  Sanctuary Point 3 D11
  Sanctuary Point 3 F16
Marie St 3 F17
Martha Elizabeth Dr 3 M2
Mary Cir 3 M3
Mathie St 1 G11
Maxwell Cr 3 D8
Merimbula St 3 M3
Meriton St 2 G12
Mernie St 3 P4
Milson St 3 E17
Moroney Av 2 J11
Mountain St 3 L8
Mustang Dr 3 K12
Nadine St 3 D10
Nebraska Rd 1 J5
Nirimba Av 3 K14
Nulla Pl
  St Georges Basin 2 L12
  St Georges Basin 3 A9
Paino Cr 3 C8
Pangari Cr 2 F8
Panorama Rd 1 J8
Paradise Beach Rd 3 F13
Park Rd 1 L7
Pelican Rd 1 J6
Pelican St 3 J13
Penguin St 3 H15
Percy St 3 H16
Piper Av 3 M3
Platypus Av 3 M13
Prince Alfred St 3 M3
Princes Hwy
  Basin View 1 A4
  Basin View 1 A8
  Tomerong 1 A4
Rauch Cl 2 G11
Reserve Rd 1 F10
Ridgelands Dr 3 K13
Riverside Esp S 1 H11
Robinsville Pl 3 E8
Rose Av 3 J9
Ross Of Australia Dr 3 M3
Roulstone Cr 3 H8
St Georges Rd 2 E9
Salinas St 3 F7
Sanctuary Point Rd
  Sanctuary Point 3 L11
  Sanctuary Point 3 M16
Shoreville Pl 3 G7
Shortcut Rd 1 K8
Sirius Av 3 M12
Stephens Rd 3 G8
Tahnee St 3 D9
Tallyan Point Rd 1 D9
Tasman Rd 2 E8
Tasman Park Cl 2 E8
Telopea Av 3 E10
Terry St 2 F9

The Basin Rd 2 D8
The Glen 3 G16
The Lane 3 E8
The No Name Rd 1 J12
The Old Wool Rd
  St Georges Basin 2 H7
  St Georges Basin 3 A5
The Park Dr
  Sanctuary Point 3 F10
  Sanctuary Point 3 J8
The Wool La
  St Georges Basin 3 A9
  St Georges Basin 3 B6
  Sanctuary Point 3 A9
  Sanctuary Point 3 B6
The Wool Rd
  Basin View 1 A9
  St Georges Basin 1 H7
  St Georges Basin 2 F8
  St Georges Basin 2 H7
  St Georges Basin 3 A5
  Sanctuary Point 3 A5
  Sanctuary Point 3 F7
  Worrowing Heights 3 A5
  Worrowing Heights 3 L5
Tide Cr 1 H10
Tilba St 3 M3
Tilbrook Av 2 J11
Truscott Av 3 K14
Turvey Cr
  St Georges Basin 2 K10
  St Georges Basin 3 A7
Ulm Rd 3 J14
Unicorn St 3 H13
Valda Av 1 C11
Vickery Av 3 J14
Vost Dr 3 E7
Wahroonga Cl 2 J12
Wallabia Pl 3 F8
Walmer Av
  Sanctuary Point 3 D12
  Sanctuary Point 3 D17
Walter Hood Pde 3 M3
Wandera Pl 3 M3
Waratah Cr 3 G10
Warne Rd
  St Georges Basin 1 K1
  Tomerong 1 K1
Warrego Dr 3 K14
Waterpark Rd
  Basin View 1 H11
  St Georges Basin 1 H7
Waters Edge Av 1 C11
Wattle Av 3 G10
Waxberry Pl 3 D11
Winn Av 1 C9
Wonga Pl 2 K12
Wood La 2 F4
Wullun Cl 3 D8
Yallara Cr 3 D8
Yuroka Cr 2 G8

MAP 1 ST GEORGES BASIN

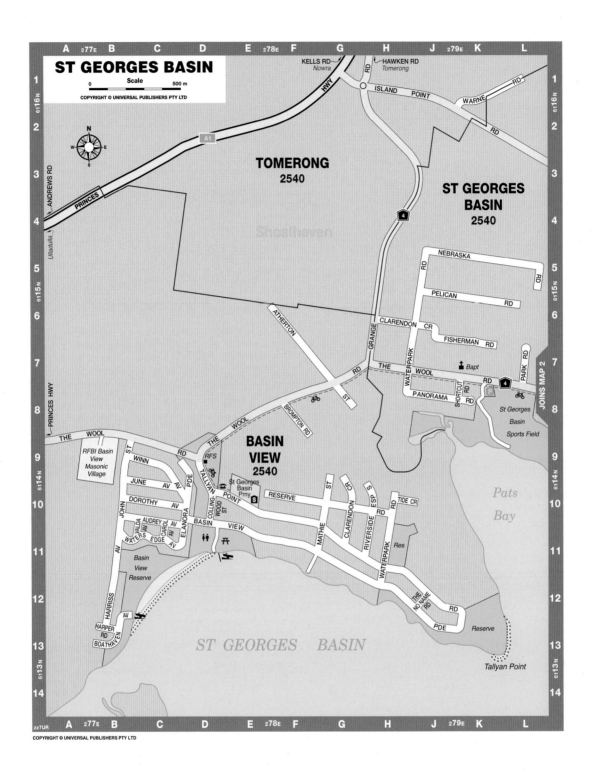

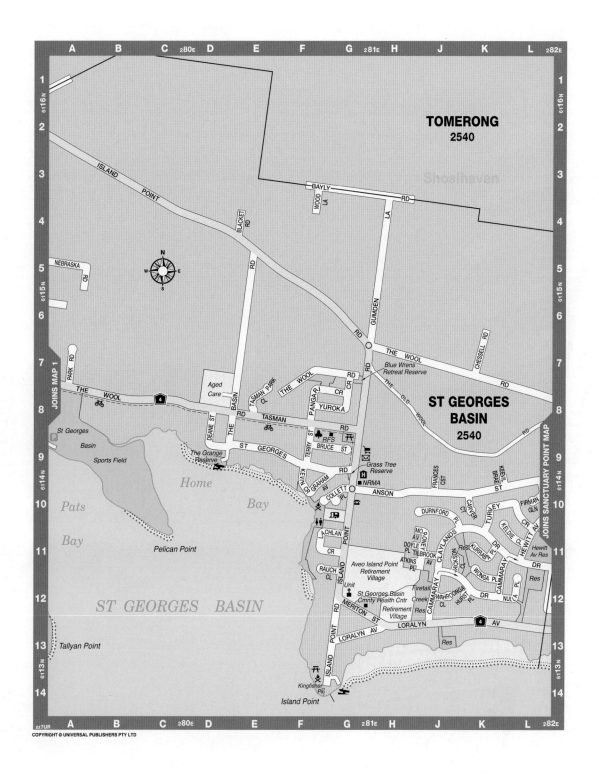

Couple getting directions from sign post directory, Sussex Inlet, Shoalhaven

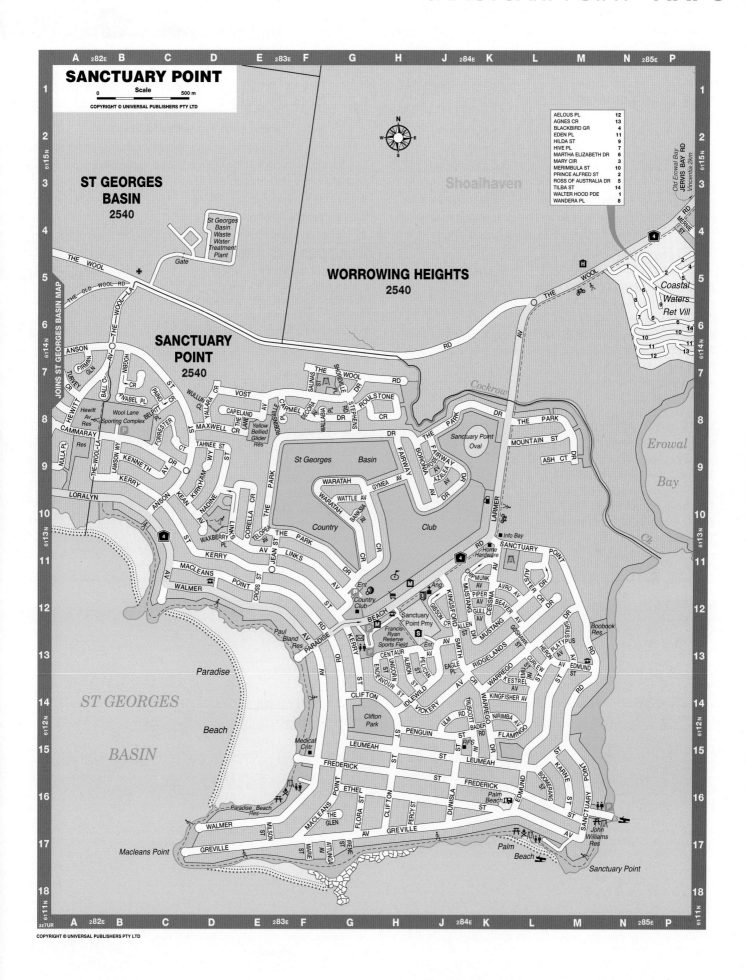

SANCTUARY POINT
2540
Scale
0   500 m
COPYRIGHT © UNIVERSAL PUBLISHERS PTY LTD

AELOUS PL	12
AGNES CR	13
BLACKBIRD GR	4
EDEN PL	11
HILDA ST	9
HIVE PL	7
MARTHA ELIZABETH DR	6
MARY CIR	3
MERIMBULA ST	10
PRINCE ALFRED ST	2
ROSS OF AUSTRALIA DR	5
TILBA ST	14
WALTER HOOD PDE	1
WANDERA PL	8

ST GEORGES
BASIN
2540

WORROWING HEIGHTS
2540

Shoalhaven

SANCTUARY
POINT
2540

St Georges   Basin

Country   Club

ST GEORGES

BASIN

Paradise

Beach

Clifton
Park

Macleans Point

Erowal
Bay

Palm
Beach

Sanctuary Point

SUSSEX INLET

LOCATION
204km south of Sydney
POPULATION
3600
NRMA ROAD SERVICE
Ph: 13 11 22

VISITOR INFORMATION
Shoalhaven Visitor Information Centre
Bridge Rd
Nowra
Ph: (02) 4421 0778
Tollfree: 1300 662 808
www.shoalhaven.com.au

A tranquil South Coast holiday town on the channel that connects St Georges Basin with the Pacific Ocean, Sussex Inlet is a very popular holiday destination for families. Sussex Inlet has enjoyed the trend of residential canal development, which has almost made it an island but has not spoilt the charm of this peaceful place. Famous among anglers for its excellent fishing, Sussex Inlet hosts a major fishing carnival held annually during the July school holidays.

ACCOMMODATION GUIDE

Anchorage Caravan Park **J6**
Badgee Caravan Park **G5**
Bentley Waterfront Motel **G5**
Cedar Pines Caravan Park & Cottages **J6**
Hotel Shang-Ri-La **J6**
Kalua Caravan Park **J6**
Ranch Motel **E12**
Riverside Caravan Park **G11**
Riviera Caravan Park **G5**
Seacrest Caravan Park **F12**
Siesta Van Park **J6**
Snappy Gums Caravan Park **B13**
Sussex House Caravan Park **K6**
Sussex Inlet Hotel Motel **J7**
Sussex Palms Holiday Resort **G11**
Talofa Caravan Park **H5**

FACILITIES & ATTRACTIONS

Boatshed & Public Wharf **K6**
Booderee National Park **K2**
Jack Finkernagel Reserve **G7**
Jacob Ellmoos Reserve **J9**
Jim Cater Park **K6**
Lions Park **E13**
NRMA **A8**
Police Station **H6**
Sussex Inlet Bowling Club **E13**
Sussex Inlet Golf Club **A7**
Sussex Inlet Moviehouse **J6**
Sussex Inlet Post Office **K7**
Sussex Inlet RSL Bowling Club **K7**
Sussex Inlet RSL Club **K7**
Sussex Inlet Sailfish Club **K6**
Sussex Inlet South Post Office **G12**
Swimming Pool **D11**
Thompson Street Sporting Complex **D10**
Totem Pole Directional Post **C8**
Trevenar Reserve **E9**
ZZ7UR

STREETS

Ainsdale St **C12**	Finch Pl **H8**	Lancing Av **A9**	River Rd **H10**
Alamein Rd **D14**	Flood Av **A8**	Lucelia Gr **F4**	Riviera Av **E13**
Anchorage Cl **E4**	Florida Cl **D3**	Lyons Rd **F11**	St Georges Av **E12**
Avocet St **D10**	Gina Av **C12**	Marlin Pl **E3**	Sandpiper Wy **G8**
Banksia St **H6**	Glanville Rd **E12**	Mary St **G11**	Seaberry St **C9**
Beachcomber Av **D13**	Goldsmith Rd **D13**	Matilda Av **H11**	Shelly Gr **E3**
Bexhill Av **B9**	Golf Course Wy **A7**	Medlyn Av **A12**	Suncrest Av **D4**
Blue Mist Cl **D4**	Gordon St **K7**	Muree St **D9**	Sussex Rd **F11**
Boatharbour Dr **C13**	Government Rd **D12**	Nielson La **J5**	Sussex Inlet Rd **A8**
Buttonwood Cl **C9**	Greentree Av **C13**	Nielson Rd **H7**	Teal Pl **E7**
Cater Cr **D9**	Harbord St **H9**	Ocean View Rd **E12**	The Springs Rd **A14**
Chichester Rd **B8**	Hastings Pde **B8**	Pacificana Dr **D14**	Thomson St **B12**
Christine St **F12**	Hoffman Dr **A13**	Paradise Cr **G6**	Thora St **G9**
Coral Ct **E3**	Ibis Pl **F7**	Peacehaven Wy **A9**	Tradewinds Av **E3**
Corang Av **F10**	Inlet Av **E4**	Pearl Cl **A11**	Voyager Av **C14**
Cormorant Av **E9**	Iverison Rd **E12**	Phillip St **G11**	Wayfarer Dr **C14**
Dotterel Pl **G9**	Jacana Cl **D9**	Plover Cl **D8**	Whimbrel Dr **F9**
Driftwood Av **D13**	Jacobs Dr **E7**	Poole Av **H5**	Wildwood Av **C14**
Edgewater Av **E14**	Justfield Dr **A11**	Ray St **F11**	Wunda Av **G6**
Ellmoos Av **H7**	Lagoon Cr **G6**	Ridge Av **G11**	
Ethel Av **H10**	Lakehaven Dr **C13**	River Rd **E1**	
Fairview Cr **F3**	Lakeshore Pde **D2**	River Rd **G5**	

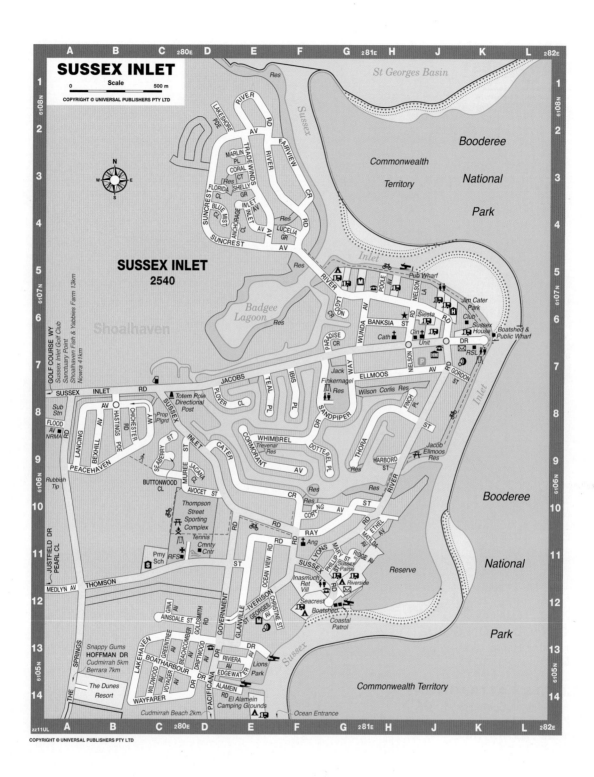

SUSSEX INLET

Scale

0 ... 500 m

COPYRIGHT © UNIVERSAL PUBLISHERS PTY LTD

SUSSEX INLET
2540

Shoalhaven

Badgee Lagoon

St Georges Basin

Booderee

Commonwealth

Territory

National

Park

Booderee

National

Park

Commonwealth Territory

Reserve

Ocean Entrance

Cudmirrah Beach 2km.

Snappy Gums
HOFFMAN DR
Cudmirrah 5km
Berrara 7km

The Dunes
Resort

GOLF COURSE WY
Sussex Inlet Golf Club
Sanctuary Point
Shoalhaven Fish & Yabbies Farm 13km
Nowra 41km

SUTTON FOREST/EXETER

LOCATION
129km south west of Sydney

MAP I SUTTON FOREST

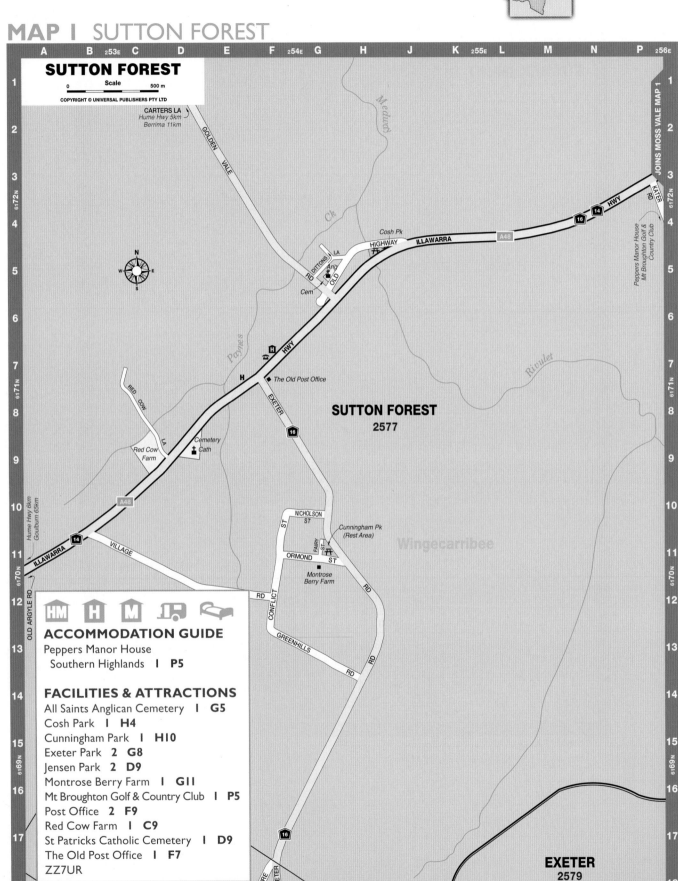

SUTTON FOREST
0 Scale 500 m
COPYRIGHT © UNIVERSAL PUBLISHERS PTY LTD

CARTERS LA
Hume Hwy 5km
Berrima 11km

SUTTON FOREST
2577

EXETER
2579

Wingecarribee

JOINS MOSS VALE MAP 1

JOINS EXETER MAP

Hume Hwy 6km
Goulburn 65km

The Old Post Office

Cosh Pk

Peppers Manor House
Mt Broughton Golf &
Country Club

Red Cow
Farm

Cemetery
Cath

Nicholson St

Cunningham Pk
(Rest Area)

Montrose
Berry Farm

ACCOMMODATION GUIDE
Peppers Manor House
  Southern Highlands   I   **P5**

FACILITIES & ATTRACTIONS
All Saints Anglican Cemetery   I   **G5**
Cosh Park   I   **H4**
Cunningham Park   I   **H10**
Exeter Park   2   **G8**
Jensen Park   2   **D9**
Montrose Berry Farm   I   **G11**
Mt Broughton Golf & Country Club   I   **P5**
Post Office   2   **F9**
Red Cow Farm   I   **C9**
St Patricks Catholic Cemetery   I   **D9**
The Old Post Office   I   **F7**
ZZ7UR

EXETER

Scale

0   500 m

COPYRIGHT © UNIVERSAL PUBLISHERS PTY LTD

JOINS SUTTON FOREST MAP

SUTTON FOREST 2577

SUTTON FOREST 2577

WERAI 2577

EXETER 2579

BUNDANOON 2578

Wingecarribee

STREETS

Badgerys Wy 2 G8
Blue Gum Rd 2 B18
Bundanoon Rd 2 F12
Buskers Av 2 C9
Carmen La 2 A11
Carters La 1 C2
Conflict St 1 F12
Cornwall Rd 2 A13
Dittons La 1 G5
Ellsmore Rd
  Exeter 1 F18
  Exeter 2 A9
  Exeter 2 B18
Exeter Rd
  Exeter 1 F18
  Exeter 2 F1
  Sutton Forest 1 F8
Fairy St 1 G11
Gatehouse La 2 P3
Golden Vale Rd 1 E2
Greenhills Rd 1 F13
Illawarra Hwy 1 A11
Indigo La 2 K9
Invergowrie La 2 C10
Jensens La 2 C12
Kater Rd 1 P3
Kelly Pl 2 C9
Little Meadow La 2 A13
Loftus Pde 2 P4
Middle Rd 2 B8
Montgomery Rd 2 H10
Morgans Rd 2 B18
Mt Broughton Rd 2 P3
Nicholson St 1 G10
Norwood St 2 F10
Old Hwy 1 G5
Old Argyle Rd 1 A13
Ormond St 1 G11
Parsland Cl 2 A13
Pile St 2 F11
Red Cow La 1 C8
Ringwood La 2 C17
Ringwood Rd 2 F12
Rockleigh Rd 2 J8
Sallys Corner Rd 2 A9
School La 2 G10
Sheil Pl 2 D7
Stonequarry Creek Rd 2 P12
Trueman Av 2 C8
Village Rd 1 C11
Werai Rd
  Exeter 2 H8
  Werai 2 H8
Westgrove Rd 2 A11
Wilsons La 2 D10
Yarwood Dr 2 C6
Yuille Av 2 G18

GATEHOUSE LA
MT BROUGHTON RD
Bundanoon Ck Water Treatment Plant
Moss Vale 7km

LOFTUS PDE

EXETER RD

Hume Hwy 5km

YARWOOD DR

SHEIL PL

MIDDLE RD

ELLSMORE

TRUEMAN AV

KELLY PL

BUSKERS AV

Jensen Pk

SALLYS CORNER RD

CARMEN LA
WESTGROVE RD

PARSLAND CL
LITTLE MEADOW LA

ELLSMORE

Reedy

CORNWALL

JENSENS

RD

WILSONS LA

INVERGOWRIE LA

BUNDANOON

PILE

RINGWOOD

NORWOOD ST

SCHOOL ST

BADGERYS RD

RINGWOOD RD

WERAI

ROCKLEIGH

INDIGO LA

MONTGOMERY RD

(Buses Only)

Indigo

STONEQUARRY CREEK RD

Ck

Reedy

(Causeway)

RD

Ck

Ck

RINGWOOD

BUNDANOON

RD

Substn

BUNDANOON LA

BUNDANOON RD

MORGANS RD
BLUE GUM RD

YUILLE AV

Ten
Exeter Park
Ang
Gen Store
RFS
H
Croquet

Exeter

zz7UA

TATHRA

LOCATION
446km south of Sydney
POPULATION
1525
NRMA ROAD SERVICE
Ph: 13 11 22

VISITOR INFORMATION
Merimbula Visitor Information Centre
2 Beach St
Merimbula
Ph: (02) 6495 1129
Freecall: 1800 150 457
www.merimbulatourism.com.au

Tathra is home to the last remaining sea wharf on the East Coast of New South Wales, an important reminder of the town's shipping past. First built in the 1860's, the wharf was preserved by the National Trust in the 1970's. Today, the wharf is home to the Tathra Maritime Museum, where the town's place in steamer history is celebrated. Below the water, the wharf is home to a host of snorkelling and scuba diving delights. Tathra is the closest beach to Bega, lying at the southern end of a lovely three kilometres curve of sand. At the other end of the beach is the mouth of the Bega River. Known as Mogareeka Inlet, this wide, shallow expanse is beloved by waterbirds.

ACCOMMODATION GUIDE
BIG4 Seabreeze Holiday Park **D5**
Esther Lodge Holiday Units & Motel **D4**
Surfside Motel **D4**
Tathra Beach Motor Village **C2**
Tathra Beach Tourist Park **E4**
Tathra Hotel Motel **H6**

FACILITIES & ATTRACTIONS
Chamberlain Lookout **G10**

Lawrence Park **D9**
Maritime Museum **H5**
Police Station **G6**
Post Office **H6**
Surf Life Saving Club **F6**
Tathra Beach Country Club **C2**
Tathra Memorial Gardens **J5**
Tathra Wharf **H5**
Thatchers Flat **E5**
ZZ7UR

STREETS

Andy Poole Dr **D3**
Bay St **E9**
Bay St **H7**
Bay View Dr **C5**
Beach St **H6**
Bega St **C9**
Cliff Pl **G6**
Davidson St **E8**
Dilkera Rd **E7**
East La **H7**
Edna Dr **D4**
Esther St **D4**
Fauna Gr **C6**
Flora Pl **C5**
Francis Hollis Dr **D5**
Haven Pl **C4**
Huggetts La **E8**
Illoura St **G8**
John Taylor Cr **E6**
Kianinny St **F9**
Killarney Rd **C9**
Koorilla St **D9**
Noojee St **E8**

Ocean View Tce **B4**
Orange Cl **E9**
Pacific St **D8**
Panamuna Rd **F9**
Panorama Dr **C4**
Pimms Ct **E9**
Pimms La **D9**
Preo Pl **E6**
Reservoir St **C10**
Sanctuary Pl **D6**
Snowy Mountains Hwy **E8**
Stafford Cr **C9**
Tathra Rd **A9**
Tathra St **G7**
Tathra St **H7**
Tathra Bermagui Rd **D1**
Thompson Dr **A9**
Tomigee St **E9**
Wallagoot St **F7**
Wharf Rd **H6**
Wildlife Dr **C5**
Yuppara St **G9**

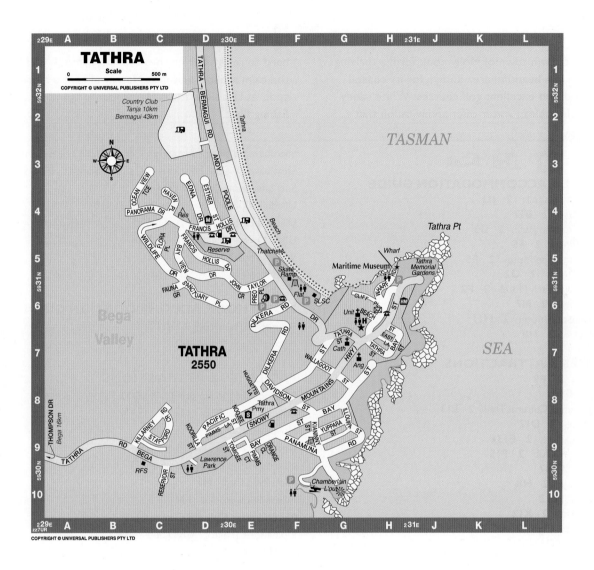

TATHRA

Scale

0   500 m

Country Club
Tanja 10km
Bermagui 43km

TASMAN

SEA

Tathra Pt

Wharf

Maritime Museum

Tathra
Memorial
Gardens

Skate Ramp

Flat

SLSC

Reserve

Thatchers

Bega

Valley

TATHRA
2550

Lawrence
Park

RFS

Chamberlain
L'out

229E

230E

231E

5932N

5931N

5930N

ULLADULLA/MOLLYMOOK

LOCATION
On the Princes Hwy
227km south of Sydney

POPULATION
12 150

NRMA ROAD SERVICE
Ph: 13 11 22

VISITOR INFORMATION
Shoalhaven Visitor Information Centre
Civic Centre
81 Princes Hwy
Ph: (02) 4444 8820
Tollfree: 1300 662 808
www.shoalhavenholidays.com.au

Ulladulla and its twin town of Mollymook form a thriving holiday centre in a beautiful area known for its coastal waterways and two excellent golf courses. White sandy beaches and clear clean water offer an invitation that's hard to resist. Surfers head for Mollymook surf beach while the calm shallow water at Narrawallee is a more sheltered spot; at Ulladulla, the safe harbour is home to a vibrant fishing fleet.

ULLADULLA ACCOMMODATION GUIDE
Holiday Haven Ulladulla **2 J11**
Ingenia Holidays **2 B17**
Mollymook Caravan Park **2 D3**
Mollymook Motel **2 F5**
Mollymook Seascape Motel **2 F5**
Mollymook Shores **2 G2**
Mollymook Surfbeach Motel **2 F2**
Sandpiper Motel **2 H7**
Ulladulla Harbour Motel **2 H11**
Ulladulla Hotel **2 H8**

FACILITIES & ATTRACTIONS
Bowling Club **2 F9**
Cinema **2 G10**
Coomee Nulunga Cultural Trail **2 L13**
Council Office **2 D12**
Dunn Lewis Centre **2 E13**
Ex-Servicemens Club **2 F15**
Fire Station **2 H7**
Kendall Cottage **2 H8**
Lighthouse **2 L12**
Lighthouse Oval **2 K12**
Mollymook Golf Club **2 G2**
Mollymook Golf Course (Beachside) **2 G4**
NRMA **2 G12**
Police Station **2 G7**
Post Office **2 G10**
Rotary Park **2 H8**

Shoalhaven Visitor Information Centre Dunn Lewis Centre **2 E13**
Shoalhaven Visitor Information Centre Ulladulla **2 G9**
Surf Life Saving Club **2 G1**
Ulladulla (Ocean) Swimming Pool **2 J10**
Ulladulla Sports Park **2 C14**
Ulladulla Swimming Pool **2 B9**
Warden Head Reserve **2 L11**
Wildflower Reserve **2 A10**

MOLLYMOOK ACCOMMODATION GUIDE
Bannisters Point Lodge **K11**
Milton Village Motel **H1**

FACILITIES & ATTRACTIONS
Bill Andriske Mollymook Oval **G12**
Bowling Club **F12**
Hospital **K2**
Library **J2**
Matron Porter Drive Reserve **F3**
Mick Ryan Park **H1**
Milton Showground **H4**
Milton Village Cultural Centre **J2**
Mollymook (Hilltop) Golf Club **B15**
Post Office **J1**
Surf Life Saving Club **G18**
Swimming Pool **K1**
ZZ7UR

MOLLYMOOK STREETS

Allunga Pl **C10**
Amaroo Dr **C6**
Angophora Av **E12**
Anker Av **G10**
Aquarius Av **D10**
Aries Pl **D7**
Augusta Pl **D14**
Bangalow St **E6**
Bannister Head Rd **F10**
Barclay St **E5**
Beach Rd **H12**
Bellbird Cl **K12**
Bishop Dr **A15**
Blake Pl **D5**
Bombora Cr **F14**
Bond Pl **H11**
Booth Av **E8**
Brookwater Cr **B14**
Bushland Av **E11**
Callemondah Cl **C10**
Capricorn Av **D9**
Carinya Cr **B7**
Carriage Wy **H3**
Carroll Av **F15**
Charles St **J2**
Church St **J3**
Cliff Av **L12**
Clifford Cl **B15**
Clyde St **E15**

Combe Dr
 Mollymook **A16**
 Mollymook Beach **A16**
Corks La
 Milton **H4**
 Milton **J1**
Croobyar Rd **J3**
Donlan Rd **G15**
Driver Av **E15**
Drury La **L3**
Everett Ct **A16**
Eyrie Bowrie Dr **L1**
Fairview Pl **E13**
Faust Cl **E15**
Forest Wy **D12**
Garrads La **A12**
Garside Rd **C13**
Gemini Wy
 Narrawallee **C7**
 Narrawallee **C8**
Gordon St **K3**
Graham St **K2**
Gumley La **K2**
Hilltop Cr **F10**
Huntingdale Dr **A17**
Ilett St **C18**
Iluka Cr **C6**
Jones Av **H12**
Kooralbyn Av **C13**

Kooyonga Cl **C14**
Latta St **E15**
Leo Dr **D8**
Libra Pl **D9**
Linden Wy **E11**
Lockhart Av **F15**
Mcleay St **D4**
Maisie Williams Dr
 Mollymook **C16**
 Mollymook Beach **C16**
Manning Av **E9**
Matron Porter Dr
 Milton **L2**
 Mollymook Beach **A12**
 Narrawallee **A12**
Miles Cl **B16**
Milton Pl **E14**
Mison Cct **A15**
Mitchell Pde
 Mollymook **F17**
 Mollymook Beach **F17**
 Mollymook Beach **K12**
Molloy St **C18**
Moonah Av **B14**
Mudges Av **E8**
Myrtle St **H3**
Niblick Av **E15**
Normandy St **E6**
North East Pl **E13**

Ocean St
 Mollymook **D18**
Oxley Cr **C12**
Parkinson St **E5**
Park View Pde **F12**
Payten Av **H2**
Plateau Pl **F13**
Price Pky **H4**
Princes Hwy
 Milton **H1**
 Mollymook **A18**
Robin Pl **D12**
Rosella Av **E12**
Ross Av **D8**
Sagittarius Wy **C9**
Scorpio Gr **C9**
Seascape Cl **B8**
Seaspray St
 Narrawallee **B6**
 Narrawallee **C8**
Seawinds Pde **C8**
Settlers Wy **A17**
She Oak Av **A18**
Skillman Pl **A16**
South Haven **E10**
Springfield Dr **A17**
Stony Hill La **J1**
Sungrove La **A12**
Surfers Av **E9**

Tallwood Av
 Mollymook Beach **F10**
 Narrawallee **F9**
Taurus Spur **C9**
The Court **E10**
The Green **A16**
The Haven **H11**
The Heights **A11**
The Meadows **B18**
Thomas St **J1**
Toorak Cl **C12**
Treetops Cr **D12**
Valley Dr **D11**
Valley View Cl **H2**
Victor Av **E8**
Virgo Pl **D10**
Wason St **J3**
Wilfords La **K4**
Wolseley St **K3**
Wood Cl **K1**
Woodalla Wy **C10**
Woodglen Cr **G11**
Wynella Pl **L2**
Yarrawonga Dr **C13**
Yarra Yarra Cl **C13**

ULLADULLA STREETS

Abbey Rd 2 A8
Aroo Rd 2 B15
Augenaut Av 2 F16
Banyalla Pl 2 A8
Belowra Cl 2 B7
Benalla Pl 2 C10
Bendoura St 2 B1
Benowa Wy 1 M8
Bishop Dr 2 A2
Black Bean Gr 2 A4
Blackburn Rd 2 C15
Boag St 2 D3
Bolwarra Av 1 P1
Booyong Av 1 P2
Boree St 2 G11
Braidwood Av 2 A18
Brill Cr 2 E17
Brushbox Dr
  Ulladulla 1 N4
  Ulladulla 1 P5
Buchan St 2 G5
Buckland St 2 D2
Budawang Dr 2 A7
Bunya Pl 1 N1
Burleigh Wy 2 H4
Burrill St N 2 H7
Burrill St S 2 H12
Byangee St 2 B7
Callistemon Ct 2 B3
Camden St
  Ulladulla 2 E13
  Ulladulla 2 F7
Canberra Cr 2 A18
Carabeen Av 1 P2
Carmen Cl 2 D10
Carnelian Cl 2 C6
Carramar Cr 2 D5
Cashman Rd 1 P8
Cassia Pl 2 A5
Chaucer Pl 2 C9
Church St
  Ulladulla 2 C8
  Ulladulla 2 E8
Clissold St 2 F4
Colden Pl 2 D8

Coller Rd 2 B15
Colony Row 2 B8
Combe Dr 2 A2
Conjola St
  Mollymook 2 H6
  Ulladulla 2 H6
Cooper Gr 2 C8
Cooyoyo Cl 1 P7
Coral Cr 2 G15
Crescent St 2 H8
Croft Av 2 E9
Croobyar Rd 1 D1
Curtis St 2 D4
Davies St 2 F2
Deering St 2 D12
Diamond St 2 D5
Dickson Cl 2 D7
Did-Dell St
  Ulladulla 2 H14
  Ulladulla 2 J7
Dolphin St 2 H7
Dowling St 2 G14
Edward Av 1 G16
Elliott Pl 2 D8
Ewin Cl 2 C9
Fan Palm Ct 1 P5
Fitch St 2 D9
Flame Tree Ct 2 B4
Forrest Oak Dr 2 B6
Frangipani Av 1 N3
Gadara Pl 1 P7
Gemalla Pl 2 E7
Geoffrey St 2 F8
George Av 1 H16
Golden Wattle Dr 2 A4
Golf Av 2 F5
Green St
  Ulladulla 1 M8
  Ulladulla 2 D9
Greenview Cl 1 L6
Grevillea Ct 2 A3
Harold St 1 G16
Henry Pl 1 G16
Hillview Pl 1 J3
Hollywood Av 2 G13

Howes Pl 2 C9
Huntingdale Dr 2 A2
Ian St 2 F7
Ilett St 2 C2
Ingold Av 2 F2
James Cr 1 E15
Jarrah Pl
  Ulladulla 1 P8
  Ulladulla 2 A8
Jason Pl 2 H13
Jindelara Rd 2 D7
Jubilee Av 2 G13
Kalang Av 2 E7
Kamala Av 1 N3
Kanuka Dr 1 P1
Kingsley Av 2 G7
Kings Point Dr
  Kings Point 1 F16
  Ulladulla 2 A16
Kiola St 2 F8
Knight Wy 2 C8
Laurel Av 1 N2
Leigh Cr 2 A7
Lilly Pl 2 G6
Lomandra Pl 2 B5
McKail St 2 C5
Maisie Williams Dr 2 D1
Martin Av 2 F17
Millard St 2 E5
Mitchell Pde 2 F1
Molloy St 2 C1
Morris St 2 C10
Mulga Pl 1 P2
Murramerang St 2 H6
Nelson Dr 2 C8
Nethercote St 2 B1
New St 2 J11
North St
  Ulladulla 2 C7
  Ulladulla 2 J7
Nurrawallee St 2 F6
Oakley Pl 1 H16
Ocean St
  Mollymook 2 D1
Osrick Av 2 H13

Owen St 2 H12
Parkland Dr 1 F16
Parson St 2 F13
Pengana Cr 2 D3
Penny La 2 B8
Periwinkle Pl 2 F16
Pettys Av 2 G14
Pindari Pl 2 E11
Pirralea Rd 1 M5
Pitman Av 2 E16
Powell Av 2 G14
Princes Hwy
  Milton 1 J1
  Mollymook 2 B2
  Ulladulla 2 B2
  Ulladulla 2 C18
Princess Av 2 A18
Red Gum Dr
  Ulladulla 1 N2
  Ulladulla 1 N3
Rennies Beach Cl 2 J14
Riley St 2 F3
Ripley Cl 2 A7
Riversdale Av 2 G4
Robertson Pl 1 M5
Rose Gum Av 2 A6
Royal Mantle Dr 2 A3
Rundle St 2 E10
St Vincent St 2 F12
Sapphire Cl 2 D6
Scarlet Gum St 2 B4
Scribbly Gum Cr 2 B5
Seaview St 2 E3
Settlers Wy
  Mollymook 2 A2
  Mollymook 2 C1
Shackleton St 2 F3
She Oak Av 1 P1
Shepherd St 2 F2
Shipton Cr 2 G5
Silky Oak Av 1 P5
Simmons Dr 2 D9
Slaughterhouse Rd
  Milton 1 K2
  Ulladulla 1 K2

South St 2 C10
South Pacific Cr 2 E17
Spencer St 2 C8
Springfield Dr 2 A2
Stack St 2 L13
Stanton Dr 2 C6
Tanja Ri 2 B1
Terence St 2 E7
Tetley Pl 1 M5
Thadalee Pl 2 J12
The Green 2 A3
The Meadows 2 B1
Timbs St 2 D4
Trapp Cl 2 D8
Tuckerman Rd 1 K4
Tudor Rd 1 H15
Tulip Oak Dr
  Ulladulla 2 A5
  Ulladulla 2 C7
Turnball La 1 L3
Turner St 2 D2
Vigilant Dr 2 D10
Village Dr 2 B8
Wallace St 2 F2
Walpole Av 2 C10
Wandella Cl 2 D11
Warden St 2 B10
Warrawee Pl 2 C10
Washburton Rd 1 K7
Wason St 2 G10
Wattlevale Pl 2 E7
White Gum Rd 1 N6
Wilfords La 1 D6
Wilga Pl 1 N1
William St 1 G17
Willunga Cl 2 D11
Windward Wy
  Milton 1 D1
  Milton 1 J1
Witherington Av 2 E12
Woodgrove Dr 1 K4
Woorree Pl 2 J13
Wyuna Pl 2 E5

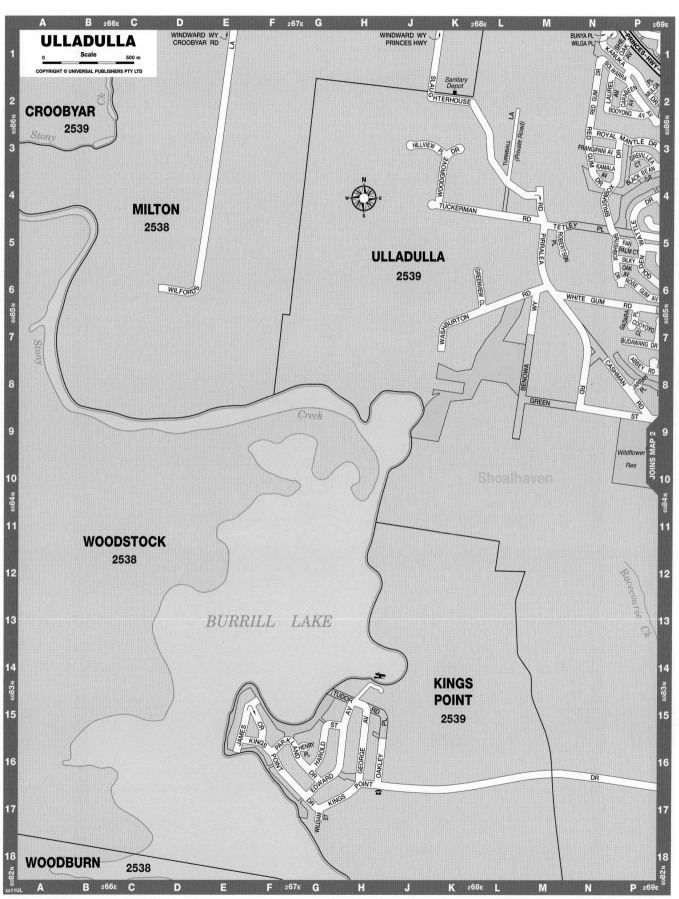

MAP 2 ULLADULLA

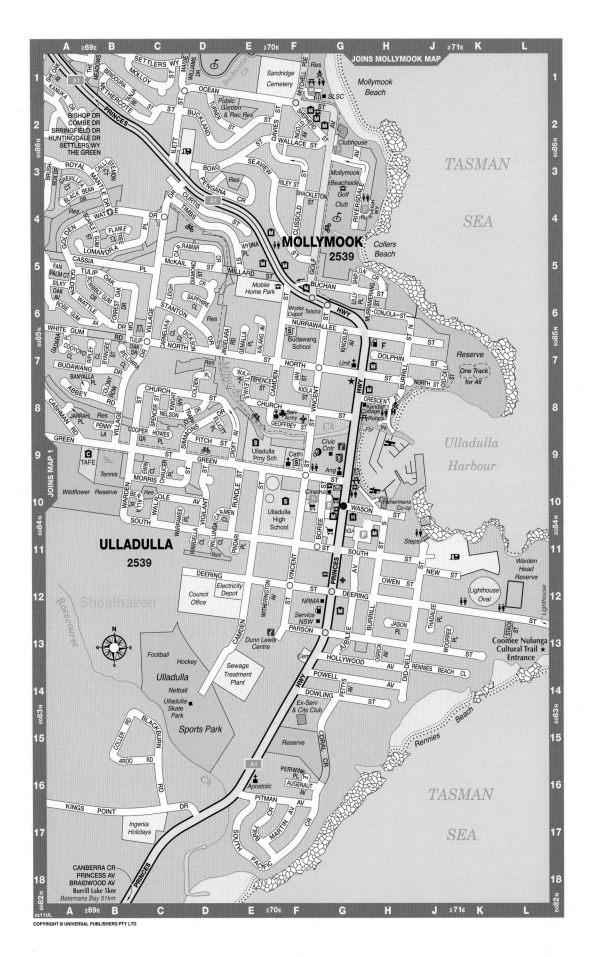

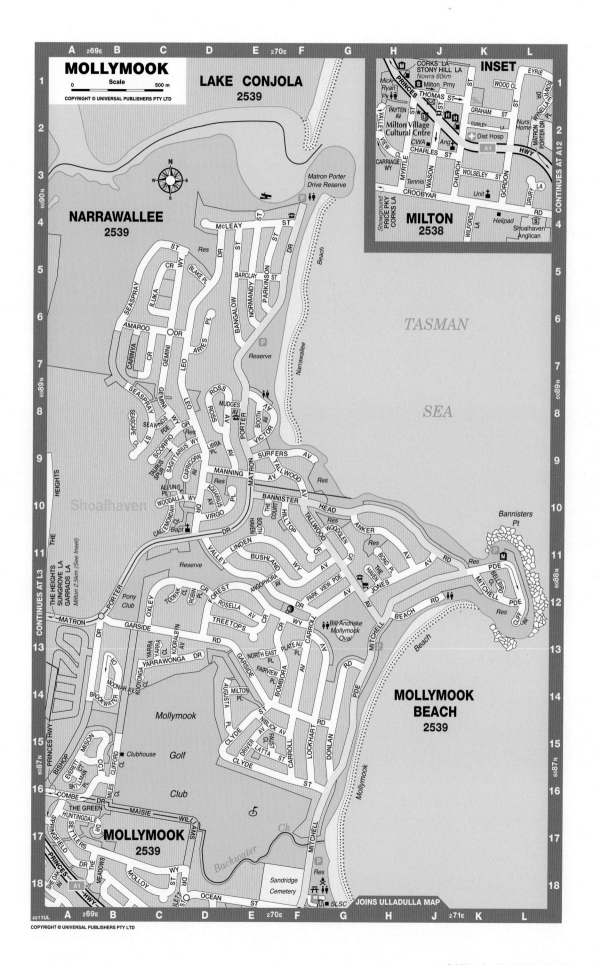

MOLLYMOOK

Scale
0   500 m

COPYRIGHT © UNIVERSAL PUBLISHERS PTY LTD

LAKE CONJOLA
2539

NARRAWALLEE
2539

INSET

MILTON
2538

TASMAN

SEA

Matron Porter
Drive Reserve

Shoalhaven

MOLLYMOOK
BEACH
2539

Bannisters Pt

Mollymook
Golf

Club

MOLLYMOOK
2539

Sandridge
Cemetery

JOINS ULLADULLA MAP